NELSON'S ARCTIC VOYAGE

NELSON'S ARCTIC VOYAGE

The Royal Navy's first polar expedition 1773

Peter Goodwin

Foreword by Vice Admiral Sir Alan Massey KCB CBE

ADLARD COLES

LONDON · OXFORD · NEW YORK · NEW DELHI · SYDNEY

Adlard Coles
Bloomsbury Publishing Plc
50 Bedford Square, London, WC1B 3DP, UK

BLOOMSBURY, Adlard Coles and the Adlard Coles logo are trademarks of
Bloomsbury Publishing Plc
First published in Great Britain 2018
This edition published 2018

A catalogue record for this book is available from the British Library.
Library of Congress Cataloguing-in-Publication data has been applied for.

ISBN: HB: 9781472954176; ePDF: 9781472954169; ePub: 9781472954183

2 4 6 8 10 9 7 5 3 1

Typeset by Deanta Global Publishing Services, Chennai, India
Printed and bound in Great Britain by CPI (Group) UK Ltd, Croydon, CRO 4YY

To find out more about our authors and books visit www.bloomsbury.com.
Here you will find extracts, author interviews, details of forthcoming events and
the option to sign up for our newsletters.

Contents

CONTENTS

Foreword
by Vice Admiral Sir Alan Massey KCB CBE

It is a great honour for me to introduce this remarkable book and its remarkable author, Peter Goodwin. The account of Horatio Nelson's first voyage to the Arctic latitudes as a young Royal Navy midshipman in 1773 is one of rare adventure, risk, inventiveness and fortitude under great duress. I was privileged to work briefly with Peter when I served as the Navy's Second Sea Lord from 2008 to 2010, and he as long-standing keeper and curator of the wonderfully preserved and restored HMS *Victory* in Portsmouth – Nelson's flagship at the 1805 Battle of Trafalgar. Drawing on his extraordinary knowledge of the ships, their operations and their crews in the tumultuous years of George III's reign, the author has documented with characteristic rigour and detail what was the Navy's first officially documented polar expedition. Two hundred men, in two modestly-sized warships, set off willingly and excitedly to seek out the North Pole and a so far undiscovered north-east trade route across the top of Russia to the Pacific. Embarked alongside the naval crews were scientists, new instruments, experimental machines, meticulously compiled logistics and the profound spirit of the Age of Enlightenment: an era marked by man's irrepressible urge to make sense of the world through exploration, science and philosophy.

This gripping tale of endeavour and its rich historical context are finely drawn. The author's well-established reputation and peerless technical grasp of how ships were built, manned and sailed in those times shines through in his broader narratives around the usually clipped, laconic entries in the two ships' logs. Perhaps most compelling – even more so than the authoritative descriptions of the ships' technologies – are his references to the human factors underlying the huge day-to-day challenges of this expedition. For this is a story of leadership, determination, personal resilience and careful management, as much as of the specific skills of navigation, seamanship, and sound maintenance that, in the end and against the odds, were able both to achieve great things and to bring the ships and their people back home safe. Unsurprisingly, both ships' commanding officers completely understood the importance of a clear aim, firm discipline (which – as the author points out – is not synonymous with tough punishment, good order, seizing the initiative and maintaining morale: cardinal principles that are still faithfully observed in today's Royal Navy. In my own personal experience of duress at sea, at peace as well as in war, those things trump all else in getting and sustaining the best of a ship and her crew: especially when bad thing happen and spirits become bruised.

Though Horatio Nelson's part in the story is a limited one – he was, after all, only 14 years of age at the time – he most certainly did his bit. And no doubt the tribulations of this Arctic voyage will have been formative on his subsequent passage to greatness. One can only speculate over what other turns history might have taken, had Nelson not survived this stern test of character, grit and fibre.

Alan Massey, Southsea, November 2018

I

Introduction

Captain's log HM Sloop *Carcass*, Sunday 1 August 1773.

Bearing & position at noon: 'Beset with Ice amongst the 7 islands Black point on the NE^t land S 67°W 3 or 4 leagues, West Island N 18° (Table Island) N 5°W.'

Situation: 'Light airs and Calms, PM laying amongst the drift Ice, and at 4 PM made fast the Ship to it, and filled our water Casks from a pool upon the Ice, at 10 PM cast the Ship loose and made fast to the Ice near the *Racehorse*, finding we drifted to the SE^t, from here, at 11 AM a large white bear coming over the Ice towards the Ships, was shot and brought aboard the *Racehorse* – at Noon the drift Ice round the ships considerably increased, setting in towards the SW^t Shore from the North and East. Some open water between the Ships and that Shore, but no passage out to the Westward where they came in PM Variation Pr Azimuth N 17°: 33′W.'[1]

Captain Skeffington Lutwidge, writing in *Carcass*'s journal in 1773, was part of a pioneering voyage to the Arctic, alongside the *Racehorse*, commanded by Constantine Phipps on behalf of the Royal Navy. Also serving in the *Carcass* was a very young midshipman named Horatio Nelson, later to become Vice Admiral Lord Nelson.

When Nelson and the rest of the expedition ventured into the unforgiving Arctic regions around Spitsbergen (today Svalbard) in 1773, few sailed this hostile area other than the European whaling fleets. As the British Royal Navy's first Arctic expedition, Phipps's voyage offered no strategic martial advantage. Although intended to answer a number of scientific questions, this was essentially another quest to seek a northerly sea passage to the Far East, the conceptual origins of which had far deeper roots. Influencing this quest was a European trade with the East that had existed since Roman times and was largely reliant on a long-established system of caravan routes traversing the vast continent of Asia with commodities reaching Europe through the city of Istanbul. Merchandise was also shipped from the equally important distribution city of Alexandria, Egypt. Whichever route was taken, trade to the East was subject to the political control of the interceding regions, especially after the onset of Muslim expansionism during the 7th century.

The desire to explore these regions further was also inspired by the writings of the Italian merchant and traveller Marco Polo. Having traversed central Asia, after reaching China by land, he recorded his experiences in around 1300 in a book called *The Book of the Marvels of the World (Livre des Merveilles du Monde)*. Following Polo's travels and the later voyages of his fellow Italian Christopher Columbus in 1492, on behalf of Spain, and those of the Portuguese sailor Vasco da Gama, who reached India in 1497, there emerged a trade race between Spain and Portugal. This situation was exacerbated by the Treaty of Tordesillas initiated by Pope Alexander VI. Signed by the royal families of Spain and Portugal on 7 June 1494, this trade boundary agreement subdivided the globe in the interests of Portugal and Spain, effectively preventing England and other northern European nations from benefiting from Eastern trade.

The original notion of finding a polar sea route to reach the rich trade markets of the East seems to have been conceived in the early 16th century by the Bristol merchant Nicholas Thorne. Trading in collaboration with an Anglo-Portuguese syndicate, Thorne was granted letters patent by Henry VII for exploration in the north-west. It was his son Robert Thorne, a merchant and writer, who first suggested to King Henry VIII that it should be Englishmen who found short cuts to the Indies and 'spiceries' by way of the north-east or north-west, or even by sailing across the North Pole, which, at that time, was thought to be an open sea. Convinced by his theory, Thorne argued that by using these routes England would reach the intended destinations far sooner than the Spaniards and Portuguese, who sailed by either the south-east or south-west routes, via the Cape of Good Hope or the Strait of Magellan.

Using a hand-drawn map based on one originally made by John Cabot of Newfoundland and Cape Breton Island in c. 1497, Thorne demonstrated that the northern tracts still open to the English were 'nearer by almost two thousand leagues' (6,000 miles/9,656km) than the southern route.[2] He also believed that the effects of extreme cold and ice were no more insurmountable than the unbearable heat met in the tropics. The idea for a northerly route was also promoted by those serving with the Muscovy Company in the early 17th century, by which time Dutch and English ships were making voyages north. This led to the discovery of the Spitsbergen archipelago, which soon became the centre of the profitable whaling industry and was jointly exploited by the Danes, Dutch, English, French, North Germans and Norwegians. Despite this intrusion, the seas above lat 80°N remained unexplored, the belts of ice forming an impenetrable barrier that deterred even the most adventurous whalers.

However, even before various European countries attempted to reach the East via alternative routes not controlled by Portugal and Spain, there had been attempts to sail through the high latitudes of the northern hemisphere. These earlier ventures were driven by a need for more land by indigenous Scandinavian peoples. It was only when navigational capability and ship technology improved sufficiently that other European countries came seeking routes into these icy seas.

Nelson's Arctic Voyage sets out to explain the organisational story behind the Royal Navy's first official exploratory expedition into the Arctic regions in HM ships *Racehorse* and *Carcass* in 1773. The main objective of the voyage was to seek – and hopefully reach – the North Pole. A secondary quest was to search for a northerly passage around the top of Russia as an alternative route to trade with the East. Using this opportunity, a further goal was the undertaking of a range of geographical and scientific endeavours as requested by the Royal Society. Why the Royal Navy became involved with this and other exploratory pursuits was simply a matter of its logistical capability compared to that of commercial groups attempting similar ventures at the time. The Royal Navy had already given support to the Royal Society with Captain Cook's voyage carrying the British naturalist, botanist and patron of the natural sciences Joseph Banks into the Pacific Ocean to observe the transit of Venus. Such ventures could only be carried out by the Navy when Britain was not at war – a somewhat rare occurrence during the 18th century.

Details of the voyage and preparations for the expedition have been taken from a number of primary sources, in particular the ship's logs of the expedition ships, *Racehorse* and *Carcass*, and the later official account written by its overall commander, Captain Constantine Phipps: *A Voyage towards the North Pole Undertaken by His Majesty's Command, 1773*, which was published in 1774. Details of the voyage itself have been supplemented by the writings of Midshipman Thomas Floyd, who kept a detailed and lively journal of his time on the voyage. These all illuminate the story of an expedition that was, in its time, one of the true journeys into the unknown and a perilous venture with an uncertain outcome.

Ship's Journal Log Book Abbreviations

Ship's commanders used a wide variety of abbreviations or informal shorthand in their journals (log books) when recording aspects of seamanship, bearings or referring to the sails. The wording was not formalised, commanders using their own style; neither were they consistent as to how terminology was applied. A number of common examples taken from the journals of *Racehorse* and *Carcass* and their meanings are explained below.

D^o – ditto.	*Miz.* – mizzen.
Est'ward, N^o ward, S^o ward', *W^t ward*, – Eastward Northward, Southward, and Westward respectively.	*NbW* – a bearing North by West. (Others given are self-explanatory: i.e. *EbS to NbE*.
Fath^s – fathoms; alternatively given as *^fms.* or. *^fm.* in the singular.	*Obs^d.* – observed.
F.T.M – fore topmast.	*P^r* – per.
hawl'd – hauled.	*Qu^r* – quarter as in a bearing or direction from the ship.
Lat^d. – latitude.	*reeft* – reefed.
L.L. – Lower Limb. This relates to the bottom part of the sun's circumference observed through a sextant when taking navigation sightings.	*Stud^g Sl^s* – studding sails.
	T G^t S^ls, – topgallant sails; may be preceded by M (main), F(fore), or Miz. (mizzen).
	Ta^kd – tacked as in manoeuvre.
leag^s – leagues.	*thro* – through.
	Wea^t – weather.

2

The early Arctic explorers

Although not Arctic explorers in the true sense, a number of Europeans did venture beyond the Arctic Circle before the 18th century. The first of these was the ancient Greek sailor Pytheas of Massalia, who undertook a voyage of exploration beyond north-western Europe in about 325 BC. Unfortunately, his description of this venture, though widely known in antiquity, has not survived, though it is acknowledged that he circumnavigated the British Isles, possibly reaching Iceland, and that he was the first person to describe the midnight sun and report about polar ice. Moreover, it was Pytheas who first put forward the theory that the position of the moon was responsible for the manner in which tides rise and fall.

Few, except native peoples such as the Inuit who lived close to the Arctic Circle, had reason to travel in these regions other than for fishing. The first significant travellers to the far north were the Vikings who, in search of new arable land, ventured considerable distances from their Scandinavian shores. By the second half of the 9th century they had begun to establish settlements on Iceland, where the Norse leader Ingólfr Arnarson founded Reykjavik in AD 874. During the 10th century, led by Eric the Red, they migrated westwards to settle on the south-west part of Greenland. In around AD 1000 Eric's son, Leif Erikson, sailed westwards of Greenland to become the first European to discover the continent of North America – nearly 500 years before Christopher Columbus laid claim to its discovery when he landed on San Salvador Island in the Bahamas on 12 October 1492. Believing he had reached India or China, Columbus duly took possession of the new land in the name of the Spanish monarchs King Ferdinand II and Queen Isabella of Aragon and Castile, for whom he was agent. Today, San Salvador Island is called Watlings Island.

According to the Icelandic saga, Erikson established a Norse settlement at Vinland, which today encompasses Newfoundland and the Gulf of Saint Lawrence as far as north-eastern New Brunswick. Later archaeological evidence suggests that Vinland is also identified with the area L'Anse aux Meadows, which was a ship-repair station located on the northern tip of Newfoundland. It is possible that the Icelandic Viking settlers ventured further north to Spitsbergen. Other adventurers voyaged north-eastwards and, by sailing close to the land, reached the remote archipelago of Novaya Zemlya (located in the White Sea, which fringed the northern-most coast of Russia). In c. AD 1010 another Icelander, Thorfinn Karlsefni, sailed to northern Vinland and reached an extensive land mass, which they called Helluland – today known as Baffin Island – at lat 69°N.

After the Vikings, few Europeans undertook exploration north-wards. Europe was politically preoccupied with Norman plans for expansion and the Christian Church of Western Europe had become embroiled in a series of religious wars against the Muslims in the Holy Land. Later, Europe was devastated by the Black Death (1346–1353), which is estimated to have killed some 200 million people.

The Renaissance, which began in Italy in the 14th century, encouraged a new artistic awareness and developments in mathe-matics, astronomy and navigation. Armed with recent knowledge and advances in technology, the seaman traders of Venice, Spain, Italy and Portugal set out on expeditions west and east beyond the Mediterranean. These pioneers included Count Vasco de Gama, Ferdinand Magellan and Christopher Columbus. In the field of Arctic exploration, the leading Europeans were John Cabot, Martin Frobisher, William Barentz, John Davis, William Baffin and Henry Hudson; it was in the footsteps of these pioneers that Captain Constantine Phipps, 2nd Baron Mulgrave, would follow when commanding the Royal Navy's first exploratory Arctic expedition in 1773, on which young Nelson sailed.

The first was the Genoese navigator and explorer Giovanni Caboto, usually known as John Cabot. In 1496, Cabot received patents royal from King Henry VII of England to 'go and find the new land'. Financed by London bankers, Cabot also received the sum of 50 nobles (£16 13s 4d) to undertake this venture.[1]

Cabot sailed to North America in May 1497 in the caravel *Matthew* of 50 tons' burden; his crew, including his son Sebastian, consisted of some 20 men. After a four-week passage Cabot landed at Cape Bonavista, in what is now Newfoundland. Some historians believe that Cabot also landed at Cape Breton Island or mainland Nova Scotia. This event is recorded by an entry in a 1565 chronicle of the city of Bristol: 'This year, on St. John the Baptist's Day [24 June 1497], the land of America was found by the Merchants of Bristow in a shippe of Bristowe, called the *Mathew*; the which said ship departed from the port of Bristowe, the second day of May, and came home again the 6th of August next following.'[2]

On 10 August 1497, Cabot was given a reward of £10 – equivalent to about two years' pay for an ordinary labourer or craftsman – and that December a pension of £20 per year, and was later awarded the title of admiral.

It seems this was not Cabot's first attempt to cross the Atlantic. A letter from Bristol merchant John Day, who traded with Spain, was discovered in the Archivo General de Simancas in 1956. Addressed to 'the Lord Grand Admiral' (presumably Columbus), the letter contains much information about Cabot's voyages and, responding to a question, Day infers that once Cabot was commissioned in 1496 that summer he: 'went with one ship, his crew confused him, he was short of supplies and ran into bad weather, and he decided to turn back.'[3]

Cabot did, however, make another voyage: Fabyan's *The Great Chronicle of London* (1189–1512)[4] reports that Cabot departed with a fleet of five ships from Bristol at the beginning of May 1498. While it was believed that this fleet was lost at sea, other historians have suggested that Cabot successfully returned to England in the spring of 1500. Also on behalf of the English crown, Sebastian Cabot sought a north-west passage and sailed from Bristol with two ships, the *Jesus* and the *Gabriel*, in 1504. Although not wholly successful in finding a suitable passage, he did fulfil his commercial aim of bringing back salted fish. For his efforts Sebastian Cabot was granted an annuity of £10 on 3 April 1505 by Henry VII for services 'in and aboute the fyndynge of the new founde landes'.[5] Making a further voyage between 1508 and 1509, Cabot reached north as far as the entrance of Hudson Bay, before sailing south along the east coast of America as far as the estuary of the Chesapeake and perhaps, according to Peter Martyr's 1516 account, 'almost the longitude of Cuba'.[6] In 1509, Henry VIII succeeded to the throne, but unlike his father he had little interest in exploration and English explorers lost royal support.

The first English Arctic explorer was the Yorkshireman Martin Frobisher (c. 1535 or 1539–15 November 1594). As early as 1560, this Elizabethan seaman and privateer had resolved to undertake a voyage in search of a north-west passage trade route to India and Cathay (China); in all he made three voyages. Having convinced the English merchant consortium of the Muscovy Company to support his first exploit, finance was raised to provide two barks named the *Gabriel* and the *Michael*, each of which were of about 20–25 tons. With an approximate keel length of 42ft (12.8m), a breadth of about 12ft (3.7m) and a depth in the hold about 6ft (1.8m), these single-decked vessels were small compared to Phipps's ship of 1773. Frobisher was also provided with a pinnace of 10 tons for inshore navigation, the cost of all three vessels amounting to £235 16s 8d. The *Gabriel* was furnished with a cabin on deck for Frobisher, the *Michael* likewise fitted for use by the director of the Muscovy Company, Michael Lok, who accompanied the voyage. With the exception of these cabins, living conditions for the rest of the crew must have been abysmally cramped.[7]

The masters commanding the *Gabriel* and the *Michael* were Christopher Hall and Owen Grifynne, while the rest of the crew comprised two boatswains, two gunners, one cook, one carpenter, one cooper, one smith and a surgeon, along with 34 seamen and one trumpeter, the latter to give signals.[8] The number of personnel carried, compared with the crew on Phipps's expedition of 1773, seems quite small.

Expecting to be away for a year, Frobisher's ships were well victualled:[9]

Provisions on Frobisher's expedition

Item	Quantity (imperial)	Quantity (metric)
Biscuit	7,642lb (3.41 tons)	3,500kg
Peas	40 bushels (approx 5,525lb)	2,500kg
Oatmeal	12 bushels (approx 194lb)	88kg
Wheatmeal	26 bushels (approx 423lb)	192kg
Rice	1,300lb (0.58 tons)	590kg
Mustard seed	5½ bushels (approx 90lbs)	41kg
Oxen	11 in number (5,292lb)	2,400kg
Stock fish (salted cod)	600 (approx 1,080lb)	490kg
Butter	5 barrels (approx 225lb)	102kg
Cheese	1 barrel (approx 45lb)	20kg
Flyches (sides) of bacon	27 in number (approx 225lb)	102kg
Vinegar	2 hogsheads (approx 123.2 gallons)	560 litres
Sweet oil	2 hogsheads (approx 123.2 gallons)	560 litres
Aqua vitae (brandy)	3 hogsheads (approx 187 gallons)	850 litres
Beer	13 tons (approx 330 gallons)	1,500 litres
Wine	5 tons (approx 1,210 gallons)	5,500 litres

The expedition was also armed with five falconets, which were effectively hand rail-mounted swivel guns that fired a round shot weight of 1½lb.[10]

Acording to the Julian calendar, Frobisher sailed with the blessing of Queen Elizabeth I from Greenwich on 7 June 1576 (17 June by the Gregorian calender) by way of the Shetland Isands. After losing the pinnace with four men in a storm south-west of Iceland, the *Gabriel* became separated but pressed on westwards.

When the *Michael* closed with the coast of Greenland, her crew, according to Michael Lok, became: 'so compassed with monstrous high ilands of ice flow fleting by the sea shore that they are durst not approache with their ship, nor land thereon with the bote. And so in great discomfort cast about with the ship the next day: and set their course bak agayn homeward to London, where they arrived the first day of September.'[11]

The *Gabriel*, with Frobisher and Hall, pressed on alone to the west. Recording in his master's log of 2 July, Hall wrote: 'Wee had much to adoe to get cleare of the yce by reason of the fogge.' On 14 July the *Gabriel* was struck by a northerly storm that briefly cast the ship on her side. As water flooded in, quick action saved the ship from foundering. Lok's account of 29 July records that: 'the captain himself first had sight of a new land of marvellous great heith. The headland wherof he named Elizabeth Foreland in the memory of his Quene's' Majestie.' Later named Resolution Island, this lies at 61°N 64°W between the northernmost tip of Labrador and the south-east promontory of Baffin Island, which Frobisher referred to as Meta Incognita ('The Unknown Shore') on the suggestion of Elizabeth I. As ice and wind prevented him sailing further north, Frobisher sailed west, reaching what was later named Frobisher Bay on 18 August where, upon landing, he and his crew met the local Inuits.

Uncertain about further safe navigation, Frobisher and Captain Hall now needed to reconnoitre the land. According to Lok: 'on this western shore the captayn with his men went on shore on an iland mynding to have gone to the top of a high mountayn to discover what he could of the straits of the sea and land about and there he saw the far the two hedlands at the furdest end of the streits and no likelyhood of land to the northewards of them and the great open betwene them which by reason of the great tydes of floods which they found coming owt of the same, and for many good reasons they judged to be the West Sea whereby to pass to Cathay and to the East India.' [12]

In this belief, Frobisher and Hall were entirely wrong. It appears from Frobisher's account that five of his seamen went missing when sent on shore with the boat and were subsequently found to have been captured. Unable to retrieve these men, the expedition sailed home, reaching London on 9 October. In contrast to Frobisher's story, Inuit folklore states that the seamen were in fact left behind by accident and were cared for by the Inuit villagers. [13]

On his return to England, Frobisher received much acclaim and was given a charter from the Crown in the name of the Company of Cathay, which funded his second expedition to the sum of £1,000. Given the right to sail in every direction but to the east, Frobisher was appointed as 'high admiral of the lands and waters he may discover'. He was given three ships: the Navy Royale's ship *Ayde* of 'nine score tuns' and two mercantile barks, the *Gabriel* and the *Michael*, which he had taken on the previous expedition. The former was now commanded by Master Fenton, the latter by Master Yorke, and both were 'furnished with victuals and provisions necesarie for one halfe year'.[14] Intending to prospect for valuable minerals, the ships were manned with 150 men, including miners, refiners, gentlemen and soldiers. The expedition sailed from Blackwall on 26 May 1577. Michael Lok, who had been appointed governor of the Muscovy Company, sailed with them. Destined for the Labrador coast of Canada, Frobisher's hopeful intention was to find a north-west passage to the East.

Shortly after their arrival at what is now the south side of Frobisher Bay, they solemnly took possession of the land in the name of Elizabeth I. Although the main objective had been to seek out a north-west passage, this was cast aside when they found what they assumed to be gold ore – a treasure with a value of some £5 4s per ton. Anticipating a considerable profit, Frobisher had 200 tons of ore loaded into three ships and brought home in July. The estimated market value of this cargo was in excess of £1,000.[15]

Frobisher's third expedition elicited very little in the way of discovery. He had been specifically directed by his commission to 'defer the further discovery of the passage until another time'. Several weeks were spent digging mines around Frobisher Bay, from which they collected 1,350 tons of ore with an expected value of more than £7,000. The prospecting project, however, proved fruitless. What's more, when smelted in England, the ore proved to be worthless iron pyrite.

In reality, Frobisher's three voyages contributed little to expanding knowledge of the far north-west. He spent much of the rest of his career as a privateer and pirate, plundering riches from French and Spanish ships, though he was later knighted for his service in the Navy Royale for fighting with Admirals Lord Howard of Effingham, Drake, Hawkins, and the lesser-known Dutchman Justinus van Nassau against the Spanish Armada in 1588.[16]

A more significant explorer from northern climes is the Englishman John Davis. Born in the parish of Stoke Gabriel in

Devon c. 1550, he was one of Elizabeth I's chief navigators and possessed exceptional skills, which were probably initially influenced by the achievements of other local navigators such as Adrian and Humphrey Gilbert and their half-brother Walter Raleigh. Davis also led several voyages in search of the north-west passage and served as pilot and captain on both Dutch and English voyages to the East Indies.

In 1583, Davis proposed a voyage to search for a north-west passage to Francis Walsingham, Elizabeth I's secretary. Two years later, Walsingham finally agreed to fund the expedition and Davis set sail on his first voyage from Dartmouth on 7 June 1585 'towards', he said, 'the dicoverie of the aforsayd North west passage with Two barks, the one being of 50 tunnes, named *Sunneshine* of London the other being 35 tunnes, named the *Mooneshine* of Dartmouth. In the *Sunneshine* we had 23 persons ... The *Mooneshine* had 19 persons.' [17]

The crew of the Sunneshine[18]

Title	Name
Captain	John Davis
Master	William Easton
Master's Mate	Richard Pope
Merchant	John Jane
Gunner	Henry Davie
Boatswain	William Crosse
Carpenter	Robert Wats
Mariners	Luke Adams, Walter Arthur, John Bagge, Robert Coxworthie, Edward Dicke, John Ellis, Thomas Hill, John Kelly & Andrew Maddocke
Musicians	James Cole, Robert Cornish & Francis Ridley
Boys	William Russell & Christopher Gorney

The crew of the Mooneshine

Title	Name
Captain	William Bruton
Master	John Ellis
Mariners	17 in number unnamed

Davis set out to trace Frobisher's route, taking in the east coast of Greenland, which he called the 'land of desolution' because of the vast amount of driftwood seen along the shoreline. Meeting native Greenlanders in 'four canoas', he was given sealskin clothes. He also recalled seeing 'foure white beares of monstrous bigness'. Circling around Cape Farewell, he proceeded to Baffin Island where he discovered and named the Davis Strait. Returning home, they reached Dartmouth on 30 September.

Sailing again from Dartmouth on 7 May 1586, Davis had four ships: *the Sunneshine,* the *Mooneshine,* the *Mermayd* (120 tonnes) and a pinnace of 10 tonnes named the *North Star.*[19] This time Davis divided his forces: two ships were sent to explore Greenland's eastern shore while he took two ships NNW up what would later be called the Davis Strait between the western side of Greenland and the east coast of Baffin Island. Unfortunately, he was unable to penetrate further than 67°N as the passage was blocked by the Arctic ice cap. The *Sunneshine* attempted to circumnavigate Greenland from the east but was also unsuccessful. It seems that Davis initially made friendly contact with the Inuit people but this changed after one of the ship's anchors was stolen, and the resulting hostilities led to the ships being attacked in the Hamilton Inlet on the Labrador coast north of Newfoundland.[20]

On a third expedition in 1587, Davis reached latitude 72°12′N and Disko Island, the second largest of the Greenland islands. Turned back by unfavourable winds, he bore south to chart the Davis Inlet on the coast of Labrador.

Despite the various setbacks Davis encountered, his expeditions proved useful, not least because throughout his voyages he kept an accurate journal, the content of which remained a model for ships' captains for centuries.

When England was later threatened by Spanish invasion, Davis commanded the *Black Dog* against the Spanish Armada in 1588, after which he continued making various adventurous voyages. In 1591, for instance, Davis sailed in the *Desire* with Thomas Cavendish in an ultimately unsuccessful attempt to search the north-west passage from the western side of the North American continent. During the voyage home in 1592, Davis sailed back into the Atlantic via the

Strait of Magellan and is said to have discovered the Falkland Islands. Here, running short of food, he and his crew were forced to kill penguins and store them on board, though because the meat spoiled and couldn't be eaten only 14 of his 76 men made it home alive.[21]

Between 1596 and 1601 Davis appears to have been the master of one of Sir Walter Raleigh's ships sailing to Cadiz and the Azores. Between 1601 and 1603 he accompanied a Dutch expedition to the East Indies and later accompanied Sir James Lancaster as pilot major on the first voyage of the English East India Company. On a second voyage for the East India Company, Davis was killed on 29 December 1605 when his ship was attacked by Japanese pirates off Bintan Island near Singapore.

The Davis Strait, which he had discovered, went on to become one of the most noted hunting grounds used by the British, Dutch and, later, American whaling fleets, rivalled only by the Spitsbergen archipelago to which Captain Phipps's expedition sailed in 1773.

Men from the Barentz expedition encountering polar bears. Rijksmuseum.

A need to compete with the trade that the English Muscovy Company had developed with Russia led Dutch expeditions to also venture to the north-east. Their first chosen explorer and navigator was William Barentz, born c. 1550 on the island of Terschelling, although he went on to die on his third voyage. Much of our knowledge about Barentz's expeditions can be attributed to his officer Gerrit de Veer, who besides keeping a diary on the second and third cruises also wrote a fluent record of the first. These detailed descriptive accounts covering all three voyages were published in Amsterdam in 1698.

Barentz sailed in the *Mercury* from Texel, the largest of the Dutch West Frisian Islands, on 5 June 1594 with a group of three ships. Each of these vessels was to sail in separate directions and attempt entry into the Kara Sea off the north coast of Russia in the hope of finding a north-east passage across the Siberian coast. During the voyage, Barentz and his crew stayed on Kildin Island off Murmansk, where a polar bear 'boldly came towards our ship to enter it' and rampaged around on board. In response, the crew 'raised four pieces [muskets] and shot her in the body'.[22]

Sailing further they discovered the Orange Islands where they found a vast herd of walruses, which they tried to kill for their tusks. It is unclear whether this name relates to the group of 191 small islands NbNW of Novaya Zemlya, later named Franz Josef Land. Barentz appears to have approached Novaya Zemlya from the south-west from Kildin Island before turning northwards, running up the west coast of the great island, passing various islands off the coast en route. However, upon meeting large icebergs and pack ice in the north, he was eventually forced to turn back.

Although Barentz did not achieve his ultimate goal and find a navigable north-east passage, the voyage was considered a success.[23] On hearing of the exploits, Prince Maurice of Orange consented to a second voyage and provided Barentz with six vessels loaded with merchandise to trade with China. The expedition left on 2 June 1595 and sailed between the Siberian coast and Vaygach Island. Searching for crystal on a nearby islet on 4 September, the boat's crew were attacked by a polar bear and two men were killed. On their return voyage they found the Kara Sea frozen and were once again forced to return home.[24]

Despite the apparent failure of this second voyage, Barentz received funds to undertake a third voyage, which proved highly rewarding in terms of its geographical achievements. Equipped with two ships, commanded by Jan Rijp and Jacob van Heemskerk, Barentz set sail in May 1596. On 9 June, Barentz and Heemskerk discovered Bear Island (known today as Bjørnøya). Located in the western part of the Barents Sea approximately halfway between Spitsbergen and the North Cape, Norway,[25] it was so named after Heemskerk sighted a polar bear swimming nearby.

Sailing further north, Barentz discovered the archipelago of Spitsbergen on 17 June – a location that Phipps's expedition would become very familiar with in 1773. Three days later Barentz came upon the entrance of a large bay, which was later called Raudfjorden. On 21 June they anchored between Cloven Cliff and Vogelsang, where they claimed ownership by setting up 'a post with the arms of the Dutch upon it'.[26]

On 25 June the expedition entered Magdalenefjorden and, finding many walrus tusks scattered there, they named it Tusk Bay. Next morning, they sailed into the northern entrance of Forlandsundet but were forced to turn back because of a shoal, which led them to call the fjord Keerwyck ('inlet where one is forced to turn back'). On 28 June they rounded the northern point of Prins Karls Forland, which they named Vogelhoek ('bird corner') on account of the large number of birds they saw there. Sailing south, they passed Isfjorden and Bellsund, which Barentz recorded on his chart as Grooten Inwyck and Inwyck – Grooten referring to the 'larger islet'.[27]

When the ships returned to Bear Island on 1 July a dispute ensued that resulted in a parting of the ways. While Rijp decided to sail north, Barentz kept to his plan to seek out a north-east passage with van Heemskerk and reached Novaya Zemlya on 17 July. Late in the season Barentz became trapped amid icebergs and ice floes and he and his 16-man (and one boy) crew were forced to overwinter on the ice. Using timber and canvas from the ship together with driftwood they collected, they built a shelter measuring just 25ft 8in by 18ft (7.8m x 5.5m), which they called *Het Behouden Huys* ('The Saved House'). With materials from the ship they also managed to fashion blankets and additional clothing to combat the cold, and kept warm by sleeping with heated stones and cannonballs.

Before sailing, the ship had been well stocked with provisions including salted beef, butter, cheese, bread, flour, hardtack barley, peas, beans and groats along with smoked bacon, ham and fish, oil, vinegar, mustard and salt. There was also beer, wine and brandy, although unfortunately most of the beer froze.[28] Gerrit de Veer recorded in his diary that rationing of the wine and bread began days after the stranding occurred, and stored food stocks were supplemented by fresh meat from hunted Arctic foxes and polar bears.[29] It's clear that every effort was made by de Veer to maintain the health of the men, including the creation of a hot water bath from an old cask, although this did not prevent the boy from dying during the winter. Despite this, Barentz and his men may be the first recorded European explorers ever to have overwintered in the ice.

By June of the following year, the ship was still completely gripped in the ice, so on 13 June the survivors, by now suffering with scurvy, took to the sea with two small boats and made their way to the Kola Peninsula. Barentz died on 23 June 1597, but seven weeks later the crew reached their destination, where they were rescued by a Russian merchant vessel. By this time just 12 men remained of the original crew, and they eventually returned to Amsterdam on 1 November.[30]

Although Barentz did not survive his final voyage, his contribution towards Arctic exploration stands testament to his perseverance and capabilities as a navigator. In the post-Viking period he was the first European to reach Novaya Zemlya but his most important discovery was finding the Spitsbergen archipelago. The discovery of these islands had a profound impact on further exploration, including that of Constantine Phipps. As a mark of his importance, the north-eastern seas between Spitsbergen and the Kola Peninsula were named the Barents Sea in his honour in the 19th century.

The voyages also highlighted the difficulties of navigating the Arctic regions: ships could be trapped in ice, crews might need to overwinter in a desperate climate, food stocks were limited, and the psychological effect of total isolation on a ship's crew could not be overestimated.

The next English sailor to follow Frobisher and seek a north-west passage was the English navigator and explorer William Baffin

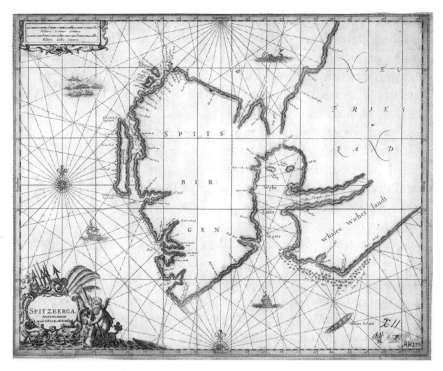

The west coast of Spitsbergen, c.1680–1711.

(c. 1584–23 January 1622). Primarily known for his attempt to discover a north-west passage from the Atlantic to the Pacific and his discovery of Baffin Island and its bay in what is now Canada, Baffin also surveyed the Red Sea and the Persian Gulf for the East India Company.

A dogged and intuitive navigator, Baffin was appointed to Captain Hall, who had previously undertaken three voyages to Greenland on behalf of Christian IV of Denmark, who was trying to re-establish contact with the Norse settlements there. Wishing to undertake a fourth voyage, Hall had persuaded four English merchants – Thomas Smythe, James Lancaster, William Cockayne and Richard Ball – to support a further Greenland enterprise.

Baffin sailed with Hall from the Humber estuary in the *Patience* on 22 April 1612, accompanied by the *Heart's Ease*. Hall was duly killed by the Inuit on the west coast of Greenland, but Baffin successfully returned to Hull on 11 September.[31] Between 1613 and 1614 Baffin was employed in the Muscovy Company controlling the whale fishery off Spitsbergen, first serving under Captain Benjamin Joseph as pilot of the *Tiger*, the flagship of the seven-vessel whaling fleet. Then, in 1614 he and Joseph served in the *Thomasine*, amid a fleet of 11 ships and two pinnaces. Although icy conditions precluded exploration to the north, Baffin did examine a 'considerable portion' of Spitsbergen's coast, returning to London on 4 October.[32]

In 1615, Baffin entered the service of the 'Company of Merchants of London, Discoverers of the North-West Passage' that had been established in 1612. Serving as pilot in the *Discovery* under Captain Robert Bylot, Baffin sailed from England on 15 March, crossed the North Atlantic and began to explore the Hudson Strait for a north-west passage to the Far East. During this expedition Baffin charted a good part of what would be named Baffin Island and recorded astronomical and tidal observations with such accuracy that all the details could be confirmed when explorer William Edward Parry sailed in the same waters more than 200 years later.

The following year, 1616, Baffin again sailed as pilot of *Discovery*, leaving Gravesend on 26 March. On this voyage he sailed through the Davis Strait, where he discovered a large bay, which today bears his name. In all, Baffin sailed some 300 miles (480km) further north than did his predecessor John Davis, but he also failed to find an ice-free nautical path to the Orient.[33]

Baffin's navigational abilities proved to be of great value to those exploring the ice-bound regions of north-east Canada in the years to come. In 1617, for example, he took service with the East India Company, first serving as master's mate in the *Anne Royal* under Captain Andrew Shilling bound for India, returning home in September 1619. Next, he was appointed master of the East India Company ship *London* and sailed from the Downs, off Deal in Kent, on 25 March 1620, reaching Surat in November, by which time the East India Company had become embroiled in attacking rival Portuguese possessions. A couple of years later, on 23 January 1622, it was recorded that he met his death while off Bandar Abbas preparing to attack Fort Queixome: 'Master Baffin went on shoare with his Geometricall Instruments, for the traking of the height and distance of the Castle wall for the better levelling of his peece [gun] to make his shot; but as he was about the same he received a small shot from the Castle in his belly, wherewith he gave thre leapes and died immediately.'[34]

Although Baffin Bay and Baffin Island were later named after him and he named their various features, the only accounts we have of Baffin's voyages were printed in an abridged publication by Samuel Purchace in 1625. Unfortunately, Purchace omitted Baffin's charts and hydrographic observations to save expense and in order to cast doubt on Baffin's discoveries, though one chart has survived. Despite the uncertainty caused by the lack of published material, when explorer John Ross led an expedition in search of the north-west passage in 1818 he was able to confirm that all of Baffin's accounts were entirely accurate.

Perhaps the last of the early 17th-century explorers and navigators was the Englishman Henry Hudson (1565–1611), who undertook three voyages seeking a northerly passage to the East. In 1607, Hudson was hired by the merchants of the Muscovy Company to find a northerly route to the Pacific coast of Asia. At the time it was believed that because the sun shone during the three-month summer of the northernmost latitudes the Arctic ice would melt, allowing ships to sail across the top of the world. With a crew of ten men and a boy, Hudson sailed in the 80-ton *Hopewell* on 1 May, reaching the east coast of Greenland on 14 June and then steering north. Eight days later he reached a latitude of 73°N and named a prominent headland Young's Cape. Hudson then set a course east, sighting what he called the 'Newland' on 27 June. This in fact turned out to be Spitsbergen. Here, he entered a large bay, which he simply named Great Indraught (Isfjorden). By 13 July, Hudson believed he had reached lat 80°23′N, (he was in fact 1° in error and consequently 69 miles (60 nautical miles/97km) south of this assumed position). Next day he entered what he named Whales Bay, the north-west promontory of which he named Collins Cape after his boatswain, William Collins. On 16 July they reached as far north as Hakluyt's Headland at lat 79°49′N, at which point Hudson thought he saw more land extending to the north-east. What he had really seen was what Phipps would later refer to as the 'Northeastland'. Meeting pack ice, Hudson was then forced to turn south. He had hoped to return home via Greenland and the Davis Strait but ice conditions made this difficult, and he eventually arrived at Tilbury Hope on the Thames on 15 September.[35]

In 1608, the English East India Company[36] and Muscovy Company commissioned Hudson in the *Hopewell* to attempt to seek a passage to the Indies, this time following a north-east passage around northern Russia. Leaving London on 22 April, Hudson sailed in the *Hopewell* almost 2,500 miles (2,172 nautical miles/4,023km), reaching Novaya Zemlya in July. However, although it was summer the ice was impenetrable and Hudson was forced to retreat, arriving back at Gravesend on 26 August.[37]

The Dutch, too, were seeking northerly trade routes. So, given Hudson's reputation, he was employed in 1609 by the Dutch East India Company to seek a passage westwards.[38] The ship provided by the Dutch was an unhandy carrack named the *Halve Maen* (Half Moon), which had a length of about 85ft (25.9m) and a breadth of 17ft 6in (5.33m). In design, the ship was more suitable for Dutch waters and, comparing her to English vessels, Hudson remarked: 'I'm afraide *she'll prove clumsy in foul weather.*' Nevertheless, Hudson set sail from Amsterdam on 4 April and headed north. Meeting considerable ice off North Cape (Norway), he then set a course west, arriving off the Grand Banks of Newfoundland on 2 July. Sailing south, he passed Nova Scotia before exploring what is now the Hudson River and the area that would in 1625, become the Dutch colony of Manhattan (New Amsterdam). Sailing further south he reached Chesapeake and explored Delaware Bay and the North River. Deciding to return to Europe in late September, Hudson eventually put into Dartmouth, England on 7 November. Here, he was detained by English authorities who were concerned about potential Dutch commercial advantage and wanted access to his navigational journals. Fortunately for Hudson, the Dutch ambassador intervened on his behalf.

Jointly funded by the English Virginia Company and the British East India Company to find a north-west passage, Hudson set off on his final voyage in 1610. Approaching the Labrador coast, he discovered the Hudson Strait and the immense inland sea now named Hudson Bay. Trapped by ice, he was forced to overwinter on the shore of James Bay. Setting forth again in the spring of 1611 he decided to press further west. However, in June, most of his crew, keen to return home, mutinied and cast Hudson, his son and seven others adrift in an open boat. They were never seen again.

After Hudson, little Arctic exploration occurred during the late 17th century. This was due in part to the fact that Britain was preoccupied with expanding the North American fur trade and competing with other nations involved with the Greenland and Spitsbergen whaling industry. Furthermore, between 1652 and 1674 Britain and Holland were at war, disputing their colonial trade monopoly with their respective trade routes. By 1688, Britain was again at war, this time against France in what became the Nine Year's War (often called the War of the Grand Alliance, the War of the League of Augsburg, or King William's War). After this conflict ended in 1697, within four years Britain was once more at war, this time the War of the Spanish Succession (1701–15). It was thus not until 1719 that the Hudson's Bay Company sent an expedition north-west to seek mineral deposits.

Led by James Knight, the company vessel *Albany*, described as a frigate, and accompanying sloop sailed from Gravesend that June and were never seen again. It was later revealed by some Inuit people they'd had contact with that the crew, confined to their hut, were suffering from sickness and malnutrition. When they were found by the Inuit in 1721 only five remained alive, barely surviving on seal meat and whale blubber. After three more died, the remaining two men survived for a short while, expecting relief to arrive. It never did, with the consequence that 'they sat down together and wept bitterly'. At length one of the two died, and the other's strength was so far exhausted that he fell down dead too, 'in attempting to dig a grave for his companion the sculls and other large bones of those two men are now lying above the ground close to the house'.[39]

Although the early Arctic explorers were men with experience and ability, none were actually able to find an alternative east or west route to the Orient – a failure that was usually due to their inability to penetrate the fields of sea ice they met in such high latitudes. Despite this, driven by pure determination, each exploratory journey contributed important additional information and experiences towards future ventures. Collectively, the accumulated knowledge helped to prepare the way for Phipps's later expedition.

Of these explorers, perhaps William Barentz was the most important in terms of the knowledge he contributed, primarily because it was he who discovered the Spitsbergen archipelago from where Phipps would make the main thrust towards the North Pole. The detailed descriptive records of Barentz's surviving officer Gerrit de Veer stand testament to the incidents and conditions encountered on the voyages. His account, first published in Amsterdam, was transcribed by writer and geographer Richard Hakluyt in his three-volume work *The Principal Navigations, Voyages, Discoveries of the English Nation,* first published in 1589 and with second editions in 1599 and 1600. This work was certainly available to Phipps and other potential explorers by 1770.[40]

3

Circumnavigation, longitude and the
Royal Society mission for exploration

Although the 18th century was interrupted by many wars, with Britain and France as the main adversaries, it also heralded the Age of Enlightenment – an era when the promotion of scientific reasoning encouraged global exploration. One such venture was Commodore George Anson's circumnavigation of the world, which ended in 1744. Although the voyage had been undertaken more as a hostile venture to attack Spanish South American possessions rather than for exploratory reasons, it did promote the concept of the exploratory voyage and encouraged others to attempt further expeditions. Unfortunately, however, the subsequent War of the Austrian Succession (1740–48) and the Seven Years' War (1756–63) curtailed any potential exploration for more than 20 years.

However, when all conflict finally ended with the Treaty of Paris in 1763, both Britain and France welcomed the opportunity to restart their exploratory pursuits. Britain took the lead with a voyage undertaken by Captain John Byron – who had previously sailed on Anson's voyage – in the 24-gun sixth-rate frigate *Dolphin*, accompanied by the 20-gun sloop *Tamar*, which set forth in June 1764 for the Pacific and East Indies.

In 1765, Byron took possession of the Falkland Islands in the name of Britain – an act that nearly led to conflict between Britain and Spain. Later in the voyage, he visited the Tuamotus and Tokelau Islands, Nikunau in the southern Gilbert Islands as well as Tinian in the Northern Marianas Islands. Returning home in May 1766, Byron's was the first circumnavigation accomplished in less than two years. From a ship's perspective, the voyage of the *Dolphin* is particularly important because, in preparation for the voyage, her underwater hull had been experimentally sheathed in copper to deter the tropical sea worm *Teredo navalis,* which was known to bore into a ship's planking, rendering many vessels unseaworthy.[1]

The year 1766 saw the departure of two further global voyages – one British and one French. The British exploratory expedition, authorised by the Royal Navy, was led by a very able Cornishman, Captain Samuel Wallis. He was given command of Byron's vessel, the *Dolphin* – a ship clearly chosen because of her copper sheathing.[2] Wallis was accompanied by HMS *Swallow* under the command of Philip Carteret, who had previously sailed as a lieutenant with Byron and whose experience would prove invaluable. By misfortune, the two ships parted company shortly after sailing through the Strait of Magellan. Despite this mishap, however, Wallis continued on to Tahiti, which he named 'King George the Third's Island' in honour of the king. As Wallis was ill on arrival, it was his first lieutenant, Tobias Furneaux, who was first to set foot on the land and, after hoisting a pennant and turning a turf, took possession. Sailing further west they reached Polynesia, where Wallis Island was named after the captain. Wallis next sailed to Batavia where many of his crew died of dysentery, before sailing home via the Cape of Good Hope, arriving in England in May 1768. Wallis's arrival could not have been better timed since he was able to pass on much vital information to Captain James Cook, who was shortly to depart on his first exploratory voyage to the Pacific in HM transport *Endeavour.*

Meanwhile, Philip Carteret in the *Swallow* continued into the South Pacific, where on 3 July 1767 he discovered an isolated group of volcanic islands. These islands had been initially discovered in 1606 by the Portuguese sailor Pedro Fernandes de Queirós, sailing for the Spanish Crown, who named them La Encarnación and San Juan Bautista. Some 150 years later, Carteret renamed them Pitcairn after the *Swallow*'s 15-year-old midshipman, Robert Pitcairn, who had been the first to sight them. A few years later, in 1789, the Pitcairn Islands would become infamous as the haven for the mutineers from HMS *Bounty.* Although Carteret correctly charted their position by latitude, because he had no chronometer his position of longitude was inaccurate by 3° an approximate distance of 140 nautical miles (161 miles/259km) at this latitude: the length of a nautical mile shortening as you travel from the Equator towards the Poles. Hence the later difficulty HMS *Pandora* had when attempting to find the *Bounty* mutineers.

Carteret also discovered a new archipelago inside Saint George's Channel between New Ireland and the New Britain Islands (Papua New Guinea) and named it the Duke of York Islands. During his voyage, he also rediscovered the Solomon Islands, first sighted by the Spaniard Álvaro de Mendaña in 1568, and the Juan Fernández Islands, first discovered by Juan Fernández in 1574. Carteret finally arrived back in England, anchoring the *Swallow* at Spithead on 20 March 1769. Unfortunately, the voyage ruined Carteret's health and though he received command of the 44-gun Roebuck-class *Endymion* in 1779, he failed to get another ship afterwards. After suffering a stroke in 1792, he retired with the rank of rear admiral in 1794 and died two years later.

On reflection, Carteret's voyage was perhaps more successful than that of Wallis, though both men gathered much global information for their country. That said, although Byron, Wallis and Carteret had successfully explored parts of the Pacific Ocean, the man who would most influence the British expedition to seek the North Pole and north-east passage was the French nobleman Louis-Antoine de Bougainville (1729–1811). Educated in law and mathematics, Bougainville submitted his *Traité du calcul intégral*, which expanded on the work of Guillaume L'Hopital published in 1696. For this he achieved instant recognition from the Academie des Sciences in 1753 and election into the Royal Society in 1756. As captain of dragoons, Bougainville acted as aide-de-camp to General the Marquis de Montcalm in Canada during the Seven Years' War, and fought beside Montcalm against the British attack upon Quebec in 1759.

Following the Seven Years' War, Bougainville was promoted to admiral in the French Royal Navy and ventured into the Pacific Ocean on a scientific expedition, circumnavigating the world between 1766 and 1769. He was accompanied by Jean-François de Galaup, comte de Lapérouse (later an explorer) and astrono-mer Pierre-Antoine Véron. Also with them was botanist Philibert Commerçon and his valet (who was in fact his mistress, Jeanne Baret, disguised as a man – the first known woman to circumnavigate the globe). In 1771, Bougainville published his account of the expedi-tion, *Le voyage autour du monde, par la frégate du roi* La Boudeuse,

Admiral Antoine de Bougainville (1729–1811). Universal History Archive/Getty Images.

et la flûte L'Étoile (*A Voyage Around the World on the King's Frigate* La Boudeuse *and the Flute* The Star).

The book described the geography, biology and anthropology of Argentina, Patagonia, Tahiti and Indonesia and its publication proved a sensation, especially his descriptions of Tahitian society, which he portrayed as an earthly paradise where men and women lived a bliss-ful innocent existence uncorrupted by civilisation. Bougainville also stressed the need to resolve the problem regarding the '*passage par le Nord*', an issue that had been raised by French philosopher, mathema-tician and man of letters Pierre Louis Moreau de Maupertuis, who believed that there would be less ice in open polar seas than near land masses. With his connection to the Royal Society, Bougainville's book and accomplishments duly came to the attention of Britain's scholarly elite, leading to a far more proactive approach to exploratory affairs.

The Royal Society, which was to promote the Navy's Arctic expedition of 1773, had its origins in a group of physicians and natural philosophers, convened by Francis Bacon in 1645, who held meetings at Gresham College, London to discuss 'new science'. Later, an expanded version of the group became known as 'The Philosophical Society of Oxford' and met at the Bodleian Library. This informal group was later transformed into a college for the 'Promoting of Physico-Mathematical-Experimental Learning'. Later, influenced by the French scientists of the Montmor Academy set up in 1657, 12 leading British academics founded The Royal Society on 28 November 1660. It was granted a Royal Charter by King Charles II on 15 July 1662 and its name was revised to the Royal Society of London for the Improvement of Natural Knowledge. One of its main activities was the publication of its *Proceedings* and *Philosophical Transactions*. Among those who had already served as its president by the late 18th century were Samuel Pepys and Sir Isaac Newton.

Reflecting upon the exploratory voyages undertaken by Bougainville and Britain's earlier circumnavigators, Wallis and Carteret, the Royal Society realised that Britain's political prestige and potential trading capabilities could be threatened if France continued to take the initiative in scientific exploration. So, on 16 February 1768 the Royal Society petitioned King George III to finance a scientific expedition to the Pacific to observe the transit of Venus across the sun, which was predicted to occur on 3–4 June 1769. The main purpose of this venture was to calculate the distance between the earth and the sun using Edmond Halley's 1716 paper to the Royal Society on how this data could be obtained.[3] With full royal approval, the objectives of the voyage now also encompassed making discoveries to the south and west of Cape Horn.[4] Exploiting the opportunity, the first lord of the admiralty, Lord Sandwich (John Montagu), surreptitiously added the Society's own mission to the venture: to search the South Pacific and find the assumed continent of Terra Australis Incognita ('unknown southern land').[5] This would only be undertaken once all the formal astronomical and scientific objectives were complete.

Rising to the challenge, the Admiralty deliberated on who was best placed to command the expeditionary vessel; this was no ordinary small-ship commission. They chose Lieutenant James Cook, who had demonstrated his superb navigational skills when charting the St Lawrence River for Admiral Saunders' Canadian invasion fleet during the siege of Quebec in 1759. Not just highly competent at handling a ship, as an officer Cook was a 'seaman's seaman, resolute and blunt' – an ideal temperament for dealing with the men under his command.

Several scholars also embarked upon the voyage. These included the naturalist and botanist Sir Joseph Banks, who was patron of the natural sciences, and the astronomer Charles Green, representing the Astronomer Royal Nevil Maskelyne. Accompanying them was the Swedish naturalist Dr Daniel Solander, a disciple of the celebrated botanist, physician and zoologist Carl Linnaeus, renowned for formalising the modern system of naming organisms known as binomial nomenclature. Also present were the Finnish naturalist Herman Spöring, two artists, a scientific secretary and two black servants.[6]

Captain James Cook (1728–79) after a portrait by Nathaniel Dance RA. Photo 12/UIG/Getty Images.

Joseph Banks, FRS (1743–1820) after a portrait by Sir Joshua Reynolds. Hulton Archive/Getty Images.

Nevil Maskelyne, Astronomer Royal (1732–1811) after a portrait by Gerard van de Puyl. The Print Collector/Getty Images.

The first announcements of the proposed voyage were made in the *St. James's Chronicle* and *Lloyd's Evening Post* in the first week of August 1768. The *London Gazetteer* reported on 18 August: 'To-morrow morning Mr. Banks, Dr. Solano [sic], with Mr. Green, the Astronomer, will set out for Deal, to embark on board the Endeavour, Capt. Cook, for the South Seas, under the direction of the Royal Society, to observe the Transit of Venus next summer. The gentlemen, who are to sail in a few days for George's Land, the new discovered island in the Pacific ocean, with an intention to observe the Transit of Venus, are likewise, we are credibly informed, to attempt some new discoveries in that vast unknown tract, above the latitude 40.'[7]

In command of HM Bark *Endeavour*, Cook sailed from Plymouth on 26 August 1768 on the first of three exploratory voyages, returning home to anchor in the Downs, off Deal in Kent, on 12 July 1771. Cook's voyage with Banks had many successes, including the discovery and charting of a large expanse of Australia, the fabled Terra Australis Incognita, and the unexpected discovery of New Zealand. Cook would make two further exploratory voyages into the Pacific, both of which touched polar regions. His second venture (1772–75) took him far to the south, where he and his crew became the first Europeans to cross the Antarctic circle, while his third voyage (1776–79) took him into the north Pacific along the coast of Alaska, eventually reaching the Bering Strait before pack ice prevented him from entering the Arctic Sea from the west.[8]

Cook's successful circumnavigational journey gave encouragement to others to embark on further voyages of discovery. It also regenerated the idea of finding a northerly passage to the East. One Royal Society member who believed this was possible was the lawyer, naturalist and antiquarian the Honourable Daines Barrington, who was elected as vice president of the Royal Society on 10 December 1772. We know this because during a Royal Society Council meeting on 19 January 1773 the following minute was made: 'The Hon. Daines Barrington having mentioned a conversation he had with Lord Sandwich about the practicability of a Navigation to the North Pole, and by it to the East Indies.'[9]

In its approach to the Admiralty, the Royal Society submitted a letter to Lord Sandwich:

'My Lord,

I am directed by the President and Council of the Royal Society, to represent to your Lordship, that they have lately had under consideration the probability of Navigation being practicable nearer the North Pole than has been generally imagined; and that there is room to hope, that a passage by or nearer the North Pole to the East Indies may be thereby found out. And as a voyage made towards the north-pole might be of service to the promotion of natural knowledge the proper object of their institution, they cannot but be much interested in the prosecution of the same. They therefore beg leave to recommend it to your Lordship who have always shewn such readiness in promoting science and geographical knowledge, whether it might not be proper to take some steps towards the making such a discovery.'[10]

Responding to the request, Sandwich laid out a proposal for an expedition to the North Pole before George III. The king replied that it would be 'His Majesty's pleasure to direct, that it should be immediately undertaken with every encouragement and assistance that could contribute, towards its success'.[11] It seems likely that the success of James Cook's recent voyage influenced the king's supportive attitude. Although Barrington was confident about his initial proposal, he was cautious, later informing the Admiralty that if it proved possible to reach the Pole the expedition should return rather than crossing the Arctic Ocean.

One Royal Naval officer who upon hearing about the expedition offered his services was Commander Constantine Phipps, the son of the 1st Baron Mulgrave, Constantine Phipps. Born on 19 May 1744, Phipps junior studied at Eton College, where he became well acquainted with the future Royal Society botanist Joseph Banks. Phipps entered into the Royal Navy in 1759 as a cadet officer and saw active service for the remainder of the Seven Years' War. Later, serving as a lieutenant in the sixth-rate *Niger* under the command of Captain Sir Thomas Adams, he sailed for Newfoundland in 1766. Also on board the ship, serving as botanist, was Phipps's former school friend, Joseph Banks. Given that the two enjoyed the scientific aspects that this voyage offered, it is not inconceivable that it was this type of experience that influenced Phipps to offer his services 'to be entrusted with the conduct of the undertaking'.[12] Perhaps his intellectual inclinations meant that the idea of exploration was more appealing to Phipps than were his mundane naval duties. As perhaps the most suitable candidate (there is no evidence of other volunteers), Phipps was duly appointed commander of the expedition to seek the North Pole in 1773.

Because the expedition was considered a scientific voyage, specialists in various fields were carried in the two ships. These included the mathematician and botanist Dr Israel Lyons and ship's surgeon Dr Charles Irving. Born in Cambridge in 1739, Lyons studied at Trinity College. After publishing his *Treatise on Fluxions* at the age of 19, he was immediately recognised as a mathematical genius. As well as this, his enthusiasm for botany resulted in a published survey of Cambridge flora a few years later. As an acknowledged authority on botany, Lyons was paid by Joseph Banks to deliver a series of lectures at the University of Oxford in 1760. Shortly afterwards, he was selected by the Astronomer Royal Dr Nevil Maskelyne to compute astronomical tables for the *Nautical Almanac*, a publication first introduced in 1767 that describes the positions of selected celestial bodies to enable navigators to use celestial navigation to determine the position of their ship while at sea. Armed with a range of talents, Lyons' position as Astronomer Royal for the expedition was secured by Joseph Banks. Besides the recording of all astronomical observations and gravitation experiments, Lyons was responsible for the recording and care of the two chronometers carried to determine the ship's longitude. Tragically, just three years after his polar experience, Lyons died of measles aged just 36. At the time, he had been preparing a complete edition of Edmond Halley's works, sponsored by the Royal Society.[13]

Although Dr Charles Irving was to be borne in the *Racehorse* as the ship's surgeon, his role was actually multifarious. Noted for his knowledge of natural philosophy and trained in chemistry,

Irving invented distilling apparatus that enabled sea water to be converted into drinkable fresh water (see page 108–110). In 1770, his innovative equipment was adopted and installed on Royal Naval ships and distillers of his design were fitted in the expedition ships *Racehorse* and *Carcass*. Irving's many other duties involved undertaking and recording a series of experiments, many related to sea water. He was assisted in his work by the African able seaman who is listed on the ship's muster book as Gustav Weston – although his real name was Olaudah Equiano – who had been working for Irving in Pall Mall since 1768. Later in life he was also known as Gustavus Vassa.

Other specialists taken on the voyage were two Greenland pilots, one carried in each ship. Hired from vessels of the whaling fleet and holding master's mates' certificates, their knowledge of the polar regions was of crucial importance to those commanding the two expeditionary ships, Commanders Constantine Phipps and Skeffington Lutwidge, Phipps being in overall command. The pilots were essential because no masters serving in the Royal Navy at that time had any experience of navigating the northernmost seas, and their practical expertise would prove invaluable once the two ships started cruising in the pack ice.

Finally, indirectly associated with the Royal Society, the other academic group with a keen interest in the forthcoming polar voyage was the Board of Longitude. Established under Queen Anne by the Longitude Act on 8 July 1714, this body was created following the disastrous loss of part of Vice Admiral Sir Cloudesley Shovell's fleet off the Isles of Scilly in 1707, when the flagship *Association* together with the *Eagle* and the *Romney* sank as a direct result of navigational miscalculation.[14]

Determining a ship's position at sea relies on two criteria: knowledge of latitude and knowledge of longitude. Latitude is a geographic coordinate that specifies the north–south position of a point on the earth's surface measured by an angle ranging between 0° at the Equator to 90° (North or South) at the poles. Longitude is a geographic coordinate that specifies the east–west position of a point on the earth's surface. It is an angular measurement ranging from 0° at the prime meridian to +180° eastwards and -180° westwards. The prime meridian runs directly through Greenwich, London.

Calculating latitude with reasonable accuracy was relatively easy since it simply involved measuring the angle between the horizon and the sun, preferably at midday when the sun is at its zenith. The angle found between 0° and 90° provides the relative position north or south of the Equator. Earlier instruments used to measure this had been the cross staff, modified into the backstaff by navigator John Davis, and the Arabic astrolabe, which was ingenious but difficult to use on a rocking ship. Each was later outmoded by the quadrant, itself superseded by the more sophisticated sextant.

Calculating longitude, however, consistently proved problematic, leaving navigators reliant upon a system of dead reckoning. This involved calculating the current position by using a previously determined position, or fix, and advancing that position based upon known or estimated speeds over elapsed time and course. Many people, including Galileo, had derived complex astronomical systems involving relative positions of the moon and the satellites of Jupiter. In 1514, the German astronomer Johannes Werner developed a better system using the moon to determine position, although the solution to longitude continued to be determined by a series of calculations formulated from measuring the position of preselected heavenly bodies and comparing results against a series of astronomical tables compiled by the Royal Astronomers.

Although the Board of Longitude had 24 Commissioners of Longitude – including key figures from politics, the Navy, and academic advisors in astronomy and mathematics – it did not formally meet until at least 1737, when interest was provoked by John Harrison's invention of his marine chronometer. This was important because a proposed alternative solution to longitude involved knowing the exact time difference between the position at midday and the known time at midday on the prime meridian – information that required the use of reliable, accurate timepieces such as Harrison's chronometer.

To encourage scientific investigation into resolving the problem of how to calculate longitude, the Board offered three prizes:

1 £10,000 (£1,300,000 in today's money) to determine longitude within 60 nautical miles (69 miles/110km);
2 £15,000 (£2,000,000 in today's money) to determine longitude within 40 nautical miles (46 miles/74km);

3 £20,000 (£2,600,000 in today's money) for a method
   that could determine longitude within 30 nautical miles
   (35 miles/56km).[15]

The board also offered prizes to anyone who was able to resolve
the matter by means of astronomical, lunar or mathematical tables.
Working on these was the Astronomer Royal, Nevil Maskelyne,
who later became a major adversary to Harrison. Other benefi-
ciaries of the prizes offered were the widow of Tobias Mayer, who
had revised lunar tables based on the Nautical Almanac; and Israel
Lyons who, with Richard Dunthorne, shared £100 for contributing methods to shorten the calculations connected with lunar
distances. Prizes were also distributed to the designers of other
chronometers.

John Harrison (1693–1776) was a self-taught Yorkshire clock-
maker who built his first pendulum clock in 1713. Perfecting his
skills, he produced a watch that lost no more than a single second
in a month, unlike most other watches produced at the time, which
easily lost a full minute per day. Harrison soon attained a reputation for creating uniquely accurate timepieces. Living near the large
seaport of Hull, he would have soon become aware of the Board of
Longitude's directive to find an accurate timepiece. Confident in his
abilities, and prompted by the potential monetary prize, Harrison
began making a timepiece that would be suitable for a shipboard
environment. Realising that a pendulum would not work in rolling sea, he spent four years perfecting an innovative 'grasshopper'
mechanism with linked dumbbell balances to maintain constant
momentum.

However, when Harrison went to London in 1730 to present
his ideas to the Board of Longitude, he not only discovered that
the Board had not met even formally since its inauguration, but
he was also greeted with reservation. Indeed, on meeting Edmond
Halley, Harrison was told plainly that the Board had no interest in
resolving the longitude issue by mechanical means. Halley instead
believed in solving such issues using astronomy and mathematics; Harrison obviously posed a threat to the established theorists
and their potential financial gain. Despite this, Harrison gained the
confidence of the leading London clock-maker George Graham,

who offered financial support. With the assistance of his brother and joint business partner James, Harrison then spent another five years manufacturing the first sea clock, later known as H1. Built of brass rather than the various hardwoods he had used previously and with protruding balancing arrangements, it resembled more a model of an oared galley than a clock; in all it was unique. After undertaking trials on the Humber river, John and James took the clock to Graham in London, who endorsed it in the following words:

'John Harrison having with great labour and expense, contrived and executed a Machine for measuring time at sea, upon such Principle, as seem to us to Promise a very great and sufficient degree of Exactness. We are of opinion, it highly deserves Public Encouragement, In order to a thorough Tryal and Improvement of the severall Contrivances, for preventing those Irregularityes in time, that naturally arise from the different degrees of Heat and Cold, a moist and drye Temperature of the Air, and the Various Agitations of the ship.'[16]

Despite opposition from the Royal Astronomer Nevil Maskelyne, the Board considered Harrison's clock to be worthy of a sea trial. With formal approval from the First Lord of the Admiralty Sir Charles Wager, Harrison and H1 embarked into the 60-gun HMS *Centurion* commanded by Captain George Proctor and sailed for Lisbon in 1736. When Proctor died at Lisbon, Harrison and H1 transferred into the 70-gun HMS *Orford* for the return voyage trials.

Although H1 lost time on the outward voyage, it performed well on the homeward leg. Calculations made by the master of the *Orford* placed the ship just 60 miles (97km) east of the true landfall correctly predicted by Harrison using H1. And, despite this not being the transatlantic voyage they had required for H1's full trial, the Board of Longitude was sufficiently impressed to grant Harrison £500 for further development.

By 1741, Harrison had developed a more compact and robust timekeeper, H2, but because Britain was now involved with the War of the Austrian Succession, there were no formal trials since it was feared that the device might fall into enemy hands. This was probably just as well, as Harrison had discovered a serious fault in his design of the clock's bar balances. With a further grant of £500, he duly developed a third sea clock with circular balances: H3. This did not perform as accurately as Harrison had hoped, but despite this flaw the clock was the first device to incorporate a bimetallic strip and the caged roller bearing.

With London clock-makers Thomas Mudge and John Jeffreys now producing accurate watches, Harrison turned his mind to the concept of making a sea watch. Known as H4, it took him six years to produce. Measuring a mere 13cm (5¼in) in diameter, it contained a unique escapement mechanism that intricately incorporated the first use of diamonds in a timepiece.

In 1761, aged 68, Harrison finally got a transatlantic trial authorised by the Board of Longitude and along with his son William he embarked H4 into the 50-gun ship *Deptford*, which sailed from Portsmouth for Kingston, Jamaica on 18 November. When independently tested 12 days before departure, H4 is recorded to have been running 3 seconds slow, having lost 24 seconds over the course of nine days on mean solar time: ie it lost 24/9 seconds per day. This equated to a loss of 3 minutes 36.5 seconds over the 81 days and 5 hours it took to sail to Kingston. On arrival, it was found to be running 5 seconds slow in comparison to the known longitude of Kingston, the error of longitude incurred being 1.25 minutes, which is approximately 1 nautical mile (1.2 miles/1.9km).

Although this was indubitably a remarkable achievement, Astronomer Royal Maskelyne insisted on a second trial that would compare H4 against the complex lunar distances system. Undertaken in the 28-gun *Tartar* with both Harrison and Maskelyne present, H4 proved accurate to within 39 seconds. Finally, the Board of Longitude and the Royal Society were fully satisfied with Harrison's chronometer. Harrison duly began working on H5, completing it at the age of 79.[17]

Rightfully, although he never received the official prize money (nobody did), Harrison was fully acclaimed for his achievements and despite some delays he received money from the Board of Longitude throughout the development process, comprising £4,315 in increments for the initial development of the chronometer and £10,000 as an interim payment for H4 in 1765. Added to this was the grant of £8,750 he received from Parliament in 1773, giving a total of £23,065.[18] This vast sum is equivalent to £1,729,875 today – he died a rich man.

Harrison's accurate chronometer H4 had a profound impact upon future voyages, especially those undertaken by Captain James Cook in the Pacific from 1768; moreover, this timepiece was to have an indirect effect upon Phipps's Arctic expedition of 1773.

4

The service history of HM ships Racehorse *and* Carcass *prior to* 1773

When preparing for the polar expedition, it was important that the Admiralty selected vessels capable of meeting the environmental rigours of sailing in Arctic seas. There were many issues to consider, the first being what size of vessel was best suited to the number of crew required and to carry out the proposed scientific experiments. Choosing too large a vessel would mean extra crew and provisions would be required, leaving a reduced capacity for specialist equipment, stores and clothing.

The only purpose-built vessels that commonly ventured into the northern seas were the whaling ships that operated out of the Dutch, Danish and Norwegian and Russian ports; the American New England colonials were not yet established. From England, these whaling fleets operated out of north-eastern ports such as Grimsby and Whitby, while the Scottish whalers used the fishing ports of Aberdeen, Dundee and Peterhead. Although vessels of this kind satisfied the needs of their industry, carrying a minimal complement of men sufficient to work the ship and to undertake the work involved in catching whales and reducing their flesh into sperm oil, they were too small for the purposes of the expedition. In addition, purchasing a whaling ship into the Royal Navy was out of the question, especially as most of the privately owned ships were far too busy operating their trade.

Availability was another factor governing ship type. Although Britain was not at war, her smaller naval ships were still actively deployed escorting convoys or policing the seas against privateers, smugglers and pirates, although the latter were in decline. The most suitable purpose-built ships to hand were bomb vessels armed with heavy mortars for bombarding coastal defences. As a single-weapon system, this concept was first introduced into the French Royal Navy in the late 17th century to a design by Bernard Renau d'Eliçagary. Using five such vessels, the French Navy had bombarded Algiers in 1682, destroying the land forts and killing some 700 defenders. Two years later, several French *galiotes à bombes* sailing with Admiral Abraham Duquesne had successfully repeated their destructive ability at Genoa.[1]

When not at war, bomb vessels were surplus to requirements and presented the ideal solution for the expedition. Although relatively small, these ships were proportionally far more stoutly built than vessels of equivalent length and breadth. As their prime function was to carry two heavy mortars of up to 13in (33cm) calibre mounted on rotating beds, their hull structure had to be exceedingly strong to absorb the resultant kinetic energy generated on recoil when firing. Moreover, their hull structure was perfect for withstanding the likely compressive forces that would be imposed upon the hull by the ice floes in which the ships would be expected to operate. Two of the bomb ships available were the *Racehorse* and the *Carcass*.

HM Ship *Racehorse*

Built at Nantes on the Loire River in Upper Brittany, western France, the *Racehorse* was originally the 18-gun French privateer *Marquis de Vaudreuil*, captured from the French in 1757 during the Seven Years' War (1756–63). After her capture, *Marquis de Vaudreuil* was officially purchased into the British Navy on 28 April 1757 and taken into dock at John Randall's shipyard at Cuckold Point, Rotherhithe,[2] where he 'fitted' her for Royal Naval service. The ship was officially renamed HMS *Racehorse* by Admiralty Order on 5 May 1757.

Specifications of the Racehorse

Builder	French built at Nantes, France
Class and type	18-gun sloop of war
Taken into RN service	28 April 1757
Renamed	HMS *Racehorse*
Reclassified	Fireship between April and May 1758
Reclassified	Bomb vessel between 1758 and 1760
Reclassified	Discovery ship in 1773
Reclassified	Bomb vessel in 1775
Renamed	HMS *Thunder* 24 October 1775
Fate	Captured by the French 14 August 1778
Tons burthen	385 66/94 bm
Length	96ft 7in (29.44m) (overall)
Length of keel for tonnage	77ft 1.25in (23.5m) (keel)
Beam	30ft 8in (9.35m)
Depth of hold	13ft 4in (4.06m)
Complement: as a sloop	120
Complement: as a fireship	45
Complement: as a bomb vessel	70
Complement: as a discovery ship	80
Armament: as a sloop	18 × 6 pdrs, 14 × ½ pdr swivels
Armament: as a fireship	8 × 6 pdrs, 8 × ½ pdr swivels
Primary armament: as a bomb vessel	2 mortars: 1 × 13in & 1 × 10in
Secondary armament: as a bomb vessel	8 × 6 pdrs, 12 × ½ pdr swivels
Armament: as a sloop	8 × 6 pdrs, 12 × ½ pdr swivels

From the point of her acceptance into the Royal Navy onwards, we know a lot about the *Racehorse* from the Admiralty Progress Books. These provide a detailed historical account of the ship's refit history, including expenses, referring to, for example, her hull, rigging and masts. Held in The National Archives at Kew (with copies in the National Maritime Museum under the ADM. 180 series), these books also record the dates on which every Royal Navy ship

– whether built, captured or purchased – entered every dockyard, docked, launched and sailed.

The entry in the Progress Book for the *Racehorse* is: 'Admty Ord^r 19th April 1757 to Purchase Ship for his Maj^{ty} and to be fitted to Serve as Frigate; Was Purchased 28th April 1757 For the Hull Masts & Yards £1700 0s 0d Furniture and Stores £158 8s. 6d^3.'

From the outset, *Racehorse* was a ship-rigged vessel (three-masted) and, although resembling a small frigate as she only carried 18 guns, she was rated in the Royal Navy as a sloop of war. The rating system related both to vessel size or type and also to the rank and pay of the appointed commanding officer. As *Racehorse* was too small to justify a full captain in command, by rating her as a sloop, her appointed officer would hold the lesser rank of commander. Having been overhauled by Randell, the ship was therefore put into commission under Commander Francis Burslem in June 1757 and went into the nearby Royal Dockyard at Deptford on 20 July 1757. After further fitting out, *Racehorse* sailed on 16 August, the cost for her hull, masts and yards amounting to £425 4s 9d. With rigging and stores costing £1,786 3s 9d, her overall costs are recorded as £2,211 8s 6d.[4]

Under Burslem's command, *Racehorse* was deployed in home waters until she was paid off in 1758, at which point the ship's company were given all wages due and dispersed. As Britain was still at war and the Royal Navy needed to retain its manpower, it is highly probable that most of the men were sent into other warships.

In June 1757, William Pitt (1st Earl of Chatham) formed a coalition with Lord Newcastle to rally a strong government to counteract the war developing in Europe, in particular because of increasing French incursions against British interests in North America. The resulting Whig government made the decision to invade and drive the French out of New France (Canada). To achieve this the British first needed to take possession of the strategic French town and fortifications of Louisbourg, near Cape Breton, north-east of the mainland of Nova Scotia with its northern and western coasts fronting the Gulf of Saint Lawrence. Meeting the specific needs of the war, an Admiralty Order related to the *Racehorse* dated 5 April 1758 directed: 'To fit her as a Fire ship'.[5] Now reclassified, *Racehorse*'s armament was reduced to just eight 6-pounder carriage guns. Whether she was modified structurally to fully function as a fireship is unclear, and extant logbooks at this period do not indicate whether she was deployed in this capacity.

Between 8 June and 26 July 1758, British forces led by Admiral Edward Boscawen, with the military commanders Jeffrey Amherst and James Wolfe, laid siege to and captured Louisbourg – an action intended to open the gateway of the St Lawrence River into the interior of New France and allow an invasion to dislodge the French at Quebec and Montreal. In preparation, an Admiralty Order dated 5 September 1758 now authorised the *Racehorse* to be 'fitted for a Bomb to carry Two Mortars 1 of 13 Ins. 1 of 10 Ins. Guns No.8; Pdrs 6; Swivels 12; Men 70'.[6]

Accommodating these large guns mounted on turntables involved strengthening the ship's timbers and fitting out her hold with two shell rooms, which, built to heavy scantlings, structurally supported the 13in (33cm) and 10in (25cm) mortar beds being fitted on the centre line of her upper deck. Her 6-pounder guns were retained for defensive needs.[7]

In her new role, the *Racehorse* was recommissioned under Commander Francis Richards, who received orders to join the invasion fleet of Vice Admiral Charles Saunders that was being assembled at Spithead for deployment in North American waters. Along with another 46 warships,[8] the *Racehorse* duly sailed for Canada on 17 February 1759, Saunders flying his flag in the 90-gun *Neptune*.

Crossing the Atlantic without incident, the main body of the fleet warships commanded by Admiral Edward Boscawen, together with 150 transports carrying 14,000 troops and marines under Major General Jeffrey Amherst, assembled off Louisbourg. After a siege lasting from 8 June to 26 July, Amherst, with the aid of Brigadier James Wolfe, captured the town and fortifications from the French after their garrison simply capitulated.

Also present in Saunders' fleet at Louisbourg was future explorer James Cook, who would be out in the Pacific when the *Racehorse* was later in the Arctic. Holding the non-commissioned post as a master, Cook had become well known for his skills as a surveyor and map-maker. Recognising Cook's aptitude as a navigator, Saunders had Cook transferred out of the 60-gun *Pembroke* into the 70-gun *Northumberland* to chart a large portion of the St Lawrence River for the fleet, including a dangerous channel known as the Traverse.

After embarking additional troops from the British garrison, Saunders' fleet weighed on 1 June and advanced up the wide mouth of the St Lawrence River towards Quebec with the *Racehorse* in company. The *Northumberland* was one of the first vessels to proceed, Cook sounding the channel and guiding the fleet as it progressed towards its final objective, the ships anchoring off Isle d'Orleans on 26 June. The next day, Wolfe began landing his troops on Isle d'Orleans; though expecting to lead 12,000 men, Wolfe found his forces only comprised some 400 officers, 7,000 regular troops, and 300 gunners.[9]

The defence of Quebec lay in the hands of the supreme commander of New France, General Louis-Joseph de Montcalm-Gozon, Marquis de Saint-Veran. One of his supporting officers was his colonel, Louis Antoine de Bougainville, who, later ranked as admiral in the French Royal Navy, became a renowned explorer

Pierre de Rigaud de Vaudreuil de Cavagnial, Marquis de Vaudreuil. The *Racehorse* was originally named after him but her name was changed following her capture in 1757, during the Seven Years' War. Engraving after a painting by Elisabeth Louise Vigée Le Brun. Library of Congress.

and navigator (see chapter 3). Also present in Quebec was the Governor-General of New France (later Canada), Pierre de Rigaud de Vaudreuil de Cavagnial, Marquis de Vaudreuil.

Along with the fleet, the *Racehorse* was disposed to counter any likely attack from enemy fireships. Although General Montcalm had soundly protected the city approaches with defensive earthworks, on the night of 28 June he took the offensive and sent seven fireships and two firerafts into the British fleet. Fortunately, these vessels were ignited too early and the diligent British seamen manned ship's boats and grappled and towed away the burning craft before they were able to cause serious damage.

To avoid similar occurrences Saunders moved his fleet into an open area of water called the Basin of Quebec just below the town, which improved its protection. The French next attempted to extricate Saunders' ships by means of floating gun batteries but, coming under heavy fire from the 28-gun *Trent*, these were soon driven back. The British seamen next landed guns and set up batteries on Point Lévi and commenced bombarding the city.[10]

Meanwhile, Wolfe's troops embarked into flatboats,[11] which, escorted by naval ships the 14-gun HMS *Porcupine* and the fireship HMS *Boscawen*, went upriver and landed on the north shore below the falls of Montmorency. Wolfe's survey of the nearby town of Beauport found rows of houses suitably barricaded for defensive musket fire from within, which made any approach on that route hazardous. As a result, Wolfe was faced with making a direct assault upon the northern shore using some 3,500 troops. In preparation, on Monday 30 July *Racehorse* 'embarked on board us 197 of the Royal American Trupes'.[12]

The main attack on 31 July opened with Saunders' ships providing a heavy bombardment. Despite this, the ensuing Battle of Beauport (also known as the Battle of Montmorency) was not a success for the British – British troops wading in the river shallows and landing on the beach came under severe volleys of French fire, the Louisbourg Grenadiers suffering considerably. The small ships could not get in close.[13] Fortunately, the appalling weather conditions (rain, thunder, lightning and gales) ended the fight, allowing Wolfe to withdraw, but only after sustaining some 450 casualties, while the French suffered just 60 fatalities.[14]

While the siege of Quebec dragged on throughout August, the situation debilitated the British forces; illness was rife within the British camps and Wolfe himself was bedridden. Far worse, with little strategic advantage being gained, morale among the British forces was low. However, the naval crews, being relatively free from illness, remained in good spirits and daily routine in the *Racehorse* and other ships such as the *Seahorse* continued unaffected.[15]

Frustrated by Montcalm's tactical inactivity, Wolfe needed to force his hand. Mobilising his troops with the American Rangers he attacked small French settlements along the St Lawrence River, destroying some 1,400 stone houses and manors – an action he hoped would draw the French army out from its fortifications to do battle.[16] Despite many colonists being killed, however, this ploy failed to motivate Montcalm into open combat, although it did effectively reduce the supplies reaching the French forces. Montcalm's situation was exacerbated because munitions from France were not forthcoming, the British Navy having successfully blockaded the French ports.[17]

With winter approaching, Saunders' fleet could not prevail indefinitely as the river would soon ice up, making his own supply chain virtually impossible. Wolfe therefore needed to act swiftly if Quebec was to be successfully taken. To this end, ships with shallow draughts were sent upstream to reconnoitre potential landing sites, an event recorded in *Racehorse*'s log[18] on Tuesday 28 August: 'sailed above the Town of Quebeck his Maj[s] frigate *Lostoff Hunter* sloop, 2 Arme [army] ships & a small sloop.' According to the log of 1 September, other vessels followed: 'Whent above the Town of Quebeck his Maj[s] ships *Seahorse* with 4 transports and arme ships.' That same day aboard *Racehorse* they: 'Sould [sold] at the mast Roger Thornton and Walter Masons things', the two crew members having died after being 'shott by accident' a few days earlier. *Racehorse*'s log also records that an additional bomb vessel, the *Baltimore*, had joined the fleet.[19]

The site chosen by Wolfe for landing the British troops was L'Anse au Foulon, located south-west of the city, just 2 miles (3km) upstream from Cap Diamant (Cape Diamond). Rising above this cove were cliffs 174ft (53m) high, leading on to a plateau called the Plains of Abraham[20], which was protected by gun batteries.

Wolfe planned his major assault against Quebec to begin on the night of Wednesday 12 September. Though risky, Wolfe intended to have his troops scale the heights by stealth in order to secure a foothold and strike at Bougainville's forces on the Plain defending the west flank of the city, hopefully drawing Montcalm out of Quebec's citadel on to the open plains to give battle. Admiral Holmes took command of the flotilla, which included the *Racehorse*, on the upper river from which various feints were made to confuse the French before the main offensive. Wolfe now needed to move his forces. According to *Racehorse's* journal of 3 September: 'General Wolf broke up the Camp at Mount Morancey. Imbark his trups over to Point Levi and landed p^r sig^l.'[21]

During the night of 4 September, lesser vessels, *Racehorse* included, sailed upstream past the city accompanied by all the flat-bottomed boats carrying troops. On Saturday 8 September *Racehorse* manned and armed her boats – the long boat, launch and cutter – and sent them over to Point Levi, joining many others assembling there, then at '½ past 8 all the boats went over to the North shore to Alarm the French'.[22]

During the evening of 12 September all craft and flatboats were filled with as many troops as possible, the boats remaining below the city being filled with marines ready to make a feint of landing early next morning. While these events unfolded, Wolfe wrote his last letter:

'HMS *Sutherland*, 8.30pm 12 September.

I had the honour to inform you today that it is my duty to attack the French army. To the best of my knowledge and ability, I have fixed upon that spot where we can act with most force and are most likely to succeed. If I am mistaken I am sorry for it and must be answerable to His Majesty and the public for the consequences.'[23]

Throughout the night, Wolfe's forces moved upriver in the flatboats and by 8am on Thursday 13 September the Heights of Abraham had been scaled by the Highlanders and fighting had commenced. Upon the result of this battle, which jointly involved some 10,000 troops, lay the fate of New France and British or French autonomy in the western hemisphere.

Racehorse's master's log entry on Thursday 13 September covers the main military attack: 'Mo^d & clear Wea^r. At 6 PM sent our Boats to Point Levi Man'd & Arm'd as did all the fleet AM our Trupes lande^d above point Diamond & Defated the French that was at that Post our Trupes Kill^d in the atack about 2000 & took 600 presoners [sic] General Wolfe was kill^d in the atack & several Officers Likewise a Great Number of the French Officers Mount Calm was woun^d & Dye^d about 10 AM At 8 D° sent our Boat to Point Levi man^d & Armd as p^r sig^l.'[24]

The master in the *Racehorse* recorded in his log that Quebec formally surrendered at 4pm on Wednesday 19 September. Looking at extant logbooks of the British ships that were present, it is likely that the *Racehorse* would have temporarily received French prisoners and deserters. On 5 October, the *Racehorse* received, by orders of Admiral Saunders, five English seamen who had been discharged out of the 24-gun *Seahorse*, a vessel in which Nelson would later serve.[25]

With British supremacy in Canada declared, the main body of Saunders' fleet sailed for England shortly afterwards, leaving behind the *Racehorse* and 14-gun sloops *Porcupine* and *Scorpion* to overwinter at Quebec, the *Racehorse* being temporarily placed under the command of Lieutenant George Miller for the duration. As winter set in, conditions deteriorated: in early December 1759, sick men were sent on shore to the nunnery hospital and much time was spent: 'Clearing the Battreys of Snow in the Low Town' and 'Cutting and Carrying wood from the Builders Yard to the Ship.'[26] Far worse, the St Lawrence River froze solid and the *Racehorse* became trapped in ice; at one point it appears that the English governor of Quebec supplied soldiers to help free the ship. This was the first time *Racehorse* was beset by ice.

Despite the British having control of Quebec city, *Racehorse*'s journal discloses that hostilities had not abated and skirmishes continued between French subjects and English troops for quite some time, the French resistance being led by the Marquis de Vaudreuil.[27]

Although Richards resumed command in early May 1760, he was superseded on 15 May by James Harmwood, who brought the *Racehorse* home to Portsmouth Dockyard on 13 December 1760. Taken into dock on 3 February 1761, the ship was graved – a procedure that involved cleaning and coating the bottom of a wooden ship with pitch or a compound of white lead often mixed with horsehair. The overall cost of this refit amounted to £1,296 6s 6d.[28] Launched just two days later, the ship sailed on 17 March to escort a convoy bound for Newfoundland. Operating in home waters, command passed to John Macartney in January 1761. Needing further refitting, the *Racehorse* arrived at Sheerness on 31 July 1762 and docked on 10 August. After graving, the ship was launched 11 days later, sailing on 31 August; the cost of this refit totalled £1,286 10s 10d, of which some £1,000 was for rigging and stores.[29]

By this time the seven years of fighting on a global scale in what was effectively the first world war was drawing towards a conclusion. With most countries involved being too financially crippled to continue, the Treaty of Paris, signed on 10 February 1763, ended all hostilities. Shortly afterwards, Macartney took the *Racehorse* into Sheerness on 13 May 1763 and paid off the ship.

The *Racehorse*: 1763–75

Although the Progress Book of the *Racehorse* states that she was not taken into dock, the nature of the work undertaken is entered as 'Gr^g & Trim^g' (graving and trimming). This source then notes the following observation: 'Surveyed afloat 7th Octr 1763 & found to be in good Condition, but that she will require a docking before she proceeds to Sea for which she may be fitted in 16 days Est^d for the hull £120 Not reported to the Admt.y.'[30] Subsequently, *Racehorse* was docked on 19 December and graved, but why the Admiralty were not notified is somewhat mystifying.

Still at Sheerness, *Racehorse* was again docked on 16 May 1771 to have her wooden sheathing 'taken off'. Before the introduction of copper sheathing to protect a ship's hull below the waterline from the wood-boring worm *teredo navalis,* it was common practice to cheaply sheath hulls using thin deal (fir or pine) sacrificial boards, the surfaces of which were studded with flat-headed iron nails. The boards were then 'paid up' with a compound of white lead and sulphur, 'sometimes mixed with horse hair', the mixture of which doubled as an antifouling agent that was 'off-white' in appearance. The process of applying this compound, known as 'graving', inevitably happened quite frequently, while deteriorated wooden sheathing boards also needed periodical replacement.[31, 32]

Because the *Racehorse* needed both resheathing and graving, she remained in dock until she was launched on 21 October. Listed as a 'general repair', the works cost £3,862 4s 4d for hull masts and yards and £462 8s 3d for rigging and stores, with a total overall cost of £3,526 6s 7d.[33]

Now rated as a 16-gun sloop, the ship was recommissioned under Robert 'Slowley' St. John Chinnery on 23 November, who remained in command of the vessel until 31 October 1772.[34] Finally sailing on 23 March 1772, *Racehorse* was deployed along the south coast of England to do work that included patrolling the straits of Dover, deterring smugglers and privateers. During this period, the ship went into Plymouth to be graved on 2 May 1772 and again on 13 October – the combined refit costs amounting to £1,319 5s 7d.[35] Given how often graving had to be done, and the fact it had to be done to every ship, it is clear that this single necessary process cost the Admiralty a small fortune every year, not to mention the reduction in actual time of the ships' operational efficiency.

Recalled, the *Racehorse* arrived at Galleons Reach in the Thames and was paid off on 31 October 1772, the crew being dispersed into other ships or released from service as there was no war to retain them; Chinnery was probably sent 'on the beach' on half pay. *Racehorse* remained at moorings until she was taken into Deptford Dockyard on 23 March 1773 to be 'Fitted for a Voyage to the North Pole', a conversion that would necessitate many alterations.[36] Once docked, her wooden sheathing was 'doubled up' – meaning she was given an additional layer of sheathing planking to her lower hull as protection against ice. Comprehensive details concerning how the *Racehorse* was fitted out for this expedition are described in the following chapters.

HM sloop *Carcass*

Whereas the *Racehorse* was initially taken into the Royal Navy as a French privateer and converted into a bomb vessel, the *Carcass* was specifically designed and built as a 'bomb' – one of 11 bomb vessels ordered at the outbreak of the Seven Years' War. Of these, four were rigged as ketches (two-masted), while the remainder, which included the *Carcass,* were ship rigged (three-masted). Part of what was colloquially known as the Infernal class, the *Carcass* was designed by Sir Thomas Slade, who held the post of Surveyor of the Navy from the Navy Board from 1755 until 1771. Perhaps the most innovative surveyor of the 18th century, Slade designed some 181 ships of varying classes, including Nelson's 100-gun *Victory*.

An Admiralty Order dated 21 September 1758 gives notice of an intention 'to Build six Bomb vessels in Merchants Yards'. A second Admiralty Order issued on 27 September 1758 records: 'The Board Agreed with Mr. Stanton to Build one in his Yard at Rotherhith & to launch her in 5 Months for £12. 2s. od. P [er] Tun, but if Launched in 4 Months then to have £12. 12s. od. P.Tun.'[37] The keel of the *Carcass* was laid down on 28 September 1758, one day before the birth of her later midshipman, Horatio Nelson.

An Admiralty Order of 11 January 1759 describes the ordnance that the ship would carry: 'To Establish on the New carcass Bomb 8 Carr[iage] Guns of 6 $^{pds.}$: 14 Swivels 60 Men when Empl$^{d.}$ As a Bomb and 14 Carr. Guns of 6 ^{pds}. & 14 swivels & 110 men when Empl$^{d.}$ As a Frigate.' When *Carcass* was nearing completion, a third Admiralty Order of 19 January 1759 recorded that it was the intention 'to name her the *Carcass*, Bomb Ship. Amount of the Hull £3,757. 11s. 6d'. Completed within four months, to the financial advantage of her builder Mr Stanton, the *Carcass* was launched on 27 January 1759. Further Admiralty Orders dated 21 September 1759 instructed the builder 'to fit her for Channel Service as a Sloop & to have 110 Men'. Specifications for the *Carcass* are as follows:[38]

Specifications of the Carcass

Class Name	Infernal
Design date	1756
Designer	Thomas Slade
Builder	Stanton
Yard	Rotherhithe
Length	91ft 6in (27.9m)
Length of keel for tonnage	74ft 13/4in (22.6m)
Extreme breadth	27ft 6in (8.4m)
Depth in hold	12ft 1in (3.7m)
Tons burthen	298. 47/94
Complement	60 (110 as a sloop)
Total armament	24
Mortars	1 x 13in & 1 x 10in
Guns	8 x 6 pounder carriage guns
Ditto	14 x ½ pounder swivel guns

The ship's name, *Carcass*, does not relate to the body of a dead animal but instead to a type of incendiary device that was used as an alternative to the explosive spherical shells generally fired from a bomb vessel's mortars. The carcass was a cylindrical iron cage filled with combustible material, rope or canvas soaked in oil or tar that instantaneously ignited during the firing process of the mortar. As a weapon, flaming carcasses were bombarded into towns or anchored fleets of ships. A contemporary description of this type of missile is given in the *1750 Guide*: 'A carcass, which they fill at Sieges with Pitch and Tar, and other Combustibles to set Townes on Fire: It is thrown out of an 18-inch mortar and will burn two Hours where it happens to fall.'[39] It needs little imagination to appreciate the destruction and terror caused by bombardment with these incendiaries, which in some instances was more devastating than bombardment with heavy shells. The origin of the name 'carcass' probably refers to earlier practices, when attacking armies catapulted rotting animal carcasses into besieged fortifications in the hope of spreading disease among the defenders.

Once launched, the *Carcass* was immediately taken up the River Thames and that same day she entered Deptford Dockyard for fitting out as a sloop. This was done at a cost of £2,144 8s 1d, of which £1,721 18s 10d accounted for rigging and stores, and she was fully armed with 14 6-pounder carriage guns and 14 ½-pounder swivel guns mounted upon pedestals along her upperworks.[40] The practice of converting bomb vessels into sloops was quite common for, once the two mortars and corresponding shell rooms had been removed, these ships served well for escort and surveillance duties. Once the work was complete, *Carcass* was put into commission by Commander Charles Inglis, and with her complement comprising 110 men she was initially deployed in home waters.

The year 1759 was to prove a successful turning point for Britain during the Seven Years' War, with her land and sea forces taking the combat initiative in each global theatre of conflict. Meeting these demands, the *Carcass* was taken into Deptford Dockyard and reconverted back into a bomb vessel, mounting one 13in (33cm) and one 10in (25cm) brass mortar, with appropriate shell rooms fitted below the respective mortars. Subsequent to this modification her standard defence armament was reduced, although the swivel guns remained.

Still under the command of Charles Inglis, the *Carcass* sailed from Deptford on 27 June 1759 to join Admiral Sir George Rodney's fleet anchored in St Helen's Roads off Portsmouth. The fleet was in position to counter the plans the French minister, the Duc de Choiseul, had in motion to invade Britain using a force comprising 48,000 men; 225 troopships; 425 transports and flat-bottomed vessels; and 337 naval escorts and storeships, which were being prepared at various French ports. For logistical reasons the intended departure point was the French port of Le Havre, with the entire force under the command of the Prince de Soubise. If successful, the invasion would provide an opportunity to rally an uprising from Jacobite sympathisers in Scotland and rekindle potential Catholic rebellion in Ireland. Acting immediately, Prime Minister Pitt directed the Admiralty to destroy the French forces while they were still in harbour. With Admiral Hawke already busy blockading the French naval ports at Brest and Rocheforte, the task fell upon Admiral Rodney.[41]

Sailing from Portsmouth on 2 July, Rodney's fleet arrived off Le Havre on 3 July and anchored in the channel leading to Honfleur. As soon as the *Carcass* and the other 'bombs' had moored within range, the entire fleet started shelling Le Havre. The ensuing bombardment continued unremittingly for some 50 hours, during which more than 3,000 shells were fired into the town at the principal targets: the magazines, the gun batteries and the assembled flotilla of invasion craft. For the inhabitants, the constant barrage must have been horrifying. The *Carcass* is estimated to have fired 500 shells alone, her on-board stock being replenished from her accompanying tender. Many of the French troops intended for the invasion came down to the shore under the cover of entrenchments and maintained an active defensive fire from the batteries, but to little effect. The bombardment caused immense damage, and the town was set on fire by incendiary carcasses fired from the *Carcass* and her accompanying five bomb vessels, causing the remaining inhabitants to flee.[42]

Left: 13-inch (33 cm) mortar shell showing hole for beech fuse and lifting handles. *Right*: Incendiary shell (carcass) of the type carried on bomb vessels. Illustrations by author.

With the mission successfully accomplished, the *Carcass* and accompanying bomb vessels departed. Rodney, with some of his frigates, remained, blockading the French port for the rest of the year, and capturing numerous prizes.[43]

Having arrived at Portsmouth on 8 July the *Carcass* went into dock four days later in order for her hull to be graved. The total cost for this and smaller works amounted to £401 17s 11d.[44] The ship came out of the dock on 26 August and took up moorings alongside HMS *Experiment*, a former 24-gun (sixth rate), which not only provided temporary crew accommodation but also served as a floating lay-apart store (naval store house) into which the *Carcass*'s ship's company transferred sails and other equipment in preparation for converting the *Carcass* into a sloop. *Carcass*'s crew also disembarked the mortar shells and removed her two mortars, along with their beds. Between Friday 28 September and 5 October dockyard carpenters dismantled the shell rooms and laid planking in the room of the bomb bed housings while completing a flush upper deck. *Carcass*'s log records little activity within the ship between November 1759 and February 1760 other than the routine receipt of beef every four to six days. What is clear is that the ship must have gone into the Great Basin in Portsmouth dockyard, for she was 'moved out of the Bason' on 14 February 1760 and moored alongside the hulk *Gloria*, from which she embarked 15.12 tons of shingle ballast to compensate for the weight change caused by the removal of her mortars. Work in the ship continued until 8 March, with men sent over from

Haslar Naval Hospital and the hospital ship *Blenheim* to assist. A further 25 seamen from other ships came on board on 17 March to provide assistance.[45]

Using personnel from the ship's companies of other vessels in refits was common practice and explains how ships could be turned round so efficiently to get back to sea. One good example of this is Nelson's future 100-gun flagship *Victory*, which was recoppered – a process that involved lining the hull with tarred brown paper before some 3,900 new copper plates were fitted, each held in place with about 40 copper nails – in just one week.[46]

On Tuesday 18 March, the *Carcass* received her cables, which were bent (secured) to her anchors while the ship was trimmed for undocking and moved down harbour to lay off the various store houses and receive her boatswain's, gunner's and carpenter's stores, which were embarked on 20 March. The three great store houses seen today on the west side of Portsmouth Dockyard were still being built. *Carcass*'s gunner's stores would have been transferred from the externally located Gun Wharf. Two days later, the crew were employed rigging the ship and bending sails to the yards, a mammoth task that took just three days. Slipping her moorings on Sunday 23 March, the *Carcass* moored outside Portsmouth: 'a Cable Catch Way Gillkicker at N.N.W.' In company were the first-rate 100-gun ships *Royal George*, *Royal Sovereign*, *St. George* and 'several other men o' war'.[47]

By 26 March the *Carcass* was operating between the Needles and Portland and on Monday 6 April her log records: 'Saw a sail and gave chace, turned out to be a French and engaged.' Putting up little fight, the French vessel struck her colours and when men from the *Carcass* went aboard her it was found that the ship was the privateer *Mercure* out of Rochelle. This prize was taken into Portsmouth and the *Carcass* continued her deployment off the south coast between June 1760 and November 1761.[48]

During this period she docked three times in Portsmouth for graving – on 1 April, 4 June and 14 November – at a total cost of £1,346 7s 9d. Entering Portsmouth again on 2 February 1762, the *Carcass* was again reconverted into a bomb vessel; the cost of reconstructing the shell rooms, bomb beds and housings, completed on 11 March, totalling £727 10s 1d.[49]

Although fitted 'to throw bombs', *Carcass's* journals reveal that her career was rather uneventful, mainly because the Seven Years' War had turned in Britain's favour by this point. She underwent successive refits during the next few years, the first in August 1762 at Sheerness. In December of that year, the *Carcass* went into Deptford Dockyard (see Plate 44), where she remained in dock until January 1764, by which time the Treaty of Paris had terminated the war against France and Spain. Laid up in ordinary (reserve), the *Carcass* was twice sheathed in timber, in August 1765 and September 1769.

On 21 January 1771, Commander Skeffington Lutwidge took command of the *Carcass*, the ship being deployed in the Irish Sea undertaking mundane coastal duties watching over trade shipping out of Liverpool. Her presence also deterred smugglers actively operating out of Dublin and the Isle of Man to supply the receptive black marketeers on the coasts of Cumbria and north-west Wales. In July 1772, the *Carcass* went into Plymouth Dockyard for further refitting at a cost of £915 19s 0d.[50] Refitting in this Devonshire base rather than her home one at Deptford was geographically practical given her operating station. What's more, from an Admiralty perspective, the decision was probably politically motivated by the desire to maintain full employment in Plymouth since there was less work available in the yard after the war. The *Carcass* remained operating on this station for nine months.

Recalled to Deptford in March 1773, Lutwidge 'paid off' the ship in early April, by which time the *Carcass* with Lutwidge had been appointed to accompany Commander Constantine Phipps in HM Sloop *Racehorse* on an exploratory voyage to the North Pole. Recommissioning the *Carcass* for this purpose, Lutwidge resumed command of the ship on 16 April 1773 and by Admiralty Order the *Carcass* was to be 'fitted for a voyage to the North Pole'.[51]

5

Commissioning and fitting out the ships

On receiving a directive from the Admiralty about the proposed
Arctic expedition, on 16 February 1773 the Navy Board issued
a warrant to Deptford Dockyard stating: '*Racehorse* to be fitted
for a Voyage to the North Pole.'[1] The same instruction, for the
Carcass, was issued to Sheerness.[2] Fitting out ships for this specia-
lised non-martial deployment necessitated much planning for
their conversion and modification. On 4 March 1773, the Navy
Board issued a warrant to Deptford Dockyard stating: '*Racehorse*
to be dismantled as far as may be necessary', the wording of
which provided considerable latitude.[3] In contrast, the Navy Board
warrant issued to Sheerness Dockyard on 27 March 1773 states:
'*Carcass* Sloop to be fitted in Preparation to other Works', implying
that the work would be less complicated.[4] Regardless, both vessels
had to have their bomb beds and associated structures removed. A
second warrant to Deptford on 9 April affirms this, instructing that
work be carried out on *Racehorse* 'to take out her bomb beds and
make other alterations'.[5]

The master shipwright at Deptford overseeing all work undertaken on the *Racehorse* was Adam Hayes, who had superseded
Thomas Slade in 1755. Overseeing on behalf of the Navy Board
was the current surveyor of the Navy, Sir John Williams, a protégé
of Slade.

Immediately after the *Racehorse* went in dock at Deptford on 27
March, shipwrights fully inspected her hull while labourers breamed
the underwater planking to remove weed and marine growth. This
done, her wooden sheathing was 'doubled up', thereby providing an additional layer of sheathing planking to her lower hull as

protection against ice. Whether or not this involved removing her previous sheathing boards before doubling was done is unclear; it all depended upon the condition of her previous sheathing. According to the journal of Midshipman Thomas Floyd, the bottom of the *Racehorse* was: 'doubled from the bows to the foremost part of the main chains [half the length of the ship] and from thence to the after part in streaks [ie single strakes] in order to repel little straggling bits of ice, which, but for them, would prove an injury to the real bottom.'[6]

Preparing the *Racehorse* for the Arctic

Commander Phipps took command of the *Racehorse* on Monday 19 April 1773, recording the event in his journal: 'Fresh gales and Cloudy weather. At 11 AM. Took Command of His Majesty's Sloop the Race Horse in the Dry Dock at Deptford and found the Shipwrights employed aboard her.'[7]

Next day, the dockyard shipwrights were 'employed lengthening the Forecastle'. This not only entailed re-laying the deck with longer planks, but also fitting additional deck beams with their corresponding supportive hanging and lodging knees (brackets) beyond the original boundary. All new planking was caulked once laid. Once *Racehorse*'s 'bomb' (mortar) beds had been removed, the focsle could be extended further aft, to provide greater cover for the crew accommodation – a modification clearly needed given the harsh environmental conditions expected on an Arctic voyage. A Navy Board warrant of 21 April 1773 to Deptford Dockyard states: '*Racehorse* Sloop to make the alterations prepared.' Addressed to 'the Master Shipwright [ie Hayes] and his assistant', it reads: 'Having Acquainted the distance of the Forecastle of the *Racehorse* Sloop from the Crosspiece of the Topsail Sheets [to] where the Booms [and] the Boats to lie', the instruction then relates to 'a proposal to; lengthen her forecastle Two beams further aft and to have a Cabbin at the after part of each side', and concludes with 'and to have a bulkhead at the Aft part of the same; These are to direct and require you to cause the same to be done accordingly'.[8]

The reference to 'Topsail sheets' relates to topsail bitts, which are fitted on deck at the base of either mast and comprise two vertical posts called bitt pins, united with a crosspiece furnished with belaying pins. The bitt pins are fitted with vertical 'shivers' (pulley sheaves) through which the topsail sheets (ropes rigged to the lower outer corner of the topsail) are rove (hauled before being made fast to the belaying pins). Although the comment about lengthening the focsle by 'Two beams further aft and to have a Cabbin' at first appears practical, in reality it would only increase the length of the focsle by 3ft 6in (1m) according to the relative draught of the ship. This increase would be insufficient to provide suitable cabins each side for the boatswain and the carpenter respectively, let alone extra crew space. Despite the initial instruction disclosed in the Admiralty Order, we see from Midshipman Floyd's personal account below that deck length alterations and cabin layouts were completely revised, providing better practical solutions to meet the needs of converting the ship for the Arctic.[9]

Although Phipps's journal notes various structural modifications to the *Racehorse*, including the extension of the focsle, it does not fully detail the scope of works required to prepare the *Racehorse*. The ship's Progress Book similarly provides scarce details. What information is available comes from two sets of *Racehorse*'s ship draughts: one dated 1757 as 'fitted for a Bomb', the other dated 1773, titled 'A Draught of His Majesty's Sloop Race Horse her Body taken off in the Double Dock and as Fitted For a Voyage towards the North Pole'. Both draughts show the ship's 'lines and inboard profile' in the longitudinal plane, the inboard profile showing deck levels with relative beam disposition. Also shown are internal transverse bulkhead arrangements together with pillars and transverse riders.[10] Only by comparing the two dated draughts can the full extent to which *Racehorse* was modified be understood.

First, both bomb beds were removed along with their hexagonal embrasure-like housings with sliding covers. The extra-thick deck planking laid under the housings was also removed. Other work involved relocating the upper portions of riding bitts for the anchor cable under the focsle. Next, the foremost shell room with its

Model showing typical bomb vessel shell room construction. Stout support pillars carry longitudinal members that support the main deck beams together with lower longitudinal timbers mounted on the heavy-built transverse floor riders. (Pitt Rivers Museum, Oxford).

integral components – pillars, longitudinal beams and shell retention housings – was removed, providing greater storage capacity within the fore hold. Following this, an entire new deck was laid the full length of the ship, together with hatchways with high coamings (raised pieces of wood at the top of hatchways) to create greater accommodation for the crew. The foremost extremity of the original fore platform in the form of a short mezzanine below decks and its storerooms for the boatswain was removed and closed off with a transverse bulkhead against which the galley firehearth was fitted, its flue passing up through to the newly extended focsle. The transversely fitted riders upon which the fore shell room was supported were retained to maintain hull strength. (Riders are effectively heavily built internal frame timbers.) It appears that the main structure of the after shell room was retained within the *Racehorse* primarily to maintain structural integrity to the hull form, which being originally French and typically having smaller timber scantlings may have been less robust against crushing ice. All the storerooms previously located in the fore peak beyond the fore bulkhead were taken down to allow

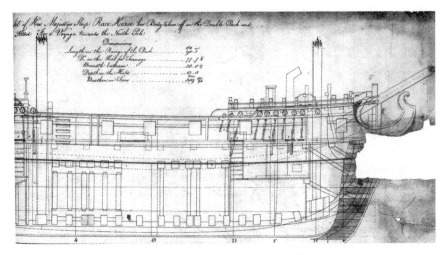

Profile view of the *Racehorse* after her conversion for the Arctic, showing the removal of the foremost shell rooms and bomb beds. NMM ZAZ 6569 (J2197).

the fitting of additional hull bracing to the bows of the ship. This comprised breast hooks, deck hooks and sleepers, supported with integrated diagonal riders, a modification that would not appear more widely until the end of the century when such components were fitted to add strength to weakened hull forms. For example, the hull of Nelson's flagship *Victory* was stiffened with breadth, top and middle riders in the 1780s.[11] In time, diagonal riders like this were incorporated into standard warship construction, introduced by the innovative Master Shipwright Robert Seppings (later surveyor of the Navy).[12]

The *Carcass* was similarly fitted with the same internal bracing system as the *Racehorse*, meaning that the finished ships became in effect Britain's first purpose-built icebreakers.

Midshipman Floyd's journal provides the following first-hand details on the fitting out of the *Racehorse*: 'within board the conveniences of the officers and men would [be] carefully studied, by the construction of cabins and births adapted to the northern climates as well as the safety of the whole by guarding against leaving too much space [for] water she might ship by high seas to act in.' He continues: 'For this purpose the quarter-deck was risen upon and continued

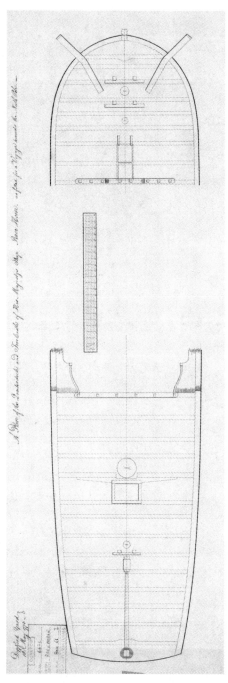

Plan view of the quarterdeck and focsle of *Racehorse* as converted for the Arctic expedition. NAM ZAZ 6572 (J2195).

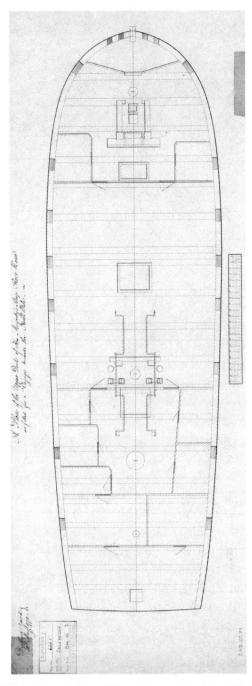

Plan view of the upper deck of *Racehorse* as converted for the Arctic expedition. NMM ZAZ 6571 (J2194).

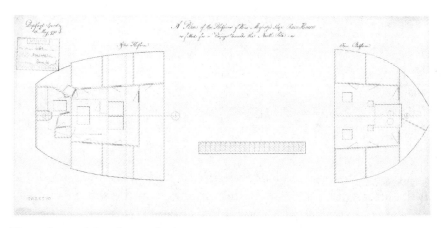

Plan view of *Racehorse* platforms as converted for the Arctic expedition. NMM ZAZ 6570 (J2193).

as far as the main mast, and the forecastle was brought twelve, or fourteen feet further aft. From the full part of the quarter-decks only after part of the forecastle, there was strong bulkheads so as to render it impassible for the water.'[13] The fact that these places below decks were subdivided into small compartments, together with the presence of stout transverse bulkheads, indicates there was a concern for keeping the ship watertight and can be regarded as a precursor of the damage-control measures built into modern warship design. Undoubtedly, considerable thought was given to adequately fitting out the ships for the hazards of the Arctic.

With all major hull work complete, the *Racehorse* was ready to be launched. On Wednesday they 'Attempted to haul the Ship out of the Dock but there not being Water enough shored her again and shut the Gates'. Besides embarking provisions, Thursday was spent getting the ship 'ready for hauling out of the Dock'. Friday proved more successful for launching for 'At 2 pm hauled out of the dock and lashed alongside the Terror Bomb [vessel]. The People employed about the Rigging and stowing way the Iron ballast.'[14] Cast in the form of rectangular blocks called pigs, these came in three sizes, each stamped with the government broad arrow and possibly the initial of the dockyard they originated from: C – Chatham; D – Deptford; or P – Portsmouth. The sizes were as follows:[15]

Pig iron ballast

Type	Size inches	cm	cwt	lb	Weight Kg
Large	36 x 6 x 6	91.40 x 15.4 x 1.5.4	1.5	168	76.204
Medium	18 x 6 x 6	45.72 x 15.4 x 1.5.4	1.0	112	50.802
Small	12 x 4 x 4	30.48 x 10.16 x 10.16	0.5	56	25.401

Although there is evidence that these were distributed as 30 pigs in the after hold, six in the brandy room, 15 in the spirit room and '15 abaft the Spirit Room', it is not known which sizes were placed where.

Racehorse's journals show that the ship was making 24in (61cm) of water in the hold over a 24-hour period. Though not an alarming quantity, 1 cu ft of water weighed 10lb (0.03 cu m weighed 4.5kg), so should this height of water extend to an area 25ft (7.6m) fore and aft and by 10ft (3m) in breadth, the weight added would have been 5,000lb (2.23 tons), which could easily affect the vessel's designed safe displacement once fully provisioned and stored.

Over the next few days shipwrights continued working in the ship, 'the People employed about the Rigging'.[16] On Monday 26 April the crew 'swayed [hoisted] the Topmasts half Mast up [that is with its head just above the lower mast cap to enable fitting the topmast crosstrees]. Received on board 23 Tons of Shingle Ballast.[17] The Ship made 6 Inches Water these 24 Hours.' This reduction clearly indicates that the hull planking was tightening up now the ship was afloat. Next day, the ship's company 'Got the Topgallant Masts up & Jib Boom out', after which they 'Stayed the Masts & Catharpened the lower Shrouds'.[18]

Both *Carcass* and *Racehorse* vessels were what was termed 'ship rigged', with three vertical masts – fore, main and mizzen – and a bowsprit 'steeved' (angled) at approximately 30° extending out from the ship's head. The fore, main and mizzen masts consisted of three sections: lower mast, topmast and topgallant, each of which were crossed athwartships with horizontal yards rigged carrying square sails. Each of these was named respectively topsail and topgallant sail, whereas the yards and sails of the lower masts were referred to as the main (or fore) course. Although the mizzen lower mast was rigged with a yard called the crossjack (cro'jack), this spar carried no sail. The purpose of the crossjack was simply to spread the bunt and clew lines of the mizzen topsail. Unlike the other two lower masts the mizzen was rigged with a gaff-rigged fore and aft quadrilateral sail, the head of which was laced to the gaff, the luff (foremost edge) and 'hanked' to the mast with loose fitted hoops. As it had no boom, the foot of the sail was loose footed and secured with tack afore, and a sheet at the clew abaft. The bowsprit of each ship was furnished with a spritsail yard and square sail and fitted with an extension called a jib boom that carried the triangular headsails, which, like the mizzen sail, were used when tacking ship.

Although not shown in the paintings of the ships (Plates 19 and 20) by John Cleveley the Younger (1747–86) the journals of both the *Racehorse* and *Carcass* clearly indicate that both ships were rigged with a square sprit topsail and yard rigged upon the jib boom. Used in conjunction with the jibs and headsails, the square spritsails and sprit topsails provided greater assistance when manoeuvring the ship when tacking and wearing. Also not shown in Cleveley's paintings, but well supported by both ship's journals, was the fact that these vessels carried additional square sails in the form of steering (or studding) sails. These were effectively side extensions to the topsails and topgallants used to provide greater sail area to drive the ship in light winds. Spread out on booms that run out beyond the extremities of the topsail and topgallant yards, these sails provide additional width to either side of their respective sails. The heads of the individual studding sails were themselves laced to their own individual yard, which was hoisted by halyard up to the appropriate boom. The sheet and tack at the foot of the sails were rove through blocks with the falls running down to deck level. The journal of the *Carcass* records that she was continuously setting her steering sails simply to keep pace with her consort, *Racehorse*.

Both ships were rigged with fore and aft triangular staysails attached to the fore stays running obliquely down from the respective mastheads. These sails comprised the lower, topmast and topgallant staysails on fore and main masts, though it is doubtful if staysails were rigged on the mizzen. Staysails proved very useful when running on a tack, since the sails balance the rig and were used to steady the vessel in gale or storm conditions. The heads of the lower masts were furnished with square platforms known as the fore, main or mizzen top, the function of which was to spread the shrouds supporting the topmasts. Similarly, the heads of the topmasts were fitted with a lighter construction called the crosstrees, which comprised three athwart ship's timbers providing spread for the supporting topgallant mast shrouds. During the course of the voyage, both the tops and the crosstrees importantly provided a high lookout point – essential when trying to navigate the ice-laden Arctic seas. Neither ship had a fourth extension in the form of a royal mast and carried no royal yards and sails, as they were too small to accommodate these.

Mast and yard dimensions of HM Sloop Racehorse *as fitted in 1773*

Dimension	Mast			Yard		
	Length		Diam	Length		Diam
	ft	in	in	ft	in	in
Main mast	74	5	21½	58	4½	14¾
Main topmast	39	7	115/8	41	1	9½
Main topgallant to the stop	19	2½	6¾	26	2½	5¾
Main topgallant pole head	5	4½	–	–	–	–
Foremast	73	0	21	33	3	125/8
Fore topmast	37	6	115/8	36	3½	81/8
Fore topgallant to the stop	19	2½	6	23	3	5¼
Fore topgallant pole head	4	0	–	–	–	–
Mizzen mast	54	2	14½	24	6	7½
Mizzen topmast to the stop	27	3½	8	23		6½
Mizzen topmast to the pole head	15	0	–	–	–	–
Bowsprit	42	4	19	37	1½	8½
Flying jib boom	30	0	8¾	–	–	–
Crossjack yard	–	–	–	37	4½	8½

On Wednesday 28 April, while the *Racehorse* 'Received some Fresh Beef', the crew was busy getting up the topmasts and topgallant yards, the latter having all associated rigging and blocks (pulleys) bent to them before hoisting. As ship's journals of the time show, it was common practice to rig the ship's masts, rigging and sails using its own seamen under the experienced charge of the ship's boatswain according to the overall needs authorised by the ship's master.

A Navy Board warrant issued to Deptford dated 26 April notes: 'These are to direct and require you to supply the *Racehorse* Sloop with ... [and] also supply her with Taylors Blocks, and the Tacks and Sheets to be of such sizes as Captain Phipps shall desire'.[19] The statement about 'Taylors Blocks' is significant. Used for rigging, these were handmade pulley blocks manufactured by Messrs Fox and Taylor of Southampton, who appear to have been the main contractor supplying blocks to the Royal Navy. Samuel Taylor also had block-making workshops in the Royal Naval dockyards of Deptford and Plymouth, and monopolised this lucrative contract until Samuel Bentham introduced a new system of mass-producing blocks to Portsmouth Dockyard in 1802.[20]

Although work on rigging the ship continued, some dockyard shipwrights still remained, fitting out with the smaller work, 'to make gratings over the Tiller as proposed', which tells us that *Racehorse's* tiller on the quarterdeck at the transom was exposed; a typical feature on bomb vessels and small craft where steering directly by hand was common. The gratings 'over the Tiller' were probably fitted to prevent ice entering where the after end of the tiller passed through the transom to engage into the head of the rudder. It is evident from the ship's draught that *Racehorse's* steering system was modified during her refit to include a standard single steering wheel and associated drum for the tiller rope to provide greater motive power to the helm. Here, the tiller rope passed from the drum through blocks at the ship's side, then back to the fore end of the tiller. This feature is verified within the ship's journal, in which tiller rope replacement is recorded.[21]

Another Navy Board warrant to Deptford on 30 April states that 'The *Racehorse* to be fitted with Ports or half Ports'.[22] This refers to the lids that closed off the port openings, but where exactly the half ports were placed is unclear. Unlike standard port lids, which hinged at their top and opened upwards, half ports are generally hinged to each vertical side of a port, opening like a door.

On Saturday 1 May the crew was 'swaying up the lower Yards, Tarring the Rigging and, Blacking the Yards & Mast Heads'[23] in the rain. The 'blacking' referred to is paint, a compound of lamp black (pigment) mixed with linseed oil and a small quantity of either thinned tar or fish glue for cohesion, the whole being thinned with turpentine if needed. On Monday 3 May, rigging the ship and making gaskets was hampered again by 'some Showers of Rain and Hail'.[24] Work for the crew throughout the remainder of the week consisted of scraping the decks after dockyard caulkers had finished paying (sealing) the seams with pitch. They were also 'Employed reeving the Running Rigging and making Swabs' together with 'scraping & paying the Masts', using rosin, a semi-sticky compound created as a by-product from the distillation of turpentine from the sap of pine trees. When cured, rosin forms a natural, inexpensive protective varnish coating for masts. It was also used for paying the sides of ships above the waterline, giving the 'bright sided' colour of warships before the advent of pale-yellow ochre linseed-oil-based paint later in the century.[25]

On Friday 7 May the ship received wood and '21 Chaldrons of Coals [for the galley firehearth] and some Fresh Beef.' Next day, 'Caulkers employed Caulking the Ports the People employed as before and stowing the Iron ballast in the Fish Room'; the quantity is not stated.[26] Work related to rigging continued, including making reef points for the sails, gaskets and foxes.[27] On Wednesday 12 May the ship 'Received a new Launch and a ten Oar'd Cutter & hoisted them in'.[28] Over the next week the journal records various preparations: dockyard joiners were 'employed in the Cabbin' (fitting out), while the crew continued embarking and stowing 'Provisions of different Species', drying the sails and bending them to their yards, which involved lacing them with tailed rope lashings called robbands. The ship also received a further 8 tons of iron ballast. Now lying off Woolwich, on the morning of Thursday 20 May they 'Completed the Hold fore and aft', which, although it suggests that all provisions were stowed, does not mention water butts. More importantly, the journal records 'Received on board Cables and Ice

Hooks', the latter being necessary for conditions of the forthcoming voyage.[29]

Next day, after the carpenter's and boatswain's stores had been embarked, there 'Came alongside a Launch to attend the Ship down the River'. Until this time, the *Racehorse* remained 'Lashed alongside the terror Bomb' but was now ready to move. At 11am they 'loosed the Topsails and got ready for going down [river]'. While this was happening the ship 'Received on board the Ice Poles and Saws'.[30]

A Navy Board warrant issued to Deptford dated 26 April states: 'These are to direct and require you to supply the Racehorse Sloop with Green Kersey floor cloth',[31] which was commonly used for covering the decks inside the cabins. Coverings of this material were used in HMS *Victory* when she was Nelson's flagship in 1805. Another warrant dated 12 May indicates that the *Racehorse* 'be supplied with coppers for freshening water'.[32] Although copper kettles were fitted upon the galley firehearth for boiling food, this particular reference relates to the special design of Dr Irving's distilling apparatus.

At 1pm on Saturday 22 May the *Racehorse* 'Cast off from the Blonde and came to Sail; At 3 Anchored in Galleons Reach with the best Bower in 6 f^m Water, veered away and Moored a Cable each way: the best Bower to the ? and Small Bower to the ? [the logbook omits the direction or bearings] Employed Rounding [in] the Cables and stowing away the Boatswain's and Carpenter's Stores'.[33] The cables were then 'rounded' in.

Lying off Woolwich Arsenal on Sunday 23 May, Phipps recorded that he had received 'our Guns with Ordnance and other Stores' from the Ordnance Yard. Phipps also records a high-ranking visit: 'At 3 came on board the Earl of Sandwich with the French Ambassador &c. Man'd Ship and gave them three Cheers on their return' as the grand Admiralty barges cast off and proceeded upriver returning to Whitehall.[34, 35]

Next day, after embarking the gunpowder, Phipps 'Read the Articles of War and Abstract of the Act of Parliament (for the encouragement of Seamen) to the Ship's Company'.[36] The 'Articles of War' comprised 35 Admiralty rules governing the duties, organisation and conduct of the entire ship's crew, the officers included. The Articles reminded the crew that they were all entirely in the service of the Sovereign Crown and that as a God-fearing and Christian country the commanding officer was to hold Divine Service every Sunday. Each 'article' – be it treason, cowardice in the face of the enemy, loss of or endangering the ship, misappropriation or simple theft – was concluded with the likely retribution; some, such as sodomy, being punishable by death.

On Tuesday 25 May the *Racehorse* let go her moorings and attempted to get under way to sail downriver, 'but the Wind not being fair Moored again with the Stream Anchor and Cable'.[37] With more favourable conditions next day – 'light airs with rain', the log records 'At 11 AM weighed and came to sail', and the *Racehorse* progressed down the Thames to rendezvous with HMS *Carcass* off Sheerness. On Thursday 27 May Phipps records: 'Fresh Gales & hazey. At 6 PM bent the Mainsail; At 8 Came too at the Nore with the Best Bower in 5½ f^m Water and veered away to 1/3 of a Cable. At 9 AM down T. Gall^t Yards and in 2nd reef T. Sails. [topgallant and topsails].' Over the next week the *Racehorse* remained 'Moored at the Nore, the Nore Light ENE 2 Miles Sheerness Garrison WSW and Minster Church SBE'.[38] As well as receiving beer and water and 'sending casks on shore', the crew were making final adjustments to the rigging by 'fleeting the Futtock Shrouds' – overhauling the shrouds and retightening their securing points or lanyards accordingly.[39] (Fleeting means moving rigging sideways to provide a better run for operation.) On Sunday 30 May Commander Phipps made his first journal entry referring to the ship *Carcass* in which the young Horatio Nelson was being carried as a midshipman: 'AM Came out of Sheerness and Anchored here His Majesty's Sloop the Carcass ... Came on board the Clerk of the Cheque and paid the People the Bounty money'[40] – the bounty in this case being the promised upfront payment for crew members signing on into the *Racehorse* for the duration of the voyage, including those impressed at the temporary 'rendezvous' officially up in the heart of London.[41]

On Monday 31 May Phipps records 'Received on board a Copper Oven'.[42] Whether this item was additional to the standard galley firehearth is unclear; the fact that Phipps recorded it implies that it probably relates to Dr Charles Irving's experimental distilling equipment being carried for trials converting sea water into fresh drinking water throughout the voyage. Other items embarked were extra purser's stores together with more water, beer and fresh beef. After unmooring and heaving in 'to ½ a Cable on the best Bower', the *Racehorse* was ready to sail.

Finally, on Friday 4 June, the weather was recorded as 'Fresh breezes and cloudy easing to light airs' and 'At 12 PM hove in to half a cable; At 4 AM Weighed and came to Sail in Company with the Carcass; Set Stud⁸ [studding] Sails; At 8 hoisted the Cutter out' in order to tow the boat astern.⁴³ The great voyage of exploration towards the North Pole had begun.

Preparing the *Carcass* for the Arctic

All refitting work undertaken on the *Carcass* at Sheerness Dockyard was overseen by Master Shipwright Nicholas Phillips who had succeeded into this post from Edward Hunt on 9 October 1772, Hunt being appointed on to the Navy Board as joint Surveyor of the Navy to John Williams.

On her return to Sheerness the *Carcass* was hauled into dock on Sunday 28 March 1773. Unlike Phipps of the *Racehorse*, Commander Lutwidge had assumed command of the *Carcass* in June 1771 when the vessel was deployed in the Irish Sea before being temporarily 'paid off' in March 1773 to commence refitting for the impending Arctic voyage, and therefore knew his ship well. A Navy Board warrant sent to Sheerness dated 26 March states: '*Carcass* Sloop to be refitted in Reference to other Works.' A second warrant of 3 April directs: 'To proceed to fitting her according to former Orders.'⁴⁴

On Saturday 10 April Lutwidge recorded: 'D° Wʳ, [ditto weather] AM the Commissioner paid Yᵉ Sloop off.'⁴⁵ Undertaking this was a matter of formality. On Friday 16 April 1773 Lutwidge started a new journal for the *Carcass* and wrote: 'Received a Commission from the Right Honʳble the Commissioners executing the High Office of Lord High Admiral to Command His Majesty's Sloop *Carcass*, fitting out at Sheerness for a voyage of discovery towards the North Pole, with an Order for her "to be victualled for Six Months with all

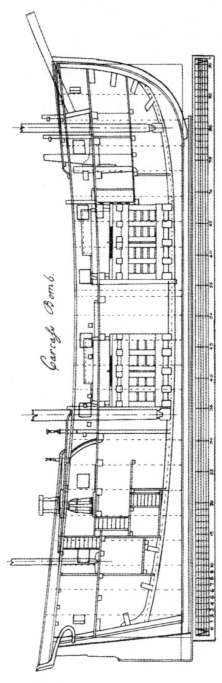

Inboard profile of the *Carcass* showing shell rooms and bomb beds. Drawing by author adapted from NMM ZAZ 5629 (J1446).

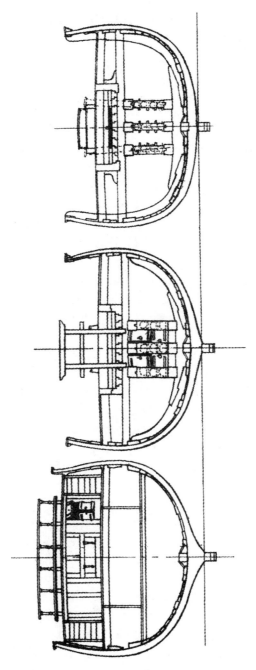

Left to right: Cross section of *Carcass* at after platform; cross section of *Carcass* at fore end of after shell room; cross section of *Carcass* through fore shell room. Drawing by author adapted from NMM ZAZ 5629 (J1446).

species of Provisions, except Beer, of which she is to have as much as she can conveniently store, and Brandy In lieu of the remainder; – to use the utmost dispatch in getting her fitted accordingly, and then proceed to the Nore for farther Orders – that none but effective men shall serve on the said voyage (her complement to be 90 Men) having given Orders that the Officers be paid by bill an Allowance equal to the Amount of Wages for their Servants".'[46] The fact that Lutwidge's crew was to consist of 'none but effective men' makes it clear that no boys or youngsters like Nelson were considered suitable for this type of voyage. Phipps in the *Racehorse* would have received a similarly worded directive. That Nelson was accepted into the ship in spite of this suggests that Nelson's uncle Maurice Suckling and Lutwidge blatantly bent the rules. This reflects the similar circumstances by which Constantine Phipps assumed overall command of the expedition, ie because he and Joseph Banks of the Royal Society had both attended Eton. The fact that Sandwich, the First Lord of the Admiralty, was also an Etonian reflects typical society alliances at the time.

A Navy Board warrant of 3 April 1773 to Sheerness Dockyard makes clear the amount of work needed: '*Carcass* Sloop to employ Men such extra on her as the Day light will permit', ensuring that Sheerness Dockyard's manpower worked at full capacity.[47] A follow-up Navy Board warrant dated 13 April initially concerning the ship's boats refers to general fitting out: 'Also that a Bulkhead may be fitted for the Afterpart of the Fore castle as the present Bulkhead of the Quarter Deck. These are to direct and require you to fit a Bulkhead at the Afterpart of the Fore castle as desired.'[48] This was done to provide greater protection from the elements. While this work was undertaken, *Carcass*'s bomb beds and shell rooms were removed as described for *Racehorse*. A Navy Board warrant sent to Sheerness on 19 April 1773 notes: 'Pursuant to an Order from the Right Honourable the Lords Commissioners of the Admit^y [Admiralty] of the 16thInst$^.$ [instant]: these are to direct & require this you to cause His Majest^{ys} sloop Carcass at your Port, to be fitted out for a Voyage towards the North Pole & stored in all respects proper for the said voyage.'[49] This same directive adds: 'And the Clerk of the Cheque is to enter Ninety Men as her Compl^{nt} [complement] according to the scheme on the other side [of the letter] hereof &c.' The warrant is signed with the initials 'GW CN'. On the reverse of the warrant is a list: 1 commander, 3 lieutenants, 1 master, 1 boatswain, 1 gunner, 1 carpenter, 1 purser, 1 surgeon, 1 cook, 3 master's mates, 6 midshipmen, 1 captain's clerk, 2 quartermasters, 2 quartermaster's mates, 2 boatswain's mates, 1 coxswain, 1 master sailmaker, 1 sailmaker's crew, 1 steward, 1 corporal. The list then gives between 40 and 50 able seamen providing a nominal total of between 72 and 82.

This figure does not fully correspond to the ship's muster list (see Appendix 8). Although the *Carcass* provisionally paid off in April 1773, the number of men of her previous ship's company with whom Lutwidge was acquainted and who had re-signed 'onto the ships books' cannot be fully corroborated. In times of peace, most seamen generally preferred to sail with a commander they knew and trusted, and there was a degree of loyalty among the seamen forming ship's companies. Most, especially those with family dependents, would 'sign on' to maintain a guaranteed, though spasmodic, income.

Work on the hull of the *Carcass* appears to have been quite extensive. On Wednesday 21 April, 'her wales were covered with 2½ Inch Oak Plank, her sides from the Wales downwards, Keel and Stern with 2 Inch Oak Plank. – additional riders in the hold, and breast hooks, sleepers &c. in the bows to defend her against the Ice. – Shipwrights employed on board in putting the sheathing upon the Keel/, which had been ripped off, as the Sloop was found to be to be very leaky after hauling out of the Dock the 17th instant (making 7in of water every hour) and had been taken into the Dock to be examined.'[50, 51]

The logbook shows that all the shipwright's work was finished within two days. While the process of doubling the external hull could be swiftly achieved using large gangs of men, the fact that the internal works were completed in the same time is remarkable. Much more complex in their form, the creation of these timbers involved extensive trimming and shaping by use of adzes, simply to fit the timbers to the internal convex surfaces. This work also necessitated boring holes through the timbers and parent structure by hand using augers before driving and clenching the fastening bolts. Following standard practice, it is probable that moulds had

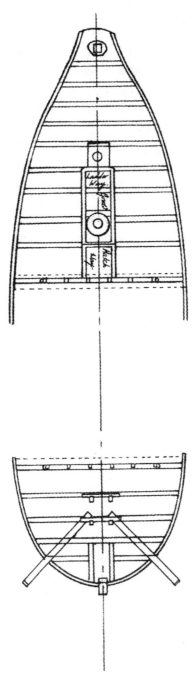

Plan of the quarterdeck and focsle of *Carcass* as a bomb vessel.
Drawing by author adapted from NMM ZAZ (J998).

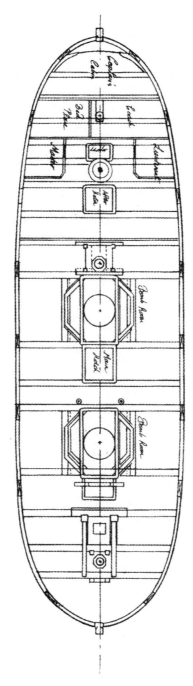

Plan of the upper deck of *Carcass* fitted as a bomb vessel. Drawing by author adapted from NMM ZAZ 5629 (J7999).

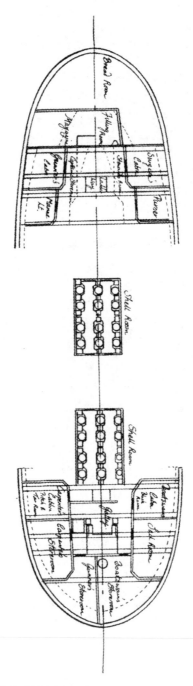

Plan of the fore and aft platforms of *Carcass* fitted as a bomb vessel.
Drawing by author adapted from NMM ZAZ 6529 (J1446).

been taken in advance in order to rough-shape the various components beforehand to allow for speedy fitting.

The weight of the additional planking and internal timbers would affect the displacement, draught and stability of the ship. Given that the weight of oak is approximately 45lb per cu ft (20.4kg per 0.028 cu m) then for every plank fitted measuring 2½in (6.35cm) thick, 8in (20.3cm) broad and 25ft (7.6m) in length, its weight would be approximately 166.5lb (75.5kg). A 2in- (5cm-) thick plank of similar length and breadth has a weight of 121.5lb (545kg). Supposing just 50 of each size plank were fitted, the weight added to the hull would be 6.424 tonnes. However, the hull weight was not completely compromised by this addition as the heavily built bomb beds and rooms had been removed. With all the major hull work accomplished by Friday 23 April, 'At 11 AM the Sloop was hauled out of the Dock, and transported alongside the Success Hulk'.[52]

Though not clear from ship's journal and Progress Books, work preparing the *Carcass* was just as extensive as that undertaken in the *Racehorse* and included the removal of structures associated with mortar housings. The only difference was that both shell rooms were completely removed, *Carcass's* hull being initially more strongly built. Storerooms in the fore peak were taken down to accommodate the additional timbers and riders to provide greater bracing to the bow.

Once afloat, Lutwidge notes: 'the Sloop not as leaky as before, being caulked between the Keel and Sheathing, as it appeared the water had got in there, and that the Leak was general, from the large Nails drove into the Sides, to secure the doubling.'[53] Following a remark about dockyard painters being employed on board ship, the log of Monday 26 April records: 'Received an Order from the Admiralty to send a Lieutenant, and One Petty Officer to open a Rendezvous in London.'[54] This is an official statement authorising Lutwidge to begin recruiting men by impressment for service in the *Carcass,* the 'rendezvous' being a temporary recruiting station set up in a tavern in which the lieutenant and petty officer lodged for the duration. Not being at war, when 'hot pressing' was forcefully and often indiscriminately pursued, recruiting was more positive; the men being sought were prime seamen from the mercantile fleet and coastal traders within the dockland 'Pool of London'. Watermen and

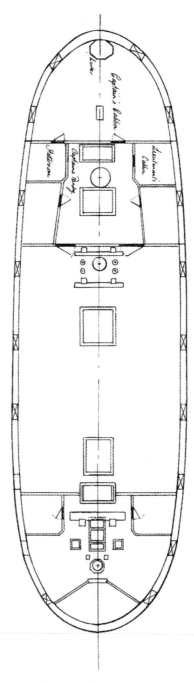

Plan view of the upper deck of *Carcass* as fitted for the Arctic expedition.
Drawing by author adapted from NMM ZAZ 6563 (J8000).

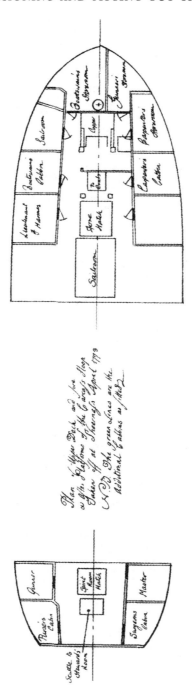

Plan view of the fore and aft platform of *Carcass* as fitted for the Arctic expedition. Drawing by author adapted from NMM ZAZ 6563 (J8000).

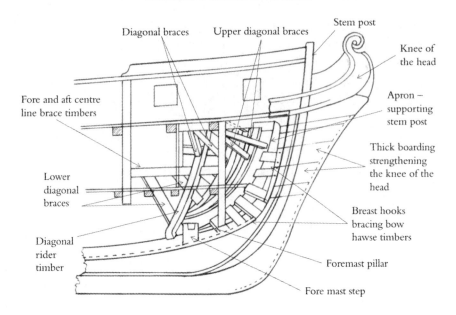

Diagonal braces

Upper diagonal braces

Stem post

Knee of the head

Fore and aft centre line brace timbers

Apron – supporting stem post

Thick boarding strengthening the knee of the head

Lower diagonal braces

Breast hooks bracing bow hawse timbers

Diagonal rider timber

Foremast pillar

Fore mast step

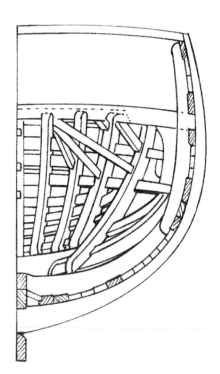

The bow of the *Carcass* showing the modifications made during her conversion. Drawing by author adapted from NMM ZAZ 6563 (J8000).

fishermen would also have been targeted. Most of those enlisting would have been looking for work, tempted by an upfront 'bounty' in receipt of the 'King's shilling'. The voyage needed 'none but effective men' – skilled, experienced, practical seamen who would work with cheerful obedience during the unusual passage upon which they were about to embark.

Throughout the rest of the week the crew were 'employed fitting the lower rigging' (the shrouds supporting the lower masts) and on Saturday 1 May, they 'got the cross trees overhead'.[55] The crosstrees are the two parallel timbers bolted to the heads of the lower masts in the athwartships plane, their undersides butting down upon the hounds of the mast (an integrally formed ledge on the fore and after face of the masthead). Once fitted, the two crosstrees were crossed by two interlocking trestletrees set in the fore and aft plane. Bolted together, the combined structure in this case served two functions: to support the top (flat wooden platform) upon the mast and to provide a supportive housing for the heels of the topmasts.[56]

Always aware of other ship movements, the other log entry of 1 May records: 'sailed hence to the Nore His Majesty's ship *Resolution*', in this case the 74-gun third rate of that name and not the *Resolution* in which Captain James Cook was already at sea on his second voyage of discovery in the Pacific. The year 1773 is the only time in history when the Royal Navy had three ships in service bearing the name *Resolution*.[57]

On Sunday 2 June Lutwidge records that the 28-gun fifth-rate frigate HMS *Lowestoffe* entered the harbour. Four years later, Nelson would be serving in this ship as a lieutenant when deployed in the West Indies. Next day, Monday 3 May, they 'Got the Tops overhead, and 25 Tons of Shingle Ballast onboard', the log entry concluding: 'a Gang of Riggers ordered on board from the Yard to assist in rigging the Sloop.'[58] In all probability the 'gang of Riggers' comprised what was termed the 'ordinary' – those seamen working on a retainer or surplus crew sent from other refitting ships; the modern jargon would be 'spare crew'.

The word 'tops' given in the journal entry relates to the flat platforms fitted at the head of the three lower masts upon their crosstrees (see above); each top named for the mast that it topped (fore top, main top, and mizzen top). They were fully planked and their primary function was to act as a spreader and securing point for the topmast shrouds and provide a stable platform for operating running rigging related to the uppermost masts and yards. They also served as a low-level lookout point.

Getting the 'tops overhead' involved considerable manpower, the use of the capstan and much dexterity. Fully assembled with their planking and fittings beforehand and with a square hole formed at the centre, these tops were first ended on to their flat after face and then hoisted to the masthead, at which point they were 'tripped' over into the horizontal plane (see Plate 18). After the square hole had been aligned they were slid down over the tapered masthead to rest upon the crosstrees and trestletrees to which they were bolted.[59] With the tops fitted, on Tuesday 4 May they 'got the Topmasts up, and rigging overhead', the masts being hoisted by means of a rope passing through an integral shiver (pulley sheave) in the heel of the topmast running up to the top tackle blocks temporarily rigged to the lower mast caps, the mast passing vertically though the hole of the respective top. Once hoisted, it was retained by means of an iron fid (tapered pin or cotter) passing horizontally though the heel and resting on the crosstrees.

Work over the next few days involved the rigging gangs getting the 'lower and Topsail yards across and rigged'.[60] The topmasts also

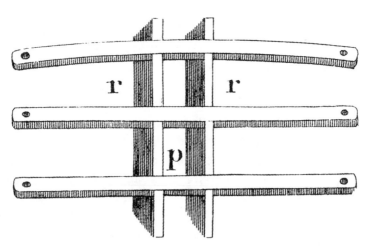

A set of topmast crosstrees, comprising three horizontal crosstrees supported by two fore and aft tressletrees. From Darcy Lever.

had crosstrees and trestletrees and although not supporting a large flat platform they did provide a receptive housing for the heel of the topgallant masts and spreader support for the topgallant mast shrouds. Moreover, they offered a precarious but advantageous look-out point – especially useful when looking for ice.

While all the rigging work was progressing and stores were being embarked, Lutwidge realised that the *Carcass* was beginning to sit too low in the water, so on Saturday 8 May he 'applied to the Admiralty to leave behind six of the Guns' to reduce the ship's displacement.[61]

Two days later, they 'stowed the Ground tier of Water', the casks of which were bedded down upon the shingle ballast embarked a week previously. Fresh water casks came in two sizes: leaguers or butts, the former containing 164–180 gallons (745–818 litres), the latter 108 gallons (491 litres). Lutwidge also notes that he 'made a demand for Provisions the same as demanded for the *Racehorse*', which indicates that he and Phipps were working in unison with the Victualling Board.[62] The weather on Wednesday 12 May, recorded as 'Strong Gales and rai'n', forced the crew to strike (lower) the yards and topmasts as a measure of safety. Moderating later, the men 'got the [anchor] Cables on board', each being some 100 fathoms (600ft/183m) long. As this involved moving about seven cables of differing circumference and coiling them below in the tiers, this work continued next day. With the weather abating on Friday, they got up the topmasts and yards. Saturday 15 May was equally busy: while a number of the ship's company worked with the gunner and his mates and 'got on board the Guns and Gunner's Stores', the able seamen went aloft and 'bent the Sails' (to their yards). A description of the complex preparatory work upon the sail at deck level beforehand under the watchful eye of the boatswain and his mates has been omitted for simplicity. In short, the sail was hoisted in a rolled form parallel to the yard using its buntlines. Next, the men aloft seized the earrings (rope eyes) at the outermost top corners of the sail to the yard arm, tensioning the head bolt rope of the sail after. They then proceeded to secure the sail along its length with robbands. This done, the men on deck manned the buntlines, leechlines and clewlines and

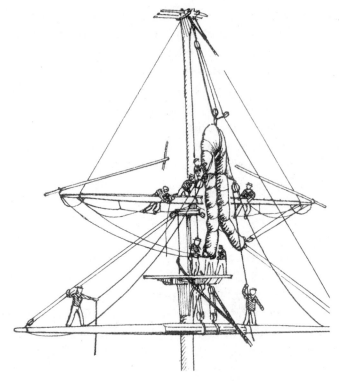

Sending up a new topsail. Illustration by Mark Myers.

furled the sail up into the yard, the respective lines secured at their appropriate cleats or belaying points. The men out on the yard then tightly bunched in the sailcloth and secured it with the rope gaskets pre-attached to the yard.[63]

Between Monday 17 and Friday 21 May the crew bent the small sails (stunsails, staysails and spritsails, the gaff mizzen included). Bending the staysails was less complicated as these were loosely secured by hanks (rings) to their respective staysail stays. Because stunsails (sometimes called studding or steering sails) were set flying with their yards when needed, these were bent to their yards ready for use, their yard halyards were also attached beforehand.

As provisioning continued, the boatswain's and carpenter's stores were also embarked, and they also 'Completed the Water to 34 Tons'. Given that a gallon of water weighs 10lb (4.5kg), this amounts to 7,616 gallons (34,623 litres).[64]

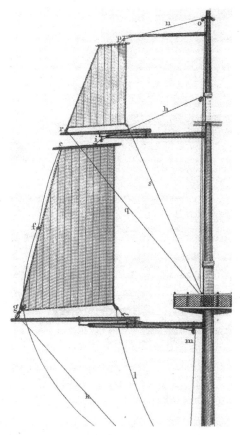

Topsail and topgallant studding (stunsail or steering) sails and their respective booms. From Darcy Lever.

With the ship ready for the voyage, Lutwidge recorded in his journal on Saturday 22 May: 'Fresh Breezes and fair, PM Hauled off into the Stream and moored a Cable each way NE and SW.'[65] The *Carcass* awaited off the Nore for her expeditionary consort *Racehorse* to come down the river.

6

Equipping the ships for the Arctic expedition

Besides special adaptations, including those to the hull, masts and rigging for the polar voyage, both *Racehorse* and *Carcass* also needed to embark equipment including boats, anchors and cables as well as provisions. Equipping a ship for scientific exploration and provisioning for Arctic conditions was a very different process from that normally undertaken and demanded an extraordinary range of procurement.

Both *Racehorse* and *Carcass* were equipped with boats for general use. However, on this occasion the boats had to be of sufficient number and capacity to carry the combined ship's companies, a precautionary measure specific to their deployment in polar regions. A Navy Board warrant of 12 April 1773 sent to Sheerness regarding the *Carcass* states: 'Captain Lutwidge late of the *Carcass* Sloop having requested as she is as soon to be recommissione'd that the undermentioned Boats may be provided as they are the most suitable for the intended voyage (Vizt). The Sloops proper Long Boat, one Launch of 26 feet, One Six oar'd Cutter, One four oar'd Gig (of large dimensions).' After referring to the refitting of the ship (see Chapter 5), the warrant then notes that: 'these are to direct and require you … to supply the Sloop with the proper Long boat and a Cutter over 25 feet, which you have in Store, unappropriated [sic]. The Launch and Gig we have contracted for here and ordered to be sent to Sheerness for &c.'[1]

The fact that Sheerness had an 'unappropriated' cutter suggests that the dockyard appeared to be concealing a number of surplus boats that were not formally designated. This matter had not escaped the notice of officials in Whitehall. Excluding the oars and boathooks, rudder and tiller for each boat listed, both the longboat and the launch would have been equipped with a single mast, sails and rigging as an alternative means of propulsion. From the warrant it can be safely presumed that the boats put under the young Nelson's charge as a coxswain would have been the 25ft (8.2m) cutter and the large gig, possibly 18ft (6m) long. The *Racehorse's* journal entry of 12 May states that the ship: 'Received a new Launch and a ten Oar'd Cutter & hoisted them in.'[2]

All of the ship's guns and associated equipment, including gunpowder and shot, were supplied to the Navy though the Ordnance Board based at the Royal Arsenal at Woolwich. As a government-controlled body, the Ordnance Board also governed artillery, equipment and all related supplies to the many regiments of the British Army. Both *Racehorse* and the *Carcass* were armed with light guns mounted upon standard wooden carriages, the main body and trucks (solid wooden wheels) being elm, the axle-trees, oak. Although ships of this size commonly carried guns for defence, they were also used for signalling, the frequency of which became particularly apparent in the foggy conditions encountered during the course of the voyage. At the time of preparation, there was reason to believe that the French might interfere with the expedition, and consequently the use of armament in an offensive role remained a possibility. The guns borne in both ships were cast-iron 6-pounders weighing approximately 1,250lb (562kg) with a bore size of 3in (76.2mm) firing as solid round shot of 6lb (2.72kg). The combined weight of the gun with its wooden carriage was approximately 1,500lb (680.4kg), which, although comparatively light, did affect the ship's displacement and stability, as is evident from the *Carcass's* journal, some being disembarked to lighten ship before sailing.

The ship's gunners also embarked all associated side arms (tools) for serving the guns, including: rammers; ladles (for loading powder, loose or cartridge); sponges (on shafts) for swabbing out the bore of the gun; and wadhooks for removing debris after firing. Added to these were prickers and reamers for the gun vents (touch hole) as well as powder horns and matches. Slow match, used for firing the guns, comprised lengths of flax cord soaked in potassium nitrate. When used, the match was held on a linstock, the firing end being forked to jamb the match. The linstock, adapting its name from the

Dutch *lontstok*, 'match stick', was generally made of wood from the ash tree and measured 18–21in (45–54cm) in length, sufficient to keep the gunner a safe distance from the flash in the gun's touch hole when firing.

At this point, firing guns by means of gunlocks with a sprung flint-lock mechanism had not yet been introduced, although the French Royal Navy had been experimenting with such devices since the 1740s. Gunpowder, also issued through the Ordnance Board, was supplied either in whole barrels, half barrels or quarter barrels, the contents being 100lb, 50lb and 25lb (45kg, 23kg and 11kg). The Ordnance Board also supplied the ships with gunners' small arms: pistols, muskets with their appropriate ball shot, cartridge, flints and cartridge paper. Muskets were commonly named a Brown Bess, supposedly after Queen Elizabeth I, but more likely from German *busche* ('gun').[3] The 'brown' relates to the dull hue of the barrel produced during the initial metal preservation process used to stave off oxidation (rust). The barrel was soaked in a mixture of oak wood shavings or bark with urine, the chemical reaction between the tannic acid ($C_{76}H_{52}O_{46}$) and uric acid (CH_4N_4O) producing a dull brown coating. Muskets were also known as 'Tower guns' or India pattern guns, the former referring to weapons officially issued 'lock, stock and barrel' from the Royal Armouries at the Tower of London, the latter to the fact that most guns were made under the monopoly of the East India Company and shipped to England. Muskets used by the Royal Navy were of the short sea service pattern with a barrel length of 39in (99cm), which were more practical for use within the confines of a ship compared with the military land pattern of 42in (106cm), which had marginally greater range. Muskets were issued with socket bayonets of triangular cross section 21in (53cm) long[4] and a firing flintlock mechanism. It would be a sea service musket that Nelson, according to the tale, would later take on to the ice in the hope of killing a polar bear (see page 213).

Other weaponry included cutlasses, tomahawks (hand axes), and (half) pikes of 7ft (2.13m) as opposed to the unwieldy 14ft- (4.3m-) long land weapon. The gunners were also provided with other para-phernalia including shot gauges, moulds for manufacturing musket shot, cartridge bags and cartridge paper. On Sunday 23 May the *Racehorse* embarked 'our Guns with Ordnance and other stores'.[5]

The *Carcass's* journal shows that Lutwidge had reduced the complement of guns to lighten the ship and compensate for the additional expedition stores.[6]

As the expedition would be carrying out celestial and astronomical observations, along with various scientific experiments, a wide range of specialist equipment and apparatus also had to be sourced and embarked. The mission to seek a northerly passage going eastwards made it important for them to accurately determine their position of longitude, the distance traversed eastwards or westwards measured in degrees from the zero-meridian aligned with Greenwich Royal Observatory. As already discussed, this required the use of accurate chronometers, which, used in conjunction with nautical mathematical tables, provided the longitudinal position. Unfortunately, John Harrison's H4 watch was too costly for the budget of the Board of Longitude so each ship instead received cheaper chronometers, *Racehorse's* one manufactured by Larcum Kendal, and *Carcass's* by John Arnold.

Larcum Kendall had run his own clock-making business since 1742 and was one of the six experts selected by the Board of Longitude in 1765 to witness the operation of John Harrison's H4. Having been asked to make a duplicate, Kendall completed his version in 1769 and presented it to the Board of Longitude on 13 January 1770. This was later given the name K1. Although marginally cheaper than Harrison's H4, K1 was still an expensive commodity at £450 (c. £75,000 in today's money), but by the time that Phipp's expedition was ready to sail K1 was already being used at sea by Captain James Cook's second exploratory voyage to the South Seas (1772–75) in HMS *Resolution*.

In 1771, the Board of Longitude asked Kendall to manufacture a similar but simpler timepiece than K1. Called K2, it was completed in 1772 at a cost of £200 – less than half the cost of its predecessor. In 1773 the Board of Longitude presented K2 to Constantine Phipps for use in the *Racehorse* during the Arctic expedition.

Based on a design initially created by John Harrison, another clock-maker, John Arnold, developed a different portable precision timekeeper. Arnold's watch was unique as it incorporated an escapement fitted with one of the first jewelled cylinders – made of ruby. The invention brought Arnold's abilities to the attention of the Astronomer Royal Nevil Maskelyne, who was in search of a watch-maker skilled enough to make a copy of H4. Arnold's timepiece (signed 'Arnold No. 1 Invenit et Fecit') was less complicated and expensive than H4. In 1772, Arnold modified the escapement so that it was now pivoted vertically and was activated by a spring. At least two pocket timekeepers with this escapement (Arnold No. 5) were supplied to Joseph Banks at a cost of £100 and, given the connection between Banks and Phipps, it is perhaps not surprising that one of these accompanied Phipps to the Arctic, having been put under the charge of Lutwidge in the *Carcass* at a cost of £450. From around 1782, Arnold's technical advances enabled the wider-scale production of marine chronometers.

The two chronometers issued to *Racehorse* and *Carcass* had strict instructions for their care, monitoring and use, including recording time loss, which had been laid out beforehand by the accompanying astronomer Dr Israel Lyons. These directions, ratified by Astronomer Royal Nevil Maskelyne, were given in the following Navy Board letter dated 21 May 1773, addressed to Phipps:

'And whereas the said commissioners have thought fit that two Watch Machines (one made by Mr Larcum Kendall and the other by Mr John Arnold) should be sent out for Trial in the said sloop under the care of Mr Lyons and that another Watch Machine (made by the said Mr Arnold), should be sent out for Trial in the *Carcass*, and have ordered three Locks of different Wards to be affixed to each of the Boxes which contain the said Watch Machines as well to prevent any improper management or ill treatment of them as to obviate any Suspicons [sic] of such mismanagement or ill treatment hereafter.'[7]

The letter then explains the control of the keys: 'And it being intended that yourself, your first Lieutenant and the abovementioned Mr Lyons, shall each have in charge one of the three Keys belonging to each of the Boxes which are to be put on board the *Racehorse*, and that the Commander, first and Second Lieutenants, of the *Carcass* shall each have in charge one of the Keys belonging to the Box which is to be put on board that Sloop. You are to receive and distribute the several Keys of the said Boxes accordingly and to be present yourself, and to see that your first Lieutenant be present every Day when Mr Lyons winds up and compares the said two Watch Machines which are to be put on board the *Racehorse*, and to take care that the respective times shewn by such Comparisons be properly inserted and attested under your respective hands, in the general Observation Book, as directed by the aforementioned Instructions.'[8]

The letter gives the same points for the *Carcass*: 'and you are to give directions to the Commander of the *Carcass* to receive and take into his Custody the Watch Machine which is to be put on board that Sloop and to be wound up every day in the manner directed by those Instruction in the presence of the first Lieutenant and to make such Comparisons of the times shewn, the said Watch Machine as shall be judged necessary and practicable for the trial thereof, and to cause the same to be properly inserted and attested in like manner, in a Book to be kept by him for that purpose.'[9]

Next, the letter advises on how comparisons should be made: 'and you are to settle such Signals with him as you shall judge necessary for obtaining the Information, if possible, of the time shewn by the Watch Machine under his Care, in order that the same may be compared with the times respectively shewn by those on board the *Racehorse*.'[10]

Always cautious about alternative eventualities and potential system failure, the Admiralty offers the following advice: 'But if it should happen that you yourself, your first Lieutenant or Mr Lyons cannot at any time by reason of or absence upon other necessary Duties, conveniently attend when the Watch Machines shall be wound up and compared as aforementioned, You are, in such Case, to take care that the Keys of the Person who cannot attend be delivered to some other Officer of the Sloop whom you can best trust therewith, in order that he may supply the place of such absentee; And you are to give similar Instructions to the Commander of the *Carcass*.'[11]

Both ships were supplied with a magnetic azimuth compass for measuring the angle of the arc on the horizon between the direction of the sun or another celestial object and the magnetic north. They could also be used to determine the angular bearings between two distinct fixed objects on the horizon, such as a headland or other natural feature when undertaking chart work surveys. Invented in 1736, these were much used before the development of reliable chronometers, and amplitude measured using a magnetic azimuth compass was regularly recorded within the journals of *Racehorse* and *Carcass*. They were relatively large and consisted of a brass case mounted in gimbals containing the compass rose, with the circumference of the card divided into 360°. They had two sights mounted diametrically opposite each other through which the sun, planet or star was viewed, and consisted of two vanes, one with a narrow slit, the other with a wider slit bisected by a thread. When making a typical observation the user looked towards the sun, which was seen through a dark glass, lining up the thread and the narrow slit on the centre of the sun to ensure that the centre of the compass was about one solar diameter above the horizon. At this point the observer pressed the stops on the side of the compass holding the card from which the magnetic azimuth or amplitude could be read. Compasses of this type were generally manufactured by Walter Hayes, Richard Glynne or Benjamin Ayres as well as Henry Gregory, who had an establishment known as 'The Azimuth Compass' in Leadenhall Street, London.

Each commander, master and lieutenant had his own quadrant or sextant, essential for undertaking astronomical observations of celestial bodies, primarily the sun and moon, to find the navigational position. The quadrant, based on the simple instrument introduced by explorer John Davis in 1594, had been developed into a reflecting quadrant by Isaac Newton in 1699 and formally introduced with further improvements made by Edmond Halley in 1730. Manufactured in ebony or lignum vitae with a triangular frame and with an integral arc of 45°, other components carrying the reflectors and sighting tube were made of brass. The arc, often inlaid with ivory, was graduated with 90 divisions of a half degree each; these were subdivided into 60 parts. Further divided into sixths, the scale on the arc provided degrees, minutes and sixths of a minute accuracy. Although the reflecting quadrant proved a well-tested navigational instrument, being limited to 90° it was incapable of measuring the angle between the sun and the moon to calculate time; a disdvantage for such an important scientific voyage.

The alternative instrument available, which provided greater scope, was the sextant devised by John Hadley in 1730. Working on similar principles to the quadrant, the frame arc of this device is one-sixth of a circle, hence the name 'sextant', which originates from the Latin *sextāns*. The arc of the sextant is graduated 0–120° divided in half degrees, giving far superior accuracy. When used to take a 'sight' or 'fix' of a heavenly body, the quadrant or sextant is held in the perpendicular. In this mode, either instrument could also be used to determine the height of land points relative to sea level. Alternatively, held in the horizontal plane, either instrument could be employed as a navigational aid to measure angles between two points on the horizon.

The telescope was another essential tool issued to each master, commander and lieutenant. At the time these were of the single draw type, about 22½in (57.2cm) long, with a wooden body and brass extension piece. It is likely that these were purchased from the telescope manufacturer Peter Dolland, who started his business in London as a maker of optical instruments in 1750. After becoming a fellow of the Royal Society in 1757, he was appointed optician to the King in 1761.[12]

Although it was intended that the expedition was to set off for the North Pole from the archipelago of Spitsbergen, we don't know what charts Phipps and Lutwidge were supplied with for the voyage, though the few available to them would have been rather rudimentary. A copper engraving titled *Spitzberg und Neu Zemble* dated 1719 does exist but this, like many early Arctic maps, was created from conjectural interpretation rather than geographical survey. Another, dated 1719 and known as *Mitternächtliche vesteland – Continent Septentrional*, which shows the North Pole at its centre and extending to a circular latitude parallel with the north coast of Spain, also lacks accuracy. The only accurate chart of the Spitsbergen archipelago was the one produced in 1758 by the French with possible Dutch intervention (see Plate 17).

One of the main reasons for the Arctic expedition was to undertake surveys of the areas visited, create new charts and update any pre-existing charts according to the new findings. The ability to more accurately calculate longitude would prove very useful in achieving this aim. Entries made in both ship's journals recorded a host of navigational data, with bearings taken at various points in order to cross-reference the positions of important geographical features. Also recorded were sea depth readings (soundings), which in addition to depth provided details about the physical composition of the seabed, such as whether it was mud, shingle or rock – useful information when anchoring. When taking the soundings, tallow placed in a hollow reccess on the bottom of the sounding lead would retrieve compounds from the seabed. The combined information gathered would be invaluable to later navigators. From the above we can assume that Phipps created his own charts for use in his book, *A Voyage Towards the North Pole: Undertaken by His Majesty's Command, 1773*. Published in 1774, this contains charts showing the course taken north to Spitsbergen and the routes sailed by *Racehorse and Carcass* throughout the archipelago.

Essential for dead reckoning calculations, three types of log were to be carried for measuring ship's speed (1 nautical mile = 6,080ft or 2026.6 yards/1,853m):

1 The common log, occasionally called a 'chip log', consisted of a log line on a reel, comprising a quadrant-shaped wooden board attached to a long line knotted at equidistant intervals of 47ft 3in (14.4m). The curved surface of the quadrant is weighted with lead to ensure the log submerges and stands vertically in the water, providing more resistance to produce a more accurate and repeatable reading. The log line is attached to the quadrant with a bridle of three lines that connect to the vertex and to the two ends of the quadrant's arc. One of these bridle lines is tied to a wooden peg that is loosely fitted into a hole in the quadrant. When given a sharp tug, the peg disengages, allowing the log to float for easy retrieval. When this log was used (often under the supervision of a midshipman) the operation required three seamen: one to hold the reel above his head, one to heave the log over the stern into the sea and count the knots as the line payed out through his hand, and a third to watch the 28-second time glass. The number of knots passing in the given time span would give the speed of the ship in knots (nautical miles per hour). The distance of 47ft 3in as a fraction of 1 nautical mile is directly relative to 28 seconds as a fraction of 1 hour in seconds (3,600 seconds). If the ship's speed was faster than 8 knots, then a 14-second time glass was used to correct the calculation. Although the difference between the knots on

the line of 47ft 3in provides true accuracy, most long lines were knotted every 8 fathoms (48ft/15.7m) for simplicity. The 14- and 28-second time glasses were kept in the ship's binnacle under the charge of the officer of the watch.

2   Bouguer's log gave Captain Phipps the opportunity to try out a more accurate method of measuring ship's speed using a log invented by the eponymous French mathematician and geophysicist in 1747. An improvement on the common log, this innovative apparatus counterbalanced the effect of wind and the sea surface on the quadrant by reducing the friction caused by the drag effect of the log line, which indirectly created a degree of inaccuracy. Bouguer's log comprised a varnished wooden cone attached to a metal weight sufficient to keep the top of the cone riding on the surface of the water. Both the cone and the weight were interconnected by a line about 50ft (16.4m) long. Bouguer's design substituted the standard log quadrant with a globe that was towed astern of the ship by a line, the end of which was attached to a lever fitted within the ship, which acted against a spring. As the vessel moved faster through the water, the pull exerted increased the angle of the lever, the inclination of which was indicated on a graduated scale relative to the ship's speed in knots. After Phipps experimented with this log on his outbound voyage, Bouguer's system was conservatively used for some 50 years.

3   The perpetual log was invented by William Foxon around 1772 and worked in a spiral manner, attached to complex clockwork mechanisms. This is probably the log that is referred to in the *Racehorse's* ship's journal as a 'diver', when they were attempting to measure the sea water current in Vogel Sound after the ships were released from the ice. In many respects the perpetual log they were using was the precursor to various new logs introduced during the 19th century. In Phipps's book, he provides observation details of both Bouguer's log and the perpetual logs in an appendix comparing the merits of both when compared with the common log.

Another item for scientific observation taken on the expedition was a pendulum apparatus made by the Scottish watch-maker Alexander Cummings for measuring the acceleration of gravity, which, based on a theory conceived by Sir Isaac Newton, varied at different places on the globe. Moreover, it would indicate the presence of large deposits of iron.[13] When Phipps and his scientific observer, Dr Irving, used Cummings' apparatus to calculate gravity acceleration on land during the voyage, they would equate the following measurements: the length of the pendulum L; the period of pendulum swing (beat) T (measured in seconds); the constant relative to the arc of swing circumscribed by the pendulum given as p (22/7 or 3.1416); and the unknown gravity G in feet per second (m/s). Thus the equation is: $G = 4p^2/T^2$. This pendulum is described and illustrated in Phipps's book (see Chapter 13).

Dip circle apparatus

Also embarked for scientific experimentation was dip circle apparatus, which was used for measuring the angle between the horizon and the earth's magnetic field (the 'dip angle'). This phenomenon had first been discovered by George Hartmann in 1544, when he noticed the needle on a compass dipped towards the northern hemisphere. Further investigation by Robert Norman in 1576 led to him submitting a hypothetical concept of how to measure the 'dip circle'. Further developed into a practical device, the dip circle proved useful for surveying, mining and prospecting. In 1772 the Rev Mitchell, a man 'eminently distinguished for his great knowledge in magnetics', designed an accurate instrument that was used as the basis for the two dipping needles manufactured by Mr Nairne for the Board of Longitude. One of these was carried on James Cook's second voyage (1772–75),[14] while the second model went to Constantine Phipps for his voyage to the North Pole in the *Racehorse*.

The instrument comprised an iron magnetic needle 12in (30.5cm) long and its axis, the ends of which were made of gold alloyed with copper resting on two friction wheels of 4in (10cm) diameter, the ends of which were balanced with great care. The magnetic needle vibrated within a circle of bell metal graduated in degrees and half degrees; a line passing through the middle of the needle to the ends pointed to the divisions. As Phipps discovered on the voyage, the dip circle apparatus also moderately determined latitude.[15] See Plate 24.

Other expeditionary equipment

The expedition's expectation of encountering a hostile environment, especially thick pack ice, led to the embarkation of a multitude of other tools and equipment. Major items included ice saws, ice poles and ice anchors. While the latter two could be easily produced by the foundries of the dockyards where the ships were fitted out, the former would have been procured from external suppliers.

Ice saws A Navy Board Warrant addressed to Deptford Dockyard on 24 March 1773 records that '*Racehorse* Sloop to be supplied with Ice Saws'. A similarly worded warrant referring to the *Carcass* but addressed to Sheerness Dockyard was also issued on the same date.[16] It appears that these saws were supplied by London-based manufacturers who were already making saws of various kinds to meet everyday industrial and rural use, including ice saws for the whaling ship companies. A typical ice saw was: 'fourteen feet in length, seven inches broad, and two lines and a half in thickness, with teeth an inch and a half deep. In the upper end of the saw are two holes, meant to receive two handles which cross each other, at which fifteen or sixteen men can work with ease'.[17]

The arrival of the ice saws on board the *Racehorse* appears to have raised some consternation among the seamen. Midshipman Floyd recorded their responses in his journal: 'they were much at a loss too, to know what were to be done with the great saws and hatchets they had seen come on board; hoping that it would please his honour [meaning the captain] to let them have free use of their hands and legs, by keeping them on ship-board, and not oblige them to turn to windward on shore, by converting them into sawyers!'[18] From this it is clear that at this stage of the preparations most of the common crew were totally unaware of exactly where the ships were going.

Ice poles Although Commander Phipps mentions that these were supplied to each ship, he gives no description and no precise details are referenced within the ship's logbooks except their usage when manually employed to free the ships from ice. The use of ice poles seems to have been fairly common for sailing ships operating in ice-bound areas, especially those engaged in the Newfoundland seal fishery. The Scottish author RM Ballantyne, whose sea adventure stories were supported by background knowledge, also makes reference to them: 'The captain shouted to the men "Bear a hand with the ice-poles!" Each man seized a long pole and stood ready for action. The ice was rushing in and the bay was full in a minute, and although the men used their ice-poles actively and worked with a will, they could no shove the pieces past them.'[19] Judging from this description they were stout wooden poles made from ash, 8ft–11ft (2.4m–3.6m) in length, used to push ice floes away from the ship's sides; whether or not they were tipped with an iron cap is conjectural.[20] Racehorse's log of 20 May records: 'Received on board the Ice Poles and Saws.'[21]

Ice hatchets As well as saws and ice poles, the ships were supplied with a good stock of ice hatchets for similar purposes. A Navy Board warrant to Deptford on 29 March simply states: 'Ice Hatchets to be provided and sent to Sheerness for the Carcass Sloop'.[22] Not only does the instruction indicate that the Racehorse would have received her hatchets locally, but the directive also specifies that Deptford Dockyard held the bulk of equipment issued to HM ships, a practice that would continue into the 20th century.

Ice anchors Also known as ice hooks, these are simply a 'large grapple used for holding the ship to an ice floe'[23] and resembled a normal ship's anchor but with only one arm and fluke, which was driven into the ice. When attached to a large, stout cable made up to a winch or capstan, these were used to warp (haul) a ship through the ice floes. They can also be driven into the ice around the ship to steady the vessel in much the same way as a sea anchor. Like a normal anchor, ice anchors were manufactured from forged iron and strength tested before being issued to a ship. It is likely that they were simply converted from damaged anchors that had lost an arm; their length was about 6ft (2m), suggesting a small kedge anchor. The *Racehorse*'s ice hooks were embarked on Thursday 20 May.[24]

Perhaps the most unexpected items embarked into the two ships were bricks and mortar, the purpose of which was to build shelters should the crew find themselves trapped in the ice and need to over-winter for the duration or await rescue. Like the ice saws, the sudden appearance of these materials caused some dismay among the men, the reaction of which is again recorded by Misdshipman Floyd in his journal: 'then would be found the vast utility of our store of bricks and mortar, for the want of which, if misfortune was to happen, we should have all, probably perished. Our people [the seamen] became now as earnest to discover, whether they were bound unto brick-layers or not, as they were before uneasy on a supposition of their being made sawyers!'[25]

Standard stores embarked

In addition to the specialist apparatus above, equipment and stores required by the key personnel, the boatswain, carpenter and gunner, had to be embarked. Specific evidence is somewhat vague as this was simply routine practice, regardless of ship or its deployment. A Navy Board warrant to Sheerness on 5 May 1773 simply states: '*Carcass* Sloop to be supplied with several stores.'[26] A second Navy Board warrant of the same date sent to Deptford and Sheerness simultane-ously instructs vaguely: '*Racehorse, Carcass* to be provided with several particulars.'[27]

The gunner, boatswain, carpenter, cook and armourer each held a wide range of items specific to their individual trade. The boatswain's stores and equipment related to rigging and included such items as blocks, coils of spare cordage, sailcloth and smaller items such as twine and marling spikes. The carpenter's stores included not only his tools but also essentials for maintenance, such as pitch, tar oakum, paint, rosin, varnish and linseed oil, together with bolts, spikes, nails and tin and copper sheathing. The journals of the *Racehorse* and *Carcass* provide little information about actual quantities of miscella-neous items embarked. Documentary evidence suggests that by the turn of the 18th century it was common practice for the gunner, boatswain and carpenter to keep accounts of their stores, including consumption of materials and the purpose they were used for, these account returns being presented to the ship's commander monthly. Unless new documents come to light, however, we cannot be sure if this prevailed in the 1770s, though sailing reports under varying conditions that included ballast and stores weights suggests that such accountability is highly likely.

7

Provisioning, supplies and ship's facilities for an Arctic voyage

Through the Navy Board, the provisioning of naval ships came under the authority of the Victualling Board, with Deptford being a key centre supplying Woolwich, Chatham and Sheerness.

The content of foodstuffs carried in Royal Navy ships in 1770 had remained much the same since a standard was introduced by Samuel Pepys nearly a century before. The weekly allowance per man generally included the following:

Basic supplies on Royal Navy ships, c. 1773

Day	Bread lb	Beer pints	Beef lb	Pork lb	Pease pints	Oatmeal pints	Butter oz	Cheese oz
Sunday	1	8		1	½			
Monday	1	8				1	2	4
Tuesday	1	8	2					
Wednesday	1	8			½	1	2	4
Thursday	1	8		1	½			
Friday	1	8			½	1	2	4
Saturday	1	8	2					
Weekly total	7	56	4	2	2	3	6	12
Weekly (metric)	3.2kg	32 litres	1.8kg	0.9kg	1.1 litres	1.7 litres	0.8kg	0.34kg

Note: The above are the basic rations only and could be supplemented with raisins, vegetables, and with an equivalent amount of flour substituting bread.[1]

Although it is not listed above, the purser also embarked a reasonable quantity of suet. The list above provided each man with a high-calorie diet – approximately 4,500 calories daily – sufficient to meet the intensive energy needs of seamen, which was equivalent to that required by farm labourers of the time.

When procuring provisions, the ship's purser used the quantities listed in the table to calculate the overall requirement of foodstuffs to embark. He would simply multiply the daily ration by the number of days (usually six months (180 days), or approximately 26 weeks), by the number of men borne in the ship. Assuming that one ship's complement comprised 90 men, then the following quantities would have been embarked:

Estimated quantity of provisions for 90 men for six months

Item	Total 1 man per week	Total 1 man per 26 weeks	Total 90 men	Total units	Total imperial tons	Total metric tonnes	Total litres
Bread	7lb	182lb	16,380lb	146.25cwt	7.313	7.20	–
Beer	56 pints	1,456 pints	131,040 pints	16,380 gallons	–	74.30	74,447
Beef	4lb	104lb	9,360lb	83.57cwt	–	4.11	–
Pork	2lb	52lb	4,680lb	41.79cwt	2.09	2.06	–
Peas	2 pints (refer to Notes)	14 pints	9,360 pints	9,360lb	4.18	4.11	
Oatmeal	3 pints (refer to Notes)	78 pints	7,020 pints	3510lb	1.58	1.55	–
Butter	6oz	156oz	140,40oz	877.5lb	0.4	0.39	–
Cheese	12oz	312oz	28,080oz	1,755lb	0.78	0.77	–
TOTAL					104.16	94.49	74,447

Notes:1: 1 pint of peas is approximately 1lb (450g) in weight
2: 1 pint of oatmeal is approximately ½lb (225g) in weight
3: Figures above for peas and oatmeal have been calculated by experimentation
4: 1 imperial ton = 2,240lb
5: 1 gallon = 10lb
6: 1lb = 16oz

While the quantities listed relate to standard provisions for providing the energy needs of men working under normal sailing conditions, they were less than satisfactory to sustain men working in extremely cold climates where daily needs could amount to as much as 6,000 or 7,000 calories simply to keep warm. Taking this into account, John Parry, the purser of the *Racehorse*, and John Strong, who managed supplies on *Carcass*, embarked a greater allowance of butter and suet to supplement the sailors' dietary requirements. They also obtained a wide range of other commodities to complement the standard victualling list. Pepper and mustard, for instance, with their warming effect, were believed to be important in sustaining the men in the extreme climatic conditions expected.

Beer was commonly carried in warships to supplement the water. Spirits, such as rum, were generally carried and were issued diluted with water. On this occasion, because of the nature of this voyage, it was recommended that brandy should be carried as well. Lutwidge mentions the supply of beer and brandy in his journal entry of 16 April 1773: 'Received a Commission from the Right Hon'ble the Commissioners executing the High Office of Lord High Admiral to Command His Majesty's Sloop *Carcass*, fitting out at Sheerness for a voyage of discovery towards the North Pole, with an Order for her "to be victualled for Six Months with all species of Provisions, except Beer, of which she is to have as much as she can conveniently store, and Brandy In lieu of the remainder".'[2]

The following letter, sent to the Commissioners for Victualling, discusses the embarkation of other varieties of alcohol: 'Having taken into consideration your letter the 12th Instant in relation to the Wine intended to be supplied to the two Sloops named in the margin (refer note) you are hereby required and directed to cause each of the said Sloops to be furnished immediately with Nine Casks of Red Port and three Quarter Casks of good old Mountain Wine for the reasons mentioned in your letter. Given &c. 21st May 1773.'[3] The letter is signed by Sandwich, Palmerston and Lisburne.

A total of 34 tonnes of water was finally embarked before sailing, equivalent to about 7,616 gallons (34,623 litres) which, accounting for a daily allowance of about 1½ pints (850ml) per man, would soon be used for cooking. However, for two reasons water would not be problematic on this voyage: first, abundant supplies of fresh water could be obtained from melting snow and ice; second, the ships were equipped with Dr Irving's distilling apparatus, which could convert sea water into fresh. Adding 34 tons of water to the standard provisions weight of 93.23 tons gives a gross of 127.23 tons, which is not excessive in comparison to the weight of other commodities embarked.

Other commodities included firewood and coal for the galley fire-hearth, and possibly portable heating stoves for the officers' cabins. The actual quantities embarked are vague but Racehorse's journal records that on Friday 7 May she received '21 Chaldrons of Coals'.[4] One chaldron weighed 25½ cwt and 1 cwt = 112lb (51kg) so the quantity embarked was 535.5lb (243kg). The quantity of coal embarked on this occasion does not, however, reflect the full amount needed for the voyage, the total quantity of which could not be fully extrapolated from the ship's journals. Coal was stored in a coal hole below the galley.

In the Racehorse, the ship's galley was located amidships on the fore platform below the main deck, abaft the foremast, the foremost boundary being the fore transverse bulkhead. The galley firehearth upon which all food was cooked had integral copper kettles for boiling food and water, ovens and a spit over the grate. Whether the whole firehearth was made entirely of iron with some part brick is conjectural since naval stove design was transitional at this period. From the ship's draught the firehearth measured 3ft 6in (1m) longitudinally and aft and probably 5ft (1.5m) in breadth. The entire stove sat upon a bricked deck measuring 9ft (2.7m) long and 5ft 6in (1.6m) broad. The galley flue passed up through to the focsle. A fixed bench table would have been fitted in the galley for use by the cook for dressing the food. All galley arrangements within the Carcass were similar, though the galley firehearth in the Racehorse was adapted for the installation of Dr Irving's distilling kettle and associated apparatus, a point noted in the Racehorse's journal of 31 May 1773: 'Received on board a Copper Oven.'[5] Phipps's recording of this suggests that the trial of Dr Irving's experimental distilling equipment on board was important to the expedition.

Dr Irving's distiller

For his invention, Irving received a parliamentary reward of £5,000 and the distilling apparatus was formally introduced into the British

Navy for general use in 1770. His initial experimental device consisted of a tea kettle made without a spout, with a hole in the lid in the place of a knob. When filled with sea water and boiled, the rising vapour passed through the hole in the lid into which the mouth of a tobacco pipe was fitted. By letting the stem incline a little way downwards, the fresh water vapour passed through the steam in the tube and was collected in a vessel fitted to its end. Moving on from his prototype, Irving fitted a tin, iron or copper tube to the lid of the kettle used for boiling water on board ship, and the fresh vapour passed through this tube into a hogshead, which served as a receiver. To ensure that the vapour condensed easily, the tube was kept cool by constantly wetting it with a mop dipped in a tub of cold water.

The testimony delivered to the lord commissioners of the Admiralty, and by officers who witnessed the experiment at Spithead, on board the *Arrogant* in January 1771, suggested that the device was effective:

'eighty gallons of sea-water did, in twenty-five minutes, after being put into the copper, and a fire made, distilled in the proportion of twenty-five gallons per hour into fresh water, perfectly well tasted, and of less specific gravity than the best spring water in that neighbourhood; and the said officers gave it as their opinion, that five hundred gallons of fresh water might be distilled in the course of twenty-four hour period using, with the same quantity of fuel, in proportion to the time, as it required in the ordinary business of the ship.

The testimony continued

'Every ship's kettle of that time is divided into two parts, by a partition in the middle; one of these is only used when peas or oatmeal are dressed; but water is, at the same time, kept in the other to preserve its bottom. Dr. Irving availed himself of this circumstance; and, by filling the spare part of the copper with sea-water, and fitting on the lid and tube, he demonstrated that sixty gallons of fresh-water may be drawn off during the boiling of the above-mentioned provisions, without any additional fuel. Regarding water preservation Irving also recommended that the water which may be distilled from the coppers in which peas,

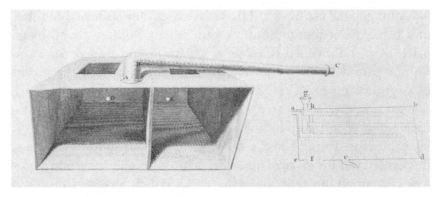

Drawing of Dr Charles Irving's distilling apparatus showing the condensing tube. Drawing from Phipp's book, NMRN.

oatmeal, &c. are dressed, as salutary for the scorbutic, and the most proper kind of water for boiling salt water provisions. On operation Irving remarked that only three quarters of the sea-water should be distilled, as the water distilled from the remaining concentrated brine is found to have a disagreeable taste; and that the farther continuation would effectively damage the vessel.'[6]

Dr Joseph Priestly, recognised for his discovery of oxygen, would later advise chemical intervention in Irving's distilling process to improve the water purity. Irving's distillers were not, though, the first to have been installed and tested on Royal Naval warships: the first trial had been conducted with the approval of King Charles II on board the 24-gun ship *Mermaid* in 1684:

'Charles R. Whereas a proposal has been made to us of an engine to be fixed in one of our ships for the making of an experiment of producing fresh water (at sea) out of salt, our will and pleasure is that on application to you by the persons concerned in the said engine you do receive on board and cause it (at their charge) to [be] fixed in some convenient place in our ship, in order to your making the said experiment in the present voyage, and reporting to us your obser-vations upon it, for satisfaction, upon your return provided that you be first satisfied that the same may be put up and made without any sort of danger to our ship by fire or otherwise.

For which this shall be your Warrant. Given at our Court at Windsor, this third day of August 1684.

To Captain William Gifford: Commander of Our Ship the *Mermaid*
By His Majesty's Command
S Pepys'[7]

Living conditions on the two ships were cramped but no more confined than those of any other sloop or sixth-rate warship of the period. On the *Carcass,* the after part of the vessel on the main deck contained two cabins for the commander, his state cabin and his bedplace. A further three cabins accommodated the lieutenants, and the centreline area was enclosed to form the wardroom. The aftermost cabins on the deck below quartered the purser, surgeon master and gunner. Cabins for the boatswain and carpenter were located at the fore end of the lower deck with their storerooms adjacent. An additional cabin next to that of the boatswain was given over to one of the scientific supernumeraries. The remainder of the crew, midshipmen and Nelson included, slept and messed throughout the two respective decks. Considering each man had additional 'Arctic clothing', conditions below decks would have been extremely cramped and, regardless of their rank or status, each crew member would have suffered damp bedding. Accommodation within the *Racehorse* would have been similarly organised.[8]

It is not clear from the records what the toilet arrangements were, although copper pissdales (urinals) were commonly fitted against the bulwarks (ship's sides) on the range of the upper deck. Alternatively, 'piss buckets' were kept below decks for use at night or when weather conditions on deck were difficult. The alternative type of toilet facilities called 'heads' are not shown on either of the ship's plans. Those for the officers may have been fitted into small compartments by the ship's badges (windows either side at the ship's quarters). Under normal circumstances the ratings may have had to use external facilities in the form of a 'seat of ease' at the ship's head. Although not evident from the ship's plans, John Cleverley the Younger's drawings showing the ships when stuck in the ice indicate that there may have been two circular 'blisters' fitted into the ship's external sides under the focsle near the head of the ship, which may have been fitted to meet Arctic conditions.

Naval officers and seamen usually supplied their own uniforms and clothing according to rank or status. This included jackets, waterproofs and boots, most of which were practical for working in ships. The unique climatic conditions of the Arctic necessitated a different approach and special clothing had to be procured and financed through a government grant administered through the Navy Board. This was done because neither the Admiralty nor the Royal Society could realistically expect the officers and seamen to carry this expense. Issued for free to each man through the ship's purser, this 'Arctic clothing' comprised sealskin boots, 'fearnought' (a rough, heavy, undyed woollen cloth) jackets and trousers, woollen waistcoats, mittens, thick woollen socks and hats of various materials – wool fur (beaver) or sealskin.[9]

Much of this clothing was similar to the attire worn by the men working in the whaling fleets; circumstantial evidence suggests that one supplier was based in Liverpool. From this it can be surmised that some clerk within the organisation of the Navy Board would have been tasked with investigating the clothing necessary, seeking suppliers and negotiating costs.

Given the magnitude of equipping both ships with all manner of scientific apparatus together with special tools and materials for the Arctic voyage, there must have been an unusual level of organisation on the part of major bodies concerned: the Admiralty, the Navy Board and Commissioners of the two dockyards involved. Although the Navy had well proved its logistical capabilities throughout the Seven Years' War supplying the ships, bringing together fleets and transports for the attacks on Louisbourg and Quebec, for example, exploration was a completely new field. Not including the complexities of obtaining varying materials and equipment not common to normal fleet support, it is evident that the Admiralty gave great consideration to the welfare of the ships' crews, ranging from ship modifications to improve living conditions, to provisioning and clothing. And although they had faced similar planning challenges for Cook's first voyage in the *Endeavour* in 1768, that expedition only involved one ship with 25 men travelling to a region with more congenial climatic conditions. Phipps's expedition involved two ships, some 200 men and truly severe climatic conditions for much of the voyage.

8

Manning the Racehorse and the Carcass
for the expedition

Due to the extreme nature of the weather likely to be encountered on the expedition, this was not a voyage for untested sailors.
Determining the number and calibre of the men needed to man the
two ships was essential. Unlike naval warships on standard operations
where some degree of conflict with an enemy was expected, there
was no need to carry extra men to operate batteries of guns. The
crew was divided into two watches with each man listed on the
Watch and Station Bill drawn up by the first lieutenant that designated individual sea duties. Unlike on larger warships, there would
be no room to carry additional 'riders' or 'idlers' – non-watchkeep-
ers. The riders in this case would include civilians selected for their
particular field of scientific expertise such as Israel Lyons (see page
33). The idlers were 'day workers' such as the cook, the surgeon
and his mate, the carpenter, and the sailmaker. This category also
included the carpenter's crew and the sailmaker's mates. Other idlers
with specific roles were the captain's clerk and the officers' steward.

Since Britain was not at war, the crew was made up of men who
saw the Royal Navy as their profession and not those who had been
pressed into service for 'hostilities only'. Although naval ships generally carried marines, none were taken on this voyage because there
was no need for regimented fighting units and insufficient room
or provision capacity in either vessel to do so. While marines were
borne in Captain Cook's ships on his expeditions to explore the
faraway reaches of the Pacific Ocean, this was as a protection against
potential native hostility rather than to control the crew.[1]

The crew of the *Racehorse*

Once the *Racehorse* was ready to sail, the total complement carried on the ship's muster book was 89 officers and men. The muster book of the *Racehorse* indicates that the total number of men entered into the ship was 122 including two 'widows men'. These were fictitious seamen entered on the ship's books in order to provide payment arrangements for the families of seamen who might die at sea en route, thereby preventing their widows from being left destitute. The number of widows men listed was usually 2 per cent of the official ship's crew borne regardless of rate. Excluding these two 'men' the actual figure listed is 120. Deducting the number of men discharged for whatever reasons along with those 'run' (deserted), a total of 31, the final crew number was 89. This figure excludes the supernumeraries: two ice pilots and one civilian scientist, so the real total number carried in the ship was 92. A transcript of the entire 1773 ship's muster book from April through to 28 June is given in Appendix 7 (see page 333).

There were three commissioned officers holding the authority of the King's Commission, eight warrant officers holding the authority of the Navy Board, some 20 petty officers of varying professional position and 50 able seamen along with two ordinary seamen and two pilots.

Captain Constantine Phipps
Born in London on 30 May 1744, Captain Constantine John Phipps (Plate 12) was the eldest son of Constantine Phipps, the First Baron Mulgrave. Through his marriage to Lepell, the daughter of John, first Lord Hervey, Phipps the Elder had inherited considerable property from the Duke of Buckingham including Mulgrave Castle in Yorkshire. In 1766, Phipps the Elder was created Baron Mulgrave in the Irish peerage during his brother-in-law Lord Bristol's six-month tenure of the lord lieutenancy of Ireland. Between 1755 and 1758, Phipps studied at Eton College alongside Joseph Banks, with whom he would later have greater association.

Phipps entered the Royal Navy at the age of 15 in 1759 at the height of the Seven Years' War, first as a serving midshipman in the 70-gun ship HMS *Monmouth* under the command of his uncle, the Hon Augustus John Hervey, later the 3rd Earl of Bristol; the *Monmouth* was deployed off Ushant to watch over the French fleet

[19]

J O U R N A L.

APRIL 19th, 1773, I received my commiſſion for the Racehorſe, with an order to get her fitted with the greateſt diſpatch for a voyage of diſcovery towards the North Pole, and to proceed to the Nore for further orders.

23d. The ſhip was hauled out of dock.

May 21ſt. The ſhip being manned and rigged, and having got in all the proviſions and ſtores, except the Gunner's, we fell down to Galleons.

The first page of the book Phipps wrote about the Arctic expedition. Author's photograph.

in Brest. When Captain Hervey was reappointed commander of the 74-gun ship HMS *Dragon* in 1761, Phipps transferred along with his uncle and was deployed on the West Indies station where, in 1762, Phipps saw action with Admiral Sir George Brydges Rodney's fleet, supporting General Monkton's military attack against the French at Martinique and St Lucia. Rodney's fleet of 40 ships comprised 13 third rates, seven fourth rates, eight frigates, eight sloops and four bomb vessels; Monkton's forces consisted of 14,000 troops. Although the attack upon Martinique began on 16 January, it was not until 16 February that the British forces took full possession of the island. Eight days later a detached squadron under Hervey was sent to take St Lucia. Overwhelmed by Hervey's ships entering the harbour, the island's governor, M de Longueville, capitulated without firing a shot.[2]

Following his first taste of action, Phipps was promoted to lieutenant on 7 March 1762 at the age of 18 by Admiral Rodney. That July he fought at the Siege of Havana in which Captain Hervey led a bold attack against the substantial fortifications of Morro Castle, during which the *Dragon* and accompanying ships suffered a severe onslaught from the Spanish defensive gunfire. In the action the *Dragon* sustained 16 killed while Phipps, with 36 others, was wounded.[3]

The extent of his wounds is unknown but appear to have had little prolonged impact on Phipps's physical well-being. When the Seven Years' War ended with the signing of the Treaty of Paris on 10 February 1763, Phipps was promoted to commander of the 12-gun sloop *Diligence* on 24 November that year. On 20 June 1765, Phipps took command of the 24-gun sixth-rate *Terpsichore* and next served as a lieutenant under Captain Sir Thomas Adams, commanding in the 26-gun frigate *Niger*, which had been deployed escorting mercantile convoys to Newfoundland and Labrador and protecting shipping in these waters.[4] Also in this ship was a fellow Etonian with scientific interests, the botanist Joseph Banks. During this voyage Phipps and Banks consolidated the friendship they had forged at school and it was thanks to this close relationship that Phipps would be chosen to command the polar expedition of 1773. Returning to home waters in 1767, Phipps took command of the 28-gun frigate *Boreas*, which was deployed in the English Channel.[5]

In 1768 Phipps temporarily turned away from his naval career when he was elected as Member of Parliament, representing the constituency of Lincoln until 1774. This move is quite understandable as there were few career prospects for sea officers when the country was not at war, many being 'on the beach' and retained on half pay. War provided a better opportunity for promotion, hence the naval adage: 'to a bloody war and a quick promotion'. More to the point, although Phipps had held command of the *Boreas,* her mundane deployment patrolling the Channel did not provide him with the chance to prove himself sufficiently to be promoted from the rank of commander to post captain (the name derives from the fact that when someone was given command of a rated ship, the promotion was 'posted' in the *London Gazette*).

With much encouragement from Joseph Banks, when the Royal Society decided to send an expedition to jointly seek out the northeast passage and the North Pole in 1773, Phipps was chosen to take command. Although we know Phipps willingly offered his services for the venture, the decision was influenced by various factors. In addition to having proven himself a reliable, steadfast officer when commanding the *Terpsichore* and *Boreas,* Phipps was also well posi-tioned socially; besides his aristocratic connection through his father and his recent election to Parliament, Phipps had been a protégé of Augustus Hervey, a man who now carried political sway. (Hervey was MP for Bury St Edmunds and had been appointed on to the Admiralty Board as First Naval Lord of the North ministry in February 1771.) The other factor influencing the choice of command was his relationship with Joseph Banks; Banks well knew Phipps's keen interest in natural phenomena. The decision made, Phipps was formally appointed commander of the expedition aged 29 years, seven years younger than his second-in-command, Skeffington Lutwidge.

Racehorse's commissioned officers

Besides Commander Phipps there were only three other men in the ship who held the King's Commission, each of them bearing the rank of lieutenant. In order of seniority, these were Henry Harvey, Cuthbert Adamson and Thomas Graves, each of whom entered into the ship on 16 April.

First Lieutenant Henry Harvey

Born in July 1743 at Eastry in Kent, first lieutenant Henry Harvey was aged 30 when serving in *Racehorse*. Through the patronage of his relative Sir Percy Brett, Harvey had entered the Royal Navy in 1751 aged just eight, his first ship being the 20-gun sixth-rate ship *Centaur*. At the age of 11 he was transferred into the 22-gun HMS *Nightingale*. How long he spent in these two vessels is not clear as it was customary for children of naval families to be entered on to the ship's books in order to gain experience prior to their formal entry into the service – an illegal practice known as 'false muster'.

Harvey was, however, undoubtedly at sea at the age of 15 and soon became a junior lieutenant in the 50-gun fourth-rate ship *Hampshire,* serving first in the English Channel and then in the West Indies and along the coast of America during the Seven Years' War. He proved very capable and was soon promoted to first lieutenant in the 28-gun frigate, HMS *Hussar*, which was captured by the French in May 1762 when she ran aground on the coast of Cuba. Released on parole after a year in captivity, he was sent home in HMS *Dragon*, where he became good friends with Lieutenant Constantine Phipps. At the end of the war, Harvey went to sea as first lieutenant in the 28-gun frigate *Mermaid*, which was deployed off North America. Following this, Harvey received his first command in the armed schooner *Magdalen*, which operated successfully against smugglers in the St Lawrence River. Returning to British waters in 1768, he was given similar duties in the English Channel, commanding the armed revenue cutter *Swift* until he was retired on half pay in 1771. His earlier friendship with Phipps had not been forgotten, and when Phipps was looking for a highly experienced officer to serve as his first lieutenant for his expedition to the Arctic, he offered the post to Harvey. Adventurous in spirit, and supportive of his friend, Harvey accepted wholeheartedly and could not have been a better officer for Phipps's voyage to the North Pole.[6]

Second Lieutenant Cuthbert Adamson

The second lieutenant was Cuthbert Adamson, who received the King's Commission as lieutenant in 1760. Unfortunately, details about his age and career before 1773 are obscure, and although he does not appear to have been of impressionable character, he must have been professionally competent to have been chosen by Phipps.

Third Lieutenant Thomas Graves

The third lieutenant was Thomas Graves who was born around 1747, the third son of Reverend John Graves of Castle Dawson, County Londonderry. Graves was also the nephew of Admiral Samuel Graves, who would ineffectively command the British fleet on the North American station in the early stages of the American War of Independence. Entering the Royal Navy at an early age during the Seven Years' War, Graves served alongside his uncle Samuel in the sloop *Scorpion* (14-gun), the fireship *Duke* (8-gun) and the *Venus* (36-gun). When the war ended in 1763, Graves was appointed into the 54-gun *Antelope* with his cousin Thomas. As midshipmen, the two went into the 74-gun *Edgar*, then deployed off Africa. Promoted to lieutenant in 1765, Thomas went into the 28-gun *Shannon* then, five years later, into the 32-gun *Arethusa* operating in the Channel against armed French privateer cutters. Aged 26 and well experienced, Graves found himself appointed into the *Racehorse*; whether this assignment was influenced by his uncle or by Phipps's personal choice is unclear, but in either case, Graves had all the qualities needed for an Arctic expedition.[7]

Racehorse*'s warrant officers*
These men were vital members of the ship's company with particular professional skills:

The master
John Crane joined the ship on 20 April. As the senior warrant officer, he had received his warrant of authority from the Navy Board. Although not holding the King's Commission, Crane held far more power on ship matters than the three lieutenants, because he was directly responsible to Commander Phipps for all matters concerning the principal navigation and manner of sailing of the ship, the master's mates (petty officers) working directly under his charge. Crane was also responsible for the ship's stability and everything to do with masts, rigging and sails, and was supported in this by the boatswain.

The boatswain
Jonathan Stanford was directly responsible to the master with regard to masts, rigging, sails, cordage and blocks. His responsibilities included the care of the sails and their proper stowage in the sail rooms, particularly ensuring that they were kept dry to prevent the spontaneous combustion that could be caused if they were allowed to get damp. He was also responsible for the ship's ground tackle, the anchors, cables and mooring buoys, and held charge of the ship's boats and their equipment. Accountable for so many areas on board, Stanford held an extensive quantity of associated stores, including rope and tar. He was assisted by the boatswain's mates.

The carpenter
Josiah West received his warrant on 21 May 1773 and entered the ship on that date, superseding the previous carpenter Jonathan Williams, who had discharged himself out of the ship the previous day. West was directly responsible to Commander Phipps on all matters concerning the maintenance and repair of the ship's hull, any related fittings and the ship's boats. He was also capable of making masts and

spars and remedial or relative repairs. Besides necessary trade tools, he also embarked spare timber paint, tar oakum and other wood preservatives, and a number of relevant tools. West was assisted by carpenter's mates and the lesser-skilled carpenter's crew, who were allocated on 4 June.

The gunner
Jonathan Fenton received his warrant on 10 June and replaced the ship's initial gunner, John Oyne, who was discharged out of the ship the same day. Fenton was directly responsible to Commander Phipps on all matters concerning the ship's ordnance, gunpowder shot and magazines. Also under his charge were all related stores and hand weapons. Fenton was assisted in his duties by the gunner's mate, William Godfrey.

The purser
John Strong received his warrant from the Navy Board on 20 April 1773 and was fully accountable to Phipps for all the ship's provisions, in accordance with the standard food issue authorised through the Navy Board, the details of which have been covered under provisioning in Chapter 7.

The surgeon
Doctor Charles Irving entered into the *Racehorse* on 26 April. As ship's surgeon, he was wholly responsible to Commander Phipps for the crew's health and diet. He held a dispensary of suitable medicines, and the prevention and treatment of scurvy was his major concern. He was capable of setting bones and undertaking a variety of limited operations but worked within the limits of the medical practices of the time. Irving was recommended to join the voyage so that he could also oversee his experimental distilling apparatus.

The cook
Alexander Sharpe came from Ladykirk, near Berwick, and initially entered the ship as an able seaman. He received his warrant as cook on 11 May, replacing Daniel Galbraith, who had been discharged out of the ship on 6 May. Although junior to other warrant officers, Sharpe held a warrant because he was responsible for operating the largest,

and most hazardous, fire source in the ship, the galley firehearth. His tasks included boiling meat and vegetables, making oatmeal porridge or gruel and baking bread; he would not be regarded as a chef in the culinary sense today. When available, he would roast joints of meat on the galley spit. On the voyage, he probably found himself baking fish and, rather unexpectedly, cooking walrus and, according to Phipps's published account, polar bear meat.

The armourer
Richard Wellsted received his warrant to enter the ship on 25 May. He was directly responsible to the gunner for the maintenance of all hand weapons: cutlasses, tomahawks and half pikes. He was also responsible for muskets and pistols. As well as this he acted as black-smith, undertaking all repairs to ironwork at the forge and anvil.

The gunner's mate
Richard Plym was 32 and initially entered the ship as an able seaman and was promoted to gunner's mate on 4 June. He was directly responsible to the gunner for the maintenance of gunnery equip-ment, match tubs and powder horns. He would also make up match (slow match) for firing the guns, the mechanical firing mechanism of gun locks using flints not having yet been introduced. As no yeoman of the powder room is formally listed in the muster book, it is possible that Plym also took this role. Here, he would have been responsible to the gunner for the safe and dry storage of all gunpow-der barrels, making up cartridges and turning the gunpowder barrels on a periodic basis to prevent the powder from solidifying. If he had been in a ship deployed for combat, his duties would have been far more complex, especially when in action.

The surgeon's mate
Alexander Mair received his warrant on 24 April when he was trans-ferred out of the *Egmont* into the *Racehorse*. In his new post, he was directly responsible to the surgeon in all medical matters and assist-ing in operations as required. Second in line to Mair was Frederick Waldon, aged 30, who came from Uppsala in Sweden. Initially enter-ing the ship as an able seaman, he was appointed surgeon's mate on 4 June. Why an additional mate was necessary in the ship is unclear,

the *Carcass* having only one. It may be that this man had previous medical knowledge, which is why he was chosen for promotion into this role.

The sailmaker

Thomas Spence, aged 22, came from Limehouse in east London, near Wapping, which was closely connected with trade shipping and docks. Spence reported directly to the boatswain for the repair and maintenance of the sails and was assisted by the able seaman appointed as sailmaker's crew on 4 June.

Racehorse's midshipmen

The four midshipmen in the *Racehorse* all seem to have entered the ship as able seaman and been made up to midshipman under Phipps's authority on 4 June. In order of age they were: George Scott, aged 24, from Limerick in Ireland; Charles Lucas, also aged 24, from Saffron Waldon in Essex; Thomas Floyd, aged 21, from Shrewsbury in Shropshire; and 19-year-old Philippe d'Auvergne from the Channel Islands.

Thomas Floyd

While little information can be found about Scott and Lucas, Thomas Floyd wrote a journal of the voyage, *A Midshipman's Narrative of [Capt. C. J. Phipp's] Polar Voyage – 1773*, which was not intended for publication, rather for sharing with family or close friends. Floyd's journal gives an invaluable picture of the voyage. Born in around 1752, Floyd was the second son of John and Mary, who seem to have been a family of reasonable social status. Thomas's elder brother, John, fought in the Seven Years' War in Europe and later found distinction when Lord Cornwallis appointed him as General Sir John Floyd to command military units in India during the Third Anglo-Mysore War (1790–92). According to various ship's books, Thomas Floyd entered the Royal Navy c. 1760 as a 'captain's steward' when aged eight, while completing his education at Greenwich. He first saw proper service under Captain John Wheelock in the former French 64-gun ship *Modeste* in early 1771. In October 1772, he went into the 74-gun *Centaur* commanded by Captain John Bentinck.[8]

Although Floyd had been informally accepted as a midshipman by the time the *Centaur* paid off in January 1773, when he went into the *Racehorse* that April, aged 21, he initially signed on as an able seaman. As with his peers Lucas and Scott, Floyd was promoted to midshipman on 4 June. Ironically, the *Racehorse* was his third ship to have been captured from the French.

Philippe d'Auvergne

A Channel Islander born in Jersey on 13 November 1754, Philippe (Plate 14) was the adopted son of Godefroy de la Tour d'Auvergne, the sovereign Duke of Bouillon. Aged 18 when he went into the *Racehorse*, d'Auvergne had entered the Royal Navy as a gazetted midshipman in 1770. He trained aboard the Royal Yacht HMS *Mary*, commanded by Captain John Campbell – a vessel that was used specifically for selected officer candidates, giving them a far easier journey than the usual training on a man-of-war. He was aided by the fact that Vice-Admiral Howe, who commanded the British flotilla at Jersey in 1756, befriended Philippe's father, Charles d'Auvergne, when he was British aide-de-camp in the islands. Midshipman d'Auvergne next served in the 32-gun *Flora*, during which period he met Empress Catherine of Russia and was influenced by a team of French scientists in Copenhagen. Throughout this time, Philippe studied mathematics and tried to solve the problem of timekeeping and barometric pressure at sea and was soon recognised for his work in this field. Phipps clearly thought him a suitable candidate for the *Racehorse* and d'Auvergne indeed proved an excellent choice, especially as he provided numerous meticulous sketches of the topography of the islands of Spitsbergen, along with images of the native flora and fauna. All were later used to illustrate Phipps's book.

Racehorse's able seamen

This group accounted for the majority of the ship's company. Each 'able bodied' man would have had considerable experience in skills of seamanship, such as operating the rigging, working aloft, handing sails and dealing with all general rope work. They also manned the ship's boats and provided the manpower at the capstan, dealing with the heavy work related to hoisting the anchors and cables, embarking stores, hoisting and striking (lowering) yards and topmasts as required according to sea and wind conditions. They also formed the guns' crews. Although averaging 25 years of age at the time of the expedition, most of these men would have been at sea from an early age.

Despite the attraction of both steady employment and potential adventure offered by the exploratory voyage, both the *Racehorse* and *Carcass* experienced some difficulties recruiting men. Of the 106 men who entered the *Racehorse* between 23 April and 28 June, four were officially discharged and 18 men (17 per cent) were listed as 'run' (deserters). Of the remainder, 22 were promoted to a higher status – for example, midshipmen or mates to warrant officers – in order to meet the needs of the ship's watch bill.

Those listed as 'run' reflect several events that made recruiting for the voyage problematic. In 1770, Spain declared sovereignty over the remote Falkland Islands, precipitating the Falklands Crisis and a potential state of war that caused many British warships to be fitted out and put into commission in case the war did arise. Ships ready for war and needing crew lured many seamen, attracted by the more lucrative earnings of prize money. Added to this, the Admiralty enticed seamen into the fleet with offers of bounty money of as much as £40. These factors, compared to little potential financial reward for a voyage in the freezing Arctic seas, certainly deterred potential recruits and were undoubtedly among the factors that drove 18 men from the *Racehorse* and three from the *Carcass* to desert. Complying with orders about only 'signing on' mature experienced men, no ordinary seamen were entered into the *Racehorse*.

Able Seaman Gustav Feston (Olaudah Equiano)
Feston (sometimes known as Weston) is perhaps the most remarkable of the men who embarked on Phipps's voyage. Entered on the *Racehorse*'s muster book as aged 28 and from South Carolina, Feston was actually a former African slave, Olaudah Equiano. Although the age given in the muster book states Equiano's birth date as 1745, his place of birth is somewhat controversial for, according to his autobiography, he was born in Essaka (today known as Isseke in Guinea).[9]

At the age of 11, Equiano was kidnapped along with his sister and the two were sold into the slave trade and shipped across the Atlantic to Barbados and then to Virginia. Like all Africans who had been taken into the slave trade, he suffered great deprivation and much harsh treatment. In 1754, Equiano was sold to Michael Pascal, a Royal Navy officer who renamed him 'Gustavus Vassa' – so the name Gustav Feston entered in the muster book may simply be a phonetic rendition of this.

After taking Equiano to England, Pascal took him on board ship where he acted as his valet during the Seven Years' War. During this time, he trained in seamanship and while in battle worked as a 'powder boy', passing gunpowder cartridges to the guns' crews. In these roles, Equiano served in the 44-gun *Roebuck* in 1757 and the 50-gun *Preston* in 1758. He then followed Pascal into the flagship of Admiral Sir Edward Boscawen, the 90-gun *Namur*, in which Equiano actively fought in the attack on Louisbourg in June and July 1758 and the Battle of Lagos Bay on 18–19 August 1759. When Pascal was wounded in this action and later given command of the bomb vessel *Ætna,* Equiano followed into this ship, which took part in the expedition against Belle-Isle on 4–8 June 1761. Writing his memoirs, Equiano gave a good account of the events at Louisbourg, the Battle of Lagos Bay and Belle-Isle.

At the close of the war Pascal sent Equiano to his sister-in-law in Britain so he could attend school and learn to read and write. His godparents, Mary Guerin and her brother, Maynard, who were cousins of Pascal, took a special interest in helping him to learn English more fully and, having converted to Christianity, Equiano was baptised in February 1759.

Later, Pascal sold Equiano to Captain James Doran of the *Charming Sally* at Gravesend. From here he was transported back to the island of Montserrat, where he was then sold to Robert King, a prominent American Quaker merchant from Philadelphia who traded in the Caribbean. Here, Equiano worked as deckhand, valet and barber for his new master. In 1765, when Equiano was 20 years old, King promised him that he could buy his freedom for £40. He also helped him to improve his reading and writing and guided him on matters of religion. Later, King not only engaged Equiano to assist him in trading along his shipping routes and in his stores, but he also permitted him to trade independently, selling goods between the Caribbean and Georgia. Equiano's success in this field enabled him to buy his freedom in 1767.[10]

King subsequently urged Equiano to become his business partner, but having almost been kidnapped back into slavery while loading ship in Georgia, he felt it was too dangerous to stay in the colonies as a freedman and began to travel extensively, working ship to ship as a deckhand before going to England. Here, in 1768: 'I hired myself to Dr. Charles Irving, in Pall Mall, so celebrated for his successful experiments in making this sea-water fresh; and here had plenty of hairdressing to improve my hand. This gentleman was an excellent master; he was exceedingly kind and good-tempered; this allowed me in the evenings to attend my schools, which I esteemed a great blessing; therefore I thank God and him for it and used all diligence to improve the opportunity. This diligence and attention recommended me to notice in care of my three preceptors, who on their part, bestowed great deal of pains in my instruction, and besides all very kind to me.'[11]

However, Equiano must have gone to sea again, since he writes: 'on my return to London, I waited on my old friends and good Master, Dr Irving made me an offer of the service again being the outside of the sea I gladly accepted it I was very happy in keeping with his gentleman once more; during which time we were daily employed in reducing old Neptune's dominions by purifying the briny elements and making fresh thus I went on till May 1773 when I was roused by the sound of fame to seek new adventures.'[12]

When Dr Irving offered his services to take his distiller on the forthcoming Arctic expedition in the *Racehorse* it was only natural, given his extensive experience in seamanship, that Equiano would volunteer to accompany his new master on the voyage. As he assisted Dr Irving during the voyage, the two men developed a friendly working relationship and, recording his time in the *Racehorse*, Equiano wrote: 'On the 20th of June we began to use Dr. Irving's apparatus for making salt water fresh; I used to attend the distillery; I frequently purified from twenty-six to forty gallons a day. The water thus distilled was perfectly pure, well tasted, and free from salt; and was used on various occasions on board the ship.'[13]

Olaudah Equiano in an etching taken from the frontispiece of his book, *The Interesting Narrative of the Life of Olaudah Equiano or Gustavus Vassa, the African.* World History Archive/UIG via Getty Images.

Recalling events later, he wrote: 'Our voyage to the North Pole being ended I returned to London with Dr. Irving, with whom I continued for some time.' Equiano then recalls: 'in the process of the time I left my master Dr Irving the "purifier of waters" and was happy amongst my friends and brethren.'

Racehorse's *supernumeraries*

This group contains personnel not involved with standing watch duties or physically operating the ship. The captain's clerk, Josiah Bates, a 22-year-old Londoner, dealt with all Phipps's paperwork and correspondence, and maintained a fair official copy of the ship's journal (logbook). Others were those listed as either carpenter's or sailmaker's crew and included men who maintained the ship. Working during daytime only, they were colloquially known as 'idlers'. Able Seaman Thomas Owen, for example, a 21-year-old from Deptford, London, was reassigned as carpenter's crew on 4 June.[14]

The unlisted supernumeraries
This group comprised those men carried in the ships for expeditionary and scientific purposes only. They had no direct role in the operation of the ships and are not listed in the ship's muster books.

The ice pilots
As the Royal Navy was unfamiliar with the Arctic regions they had to recruit men from the Greenland whaling fleet who had a unique knowledge of the polar seas off the Spitsbergen archipelago and beyond. In all, four Greenland men were employed, two serving on each ship to provide assistance to the vessel's commander. Those appointed into the *Racehorse* were Christopher Horner and Jonas English.[15] Those carried in the *Carcass* were Joshua Edwards and John Preston.[16] Each of these men held the equivalent of a Board of Trade Masters certificate.

The scientific supernumeraries
These included the mathematician and botanist Israel Lyons (see Chapter 3). Although Dr Charles Irving could have been categorised for his scientific role, he was logged on *Racehorse*'s books in his capacity as surgeon.

Of the other able seamen in the *Racehorse*, nothing significant can be ascertained about their origins other than that quite a number were of mixed nationality.

The crew of the *Carcass*

The *Carcass*'s muster book (Appendix 8) gives the number of men entered into the ship as 114 which, excluding the two mandatory 'widows men' gives an initial total of 112. Deducting the 34 discharged and deserted, the final crew number is 78. This figure excludes the two ice pilots, so the total carried on the voyage was 80. Like the *Racehorse* the *Carcass* carried three commissioned officers.

Captain Skeffington Lutwidge
Born in Whitehaven on 13 March 1737, Skeffington Lutwidge (Plate 13) was the son of Thomas Lutwidge and his second wife,

Lucy Hoghton. The date on which Lutwidge entered into the Royal Navy after his school years is uncertain, but assuming he was 15 years old this would give a date of c. 1752. What we do know is that he received his commission as lieutenant on 15 August 1759 while serving in the 24-gun sixth-rate HMS *Echo* – the same year that Constantine Phipps entered the Navy.[17] The fact that he was aged 22 when ranked lieutenant could suggest two things: perhaps he was slower to progress than his peers, or he could have joined the Navy a few years later, in 1754 or 1755.

As lieutenant, Lutwidge was given command of the armed cutter HMS *Cholmondely* on 6 March 1763. Swift and shallow-draughted, armed cutters were a relatively new type of vessel employed in the Navy at this time and were proving to be a valuable and inexpensive asset for defence in coastal waters. *Cholmondely* was deployed off Liverpool until 6 June 1766.[18]

Having been promoted to the rank of commander on 21 January 1771, Lutwidge was given command of the bomb vessel HMS *Carcass*, which was deployed in the Irish Sea to act against the privateers who preyed on the coastal mercantile trading vessels.[19] Lutwidge would also have been watching out for smugglers operating out of Dublin and the Isle of Man, who maintained a lucrative illegal business with the ports of Cumbria and Lancashire. Although the *Carcass* was paid off in March 1773, Lutwidge remained in command, overseeing the refitting and conversion of the ship in preparation for the planned Arctic voyage at Sheerness Dockyard throughout March and April of that year, under the overall command of Constantine Phipps. Why Lutwidge was chosen to accompany Phipps as second in command is unclear; he certainly did not appear to have the influential social connections of his peer. His appointment was perhaps simply based upon the fact that he had proven a good sea officer and that he already held command of the *Carcass* – he knew the ship and he knew her men. More to the point, the crew knew him, so drawing them together willingly for the venture presented fewer problems.

In assembling his crew, Lutwidge agreed to take on Midshipman Horatio Nelson as coxswain of the ship's boats. This arrangement was brokered by Nelson's uncle Captain Maurice Suckling, under whom Lutwidge had served on a number of occasions, including his time spent acting against privateers in 1771. In company with HMS *Racehorse*, the *Carcass* sailed from the Nore on 10 June 1773 and returned that September. On going out of the *Carcass* on 14 October, Lutwidge was made post captain on 15 October 1773 in recognition of his services during the exploratory polar cruise.[20]

Carcass's commissioned officers

Besides Commander Lutwidge, there were only three other men in the ship who held the King's Commission. Each held the rank of lieutenant and received his commission to enter into the ship on 16 April 1773.

First Lieutenant John Baird

Baird received his initial King's Commission as lieutenant in 1757 but little is known of his origins. He was appointed into the *Carcass* on 16 April and joined the ship five days later. Although Baird proved capable and popular with Lutwidge and the crew, he appears to have had 'little interest' in the service and never attained sufficient recognition for promotion to minor command, let alone to be shortlisted for captaincy. As a result, he disappeared into obscurity after the Arctic voyage.[21]

Second Lieutenant Josiah Pennington

Carcass's second lieutenant was Josiah Pennington. Like his fellow officers, Pennington entered into the *Carcass* on the day of their appointment, 16 April. Although we know nothing of his abilities as an officer, he may have been of a cantankerous nature, for some time after the voyage we learn that he was killed in a duel over a matter concerning his honour as a gentleman. Had he survived and maintained his 'honour', he would have been severely reprimanded; the Admiralty frowned on their commissioned officers resorting to this means of settling personal quarrels.

Third Lieutenant George Wykam

The third lieutenant was George Wykam, of whom little is known.

Carcass's warrant officers

The duties and responsibilities of the *Carcass's* warrant officers were identical to those on board *Racehorse*. Except for the information recorded in the ship's muster book, such as the date of entering the ship and receiving a warrant according to their office, we know little about these men.[22]

Carcass's midshipmen

These were John Creswell, aged 20, and Josiah Ferris, 25, both from London; Charles Deane, 18; and Edward Rushworth, 24; together with Robert Hughes and Horatio Nelson. Only Hughes and Nelson had entered into the ship direct as midshipmen, the other men being promoted from able seaman to midshipman on 1 May 1773. With the exception of Hughes and Nelson, little is known about these men.

Robert Hughes

Midshipman Robert Hughes was 18 years old when he entered into the *Carcass* just after Nelson on 13 May. Listed under ship's book number 63, he is recorded as coming from Greenwich.[23]

It was Hughes who befriended Nelson during the voyage and was Nelson's fellow miscreant who left the ship supposedly in search of a polar bear, although he is never named in Nelson biographies. When the *Carcass* paid off, Hughes went into the 74-gun ship the *Dublin*, but would serve in six further ships before passing his examination for lieutenant in 1780. Unfortunately, he died that same year before his rank had been confirmed.

Horatio Nelson

Midshipman Nelson (Plate 15) is listed under ship's book number 39 in *Carcass*'s muster book. His entry was recorded on 7 May 1773 and his place of origin simply given as Burnham, Norfolk. His age, rather oddly, is recorded as 16[24] although he was born on 29 September 1758 and was just 14 years and eight months at the time. It seems that his age was officially falsified to comply with the order that men entered for this voyage must be at least 16 years of age with some years of experience.

Before signing into Lutwidge's ship, Nelson had served in two Royal Navy ships and one West India merchantman. His entry into the Royal Navy came through the influence of his uncle, Captain Maurice Suckling, who had served in the Royal Navy during the Seven Years' War. During this war, Suckling had fought with distinction, commanding the 60-gun third-rate *Dreadnought* against the French in the Battle of Cap-Français off Saint-Domingue on 21 October 1757. As a midshipman, Nelson was initially entered on to the ship's muster book of the 74-gun third-rate *Raisonable* on 1 January 1771 under Suckling's current command. He did not actually go into the ship, which was then lying at Chatham, until 15 March, after he had finished his term at school. At that point, he was just 13½ years of age.

The Falklands Crisis that arose in 1770 led to much of the Navy, including the *Raisonable*, being prepared for war, but the ending of the crisis in January 1771 meant that the *Raisonable* was demoted to act as a guard ship and was moored on the River Medway until 15 May 1771 when she was paid off, with Suckling and the ship's company transferring into the third-rate 74-gun *Triumph*, Nelson included. Like the *Raisonable*, the *Triumph* was acting as a guard ship and there was little activity to further Nelson's training. To give him experience of seamanship and life at sea, Suckling arranged for Nelson to go aboard the merchantman *Mary Ann* under her master, John Rathbone, who had previously served with Suckling. As an able seaman, Nelson sailed from the Medway in the *Mary Ann* on 25 July 1771, bound for Jamaica and Tobago.

When the ship returned to Plymouth on 7 July 1772, Nelson had been away at sea for almost a year but had still not reached his 14th birthday. Returning into the *Triumph*, Nelson had to readjust to the harsher naval discipline of a man-of-war. His greater confidence following his experiences in the *Mary Ann* encouraged Suckling to give Nelson command of the ship's tender, operating the boat running despatches between ship and shore. Nelson also took charge of the ship's cutter, navigating the salt marshes, waters and mudflats of the Swin Channel and Medway, leading to Chatham and Sheerness dockyards. Within a short time, he could deftly navigate through the sandbanks of the greater Thames estuary, taking the boat upriver as far as the dockyards at Deptford and Woolwich. Nelson later remarked: 'thus by degrees I became a good pilot for vessels of that description from Chatham to the Tower of London, down the Swin, and the North Foreland and confident of myself amongst the rocks and sands.'[25] These experiences of shoaling channel waters would stand him in good stead at the battles of the Nile (1798) and Copenhagen (1801).

It was during these boating forays that Nelson would have seen the *Racehorse* and *Carcass* fitting out for their polar expedition. After making enquiries, he asked to go on the voyage as a coxswain. Nelson biographer Tom Pocock suggests that Lutwidge had seen Nelson's impressive handling of the *Triumph*'s tender off Sheerness, which implies that he may have chosen the young midshipman himself. While no evidence supports Lutwidge and Nelson having met beforehand, it is quite likely that they did, as Suckling was well acquainted with Lutwidge, the two having served together previously. Although Nelson was too young to accompany such a potentially hazardous expedition, it appears that Suckling made the arrangements through Lutwidge.[26] So, confusingly, Nelson is shown entering into the *Carcass* on 7 May 1773 apparently aged 16 but in fact celebrated his 15th birthday just ten days after his return from the Arctic. When he was paid off from the *Carcass* on 14 October he received wages of £8 2s 2d after deductions of 10s 4d. Next day, Nelson returned to his uncle's ship *Triumph*.

Carcass's able seamen

The remainder of the ship's company carried out duties identical to those described for *Racehorse*. The average age of the men in both ships was 26, a figure slightly higher than that found in other naval vessels, the difference reflecting the initial order for 'experienced men' – namely able seamen fully experienced in working aloft, handing sails, sail drill and anchor-related work. Just as important, men of this calibre were well acquainted with the rigours of shipboard life below decks. Maturity also brought with it obedience, the absolute attribute expected in situations that involved potential danger.

Able Seaman Nicholas Biddle

Biddle entered the *Carcass* on 4 May under ship's book number 50. Reappointed as coxswain by Lutwidge on 11 May, Biddle would, in his role operating the ship's boats, become well acquainted with Horatio Nelson, although he was eight years older.

An American colonist, Biddle (Plate 16) was born in Philadelphia in 1750, one of nine children of the William Biddle (1698–1756) whose Quaker family emigrated from England to America in 1681 to avoid religious persecution.[27] Biddle first went to sea at the age of 14 as a ship's boy aboard a merchant vessel trading with the West Indies. As he was still a British subject, he entered into Britain's Royal Navy in 1770, although whether he was pressed or volunteered out of a merchant ship is uncertain. He initially signed into the *Carcass* as an able seaman but, clearly showing considerable aptitude, he was appointed as coxswain on 11 May. Any reference to the use of the ship's boats made in Lutwidge's journal during the voyage would have involved Biddle.[28]

Carcass's supernumeraries

This group contained men not keeping standing watch duties, such as the captain's clerk, 17-year-old James Robinson from London. Others belonged to the carpenter's or sailmaker's crew, such as 29-year-old Thomas Lawrence from Liverpool; Londoner Edward Bernman, aged 28; and William Hall, also from London, who maintained the ship. Unlisted supernumeraries were carried for scientific purposes.

Overview of the ship's muster books

The total number of men entered into the muster books of *Racehorse* and *Carcass* for the Arctic voyage was 232. However this figure is misleading because 65 men were either discharged or 'run' (deserted). Some volunteers who joined in good faith found themselves discharged as late as 28 June 1773, partly due to the need to reduce manning levels relative to the quantity of provisions that had to be disembarked to lighten ship. This particularly applied to *Carcass* where 20 men rather than the 22 given in the ship's journal, were discharged for this reason after the ship was found to be riding too low on her waterline, making her unstable.

Carcass's muster book does show that Lutwidge used this opportunity to discharge two ordinary seamen. Also discharged on 11 June was Able Seaman Thomas Mitchener, sent out of the ship after being found 'unfit to proceed the voyage' or service. He was put ashore when the ship was anchored at Whitby[29] and his place was taken by a volunteer recruited from the town.

The muster book also reveals that several men were promoted or reallocated duties at the start of May, including Able Seaman Richard Seale, who was made master's mate, and Able Seaman Charles Dean, who was promoted to midshipman. Others were Able Seaman Patrick Farrell, who found himself made yeoman of the powder room on 11 May, only to be later discharged 'to lighten ship' (and possibly because of the realisation that the role was hardly essential on a scientific voyage).

All the alterations to the crew's status shown in the muster book indicate that when Lutwidge and his officers convened to work out the ship's watch and station bill, the abilities of individual men were reassessed to shape the ship's company into an effective working unit. Most mystifying is the case of the ship's cook, Thomas Yarworth, who was discharged on 12 May and replaced by Alexander McLean 'per Warrant 11 May'.[30] Navy Board correspondence reveals that Thomas Yarworth was actually blind and that after his dismissal from *Carcass* he seems to have been passed from one ship to another at Sheerness as each in turn discovered that his disability was not conducive to safe cooking at sea.

Of the 116 men who entered the ship between 23 April and 28 June, including Commander Lutwidge and the two 'widows men', only three men are listed 'R' (Run) as deserters, while 22 were officially discharged and 15 promoted to a higher status – midshipmen or mates to warrant officers to meet the needs of the ship's watch bill. The total number of men in the *Carcass* after this date, including the two ice pilots, was 91.

The men who had run earlier from both the *Racehorse* and the *Carcass* may have deserted into other naval ships that offered far better financial rewards. Although this could have been the case, it does raise the likelihood that men could surreptitiously move into other warships without the naval authorities knowing. A captain short of crew was certainly not going to ask questions when all he needed on the ship's books was a name, age and place of origin, all of which could be given falsely. Proving this would mean examining all extant muster books of ships crewing up at the time. The men listed as 'run' in both *Racehorse* and *Carcass* may simply have deserted once they realised that the voyage on which they were about to embark involved unknown hazards. Alternatively, they may have simply deserted to seek employment in the mercantile fleet or return perhaps to the fishing fleets rather than the Royal Navy, where 'signing on' could mean being 'turned over' from one ship to another for an indefinite period without being able to quit.

In many respects, the Royal Navy at this period worked on a similar principle to the mercantile fleet, whereby men signed on for the duration of a voyage, or a commission, until the ship paid off. It was only in times of war that difficulties arose when an entire ship's company could be 'turned into' another vessel at a naval captain's discretion. More commonly, an admiral or captain took with him his favoured officers, clerks, valets and servants. How many of Lutwidge's original ship's company who had been paid off from the *Carcass* re-signed into the ship that April?

Why fewer men deserted or 'run' from the *Carcass* compared to *Racehorse* is hard to account for. While the several reasons given above explain most causes, it may well be that most of the men on *Carcass* had worked with Lutwidge beforehand. Lutwidge, an experienced 'small ships' commander, used to working closely with his crew, was probably a better 'people man' than the politically minded Phipps.

Final complements of the *Racehorse* and *Carcass*, 28 June 1773

The total combined crews carried in the *Racehorse and Carcass* on the day they sailed on the exploratory voyage was 167 men: 89 in *Racehorse* and 78 in *Carcass*. With the supernumeraries: four ice pilots and one scientist/astronomer, the final total who sailed from the Nore was 172 men: 92 in *Racehorse* and 80 in the *Carcass*.

The general complement for these ships when rated and manned for war as a sloop was 120. Therefore the expedition crews in *Racehorse* and the *Carcass* were undermanned by 23 per cent and 33 per cent of their nominal total. However, both ships carried a nominal crew of 80 when operating as bomb vessels so in fact the manning figures for the Arctic expedition were not too dissimilar.

9

The voyage north and the Spitsbergen archipelago

The first aim of the Royal Navy's polar expedition was to sail north beyond the Shetland Isles for the remote archipelago of Spitsbergen that lay in the Barents Sea within the Arctic Ocean off the northern coasts of Norway and Russia. Geographically located between latitude 74° and 81°N (longitude approximately 20°E) and just 650 miles (1,050km) from the North Pole, this remote island group was the only practical land mass from where Phipps could operate the main thrust of his objective to seek the North Pole. Known today as Svalbard, which is the northernmost part of continental Norway, in Phipps's day the Spitsbergen archipelago was principally a whaling station.

The entire archipelago consists of three main islands: the largest, Spitsbergen, Nordaustlandet and Edgeøya. The smaller islands are Barentsøya (Barents Island), Kvitøya, Prins Karls Forland (Prince Charles Foreland), Kongsøya, Wilhelm Island and Svenskøya. To the south-east is Hopen and further afield directly south is Bjørnøya (Bear Island), which Phipps in 1773 refers to as Cherry Island. Remotely placed to the south-west is Jan Meyan Island. There are also many islets and skerries (small rocky islands too small for habitation). Excluding the westward-lying Jan Meyan Island, the collective land mass covers some 24,722 miles^2 (64,029km^2) with a coastline 2,229 miles (3,587km) long. The archipelago has five mountains, the highest of which is Newtontoppen at 5,620ft (713m). Other principal geographical features are 15 glaciers and ten rivers, seven fjords and two sounds. The main island of Spitsbergen is divided from Nordaustlandet by the Hinlopenstrasse Channel.[1]

It is likely that Svalbard was visited in earliest times by indigenous peoples from the northernmost parts of Scandinavia and the

Kola Peninsula of modern Russia. Except for the Vikings, thought to have landed on the islands after sailing east from Iceland in the 12th century, the barren landscape did not invite attempts at settlement. Following Dutch explorer and navigator Willem Barentz's landing in 1596, however, it was not long before hunting expeditions set out to kill Arctic mammals for their oil. The first, led by Steven Bennetto of the Muscovy Company, ventured to Bjørnøya to kill walrus in 1604. As the hunting expeditions returned annually, these mammals soon became almost extinct. A potential new oil source was discovered when English explorer and sealer Jonas Poole reported seeing a 'great store of whales' off Spitsbergen in 1610. Almost at once Europeans began hunting bowhead whales for their oil and a new industry developed, primarily dominated by Danish, Dutch and English companies with France participating on a lesser scale.

By the late 17th century there were between 200 and 300 ships operating with perhaps 10,000 men around Spitsbergen. Once the practice of whale hunting was established, outposts were needed for the mooring of ships along with facilities for rendering down whale flesh into its oil. At first these were simply seasonal stations with tents but more permanent sites were soon needed, the Dutch whalers from the Noordsche Compagnie being the first to construct timber buildings and set up large copper kettle ovens for boiling whale blubber. Settlements developed as follows:

Date	Nationality	Site	Notes
c. 1610	Dutch	Laegerneset	Seconded to the English in 1615
1615	English	Engelskbuktain	Abandoned c. 1650
c. 1617	English	Gravneset	Abandoned to the Dutch c. 1628
1618	English	Gåshamna	Two sites occupied until 1655
1619	Dutch	Smeerenburg	Located on the SE promontory of Amsterdam Island
1620s	Dutch	Ytre Norskøya	Rivalling Smeerenburg, abandoned in 1670
1631	Danish	Kobbefjorden	Abandoned in 1658
1636	Dutch	Harlingen Kokerij	Located in Houcker Bay
1633	French	Port Louis	Abandoned in 1637

The main centre of Smeerenburg, which simply means 'blubber town', contained some 16 buildings housing around 200 whaler men and eight blubber-boiling stations with cobbled alleyways between the buildings for drainage. Rivalry for the lucrative whale oil market soon expanded, with the Danes as main competitors. Needing to protect their assets from their rival Danish competitors, the Dutch built a fort at Smeerenburg in 1731 and also protected their outstation at Jan Mayen Island.[2] Such extensive whale hunting soon took its toll on numbers and the bowhead whale virtually became extinct. As Dutch operations declined, settlements were subsequently disbanded and Smeerenburg was reduced to a refuge for passing whaling ships that were now operating in new hunting grounds off Greenland. Despite its demise, however, Smeerenburg proved a welcome sanctuary for Phipps's exploratory ships in 1773 after their ordeal trapped in the ice.

The island group was given the name of Spitsbergen (or Spits Berg), from *spitz* meaning 'pointed' and *bergen* meaning 'mountains' in Dutch. Oddly, the English referred to the islands as 'Greenland'. There was no formal agreement about sovereignty at the time of Phipps's expedition; the islands were mutually recognised as *terra nullius* – an international status of 'no-man's land'. This meant that the archipelago was open to anyone who wanted to exploit its natural resources without restrictions and taxation. This mutual consensus, agreed upon since the 17th century, remained in place until 1905 when Norway broke up the Swedish-Norwegian union and annexed what is now named Svalbard.

Although the archipelago was frequently used by various national whaling fleets, it was the French who created the first chart of Spits Berg in 1758 (Plate 17). In all probability, it was a copy of this chart that Phipps relied upon, the Admiralty not yet having formally surveyed the area. The innumerable navigational data, including bearings and sightings, meticulously recorded in Phipps's and Lutwidge's ship's logbooks were used to consolidate their remit to update whatever charts the Admiralty held. In effect, the second formally organised scientific mission was the current British expedition being undertaken by the Royal Navy during which its commander, Constantine Phipps, would collect zoological and botanical samples as well as measure water temperatures.[3]

The outbound voyage for this notable expedition involved sailing up the east coast of England then heading north towards the Shetland Isles, the last land before Spitsbergen. Their initial departure from the anchorage at the Nore, in the outer reaches of the Thames estuary off Sheerness, was delayed due to extremely inclement weather. Midshipman Floyd in the *Racehorse* recalled: 'Æolus, persevered in his unkindness till 2nd June, when after a very stormy night blowing from the N.N.E. attended with thunder, lightning and heavy rain, the wind suddenly shifted to the N.W. this we were as expeditious as possible preparing sea and in less than half an hour, having by that time anchored at the bows, we were under sail; but alas! We had been so but a few hours, and indeed only long enough to push on three or four miles, when the wind became again unfavorable, and obliged us, very contrary to our inclination, to come again to anchor.'[4]

Making final preparations to sail on Thursday 3 June, the *Carcass*'s journal records the wind as 'Fresh Gales coming from the NNE the weather being cloudy', Lutwidge next recorded 'at 3 PM weighed p^r [per] Signal from the Nore in company with his Majesty's Sloop *Racehorse*, the Hon^{r}ble Constantine Phipps Esqr. Commander'. Justifying his situation, Lutwidge added that orders received from 'the Right Hon^{r}ble Lords Commissioners of the Admiralty' instructed him to put himself under Phipps's command. Lutwidge next wrote: 'at 4 Anchored with the Best Bower in 15 fathoms (90ft/27m) between the Warp and the Nore, *Racehorse* in Company.' Having anchored between the Warp and the Nore, Lutwidge wrote 'Sheerness Garrison distance 6 or 7 miles'. Once anchored, bearings were taken from three points and recorded so that they could later check that the anchor had remained firm.

Next day, *Carcass*'s log recorded: 'First part fresh Breezes and Cloudy, middle and latter light airs, ½ past 6 am weighed p^r Signal, at eight abreast of the Blacktail beacon, received a memorandum from Capt Phipps (on separation) to rendezvous at Brassey Sound in Shetland.' This appears to be a precautionary order given relative to the expected vagaries of North Sea weather. At this point in time, Blacktail Beacon was just a tall wooden post surmounted with a marker and lantern on the edge of Maplin Sands.[5] The *Racehorse* seems to have used this opportunity to hoist out her cutter with the

Simple chart of Thames estuary showing the Warp and the Nore.

intention to tow the boat while still in relatively sheltered waters. The journey to Spitsbergen before them was some 1,620 nautical miles (1,864 miles/3,000km).

Progress out of the greater Thames estuary was somewhat slow. Looking out from the deck of the *Carcass,* young midshipman Nelson would have been quite familiar with all the landmarks, having spent many hours in his former ship's boats navigating the sand banks and marshy creeks, abundant with wildfowl, that fringed the estuary.

At this period, the approaches to the Thames would have bustled with all manner of vessels. As well as the naval men-of-war entering or leaving the dockyards of Deptford, Woolwich, Chatham and Sheerness, there would be proud East Indiamen bearing spices from

India, and porcelain and silk goods from China. Less noble were the bluff-bowed, sturdy, cat bark colliers (similar to Captain Cook's chosen exploratory vessel *Endeavour*) going upriver with their black cargo from Whitby and Tyneside. Elsewhere, there were Baltic traders importing timber, hemp and tar for the naval and mercantile dockyards. Also congesting the waters were a host of wherries and spritsail barges from East Anglia bearing farm produce that at this time of the year ranged from barley, oats and rye to turnips and the like, including hay for the many horses in London. Other trading ships approached with wine and barrels of salted fish; every vessel funnelling into the estuary was feeding the expanding mercantile centre of London.

On Saturday 5 June Phipps tacked ship at 5pm 'and passed the Buoy of the Ragged Bough'. By 4.30 pm they had put in first reefs of topsails and set topgallant sails to maintain speed in lighter winds. By midnight when the *Racehorse* was 'off Orfordness WbN 2 or ? Miles', they 'hoisted in the Cutter, at 3 AM Tack'd and in 2nd reefs of T.S$^{ls.}$ at 4 Brought too'[6]. The town of Loestoff [Lowestoft] was at 'NbE½E 2 Leagues' and Phipps recorded that he let out some of the reefing to increase the sail area. *Carcass* was 15 nautical miles south. Lutwidge notes 'at 4 PM Ramzey [sic Ramsey] Church [Harwich] NNW 2 Miles, at 6 Tk^{d} to S^{o}ward, ½ past Tk^{d} to N^{o}ward, at Midnight Orfordness Lights ENE 1½ Mile, at 4 AM in 1$^{st.}$ & 2$^{nd.}$ reefs topsails, at 9 out 2nd reefs'. Both ships experienced difficulties working northward up the Suffolk coast avoiding sandbanks and contending with variable tide runs.

On Sunday 6 June *Racehorse* noted fresh gales and hazy to cloudy weather. 'At 2 PM in T G$^{t.}$ Sails & hauled up the F. Sail [fore sail]. Fired a Gun & made the Signal to Bare [sic] away; Southwould [sic Southwold] NW 3 or 4 Leagues'. Continuously having to reduce sail, to keep pace with *Carcass*, Phipps was aggravated by her slow progress and 'at ½ past 2 lowered the T. Sails & bro't to with her head to Eastward, Spoke the Carcass & bore away'. One can envisage an agitated Phipps at the ship's rail, shouting through his speaking trumpet to tell Lutwidge to 'keep up'. The voyage had already started later than planned; too late an arrival in the Arctic meant the season in the north would be short. By 3pm *Racehorse* had 'made Sail; at ½ past 7 Anchored with the best Bower in Ouzley [sic Hollesley] Bay][7] 5½ ᶠᵐ· Water.' Phipps continued to moderate the sails, to slow down and allow *Carcass* to keep pace. That Sunday Lutwidge recorded 'Dunwich Church NNE dist. 3 Miles'; he then wrote 'turning down along the English Coast; at 3 pm bore away a Pʳ· Signal and at 8 anchored in Hozely [sic Hollesley] Bay with the Best Bower in 6 fathoms'. His phrase 'turning down' appears out of context considering he was working *up* the coast of East Anglia.

With stiffer winds the next day, the *Carcass* sailing N6°E, they took in the first reefs and 'got down the Topgallᵗ Yards', a prudent move to reduce the leverage effects of topweight; with the sea state being 'a great Swell', the ship would roll heavily, creating discomfort below decks and difficulties for the cook. At this point the two ships lay some 4 leagues (12 miles/19km) off Great Yarmouth. Phipps, realising that the *Racehorse* was again surging ahead: 'at ½ past 10 shortened Sail for the *Carcass*, at 11 spoke her & decided that they would make more Sail.' The weather on Tuesday 8 June was cloudy with light airs and Phipps recorded: 'at 8 the Magnetic Amplitude 33°0´, Sounded several times from 12 to 20 ᶠᵐ·' (12 to 20 fathoms: ie 72–120ft or 36.6–23m). Progressing north the next day, Phipps records: 'at 7 Dimlington NWbW 5 or 6 Leagues.'[8] It appears from the logs that both ships were sailing with their steering sails set as the winds were still light.

Intending to stand off the fishing town of Whitby, both the *Racehorse* and *Carcass* anchored overnight in Robin Hood Bay before 'working up to Whitby'. Weighing anchor on Thursday 10 June they stood off and on Whitby bearing away 'to the N ʷᵈ·[then] turning to Windward'. The various manoeuvres made by tacking and wearing reflect the variable veering winds they experienced and the need to keep plenty of sea room to avoid getting too distant from the coast while waiting for the tide before getting inshore to Whitby to reprovision and water as intended. At 4pm on Friday, Phipps records: 'At 1 & 3 PM Tack'd ship and came to with the best Bower in Whitby Bay in 15 ᶠᵐ· Received 1298 Pounds of Fresh Beef and some Water.' Fresh beef was embarked to supplement their stock of salted meat. The *Carcass* had also anchored and sent a boat on shore for provisions. Besides Nelson or Biddle possibly coxing at the helm, also in the cutter was Able Seaman Thomas Mitchener, the person who was being discharged out of the ship as 'Unfit to proceed the voyage'.[9] Mitchener, of course, would have to make his own way home to Petworth in Sussex – some 300 miles (483km). While in Whitby, Able Seaman John Lore entered into the *Racehorse*, replacing Able Seaman Andrew Sproul, who had deserted out of the ship in this port. Not wishing to delay any longer, Phipps prepared to sail: 'At 11 AM fired a Gun and made the Signal to Weigh; at Noon fired a Gun & made a Signal for the Boat, Weighed as did the *Carcass*.'

Continuing his log on Saturday 12 June, Phipps wrote: 'at 1 PM fired a Gun & made a Signal for the Boat' that was returning with additional provisions. 'At 4 Wore and made Sail At 7 shortened sail for the *Carcass*. At ½ past 7 made Sail, at 10 set the F.T.M. [fore topmast] studding sails.' When the weather turned to fresh gales and

The Arctic expedition's route north as far as the Shetlands. Map taken from Phipp's book of the voyage.

rain an hour later, they 'hauled down D° & lowered the T. Gᵗ Sails', but set them again an hour and a half later as the wind moderated. The course set was N15°E. At noon on Sunday the *Carcass* was '1 Mile astern' while on Monday 14 June the *Racehorse* briefly hove to and 'hoisted a Boat out to pick up the Dead Light¹⁰ that was dropt overboard which we could not find'. The log records that they had to bring the ship 'to with her head to the Eastward' to retrieve the boat on the lee side of the ship because of the sea state.

In the face of strong gales, with the ships labouring in heavy, choppy seas, the expedition's progress from Whitby had been good; they were now closing in upon the Shetland Isles, which lie some 255 nautical miles (293miles/472km) north of mainland Scotland.

On sighting the islands, Phipps recorded: 'at 11 saw the Land from the Mast head bearing from NNW to WNW Distance 6 or 7 League.' Closing further, he noted: 'At 12 saw the Land from the Deck bearing NW 6 Leagues. At 5 Samborough head [Sumburgh Head] WbS 9 Leagues. Sounded 66 ᶠᵐ At 8 Hang Cliff W½ 4 Leagues; At 9 Tack'd Ship.'¹¹

Recording the landfall in *Carcass*'s journal, Lutwidge wrote: 'saw the Islands of Shetland bearing NW to NNW', and by 4am they were lying to off Bressay Island taking soundings, bearings and coordinates.

It appears that Royal Navy warships were seldom seen in the Shetlands and were a cause of great curiosity to the locals for, recalling events, Midshipman Floyd wrote: 'In the evening of the day we arrived on this coast, two boats came from the shore on their way a fishing. These islanders had never before seen a ship of war and expressed themselves with wonder at our magnitude, and were very curious in examining the different parts of her. After staying on board long enough to get drunk, they left us, but at night returned with fish which we bought.'¹²

By Wednesday they were attempting to clear the Shetland Isles and with the wind reduced to light breezes it was 'foggy and Calm', conditions that caused the two ships temporarily to lose contact. Phipps recorded: 'At 1/4 past 1PM fired a Gun and made the Signal for the *Carcass* to Ware¹³; & stand the other way; at ¾ past she bro't too; at 2 she wore, made sail and stood towards us; at ½ past 3 we Wore Ship. From 4 to 9 fired 7 Guns; and from 8 to 11 fired

6 Muskets every half hour as Signals for the *Carcass* – which he answered every time.' Phipps then made more sail to draw away from the islands: 'At 10 set Stud^g Sails; at 11 the North end of Shetland NbW 6 Leagues. At Noon the *Carcass* in Company.' Verifying this account, Lutwidge penned in *Carcass*'s journal: 'Light airs' and thick fog ... PM lost sight of the *Racehorse* who fired guns every half hour.' Sighting the *Racehorse* the next morning, the *Carcass* received signals to steer north-east.

Realising how easy it was for each ship to lose sight of the other, Phipps now made preparations for the next leg of the voyage and, needing to ensure that the ships could rendezvous at Spitsbergen, he sent new orders over into the *Carcass* to achieve this aim. Reflecting this, *Racehorse*'s log of Thursday 17 June states: 'at ½ past 7PM made the *Carcass*'s Signal for a Lieutenant and bro't too [hove to].' In response, *Carcass*'s log read: 'the *Racehorse* brought too and made the signal for an Officer, sent a Lieu^t on board and received an Order for signals to be observed in a fog, also a Mem° [memorandum] from Capt Phipps (in case of separating); if the wind shou'd be Easterly then to make the best of my way to John Mayens Island if Westerly to Cherry Island; on my arrival at either of those places to wait three days, and in case of his not arriving within that time; then to make the best of my way to Bell sound in Spitsbergen and to wait there eight days; In case of His not arriving there in that time, to proceed to Hackluits [sic] headland, waiting in the harbour there till the 20th of July; and in case of his not joining me on that day or within eight days after my arrival there, then to open the Packet (sent with the Mem°) for my further proceeding. – On leaving any of the Places of Rendezvous, then to erect some conspicuous mark and leave a letter informing him of my departure &c.' Phipps was leaving nothing to chance, his suggestions for an alternative rendezvous highlighting the fact that adverse weather and circumstances made communication between two ships erratic. The orders given, the *Racehorse* proceeded on a course of N 6°E; the *Carcass* N 9°45′E; the difference of 3° between them is inexplicable.[14]

On Sunday 20 June Phipps records the weather as 'Fresh breezes and hazy latter part little Wind & cloudy At 1 PM down TG. Yards in Spritsail yard & 1st & 2nd Reefs of the topsails, at 4 out 2nd Reef of Main TS.[1]' He then stated that the 'Carcass made the Signal for the Time Keeper which was answered'. This indicates that the two ships corresponded in order to check their chronometers, Lutwidge recording that his timekeeper was 11 minutes 15 seconds slow. At midnight, Phipps observed his position as 66°54′N. while in the Carcass the variation taken using three azimuths gave a position of N 25°4′W. Trying to make greater progress in Racehorse, they raised up the topgallant yards and reset the inner spritsail yards, the men at the pinrails of the bitts hauling on the topgallant tye halyard sheets, others on the focsle pulling on the spritsail yard outhauler and related sheets; all sails sheeted home, the seamen coiling and making up the ropes accordingly.

On Monday 21 June Phipps records: 'At 3 PM tried soundings with 780 [fm.] line but could get no ground – Thermometer 33° on the Surface– at 7 set Studg Sails At 1 AM saw a sail to the N° ward'; At 3 hoisted our colours & fired a Gun.' Although Phipps made his intentions to speak with the lone vessel clear, in light winds it was another two hours before they would close contact. Remarking on this in Carcass's journal, Lutwidge simply wrote: 'Racehorse brought too [sic] a Snow standing to the S°ward.' Having hove to near the stranger, Phipps called for a lieutenant to accompany him and 'hoisted out a boat & sent her on board the which proved to be a Snow[15] from Green-land bound to Hamburg'. Undoubtedly Phipps was eager for information about weather, and of course a courteous exchange with other mariners in these isolated seas always proved useful. Eager to get under way, Phipps then wrote: 'At ¾ past 7 hoisted in the Boat, Wore ship and made Sail.'

Tuesday 22 June saw light winds and cloudy weather, the two ships encountering drizzling rain. Both ships were sailing on a course directly north. The Carcass, again straggling behind, forced Phipps to shorten sail, first reefing the mizzen topgallant sail and later putting in the first reefs in the main and fore topgallants. A lone ship was seen standing to the south-west. It was at this point that they 'reeved a new Tiller Rope'. This rope, which ran from the drum of the ship's wheel to the foremost end of the tiller via pulley blocks, had obviously worn through constant movement as the ship steered in the heavy seas. Although Racehorse had barely been at sea for a month, this would have been a common problem in all vessels of this period and the task of replacement was simply routine maintenance, the tiller being steered by hand as the new rope was rove.

That same day in the *Carcass* 'all hands' were called by the shrill whistles of the 'bosun's pipes' to 'clear lower deck' and muster up on deck for Lutwidge to 'read out the Articles' to the ship's company. Reading out of the Articles of War was a mandatory weekly requirement of the Admiralty, the rules of which differentiated Royal Navy warships from any other British mercantile ships, including fishing vessels. These Articles, introduced under King Charles II when Britain's fighting navy became formally established as the Royal Navy, were intended 'for the regulating and better Government of His Majesties Navies, Ships of War, and Forces by Sea; wherein under the good Providence and Protection of God, the wealth Safety, and strength of this kingdom is so much concerned Be it enacted by the Kings most Excellent Majesty with the advice and consent of the Lords and Commons in the present Parliament assembled by the Authority thereof...'. Amended by the Admiralty under Lord Anson in 1749 and again under the parliament of George II in 1757, the Articles contained 36 specific regulations and laws together with corresponding penalties (including death). Besides upholding the Christian religion of the country, many of the points covered failure of duty, espionage, disobeying orders, drunkenness, desertion, cowardice or failure to pursue the enemy. Also included were theft and false musters. All matters concerning treason, murder and sodomy automatically carried the death penalty.[16]

As Lutwidge carried out this formality the entire ship's company (the young Nelson included), grouped in their divisions with their appointed divisional officers, would have stood silently swaying with the motion of the ship as the rain fell upon them.

Rain continued the next day, the weather turning foggy, and 'at ¼ past 2 shortened sail for the *Carcass*'. Phipps next recorded: 'at 6 heard the report of 3 Guns in the SW Q^{ur} [quarter].' The fact that *Carcass*'s journal also records this occurrence and states 'the *Racehorse* in company' means that the source of gunfire does appear mysterious. Given the heavy fog, it was possibly a whaling ship signalling a recall for her whale boats to return.

On Friday 25 June Lutwidge records the weather as light breezes and thick fog, turning to 'Fresh Gales with Snow and Sleet'. In the *Racehorse* the carpenter, Josiah West, and boatswain, Jonathan Stamford, jointly prepared to undertake rigging alterations, the former with chisels, augers, rule and mallet ready while his carpenter's crew set up trestles across the deck, then: 'At 3 PM unbent the Miz. T. Sail and got the Yard down to cut Sheave holes for the Reef Tackle Pendants; at 6 got up D°. [ditto] bent the sail & set it.' Sheave holes are horizontal or vertical slots to receive a pulley 'shiver' or sheave. Reef tackle pendants generally hang from the yard arm, so why this was done is unclear. While they could have been simply making good an oversight of dockyard workmanship, it may be that Phipps and *Racehorse*'s master needed to implement a more efficient system to meet the climatic conditions in which they were operating. Whatever the case, this modification, comprising a suitable vertical sheave hole cut near the end of the yard, certainly pre-dates a later practice that was widely adopted.

Saturday 26 June saw the *Racehorse* sailing N 58°E and the *Carcass* steering N 75°E. Lutwidge recorded: 'First part Fresh Gales and Cloudy with snow and sleet', though the weather did improve later. Phipps's log entry then states: 'At ½ past 7 PM the *Carcass* made the Signal for the Time Keeper.' Chronometers in both ships were checked, Lutwidge recording his at 4pm as 1 hour, 5 minutes and 45 seconds slow and at 5.30pm as being 1 hour, 5 minutes and 51 seconds slow. Some hours later 'all hands' in the *Racehorse* were called to bracing stations, the log stating: 'At 1 AM Tack'd ship.' Called up again 5 hours later, the topmen went aloft and 'took out all reefs'. This appears to apply only to topsails and courses, for shortly afterwards the men on deck manned the tye halyards and hoisted up the topgallant yards and, hauling on the outhauler, ran out the sprit topsail yard. This done, they threw off the clewlines and buntlines from the pinrails; the topmen shaking out the canvas while others hauled in the sheets taut. All sails were now set.

The weather on Sunday saw light winds with snow, both ships sailing with studding sails set. On *Racehorse*, Phipps recorded: 'At 5 PM the *Carcass* made the Signal of the Longitude observed by the Sun & Moon 10°26´´', while Lutwidge recorded the 'Variation by the mean men of 3 Azimuths N15° 20´W'.

By Monday 28 June both vessels were sailing in moderate breezes with snow, *Racehorse* sailing N 10°W under topsails and topgallants, setting her fore and main topmast studding sails as the wind became lighter. As the snow turned to rain, the decks became treacherously slippery with slush.

Tuesday 29 June saw Phipps's expeditionary ships closing towards Spitsbergen. *Racehorse*'s log records: 'at ½ past 5 bro't to hoisted out the Boat; at 6 hoisted her in again; at 7 sounded 290 ^fm. (1,740ft or 530m) no ground'. Sounding with a deep-sea lead and line to this recorded extreme depth was no mean task. Given that the lead itself weighed 28lb (14kg), and the line (dry) 43lb (19kg) per 100ft (30.5m), the overall weight when retrieving the lead and line on this occasion was some 776lb (350kg). Adding perhaps 10 per cent for the line being wet, the overall weight when vertically hoisted would be about 886lb (400kg); the leadsman definitely would have required two men to assist retrieval.

Racehorse then appears to have twice 'brought to' to wait for the *Carcass*. Phipps's journal continues: 'at 11 saw the Land bearing from ENE to NE½E; at 1 AM South Point E½N. 14 Leagues; at ½ past 2 Tack'd Ship; at 8 the extremes of the Land from ENE to NNE 12 Leagues. Read the Articles of War & Abstract of the Act of Parliament to the Ship's Company.' In *Carcass*, Lutwidge states: 'At 5PM in steering sails, at ½ past 10 PM saw the land of Spitsbergen from ESE to NE 18 to 20 Leagues dist.' This estimated visual distance, which relates to 57 nautical miles (66 miles/105km), does seem quite considerable. However, taking into account the highest point on the archipelago, ie Mount Newtontoppen (5,620ft/1,713m), and the relative sighting height at the mast head together with the general atmospheric clarity at this latitude, the calculation Lutwidge recorded in the journal is certainly reasonably accurate. Taking three azimuths, Lutwidge determined his ship's position as 10°51′W.

In *Carcass* on Wednesday 30 June, Lutwidge recorded that he hove to at 2pm and: 'at ½ past 4 sounded 112 fathoms [672ft/204m] soft blue mud, at 5 made sail to the NE, at Midnight Lat^de. by Obs^n 78.00′N; at 5 AM Tk^t to the Westward, at 7 saw two sail in the NW.' Regarding celestial observations Lutwidge recorded that the altitude of the sun at midnight was 11°4′, the moon 34°54′ and, taking three azimuths with an average mean of 5 at the time of 2pm, 5pm and 10pm, his calculated position is given as N 15°52′W; N 19°25′W, and N 15°16′W respectively.[17]

In *Racehorse*, Phipps recorded his course as N 37°E, weather hazy then foggy, the ship progressing cautiously. He then wrote: 'At 2 PM bro't too with the Main Topsail to the Mast, hoisted a Boat out & Sounded 110 [fathoms] no ground; at ½ past 4 hoisted the Boat in & made Sail; at 8 Tack'd ship; at Midnight carried away the Tiller Rope & reeved a new one at 8 am Black Point 4 or 5 Leagues. Saw A Ship in the NW Q[ur.] standing to the NE At ½ past 9 Tack'd Ship – The *Carcass* in Company.'

On Thursday 1 July the weather was clear and Phipps records seeing two sail in sight – undoubtedly whaling vessels – and that soundings taken of 110 fathoms (660ft/201m) revealed 'muddy ground'. Besides various bearings and distances, the journal also records: 'At 10 spoke the Rockingham Reed, Master of *London*'; the vessel recorded as a 'greenlander'. Concluding for the day, Phipps entered: 'from 6 to 9 AM Calm ... set Stud[g] Sails. The *Carcass* in Company.'

They had now reached the Spitsbergen archipelago. Down in his cabin that same day, Lutwidge recorded: 'Light airs and Clear Wea[r] [weather] with calms at 7 PM T[kd] to the W[t]ward Black point ENE 5 or 6 leag[s] [leagues], at Midnight Latitude by Observation 78°:6′N, at 3 AM saw a sail to the Westward, at 8 Snowhill NE½E 5 or 6 leagues, Black point 6 or 5 leag[s] *Racehorse* in Company. At Noon Altitude [of the sun] LL 34° :44′.'

Next day (Friday), Lutwidge wrote: 'Capt[n] Phipps sent on board to me to take some Angles between the *Racehorse* and the different headlands, at 7 PM sounded 123 fathoms (738ft/225m) soft black mud, Black point SE abo[t] [about] 8 leag[s] at 3 AM saw 3 Sail to the SW, at 8 AM *Mount Parnassus* EN½N 5 or 6 leag[s], *Racehorse* in Company.' The position of Mount Parnassus noted indicates that the ships were to the west of the island of Prins Karls Forland, which was itself divided from the mainland by the Forlandsundet (Forland Sound).

The next few days were spent similarly taking bearings of the land and fixes of the sun and using azimuths to calculate latitude and longitude data, which was used to amend existing charts or create new charts.

On Monday 5 July the *Carcass*'s log records her course at noon as 36°W and reads: 'First part Calm and Cloudy, middle and latter thick foggy Wea^r, 15 sail in sight sounded 15 fathoms (90ft/27m) at 4 PM rocky ground, Magdalena Head NNE ½E 4 lea$^{es.}$ at ½ past 11 came on a thick fog, lost sight of *Racehorse*, which had anchor'd close in shore in the Afternoon; ¾ past 12 heard her Guns which we answered, and at 2 Am got sight of her, set Steering sails, ½ past 3 Am Magdalena bay NE 4 or 5 miles, at Noon a thick fog.' The 'fifteen sail' seen were probably a whaling fleet; there would have been little other reason for vessels to venture this far north.

Reunited, the ships continued sailing northwards. From the closing remarks in Lutwidge's log of Monday 5 July it appears that both the *Racehorse* and *Carcass* must have anchored and lowered their boats and, with Nelson at the helm of the cutter, Lutwidge was rowed over to go aboard his consort. Completing his journal that day, Lutwidge wrote: 'at 7 PM went on shore from the *Racehorse* with Capt Phipps, who had anchored in a small bay about 2 miles from the Land, it was barren, rocky mountainous, and almost covered with snow. A Stream of Water ran down the mountains from the snow, at which the *Racehorse* filled some water Casks. There was a quantity of drift wood on the Beach and near it above the high water marck [sic]'. Devoid of vegetation the land appeared to be no more than a hostile wasteland.

Following their arrival at the Spitsbergen archipelago (see Plate 17), what did this frozen land offer to Phipps's expedition? In July, the average temperature was marginally above freezing point ranging from 3–7°C (37.4–44.6°F). Should misfortune force them to overwinter, and they were sufficiently equipped to do so, temperatures in January dramatically fall to between −13°C and −20°C (8.6°F to −4.0°F). Despite Spitsbergen's northerly latitude, one advantage in Phipps's favour was that temperatures were moderated by the North Atlantic Current (NAC), particularly during winter, and temperatures were higher compared to those at similar latitudes in continental Canada and Russia. The temperatures of the interior fjords and valleys, sheltered by the mountains, were slightly lower than those found on the coast. The NAC generally kept the surrounding waters open and navigable for most of the year[18] but the temperatures that Phipps's expedition experienced would have been some 4°C (7°F) lower than they are today.

While the journals of both Phipps and Lutwidge provide good accounts of the weather conditions, neither man would have been fully aware of what exactly generated the conditions they were experiencing. Today, we know that the archipelago is the meeting place for cold polar air from the north and mild, wet sea air from the south – the combination of both creating low pressure and changeable weather with fast winds. This was particularly predominant in midwinter: at Isfjord strong breezes prevail some 17 per cent of the time whereas in summer this figure falls to only 1 per cent of the time.[19]

What is evident from the entries made in both ship's journals is that fog was particularly prevalent away from land. Visibility in sea fog would have been under 1,000 yards (1km) – a fact that meant the two ships often lost sight of each other. With regard to rainfall, Phipps's expedition would have experienced frequent but small quantities of precipitation in western Spitsbergen, whereas on the east side of the archipelago there was more rainfall with snow due to the mountains. Sea ice was to become extremely problematic the further they probed north-east. Ironically, the ship's journals reveal that while water was instantly freezing on one side of the ship, the tar on the opposite side of the ship's hull was melting due to the constant heat of the sun.[20] Oddly, both journals appear to omit any reference to men being frequently engaged chipping the upper decks clear of ice, as might have been expected.

In his book, *A Voyage Towards the North Pole: Undertaken by His Majesty's Command, 1773,* Phipps wrote of the Spitsbergen archipelago:

'The stone we found was chiefly of a kind of marble, which dissolved easily in the marine acid. We perceived no marks of rain and minerals of any kind, nor the least appearance of present, or remains of former Volcanoes. Neither did we meet with insects, or any species of reptiles; for not even the common earthworm. We saw no springs or rivers, the water which we found a great plenty, being all produced by the melting of snow from the mountains. During the whole time we were in these latitudes there was no thunder or lightning. I must also add, that I never found what is mentioned by Marten (who is genuinely accurate in his observations and faithful in his accounts) of the sun at midnight resembling the appearance of the Moon; I saw no difference in clear weather between the sun at midnight and any other time, but arose from a different degree of altitude; the brightness of a light appearing there, as well as elsewhere depend upon the obliquesity of his rays. The sky was in general loaded with hard white clouds; so that I do not remember to have ever seen the sun and the horizon both free from them even in the clearest weather.'

He also described the ice: 'We could always perceive when we were approaching the ice, long before we saw it, by the bright appearance near the horizon, which the pilots call the "blink of the ice". Hudson remarked, that the sea where he met the ice was blue; but the green sea was free from it. I was particularly attentive to observe this difference, but could never discern it.'[21]

The journals of both the *Racehorse* and *Carcass* make few references to the animals the expedition encountered, most mentions of them focusing on what they killed rather than scientific observation. In the appendix of his book titled *Natural History*, Phipps excuses the lack of natural observations, saying that other pressing duties 'rendered it impossible for me to make many observations on its natural productions'. Under the subtitle '*Mammalia*', he refers to just six species: the 'Artick Walrus, the Common Seal, the "Arctick Fox", the polar bear, "Rein Deer", the Common Whale and the "Fin Fish".' Listing the walrus as *Trichechus rosinarus,* Phipps observes that 'this animal, which is called by the Russians Morse from hence our seamen corruptly [name] Sea Horse and in the Gulph [sic] of St. Lawrence Sea Cow, is found every where about the coast of Spitsbergen, and generally where-ever there is ice, though at a distance from the land. It is a gregarious animal, not inclined to attack, but dangerous if attacked, as the whole herd join their forces to revenge any injury received by an individual.' He was doubtless recalling the incident when angered walruses attacked some of the ship's boats, their seamen narrowly escaping death when Nelson brought his cutter to the rescue. He lists the common seal as *Phoca vitulina,* but makes no comments about it. Of the Arctic fox, which he names *Canis lagopus,* Phipps wrote: 'Found on the main land of Spitsbergen and islands adjacent, though not in abundance. It differs from our Fox, besides its colour, in having its ears much

An 18th-century illustration of a walrus. Rijksmuseum.

more rounded. It smells very little. We ate of the flesh of one, and found it good meat.'

Phipps is considered to be the first European to record detailed observations about the polar bear, *Ursus maritimus*, and wrote the following in his journal:

'Found in great numbers on the mainland of Spitsbergen; as also on the islands and ice fields adjacent. We killed several with our musquets and the seamen ate of their flesh though exceedingly coarse. This animal is much larger than the black bear; the dimensions of one were as follows:

Length from the snout to the tail – 7 feet 1 inch: Length from the snout to the shoulder bone – 2 feet: Height at the shoulder - 4 feet 3 inches: Circumference near the fore legs – 7 feet: Circumference of the neck close to the ear – 2 feet 1 inch: Breadth of the fore paw – 7 inches: Weight of the carcass without head, skin or entrails – 610 pounds.'

An 18th-century illustration of a polar bear. Hulton Archive/Getty Images.

Of the reindeer, recorded as *Cervus tarandus*, Phipps wrote that it was 'Found everywhere on Spitsbergen we ate the flesh of one we killed and found it excellent venison'. In his notes about the common whale and fin fish, listed as *Balaena mysticetus* and *Balaena physalus* respectively, it is not clear whether he is referring to the native bowhead whale or other species; the fin fish possibly relates to the fin-whale that was found in these waters.

Today, 30 varieties of birds inhabit the Spitsbergen archipelago, the most numerous being the little auk (*Alle alle*). In his subsection entitled '*Aves*', however, Phipps only appears to record 13 species, which include the greater tern (*Sterna hirundo*) and the snow bunting (*Emberiza navalis*, now called *Plectrophenax navalis*), which Phipps simply names as a 'greater Brambling'.

Phipps's appendix also makes reference to '*Amphibia*', '*Pisces*' and '*Insecta*'. In the former he records the sea snail (*Cyclopterus liparis*), in the latter the prawn (*Cancer squilla*) and the crab (*Cancer boreas*). Of the fish, he only notes the coal fish (*Gadus carbonarius*), remarking that

'Though we trawled several times on the North side of Spitsbergen, and the seamen frequently tried their hooks and lines, yet nothing was taken except a few individuals'.

Like most Arctic countries, the entire land mass of Spitsbergen is covered by permafrost with only the top 3.3ft (1m) of earth thawing during summer. As a result there is little vegetation, most of which consists of algae, mosses and lichens. Despite the harsh conditions, the archipelago surprisingly hosts 164 vascular plant species, which are slow-growing and seldom exceed a height of 4in (10cm). The most fertile areas are found within the inner fjords and in some other areas, especially in warmer valleys, where the plants produce carpets of blossoms. Phipps, however, makes little reference to plant life in his book. Although he may have gained some botanic knowledge through his earlier forays with his friend Joseph Banks, he may have thought it superfluous or simply had little time to investigate. Typical plants seen would have included the bright pink woolly louse wort (*Pedicularis dasyantha*), the Arctic harebell (*Campanula uniflora*) and the yellow arctic whitlow grass (*Draba bellii*). Also common are the Arctic bell-heather (*Cassiope tetragona*) and, perhaps most significant, the pale yellow Svalbard poppy (*Papaver dahlianum*). The archipelago also hosted scurvy-grass (*Cochlearia officinalis*), mountain sorrel (*Oxyria digna*) and the bog bilberry (*Vaccinium uliginosum*) – rich in vitamin C, the latter formed the main diet of the reindeer.

The main objective of Phipps's expedition was to seek the North Pole and, if possible, a north-east passage. He therefore had little opportunity to search for new mineral sources or make serious geological observations. As a result, neither Phipps nor Lutwidge makes much reference to the islands' minerals except for passing comments on the physical terrain and topography and its appearance, something that Phipps excuses in his later book.[22] Naturally, further scientific and navigational observations would be made as occasion provided but time dictated that Phipps and Lutwidge continue probing towards the North Pole. Phipps was evidently a competent naturalist having learned much from Joseph Banks during his earlier exploits.

10

Probing north amid the ice floes to Vogel Sang

Having reached their initial destination of Hakluyt's Headland and the whaling station of Smeerenburg, *Racehorse* and *Carcass* prepared for the next stage of their voyage – to sail further northwards into unknown waters towards the North Pole. As it was already late in the season, they needed to press on with the expedition as soon as possible to maximise the time available to them.

Thursday 1 July
Racehorse's log reveals the weather as being moderate and cloudy, and later clear. At 1pm they sounded 110 fathoms (660ft/201m) into muddy ground with the ship laying some 4 leagues west of Black Point ad at 10 spoke Reed, Master of the Rockingham, doubtless an English whaling ship. With little wind, *Racehorse* set her steering sails, the *Carcass* sailing in company.[1] The log recorded latitude as 78°6′N and the altitude of the sun at noon as 34°44′.[2]

Friday 2 July
Phipps noted that 'PM the Carpenters employed paying the Sides & Bends Varnish of Pine'. This substance, often referred to as rosin, provided a good waterproof preservative for the ship's planking. The 'Bends' refers to the planking running along the wales, which curved outwards along the ship's waterline. The log continues: 'at ½ past 1 hoisted a Boat out; at 4 shortened Sail & bro't too with the Main TS[1] [topsail] to the Mast … at ¾ past 10 made Sail and bore down to the *Carcass*. – Fired a Gun & made a Signal for our Boat; at ½ past 11 hoisted in the Boat & hauled our Wind – Tack'd Ship; at Noon set Studd[g] Sails and hoisted out a Boat.'[3]

In *Carcass*'s log Lutwidge wrote: 'Cap[tm.] Phipps sent on board [hence the boat] to me to take some Angles between the *Racehorse* and different islands at 7 PM sounded 123 fathoms [738ft/225m] soft black mud.' Latitude is recorded as 78°25´N; the altitude of the sun at noon 34°30, the chronometer given as 1 hour, 10 minutes and 23 seconds slow.[4]

Saturday 3 July

The day was calm with light airs. Phipps recorded that: 'at 2 PM sounded 55[fms.] [100m] at 3 bro't to; at ½ past 3 made Sail at 5 bro't too, hoisted out a Boat & Sounded 55[fm.] large Stones- Ships draft [draught] of Water 13ft. 8ins forward & 2ft. 8ins. aft; at ½ past 7:30 bore away; at 3 AM hoisted in the Boat.'[5]

With the boat already out to take soundings, they used this opportunity to read off the ship's draught marks as a precautionary measure. This was because any change in water density in this latitude could alter the level at which the ship rode.

Lutwidge's journal for that day also records taking angles (bearings) between the *Racehorse* and the land. Soundings recorded as 55 fathoms (330ft/100m) reveal the seabed was now soft brown mud. He also records that the altitude of the sun at midnight was 11°16´ and the variation by the mean of three azimuths was calculated as 18°36´W.[6]

Sunday 4 July

In his journal, Phipps recorded that the north end of the foreland bore 4 miles (6.4km) south-east: 'Sounded 23 to 20[fm.] Rocks and Sea Egg Shells [probably urchins]. At 11 spoke a Greenland Ship belonging to London – shortened sail for the *Carcass*, at Midnight down Studd[g] Sails, bro't too the Main T.S[l.] [topsail to the Mast] & sounded 119[fm.] muddy ground-Ten Sail in sight. At ¼ past 1AM bore away and made Sail. At 4 Magdalena Point NNE½E 5 or 6 Leagues; Cape Cod S½W 9 Leagues; at 9 hoisted out a Boat & sent to on board the *Carcass*. At noon 14 Sail in sight.'[7] The log does not disclose that Phipps and his astronomer, Israel Lyons, went on shore with instruments to make celestial observations.

View of the land where the *Racehorse* anchored at 6pm on 4 July 1773, showing the glacier meeting the edge of the sea, soon to form icebergs. Illustration taken from Phipp's book of the voyage, NMRN.

In the *Carcass*, Lutwidge recorded little other than general observations, bearings and soundings, with the altitude of the sun at noon
given as 33°6′. With regard to sightings of other vessels, he states: 'at
Midnight 11 sail in sight.'[8]

Monday 5 July
Racehorse's journal notes: 'First part Calm, latter light breezes &
foggy-at 5 PM hoisted out the Cutter; at ½ past 5 sent her on Shore
for Water & came to with the Stream Anchor in 15^{fm} Water 3 or 4
miles from Shore'; some 3 miles (5km) off Magdalena Point.

As for the *Carcass*, according to Phipps's log she bore 'SWbW
4 Miles standing to the Eastward'. Weighing anchor at midnight
they came to sail and: 'fired a Gun as a Signal for the *Carcass*, at ½
past 12 repeated D°. [ditto] at 2 AM fired a Gun & bro't to with
Main TS^l to the Mast'. Sailing again half an hour later they saw rocks
bearing north by north 2 or 3 miles and avoiding danger they hauled
off then shortened sail to allow the *Carcass* to catch up.[9, 10]

In *Racehorse*, Phipps 'Shortened sail for the *Carcass*: at 4 fired a
Volley of small arms as a Signal for the *Carcass*'. Lutwidge 'answered
the *Racehorse*'s small arms [fire] having lost sight of her in the fog'.
That same day the *Carcass* hauled her wind to the westward and
tacked to the south-east where 'at 3 PM lost sight of the Ice in the
NE'. Lutwidge recorded: '15 sail in sight … at ½ past 11 came on
a thick fog, lost sight of the *Racehorse* which had anchored close
in shore in the Afternoon; ¾ past 12 heard her Guns which we
answered, and at 2 am got sight of her, set steering sails.' Setting these
additional sails increased speed.[11]

Tuesday 6 July
From this point onwards the two ships began to encounter ice.
According to the *Racehorse*'s journal the day commenced with light
breezes and fog with clear weather later. Phipps noted: 'At ½ past
1 PM hauled down the Studd^g Sails & steered NNE. – Saw several
pieces of Ice; at 2 Tack'd Ship and stood from the Main body of it
then bearing EbN to WSW distance ¼ quarter of a Mile. Shortened
sail for the *Carcass*; at 4 fired a Volley of Small Arms as a Signal for
the *Carcass*. Using muskets used less gunpowder.' The log entry next
reads: '5 to 8 sounded from 50 to 90 fm. no ground. At 8 bore down

on the *Carcass*; at 10 the fog cleared away and at ½ past 10 saw the ice bearing from NW to E^t. [East] but the fog coming on again, hauled our Wind. At 2 heard the surf break on the Ice & Tack'd Ship; at 4 saw the *Carcass* at 5 AM the Ice bearing from ESE to NW. Distant 4 or 5 miles at 6 the Fog cleared up and at 6:30 saw the land bearing from South to SSE, 7 or 8 Leagues.'[12]

For the time being the ice presented no real threat, but this would change. Just after noon, Phipps hailed Lutwidge to steer NNE, the *Carcass* passing small pieces of ice. Lutwidge then wrote: 'at 1 PM heard the Surf beating a little on the starboard bow, at 2 pm saw a large body of Ice close to us (about ½ of a mile distant) extending from ENE to NW it appeared quite compact and heavy, and very uneven, like rough craggy land; with a great surf beating against it, hauled our wind to the Wst.ward & Tak^d to the SE, at 3 lost sight of the Ice in the NE, answered the *Racehorse*'s small arms having lost sight of her in the fog, at 4 saw the *Racehorse* again.' At 6.30 the *Carcass* tacked to the NW and with visibility clearing some three hours later they 'saw the ice bearing from NW to East, [and] bore away after the *Racehorse* to view it [the ice] found it quite compact and heavy as in the Afternoon'.

At 11.30 Lutwidge hauled up to the south-east and within an hour thick fog had descended, which caused the ships to lose sight of the ice, although the uncanny noise of the surf prevailed. The altitude of the sun at noon is recorded as 32°33′.[13] Entirely inexperienced in Arctic conditions, the stresses imposed upon both commanders must have been daunting, and the crewmen, especially those used to more tropical climes, must have felt very uncomfortable and even alarmed.

Wednesday 7 July
The weather is recorded as moderate and cloudy with little wind, turning to rain. The ships were sailing in 80 fathoms (480ft/146m) of water with four other vessels in sight. At the start of the day, Phipps wrote: 'At 1 PM saw the Ice from NE to NW, at 2 the Ice ¼ mile [400m] distant.' By midnight, Hakluyt's Headland bore SWbS some 4 leagues (12 miles/19km). Tacking at 12.30, the *Racehorse* 'stood from the ice, the main body of it ½ a Cable [304ft or 93m] distant. At 5 AM steering along the edge of the Ice.' She then bore away south easterly and 'steered in amongst the loose Ice to the ^Est.ward as near the main body as we could find openings'.[14]

In the *Carcass*, 3 miles (5km) to the north-west, Lutwidge wrote: 'at 2 PM Tak^d to the S^{o}ward, the Ice bearing from WNW to NEbN, at 8 Cloven Cliff EbS 4 or 5 leagues'. (Cloven Cliff, today called Klovingen, is a cleft-shaped island lying north-west of Hakluyt's Headland at lat 79°51′N long 11°29′E.) Continuing his journal, Lutwidge wrote: 'as we stood in shore cou'd see the Ice stretching along to the Eastward ½ past 8 Ta$^{kd.}$ to the NE $^{wd.}$ ½ past 12 Ta^{kd} to the SW, having stood amongst the drift Ice.'

Sailing eastwards, it was recorded 'at 8 Vogel land [Vogelsund] SWbW 4 or 5 lea$^{s.}$'. Making headway in light winds against large drift ice was tough going, so Lutwidge 'got the Cutter and longboat out to tow the Ship up to the *Racehorse* thro' the loose ice'. As ship's coxswains, both Nelson and able seaman Nicholas Biddle would have been fully involved with the boats towing the *Carcass* east-wards through the ice towards her consort. Lutwidge then recorded: 'at Noon got the Tackles on the Rudder, ready for unshipping it: took up several pieces of drift Ice alongside, which we found

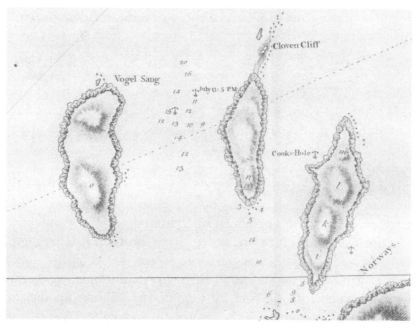

Chart showing the islands of Vogel Sang and Cloven Cliff. From Phipp's book of the voyage, NMRN. The figures give water depth in fathoms; the anchors show the anchorage sites.

View of an 'iceberg' and pack ice, similar to that with which the expedition was having to contend at this time. The 'iceberg' is actually the seaward end of a glacier. From Phipp's book of the voyage, NMRN.

quite fresh'.[15] Unshipping the rudder was a precautionary action undertaken to avoid damage if chunks of ice forced it upwards, unhooking its pintles out of their gudgeons.

Thursday 8 July

At this point in the expedition, the ships began to experience grave difficulties with the ice and, by the end of the day, the mettle of the crewmen in both ships had been sorely tested.

In the *Racehorse*, Phipps recorded: 'hazy Weather. Ranging along the main body of the ice as the loose pieces would permit. luffing up & bearing away as we found the openings.' Luffing was a means of taking weigh off the ship by temporarily hauling up the sails, the effect of stopping giving a chance to manoeuvre. After taking precautionary soundings, at 1am Phipps: 'sent the boat to 2 large pieces of Ice where we filled 3½ hogsheads [about 190 gallons/864 litres] and 5 Barracoes [sic] of Fresh Water.' Still sounding, they then found the water shoaling very quickly from 20 to 14 fathoms (120–84ft/37–26m) and took bearings as their position was becoming critical: 'The outer part of Gekloof -de Clip W½N 7 leagues, Vytkyk WbS 4 leagues & Red cliff S½E 5 leagues.' Finding the ice more open to the ENE, Phipps hauled up and brought his vessel into a depth of 28 fathoms (168ft/61m); the *Carcass*, he observed, was about half a mile astern. 'At ½ past 4 the Ice setting very close & little Wind was stopt between the two fields before we get clear of them.' He then noted: 'The *Carcass* was very near running on board us.'

According to Midshipman Floyd, this was not so much due to *Carcass* making progress but because the *Racehorse* had: 'struck pretty large pieces [of ice]: Some of these remained so long at the ship's bows as to deaden her way. One in particular stopped us that the *Carcass*, who was not far astern, was on the brink of running aboard us.' Collision was averted: 'our people were so brisk in getting on board the fore tack (the foresail having been hauled up) and hoisting the staysails, together with the management of ice poles, that we just disengaged ourselves as the bowsprit [of the *Carcass*] was over our taffrail: the piece of ice that had impeded our progress getting foul of her stem, she, in turn was stopped until she could clear it.'[16]

Phipps next wrote: 'At 5 Tack'd in a small opening & laid the Main T.S[l.] to the Mast to look for an opening to proceed, but found the Ice closed.' The severity of the arising conditions prompted Phipps to seek expert advice so he 'Sent a Boat on board the *Carcass* for her two Ice Pilots'. This, according to Lutwidge's log, was at about 3pm and, after discussing the situation with the pilots, Phipps 'sent them on board the *Carcass* again – every light air of wind springing up from the NbE filled the Main T.S (the Ship's head to Westward) and endeavoured to get out of the Ice. At 6 was closed with loose Ice.'[17]

Rallying his officers and his boatswain, Phipps gave instructions that had been recommended by the ice pilots: ropes and necessary equipment were brought up on deck, and they then 'got out the ice hooks from the Quarters, on both sides and set the Ice Poles at the same time to clear the ice from the Ship'. Our Boat hoisted up alongside the *Carcass* to prevent her being stove by the Ice setting on the Ship'.[18]

Both ice hooks were laid out on the ice from the stern, their ropes carried inboard and turned up upon the capstan where, with the seamen turning at the bars, they warped the ship along as required while others, handing the ice poles, broke ice away from the ship's hull along the waterline; slowly the *Racehorse* moved free. From the fact that the ice hooks were initially passed over the quarters, it could be assumed they were carried towards the bow and secured. By hauling in over the quarters the ship could be steadied at the stern while being shunted forwards.

The log next records: 'at ½ past 7 cleared ourselves of the Ice, got into an opening and steered WNW into clear Water, between the Ice and the Shore.' As there was so little wind to drive the ship, they next 'hoisted out the 6 & 10 Oar'd Cutters, and with them & the 4 Oar'd Cutter [now returned from *Carcass*] towed the Ship. At midnight the Boats towing the Ship through the loose Ice'. No doubt the boat's crews were periodically relieved for respite. Bearings taken at 7am 'record: 'the Yaudhook SWbS 5 or 6 Leagues at 8 set T.G^t Sails: At ½ past 8 sent the Boats ahead to tow, being near the main body of the Ice with little-Wind & a great Swell setting right upon it. – At ½ past 9 a great point of Ice about the length of 2 cables [1,200ft/366m] from us.' The wind picked up and 'at ½ past 10 br't too hoisted in the Boats & made Sail'. The log then records: 'Soundings from 1 to 3 PM – 25, 24, 20 & 19 $^{fm.}$ Rosil [?] with Stones & live Worms; and from 3 to ½ past 4 PM. 16, 15 ½, 14. & 28 $^{fms.}$ Black Oase [ouze] with Stones.'[19]

In the *Carcass*, the events of Thursday reveal similar difficulties. Lutwidge wrote: 'PM the Boats ahead towing the Ship up to the *Racehorse* (to the E$^{st.}$ward) thro' the Ice, at ½ past 3 hoisted in the Boats.' No doubt Nelson, Biddle and the relevant oarsmen were relieved to be back aboard ship in relative warmth. The log then states: 'at 5 got up close to the *Racehorse*, the Ice being then compact to the Eastward there was no possibility of getting thro' it. Cap$^{tn.}$ Phipps sent on board for my Pilots, sounded 25 fath$^{ms.}$ soft light mud, the Vogel land bearing WNW a^{bt} 7 lea$^{gs.}$ ½ past 5 PM found the Ice enclosing the Ship very fast, and endeavoured to make sail to get out, the Pilots return'd from the *Racehorse*; [after their advisory discussions with Phipps] and a few minutes after, both ships were set fast.' Following the same guidance the 'Greenland pilots' had given to Phipps, Lutwidge called for his officers and his midshipmen, Nelson included, and with 'all hands' mustered on deck gave his orders to try to alleviate their precarious situation. His journal notes that they: 'Got out Ice Anchors, and Ice Poles to hawl the Ship out to the NW and at 7 we were clear of the close pack'd Ice, at 8 the *Racehorse* got out, and both Ships made sail to the NW.' Having taken detailed bearings of the land, he then wrote: 'at ½ past 8 had the Ice under our lee; and very near us, with a swell setting upon it; tow'd the ship off with the boats.'[20]

Although Lutwidge is generally quite precise in his journal, he oddly fails to make mention of the near collision with the *Racehorse*, and he omits to say when the boats were hoisted out again. He also fails to indicate how the ice anchors were laid out. Were they run out from each quarter as Phipps had done, or off either side of the ship's head?

Although not evident from the *Carcass*'s journals, coxswains Nelson and Biddle would have been fully involved with the towing operations and would have faced the hazard of ice stoving in the frail planking of their boat's hulls.

With the exception of the four experienced Greenland pilots, the sights observed by the ship's captains, by Nelson and fellow crewmen, must have been completely overwhelming. Despite the vigilance and seamanship of both crews, they were completely unaccustomed to the polar conditions they faced, yet they rose to the situation with fortitude. Once they had completed their arduous duties, all would have welcomed a hot meal at the end of the day.

With the initial danger over, both ships made sail to the northwest, the drift ice cracking loudly under their bluff bows; the additional internal modifications made to strengthen them in the dockyards proved worthwhile. The constant noise of ice fracturing under the stern would have reverberated through the ship and made sleeping difficult. It is also likely that the strains exerted upon the hulls of the two ships would have led to a state of continuous apprehension among the crew. This was just the beginning; at this point they could at least still reasonably navigate their ships. In the days to come they would be challenged by dense fog, which, together with light breezes that provided little motive power, made piloting the ships extremely demanding. If their first experience of getting caught in ice appeared difficult, it was not as frightening as the yet more dangerous conditions they would meet later.

Friday 9 July

Except for noting the weather – fresh breezes and cloudy turning to fresh gales with fog – *Carcass*'s log says little. Strangely, Phipps records a variation in wind conditions and mentions rain later. At this time, there was no Beaufort scale relative to wind velocity and the wind category was a matter of individual interpretation. Both ships were still sailing off Hakluyt's Headland, the *Racehorse* with her topgallant sails set, but, with the wind beginning to increase, Phipps tacked ship, took in his topgallant sails and bore up towards the ice to attempt another opening. He next steered southward and 'at ½ past 7 bore away & steered NW', changing course to WbN some two hours later. *Racehorse*'s log then states: 'at 10 in 2nd Reefs of the T. S^{ls} & spoke a Ship from Hull'. According to Floyd, this vessel may have been named *The King of Prussia*, 'who sang the same song as the rest of the Greenlanders!'[21]

Concluding the day's events, Phipps wrote: 'At 5AM Tack'd Ship Vogle [sic] Sound SSW 2 or 3 miles – Two Sail in sight.'[22] Like the one recorded earlier, these ships came from the east coast Yorkshire port of Hull, from which whaling ships had been commonly operating to Spitsbergen and Greenland since the 17th century. Supporting half of Britain's whaling fleet by 1800, Hull employed some 60 vessels and 2,000 people.[23]

Saturday 10 July

Compared to three days earlier, sailing progress appeared easier, although danger remained. The day found the *Racehorse* in light breezes and fog: 'steering NW, N$^{o.}$ & NbE; at 6 Running amongst the loose Ice.' Coming round by half a point, Phipps tacked ship five times between the hours of 7 and 10 and one hour later small arms (muskets) were fired as a signal to the *Carcass*. Phipps then tacked and began taking soundings while *Racehorse*'s leadsman, inconspicuous in the mist shrouding the focsle, shouted 'by the mark' as the ship cautiously progressed on a course between NNW and NW. Phipps next called his gunner, John Fenton, to the deck and 'at ½ past 2 Wore [ship] & bro't: too: Fired a Gun for the *Carcass*; at 3 Wore [ship]. From 3 to ½ Past 3 fired 4 guns & a Volley of small arms: the *Carcass* answered the last Gun; at ¾ past 3 filled, Tack'd & fired a Gun: which the *Carcass* did not answer.'[24]

It seems to have been prearranged between the two ship's commanders that if poor visibility prevailed Phipps had to signal the *Carcass* by gun every time he changed tack. Dense fog, sea conditions and wind direction could deaden sound so much that Lutwidge's ship may have failed to hear some of the gunfire reports. This is mentioned by Midshipman Floyd in his account of the voyage: 'We soon lost sight of the *Carcass*, to whom we were obliged to make signals to let her know the course we steered, besides the general signal of a gun every half hour to know where each of us were. At four and a half hours after, our guns not being answered, we concluded she [the *Carcass*] was so far away as not to be able to hear them.' Later, the separation between the two ships was still significant: 'At nine, the weather clearing, we perceived the *Carcass* W½S distant four or five miles; the zigzag she had made among the ice could be the only reason assigned for our separation, and the strength of the wind from their direction, prevented their hearing our guns.'[25]

The ice they encountered was so extensive that it was 'without an opening big enough in which to put a minikin pin'. Floyd describes how they tried to force the *Racehorse* through as the ice was closing: 'when quickly dropping the foresail and putting the helm weather, we shot through an opening which, had it not been for the velocity of the ship, would not have been near big enough: running against it with a shock so great as to knock many of us off our legs.'[26]

The sudden jarring impact upon the ship was so tremendous that Phipps, later describing the event in his book, wrote: 'the ice fast closing upon me, obliged me to set the foresail, which with the fresh wind and smooth water, gave the ship such way as to force through it with a violent stroke.'[27] By setting the foresail Phipps fully understood that the wind forces acting upon this sail would tend to drive the bow of the ship downwards, providing power as needed in this situation. Using topsails would have had an adverse effect as the wind pressure upon these sails would lift the bow. As the ship constantly battered into the ice her hull absorbed the kinetic forces generated, while the additional structural modifications built into the bow of the ship at the dockyard well proved their design. For the men in the ship, the ceaseless reverberations transmitted into the hull timbers must have been quite unnerving. Following in the *Racehorse*'s wake, the *Carcass* would not have sustained the same shock.

Phipps's journal entry concludes: 'at 4 Tack'd & fired a Gun; at ¼ past 9 saw the *Carcass* bearing SW½S 5 Miles'... at ½ past 9 Tack'd. Fired a Gun every half hour which the *Carcass* answered, At 10 Tack'd; ¾ past 10 Bore away; the *Carcass* in sight.'[28]

Midshipman Floyd recollected of the same events: 'At five on the morning of the 10th, we saw the land Cloven Foot [Cliff] bearing SE, not farther distant than four miles; we dropped the lead and sounded twenty fathoms [120ft/37m], rocky ground. The weather moderating and the swell falling, we stood under an easy sail to the eastward, towards the place we had first been locked in, with hands stationed aloft looking out for an opening.'[29]

In his log Lutwidge recorded: 'thick foggy Wea[r] standing to the NW, At 3 PM amongst the drift Ice the main body of Ice ahead, saw many Whales, at ½ past 7 hawled our Wind, handed the Mainsail, and kept turning to Windward all Night amongst the Ice Tacking frequently and bearing up occasionally for the large pieces [of ice] we could not weather.' In effect, they turned closer to the wind, checking the ship's forward motion to avoid, in this case, collision with ice. Lutwidge had more to contend with: '[at] past 12 lost sight of the *Racehorse*, fired guns every half hour; at 3 PM observed the Ice drifting fast to the SE and much larger and heavier than before, some of the pieces extending 2 or 3 miles, which the Pilots call Flaws [sic floes].' Weather clearing, he bore away from the wind and rejoined *Racehorse*. Lutwidge recorded the altitude of the sun at noon as being 31°52′, and that his chronometer was running 1 hour, 12 minutes and 23 seconds slow.[30]

Sunday 11 July

The *Racehorse* was running under topsails, topgallants and the sprit topsail along the main body of the ice. Phipps notes that they 'Reeved a new Tiller Rope', indicating that the continuous small rudder movements taken mainly to avoid the ice incurred considerable localised wear upon the rope itself, which might lead to it parting, hence its replacement before this could occur. With the wind increasing, he next recorded: 'at 8 down T. G[t] S[ls] & in Spritsail T.S[l] Yard.' This indicates that the ship had a sprit topsail yard set up on the jib boom, rigged with a traveller, incorporating an in-hauler and an out-hauler. In this instance, the two would act in a similar way to square-sail yard halliards. Later, 'at ½ past 1AM in 2nd Reef T.S$^{ls.}$ at 3 Tack'd; Cloven Cliff SE 6 Miles'. Tacking again at 7am, Phipps then bore away, took soundings, took out the second reefs, then all reefs, and shortly afterwards, with the wind becoming lighter, set the topgallants.[31]

Close analysis of both ship's journals reveals Phipps and Lutwidge's differing responses to the events and technical challenges of each day. Lutwidge writes that he was: 'sailing amongst large loose pieces of ice to the Eastward, ½ past 1 hawled our wind to the SE. and stood out of the Ice, the main body of it stretching away to the Eastward, and so close there was no possibility of entering it.' He notes that the sea state suddenly changed: 'at 7 a great swell from the SW'. The ship began lazily rolling, the action straining the masts and standing rigging. *Carcass's* master, James Allan, with speaking trumpet in hand, took immediate charge and called to 'down Topgalla^{nt} yards'. The seamen called to the bitts and pinrails, threw off the rope turns and deftly handed the tye halyards, lowering the yards to reduce all top-hamper (uppermost rigging), the weight of which would add to the heeling momentum and further stresses. Topgallant sheets and clewlines were simultaneously hauled or eased as required. This done, the *Carcass* proceeded under single reefed topsails and the main course. The fore course (fore sail) was not set to allow a full view of ice ahead but, finding that the ship was still riding uneasy with the heavy swell at 2am, they second reefed the topsails. Next morning, Lutwidge rehoisted the yards and set the topgallants. The closing remarks in his log are: 'At Noon sounded 38 f$^{ms.}$ [70 m] loose gravel and shells, a great swell from the SW; *Racehorse* in company.'[32]

Monday 12 July
This was a hazy day with little wind and the sea was calm though with 'a great Swell from the Westward'. This sea state dominated the motion of the ships, which, with light airs, made no way in the uneasy, slow, heaving seaway. Progress towards the North Pole was eluding them; there was so little wind that Phipps had to act decisively: 'At 2 PM hoisted a boat out to turn Ship's head around to the Westward.' Floyd records that the towing was undertaken 'with some difficulty, clear of a reef of rocks which lay three or four leagues off the land'.[33]

The journal continues: 'At 8 Cloven Cliff SWbW, 4 or 5 Miles.' This positions the *Carcass* about 4½ miles (7km) NEbE of the hoof-shaped island. 'At 10 the Boat towing the Ship.' ... From 10 to 12 sounded 30, 15, &16 fm. Gravel & Shells. At 2 Tack'd; the Reef SSE2 Miles; the Boat towing the Ship's head to the Northward; at 4 the Rock S°·[South] 2 or 3 Miles From 4 to 8 the Boat towing the Ship's head to the NW.'[34]

The *Carcass* was also being towed. In his journal, Lutwidge recorded the weather as cloudy and calm, Hakluyt's Headland bore WSW some 9 miles (14.5km) and that there were 'several Ships at Anchor in the Norways' (this name relates to the safe anchorage in Norway Bay). Then, 'at 5 tow'd the ship off with the Longboat to the NW. finding the Western swell, and the Current setting onto the Eastward and in with the Shore. ½ PAST 11pm sounded 11½ fathoms [69ft/21m] hard ground. Cloven Cliff bearing SWbW, and the Boat Rock ab^t a mile.' Completing his daily entry, Lutwidge recorded the altitude of the sun at noon as 31°4′ with his chronometer at 3pm 1 hour, 46 minutes and 39 seconds slow and at 5 pm, 1 hour, 43 minutes and 58 seconds slow.[35]

Tuesday 13 July
Except for land bearings and the swell from the west, Phipps recorded little of consequence other than 'at Midnight saw 7 Ships at Anchor in Norway Bay', and his closing remark that 'at Noon the *Carcass* [was] 4 Miles to the Eastward'.[36] The expedition's slow progress must have been extremely frustrating, while the time needed to get to the Pole was passing all too quickly. Lutwidge's log recorded: 'a Current or Tide setting to the Eastward, and a great Swell from the Westward, a compact body of Ice 4 or 5 miles to the Eastward of the Ship which extended close in to the land in the SE and stretching away to the Northward.' He then wrote: 'At 8 pm came too with the Stream Anchor in 26 fathoms [156ft/47.5m] Hackluyt's Headland WSW, AT 9 a breeze springing up from the NE, up Anchor and made sail to the Westward.' Being under sail was short-lived: 'at 8 Calm, finding the Ship setting with the Current to the Eastward came too with the Stream Anchor in 26 fathoms.' This was done to prevent drifting further east. Weighing again two hours later, the *Carcass* made sail to the west.[37]

In all respects, the two exploratory ships were being prevented from venturing to the North Pole. Ice, sea currents and wind were against them, but despite these disadvantages Phipps and Lutwidge doggedly pursued their mission. Not only had the voyage become a professional and personal challenge for the two ship's commanders, but there were also broader issues at stake should they fail. It was extremely important to prove to the king, the Royal Society, and their lordships at the Admiralty that the Royal Navy could be entrusted to successfully fulfil their first officially appointed polar expedition.

Wednesday 14 July
Reducing sail at 3pm, the *Racehorse*'s topmen took in the first and second reefs of her topsails; the topsail sheets were then reset. Then, manning the sheets, clews, leech and bunt lines, they took in her top-gallant sails. She then tacked and began turning into Vogel Sound where she anchored in 10-fathom (60ft/18m) water at 5pm. The log records: 'at 9 the *Carcass* Anchored 1 Mile to the S°ward of us; at 6 saw 4 sail the NE Qu[r.] at 8 sent the Boat on Shore for Water.'[38]

The *Carcass*, as Midshipman Floyd informs us, would delay anchoring because she had been 'drove much to the eastward by the current, so that she was obliged to make several boards and carry stiff sail to get in'.[39] (The term making a 'board' was to make a tack, and 'stiff sail' was to carry a hard press of canvas.)

That same day the *Carcass* 'close Reef'd the Topsails seeing the *Racehorse* who was 2 or 3 miles to the Westward of us ... at 6 out 3rd reefs, turning up to Vogel Sound [note different spelling to Phipps's] where the *Racehorse* had anchored, ½ past 9 came too there with our Best Bower in 15 fathoms [90ft/27m] ... Cloven Cliff bearing E½S about 1½ Miles at 2 AM light breezes & hazey, the Boats employed watering on the SE[st] side of the sound.'[40]

Appointed as coxswain, young Horatio Nelson would again be overseeing the loading of empty casks into the cutter and taking charge of the watering party. Floyd noted that their anchorage in Vogel Sound was not exposed to hard prevailing winds as it 'lies in latitude 80° 0′ 45″ as determined by Mr Lyons the day after we came in, and is as fine a place for shelter as ever I saw, open only to northerly winds, and never dangerous by reason of having a harbour under lee'.[41]

Probing north-easterly amid drift ice to the Seven Islands

Thursday 15 July to Sunday 20 July

For the past two weeks both ships had been battling against appalling conditions: dense fogs, hard winds and calms, as well as the alarming experience of sailing in heavy drift ice. To make matters worse, the pack ice accumulating to the east appeared to be preventing them making further passage round to the north-east. Having endured these trials without respite, both ship's companies would have been exhausted.

Now safely anchored in Vogel Sound, Phipps and Lutwidge used the opportunity to rest their crews. Although not documented, both crews probably received extra-nourishing food to restore their health. Medically, most of the men appear to have remained in good shape. Phipps states in his book that they made 'the most minute precautions necessary for the preservation of their health', adding: 'we found the advantage of the spirits which had been allowed for extraordinary occasions as well as the additional clothing from the Admiralty.' He noted that: 'Not withstanding every attention several men were confined with colds which affected them with pains in their bones but from the careful attendance given them, few continued in the sick list above two days at a time.'[1]

Surprisingly, nobody seems to have been injured, as would generally be expected when working in wooden sailing vessels. This reflects professional seamen's tendency to safeguard themselves in whatever activity they undertake, whether it be out on a yard handing sails with 'one hand for the ship and one for yourself' or simply standing clear of the bight of a rope or keeping fingers clear of a block shiver.

Both commanders also used this period at anchor to undertake the maintenance of the fabric of the ships, rigging and sails, even though the weather was squally with gales and fog.

By Friday the *Racehorse* completed her water. Her log entry on Saturday reads: 'at 9 carried out the Kedge Anchor to steady the Ship', a precautionary measure to counteract forces from the swell playing on the ship and potentially dragging her main anchor. The day's entry concludes: 'AM the People employed scraping the Topmasts & Tallowing them & paying the lower Masts with Tallow and Varnish of Pine.'[2] Salt from wind-borne sea water would have had a detrimental effect on the pine spars so they were liberally treated with preservatives to help the masts retain their suppleness. Both tallow and varnish were carried aboard naval vessels with the carpenter's stores. Tallow was made from rendered-down animal fat and commonly applied to coat the rope sail gaskets. 'Varnish of pine', sometimes called rosin (or rozin), is a viscous by-product of the process of distilling pine sap into turpentine. Rosin 'varnish', turpentine and 'Stockholm tar' were all imported from the Baltic states and Scandinavia.

The anchorage allowed the sailmakers, Thomas Spence of *Racehorse* and John Bread of *Carcass*, to make good any repairs, while the pursers, John Strong and Jonathan Parry, re-evaluated all provision stocks. Little did these men know that their services would be called upon for unexpected necessities in early August. As for the ship's boatswains, Jonathan Stamford of *Racehorse* and John Cunningham of *Carcass*, they detailed their mates with working parties to check rigging blocks and reeve new ropes where required, with others examining the boats and notifying the carpenters of defects.

On the Sunday, the *Racehorse* 'Received a Boat load of Water; at Midnight veered to ½ a Cable'. Using the capstan, they hove in short on the best bower anchor cable and after sending the boat for more water 'at ½ past 11 Weighed the Kedge anchor & hoisted in the Boats'.[3]

Lutwidge's journal provides a variable picture. Thursday's reading described: 'all the boats employ'd watering; By the Master's

observations on the shore at the watering place, it was high water at
10pm, and the tide appeared to flow and ebb 5 or 6 feet; at midnight
saw a great deal of ice in the NE, about 2 miles distant almost
entirely across the entrance of the sound, and some small pieces
drifted in; AM went on shore to a small island, about 2½ miles to
the S°·ward of the ships, where Cap^{tn.} Phipps had landed and fix'd
a tent, for making observations & making angles of the different
points of land &c.'[4]

It seems likely that the 14½-year-old Horatio Nelson, in his role as
the ship's senior coxswain, eagerly presented himself to accompany
Lutwidge on shore. Although Phipps makes no mention of going
on shore, he would have been checking bearings against his vague
existing charts and amending them accordingly. What few charts of
Spitsbergen did exist at this period would have been relatively inaccurate; the earliest map of the island group had only been created in
1758, the year of Nelson's birth.

On Friday 16 July, *Carcass* 'Completed watering the Ship, in all 34
tons her draught of water 13 ^{ft}:3 ^{ins} forward, 12 ^{ft.}·9 ^{ins} abaft' – a quantity of water that amounts to 7,616 gallons (approximately 34,620
litres). As with all loading, the change in weight not only altered the
vessel's displacement but also changed the ship's draught of water
(the depth of water between the tread of the keel and waterline afore
and abaft). The longitudinal trim of the ship would also be inversely
altered. Freeboard, the parallel height between waterline and upper
deck, is also affected and diminished as draught is increased. Each
of the above factors influenced the relationship between the two
points: the ship's centre of gravity and the metacentric height, the
comparable positions of which determined the righting movement
of the vessel – ie the ability of a ship to roll easy from side to side
upon its longitudinal axis without instability affecting the manner
by which it could be safely sailed.

Lutwidge also notes that he 'found the flood to set out of the
Sound NEbN and the Ebb SWbS'. Concluding, he wrote: 'AM
hove up the Anchor to see it was clear,[5] let it go again and steadied the ship with a hawser to the Westward.' Observations given in
the log state: 'Variation observations recorded by azimuth taken on
board ship N18°33′W and by the Astronomical Quadrant on Shore
N19° 30′W.'[6]

The view from Cloven Cliff to Hakluyt's Headland on 18 July 1773.
Taken from Phipp's book about the voyage, NMRN.

k

m

A pair of shroud deadeyes and a lanyard. k = shroud; m = lanyard.
From Darcy Lever.

Throughout Saturday most of the crew were 'Employed overhauling the rigging, AM set up the lower and topmast rigging'. This
necessitated tightening up any slack sustained in the shrouds, which
was done by hauling up upon the lanyards to lace the pairs of deadeyes together; the lowermost firmly fixed to the channel boards, the
uppermost turned into the end of the shroud.

Before they began this task they liberally greased the deadeye
lanyards with tallow to ease movement. Next, a length of temporary
rope called a selvagee was bent to the shroud with a rolling hitch at a
sensible working height. The loose end was made up into an eye into
which the hook of the single block forming part of a luff tackle was
hooked. The hook of the double block was then hitched to the hauling part of the deadeye lanyard. The fall of the luff tackle was hitched
to a second double-purchase tackle that, when pulled indirectly, pulled
through any slack in the shroud via the deadeye lanyard, the uppermost
turned into the lower end of the shroud. This done, they then reseized
the lanyard.[7] Not easy, this was a task involving strenuous brute force.

Sunday saw the *Carcass* very much ready to put to sea: 'at 10 AM loosed topsails as P^r [per] Signal, and took up the Small anchor', the latter relating to the kedge anchor.[8]

Monday 19 July

The entry in *Racehorse*'s journal reads: 'At 2pm hove short on the best Bower; at 3 Weighed & came to sail with the *Carcass*; ½ past 3 out all Reefs & set the T.G^t S^{ls}.' Taking a course NE by SSE the ship hauled to the southward at 10pm. One hour later Phipps wrote: 'the W^{t}ermost [westermost] Land SSE & the main body of the Ice from WNW to SbW.'[9]

The *Carcass*, it appears, with her boats already hoisted in, had weighed and sailed two hours earlier than her consort and at 2pm tacked to the northward. Five hours later, Lutwidge records seeing 'much drift Ice to NNW; At 8pm Hackluyt's Headland SWb½W 9 or 10 lea^s; ½ past 10 hauled our wind, the main body of the Ice $^{abt.}$ ¼ of a mile distant stretching from NW to SbW, at 11 Tack^d to the S^{o}ward.' Soundings taken at 2pm revealed 25-fathom (150ft/46m) water with the seabed light brown sand and covered by stones. The ice was now bearing SWbW ½W and by 7am they were once again sailing among drift ice.[10]

Tuesday 20 July

At 1pm the *Racehorse* was 'Running amongst the loose ice & steering from NbE to NEbN & NbW. One Sail in sight to the S^{o}ward.' At midnight Phipps hove to and sounded 140 fathoms (840ft/256m) no ground. He then bore away and made sail and 'At 1AM hauled up the FS^{le} [foresail] & in T.G^t S$^{ls.}$ to pass a stream of Ice'. Not only did these frequent precautionary sail changes reduce the ship's speed, but the action of hoisting the foresail gave greater visibility ahead from the helm. The log notes that 'at 2 AM set the F. Sail; at 4 Running close along the ice; at 6 in 1st Reef of Miz.TS$^{le.}$ at ½ past 9 in 1st Reef of Main & 2nd Reef of Miz.TS$^{ls.}$'.[11]

In *Carcass*, Lutwidge recorded: 'thick Cloudy Wea^r with Sleet – all these 24 Hours sailing along the main body of the Ice to the Westward and thro' several streams of Ice, when we had the main body to Windward.'[12]

Wednesday 21 July

According to *Racehorse's* journal the two ships were at latitude 79°2′N. The weather, it appears, had deteriorated to 'hazy with Snow & Sleet' as sea ice conditions prevailed as before. Finding ice dead ahead of them, Phipps tacked the *Racehorse* at 1pm and was forced to tack again 30 minutes later, and 'at 3 on seeing an opening in the ice bore away, at 6 steering along the edge of the Ice; at ½ past 9 being embayed on the Ice haul'd up a point to clear it'. Amid worsening conditions, the watch officers and helmsmen continuously manoeuvred the ship to get into the stream of loose ice.[13] Aloft in the crosstrees, lookouts peered attentively across the sea of ice about them, shouting down their observations and bearings to the men on deck at the helm.

In the *Carcass*, Lutwidge and his officers resolutely followed their lead ship. Repeating much of what he had written the previous day, Lutwidge recorded: 'All these 24 Hours coasting along the main body of the Ice, and running thro' many loose streams which had drifted off from it.' After taking a navigational fix: 'By the lat^de observed found we have a S°erly current, 36 miles more than the log gives' – the log here being the log reel apparatus used for determining ship's speed. Recording the altitude of the sun at noon this is given as 30°46′. The chronometer at 9am was 1 hour, 17 minutes and 5 seconds slow.[14]

Thursday 22 July

The latitude recorded in *Racehorse's* journal is 80°1′N. whereas their position – bearing and distance at noon – is given as 'North end of Vogle [sic] Sound S82°15′E 10 Leagues; the distance run is 40 miles'. For the most part, the *Racehorse* was tacking and bearing away while running through loose ice. At 7pm they 'haul'd up the F.S^le & lowered the T.G^t S^ls to wait for the *Carcass* [as she] passed a stream of Ice'. Soundings taken gave 200 fathoms (1,200ft/366m) 'no ground'.[15]

Journal statements given by Lutwidge for the *Carcass* make similar comments about the drift ice, the ship tacking or hauling her wind to avoid 'heavy pieces'. Of note, her timekeeper recorded 'at ¾ past 5' the chronometer was running 1 hour, 34 minutes and 38 seconds slow.[16]

Friday 23 July

In *Racehorse's* log, Phipps notes: 'Fresh breezes & hazy latter part light Airs with Rain. At 5pm out 2ⁿᵈ Reefs of F & Miz. TSˡˢ· at ½ past 6 Bore away.' Finding the wind falling off to light airs, Phipps made more sail: 'at 7 out Reefs and up T. Gᵗ. Yards & out Spritsail T.Sˡᵉ Yard; at 8 the extremes of the Land from SSE to ESE, off Shore 7 Leagues.' Although the ship would tack several times off and on the ice between 12 and 3 o'clock, they were still just 7 leagues (21miles/34km) from the land.[17]

Following closely astern, the *Carcass* undertook similar courses of action: 'at 8 out reefs and got up Topgallant Yards... at Midnight Latᵈᵉ by observation 80°10´.30N. Tᵏᵈ to the SE having stood close up to the main body of the Ice.' The altitude of the sun at midnight observed by Lutwidge was 10°7´.30S. However, whichever direction they attempted to navigate through the ice to the north, the chance of finding a free opening eluded both ship's commanders.[18]

Saturday 24 July

Racehorse's position as recorded in Phipps's journal was now latitude 80°16´N. There was little wind and 'a great Swell from the Southward. At ½ past Noon Tᵏᵈ· for the Ice. at ½ past 7 Sounded 210 ᶠᵐˢ· [384m] muddy ground ... at 10 Tack'd; at 2 AM Wore Ship in the loose Ice which carried away the Pipe of the Head-Pump & broke some of the Moulding in the Stern.'[19] Although the damage sustained appears rather minor, the log entry suggests that the loose ice they were now encountering was becoming much larger, and more treacherous. In many respects, they had been lucky so far.

In the *Carcass*, Lutwidge recorded: 'Light Breezes and thick Weaʳ, with rain.' He notes mandatory bearings, and the various directions in which he tacked: '½ past Noon Tkᵈ to the SE at 4 saw the land from EbS to SbW, at 11 Tkᵈ to the NEˢᵗ· Hackluyt's Headland 10 or 11 Leagues, at 2 AM the Main body of the Ice, from NE to WNW, ½ PAST Tkᵈ to the SE, ½ past 10 Tkᵈ to the Nºward. at Noon the Racehorse about a league to Windward'.[20]

It seems that despite their efforts, the ships had not yet been able to distance themselves very far from Hakluyt's Headland, which was about 32 miles (51km) away. In his later book, Phipps emphasises the lack of progress: 'when I left the deck, at four in the morning, we were very near the spot where the ships had been fast in the ice on the 7th in the evening.' As a result they had gained little in the way of distance.[21]

Sunday 25 July

At noon, Phipps recorded *Racehorse*'s position as 'Red Beach SSW 3 or 4 Miles'. In moderate breezes, she tacked at 3pm towards the ice sheet, taking in her topgallants as the wind freshened. By 9pm she was steering various courses through the ice from NNW to SSE. Two hours later her topmen went aloft to put in first and second reefs of the topsails, thereby reducing the sail further. Phipps next noted: 'AT 2 AM Running amongst the loose Ice Red Head SSW 5 or 6 leagues.'[22]

In the *Carcass*, Lutwidge tacked ship four times between 1pm and 6.30pm then 'at 8 hawled in amongst the drift into the Ice, running to leeward close by the Main body'. He then wrote: '½ past 10 in 1st & 2nd reefs, blowing very fresh, run along much heavy drift Ice to the NE, till ½ past 3AM when we Tack'd to the Northward to weather some heavy pieces ahead.' Lutwidge next discloses: 'these 24 hours, sailing amongst the drift Ice, the pieces much smaller as we stood to the Eastward and many of them appeared discolored and rotten; at Noon found the Current setting us fast to the Eastward, and with the land.' This fast-running current was to become problematic.[23]

Monday 26 July

Racehorse's log gives the course S61°E, lat 80°17´N, long 4°43´E, the weather light airs later turning to calm with thick fog. This day saw the two ships reach Moffin Island, which was first mapped by the Dutch cartographer Hendrick Doncker in 1655 and was remotely located north of the mouth of Wijdefjorden on the northern coast of Spitsbergen. Today, the geographical coordinates of this low-lying island by accurate GPS are lat 80°01´.00N, long 14°29´.59E. Note that Phipps and Lutwidge use different spellings – one referring to it as Moffin Island, the other as Moffen's Island.

As they made their approach, Phipps recorded in his journal: 'at ½ past 2pm Red Beach Hill W45°S 3 or 4 Leagues Moffin Island EbN 5 or 6 Miles; at 5 hoisted out a Boat to try the Current; at 10 East end of Moffin Island S15°E & West end off Shore 4 or 5 Miles.' From the boat, they suspended the trial experimental log to measure the flow speed of water. The kind of device they were using is unfortunately not disclosed and it is not even mentioned in Phipps's 1774 published account. Thick fog now descended upon them and 'at 2pm lost sight of the *Carcass*. At 4 made the Fog Signals, at 6 saw the *Carcass* bearing SE½E 1 Mile'. Soundings taken varied from 10 to 24 fathoms (60–144ft/18–44m) 'small stones and shells and some parts Rocky'.[24]

Whereas Phipps's journal says little about Moffin Island, Lutwidge provides a far more detailed picture of the day's events. At 1pm the *Carcass* was standing to the NE taking soundings of 75 fathoms (450ft/137m): 'the East End of Deerfield 4 or 5 five Lea^s.' After taking further soundings Lutwidge wrote: 'at 6 Calm, tryed the Current which set 1 mile an Hour SEbE, the West end of Moffen's Island then bearing S50°E 2 or 3 miles dist.' Lutwidge then decided to investigate the island and hoisted out a boat and gathered a landing party: 'at 10 sent the Master on shore to Moffen's Island, the body of it bearing EbS. about 2 miles, at 12 a thick fog and Calm till 9 AM.' As the log then notes that the island was 6 miles (9.5km) distant at 10pm, it can be assumed that the shore party had returned, the ship having made sail. And while there is no evidential proof, it is probable that Nelson, in his dual role of midshipman and coxswain, accompanied the ship's master, James Allen, on to the island. It is also possible that Lutwidge gave the privilege of landing to his master as a matter of courtesy.

Lutwidge's journal then gives a description of the island, drawn from the observations disclosed by James Allen's debrief after his return:

'Moffen's Island is remarkably low flat land nearly of round form, and about 2 Miles in Diameter with a Lake or pond of fresh water in the middle of it, all frozen over except 30 or 40 Yards at the edge, was water or loose pieces of rotten Ice. The Ground from the Sea to the Lake is from ½ a Cables' length to ¼ of a mile over and the whole island covered with Gravel and small stones without Verdure or Vegetation of any kind. They saw but one large piece of drift wood about 3 fathoms [18ft/5.5m] long and as thick as the ship's mizzen mast, with the root on it, which have been thrown up over the high part of the Land and lay upon the Declivity towards the Lake. every two or 3 Yards they found Birds' nests with Eggs or young Birds. they saw Beares and a great number of Ducks, Geese, and Sea fowls. There was an Inscription on the Grave of a Dutchman buried there in July 1771. it was low water when the boat landed at 11 o'clock and appeared to flow 7 or 8 feet- all that time the tide set the Ship from the Island to the NW, which before had set us to the SE upon it. On the West side which they examined, is a fine white sandy bottom with 2 fathoms [12ft/3.7m] water a Ship's Length from the beach to 5 fathoms [30ft/9m] ½ a mile from it. it bears from Hackluyt's Headland by account N75°E dist. 55 miles.'

Taking a fix at noon, Lutwidge recorded lat by account as 80°2′N and long from Greenwich 16°54′E.[25]

Tuesday 27 July
Sailing with her boat still on tow astern, the *Racehorse* progressed eastwards towards the northerly land mass of the Spitsbergen archipelago referred to as the Northeastland, the *Carcass* in company about a mile distant. Manning the yard tackles at 4pm, *Racehorse's* seamen hoisted in their boat and, currently unhindered by ice, both vessels continued easterly. At 1am they sighted 'the Eastermost Land bearing EbS'. Sadly, Phipps next recorded. 'Departed this life Swin Christian.'[26] Although the cause of this man's death is not given, *Racehorse's* muster book number 87 lists him as Able Seaman Swin Christian from Gottenburg, aged 30.[27] Had Christian died when the ships were off Moffin Island they would have buried him on shore, but since they were now at sea they would 'commit his body to the deep'.

Amid calm and foggy weather Lutwidge 'sent a boat amongst the drift Ice about a mile to the NE; at 4 she returned with a Sea horse which they had killed, and tow'd on board'. The log then makes references to Vogel land being some 20 leagues distant to the southwest and 'at 12 the NE^st[Northeast] land bearing East'. They now

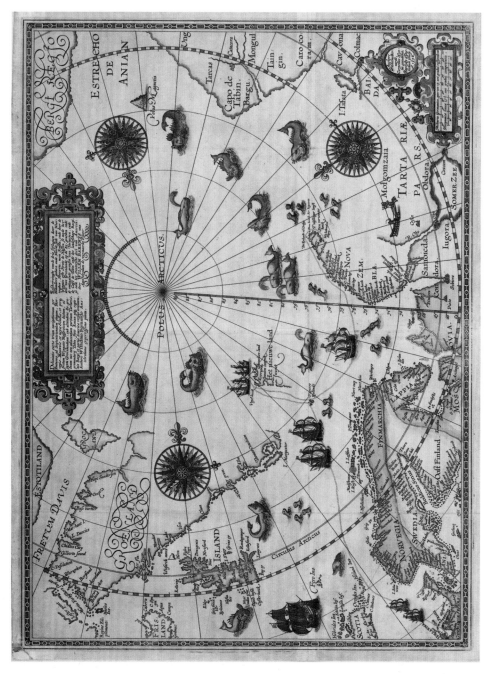

1. Chart showing the places visited by Barentz on his third voyage. Denoted simply as 'Island', the Spitsbergen archipelago group is shown to the left, slightly south of the Greenland coastline. Fine Art Images/Heritage Images/ Getty Images.

2. Whaling grounds in the Arctic Ocean by Abraham Storck, depicting Dutch whaling ships off Spitsbergen, a whale being hunted (centre) and polar bears on the ice (left). Rijksmuseum SK-A-4102.

3. The whale-oil refinery near the village of Smeerenburg, Cornelis de Man, 1639. Rijksmuseum, SK-A-2355.

4. *The Dockyard at Deptford c.1770–75* by Richard Paton. This view depicts a royal yacht (left) firing a salute to a state barge, also flying the royal standard (centre). Royal Collection, 184970-1309797788.

5. *A Morning, with a View of Cuckold's Point* by Samuel Scott. The site of Randall's Yard, it is now occupied by the Millenium Dome. Tate Images N05450.

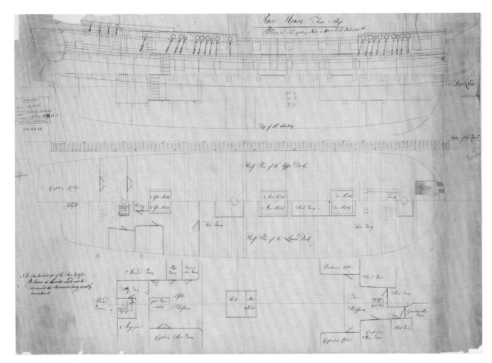

6. Plan of *Racehorse* showing her layout prior to her conversion into a bomb vessel in 1758. National Maritime Museum, J2200.

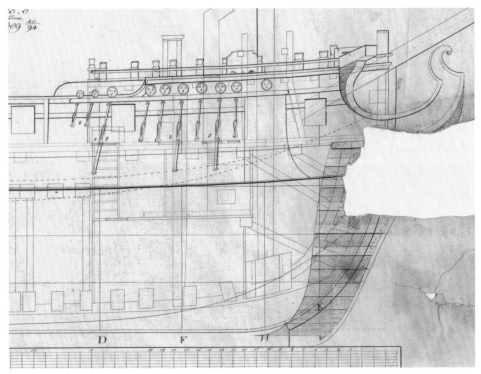

7. Profile plan of *Racehorse* showing her modified bow construction, 1773. National Maritime Museum J2197.

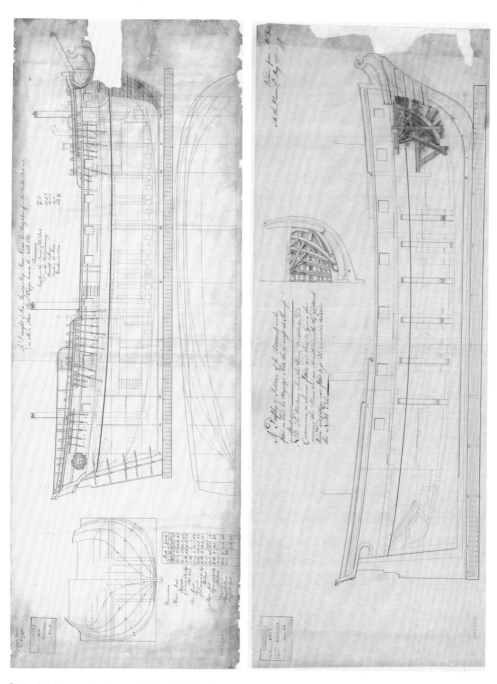

8. *Left*: Lines profile of *Racehorse* in 1773. National Maritime Museum J82197.

9. *Right*: Inboard profile and details of *Carcass* in 1773. National Maritime Museum J8000.

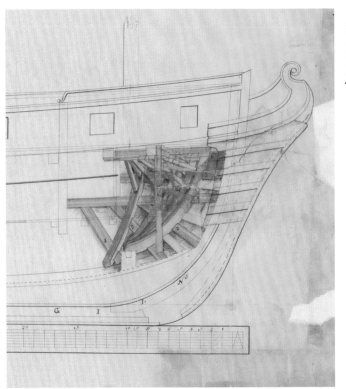

10. *Carcass* showing bow construction profile 1773. National Maritime Museum, J8000.

11. Sectional view of *Carcass* bow constructon 1773. National Maritime Museum J8000.

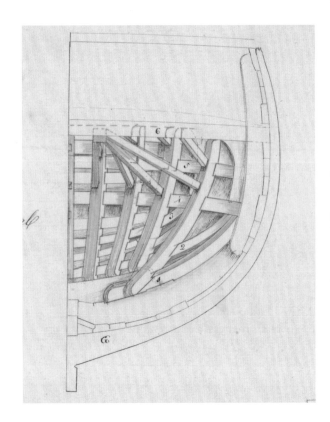

12. Constantine Phipps porrayed on the ice with a half pike in his hand, urging his men hauling the boats. Note that he is shown in his formal naval uniform, rather than dressed for the actual conditions shown. Painting by an unknown artist. National Portrait Gallery/Historic Collection/Alamy Stock Photo.

13. Skeffington Lutwidge by Gilbert Stuart. Chrysler Museum of Art.

14. Philippe d'Auvergne in middle age, artist unknown. The Picture Art Collection/ Alamy Stock Photo.

15. A painting, thought to be of Horatio Nelson as a young midshipman, artist unknown. Lebrecht Music & Arts/Alamy Stock Photo.

16. Nicholas Biddle by Orlando Lagman. Zip Lexing/Alamy Stock Photo.

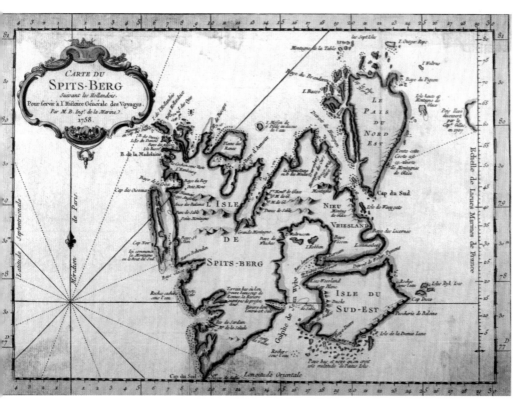

17. French chart of Spitz Berg (Spitzbergen) 1558. Chronicle/Alamy Stock Photo.

18. Getting the top over the masthead. Detail from an engraving by Richard Short 1750. 'This plate … being the Stern Views of His Majesty's Ships Monarque of 74 guns, Fougeux and Trident, of 70 guns each, three of the Six French Men of War taken by the British Fleet under the Command of Sir Edward Hawke Kt. of the Bath &c. 14 October 1747'.

19. *Racehorse* and *Carcass* trapped in the ice, 31 July 1773 by John Cleverley the Younger. This scene also shows the men playing leapfrog on the ice. National Maritime Museum, PAE 3969.

20. *Racehorse* and *Carcass* trapped in the ice, 7 August 1773 by John Cleverley the Younger. National Maritime Museum PY 3970.

21. (Above) HMS *Assistance* trapped in the ice, 1850, by Thomas Sewell Robins. Although nearly 80 years after the expedition described in this book, the use of ice anchors shown here, would have been very similar for *Racehorse* and *Carcass*. National Maritime Museum PAE 4239.

22. (Right) Watercolour of Midshipman Nelson's encounter with the polar bear by Myles Birket Foster. Midshipman Hughes can be seen in the background, the *Carcass* behind him. National Maritime Museum PAE 5378.

23. *Wreck in the Sea of Ice* thought to be an early work by Caspar David Friedrich, 1798. This painting shows clearly the potential danger of ice build-up – the ship here has foundered in the ice and her crew has been forced to abandon ship. Kunsthalle Hamburg.

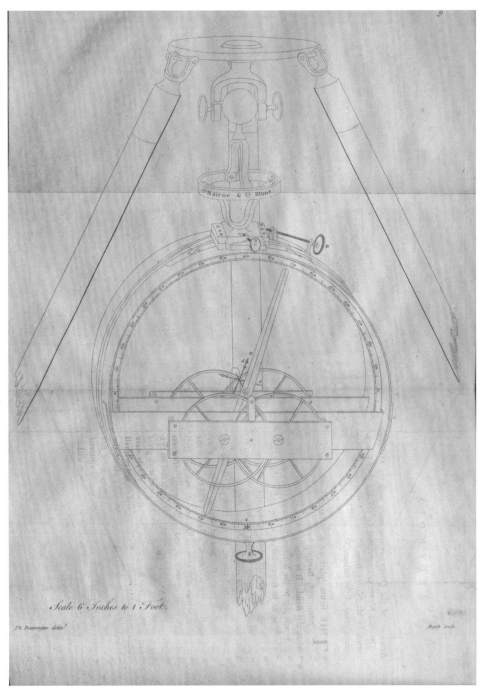

24. Pendulum apparatus designed by instument makers Thomas Blunt and Edward Nairne and manufactured by watchmaker Alexander Cummings. Drawing taken from Phipp's book, NMRN.

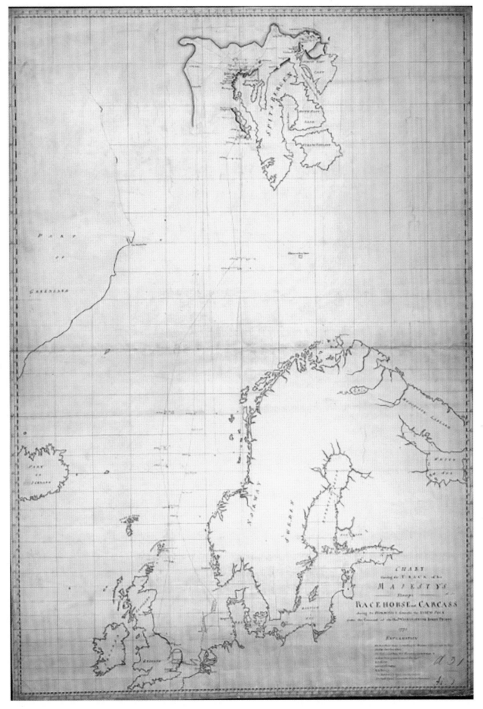

25. The route taken by the Arctic expedition in the summer of 1773 with the Spitsbergen archipelago shown at the top. Chart taken from Phipps's book, NMRN.

26. *HM Sloop* Racehorse *North Sea Storm Arctic Expedition 1773*. Her perilous situation on Friday 17 September as recreated by marine artist, Gordon Frickers.

appeared to be progressing towards the north-easterly island of the Spitsbergen archipelago, the *Carcass* tacking several times as required, her log entry concluding: 'all these 24 Hours turning up towards the NE[st]land.' The variation per azimuth is given as 14°42′W, the timekeeper recorded as running 2 hours, 14 minutes and 56 seconds slow.[28]

Wednesday 28 July
At noon the *Racehorse* tacked 'for the Ice, br't to & sounded 79f[m.] muddy Ground; at ½ past made Sail'. Throughout the afternoon, the vessel occasionally hove to and made sail until tacking again at 6pm. Phipps's journal records that 'at 8 Interred the Deceased'. At this point the entire ship's company were mustered on deck to pay their last respects to their dead Swedish shipmate. Phipps, prayer book in hand, presided over the solemn short burial service. Before them, lying on a loose plank resting on the gunwale, was the body of Swin Christian sewn up in his hammock by the sailmaker Thomas Spence, weighted with round shot. As Phipps's service reverently drew to a close, the boatswain's mate, his silver call in hand, 'piped the still' as the plank was quietly tilted, committing the body to the sea. (Contrary to popular belief today, seamen were not always buried at sea; instead, in compliance with Christian ethics they were nominally interred on land whenever possible pending ship's location. For practicality, however, battle casualties and diseased men were commonly interred 'over the side' at the earliest opportunity.)

The journal concludes: 'at 12 the Southermost part of the Island SE Lat[de] ob[sd] 80°37′ N.' At 1am the ship tacked and three hours later *Racehorse*'s watch officer sighted the easternmost land bearing SE½S 7 or 8 Leagues and 'at 5 & 6 Tack'd'.[29]

Contending with fog, the *Carcass* was initially standing to the SE: 'at 6 AM Snow Hill on the NE[st] land bore E¼S, ½ past tacked to the N[o.]ward at Midnight latitude by observation 80°33′N, North part of the NE[st.] land bearing S81°E with part of it S52° E, the land we supposed The West side of Weygatt's Heights SbE.' After making several tacks, Lutwidge recorded: 'all the 24 Hours turning up to the E[st.]ward towards the NE[st] land.' By morning they were closely sailing along with the drift ice to east of them:

'at Noon the main body of Ice bore North; about a mile ahead of the ship.'[30]

The two ships were now working north-easterly around the top coastline of what they called the Northeastland with little hindrance from drift ice. Checking his chronometer at 3pm, Lutwidge recorded it running 2 hours, 24 minutes and 14 seconds slow. The variation by azimuth taken at 4pm gave N18°56′W. Making further observations, the altitude of the sun at midnight was 9°26′ and at noon 28°6′.[31]

Thursday 29 July
At noon, the *Racehorse* 'Tack'd br't to & sounded 101f^fm. [185m] muddy Ground; at ½ past made Sail, steering various courses thro' the Ice from ESE to W^d. [westward], at 5 Running amongst the Ice, steering mostly SEbS, the Eastermost Land E½ N, 7 or 8 leagues'. After tacking at 10.30pm, by 3am they found themselves dangerously close to the ice. Taking evasive action, Phipps quickly tacked ship and 'at ½ past 3 up F^r.S^le. [foresail] & backed the Miz. T.S^le'. Manning the foresail buntlines and clewlines, they brailed up the sail to its yard; others manning the braces hauled round the mizzen topsail, the wind setting it aback. These actions immediately took all weigh off the ship and avoided collision with the ice. Between 5am and 11am the ship tacked several times to beat away from the ice, the ships running just 3 miles (5km) off the land. Final remarks entered in the journal that day state: 'at Noon the middle of the opening South. Read the Articles of War to the Ship's Company.'[32]

The above journal details from *Racehorse's* log do not appear to reflect what Phipps had disclosed for 29 July in his book. According to this 'public' account, Phipps had written that 'two officers went with a boat in pursuit of some sea-horses [walruses] and afterwards to the low island'. Could this be Little Table Island? He then mentions the use of Bouguer's log to measure the current and records: 'At six in the morning the officers returned from the island; in their way back they fired at, and wounded a sea-horse, which dived and brought up with it a number of others. They all joined in the attack upon the boat, wrested an oar from one of the men, and were with

Men in boats fighting off a walrus attack. The image is not contemporary to the Arctic expedition but the boats, clothing and equipment would have been very similar to that shown here. De Agostini/Biblioteca Ambrosiana/Getty Images.

difficulty prevented from staving, or upsetting her [the boat]; but a boat from the *Carcass* joining ours they dispersed.'[33] This description apparently relates to the episode when Nelson arrived in his cutter to help the situation (see page 213).

Like *Racehorse*, the *Carcass* persevered under light breezes amid dense fog: 'At ½ past Noon T$^{kd.}$ to the SE, having stood within the Ship's length of the Main body Ice into a deep bight, hauled up amongst the drift ice which was heavy and close at 5pm got out of it.' Around 6pm the fog lifted, enabling Lutwidge to record bearings of Snow Hill on the north-east land. Looking around, he records: 'a great fog upon the land that we could not well judge the distance, at 9 sounded 18 fathoms [108ft/33m] hard ground, ½ past 10 Tk^d to the NE.' Taking observations at this time, Lutwidge recorded latitude as 80°25′N.

Throughout the night his ship tacked four times: SE, NE, S and SW. Every time they tacked, the bosun's mates called 'all hands' on deck to bracing stations, their shrill pipes sounding throughout the ship. Here, each man went to his position as authorised in the Watch and Station Bill to man the pinrails and cleats. Upon the master bellowing the order 'helms'lee', all sprang into action, hauling round the yards of the square sails on their braces, or letting go as required. The same was done for the main and fore coarse tacks and sheets. Others, manning the tacks and sheets of the headsails, waited in anticipation for the ship's head to cross through the wind, the sails flapping. As the wind filled the sails they rapidly hauled in the sheets and made fast the ropes. In home waters this process would have been relatively easy, but in Arctic conditions the hard icy ropes and ice-covered decks must have been quite precarious. Tacking in extremely light airs was not always successful, especially as square-rigged ships often 'miss stays' – fail to come about on to another tack if insufficient momentum through the water has been gained beforehand. By missing stays, the vessel can virtually stop dead in the water. Should this happen, they would resume course to gain sufficient speed to attempt another tack change. Alternatively, they would wear ship.

Chronometer readings taken at 4.45pm show it running 2 hours, 32 minutes and 39 seconds slow; taken again at 5.15pm it was then 2 hours, 33 minutes and 46 seconds slow. The altitude of the sun was twice recorded, at midnight 9°2′; at noon 28°5′.[34]

Friday 30 July

Now at a latitude of 80°31′N, the *Racehorse*'s log reads: 'Light Airs & clear intermixt with Calms. at 3pm Tack'd; at 4 Sounded 15^{fm}, the Southermost point of the Large Island SSE 3 leagues & the South part of the E'most Land SbE ½ E.' Tacking and handing the sails, she was 'Running thro' the Ice'. The log then records: 'at 8 N°, (1) SSE¼E - N°, (2) SE - N°, (3) NE, & N°, (4) – SSW'. Phipps next hoisted out a boat and 'at 9 made a Signal for the Boat, at ¼ past 9 & at 12 repeated D°'.[35]

Although the significance of the numbers given in brackets appears obscure, with the exception of Table Island, Little Table Island and Walden Island, the smaller islets forming the Seven Islands were not formally named, instead being simply recorded numerically in the ship's journals.

Did the need to repeat signals have anything to do with the two officers pursuing 'sea-horses' as mentioned above, as well as the instance mentioned in Phipps's book on 29 July? And did the officers simply miss the recall signals? What appears more likely is that they were unable to respond because they were too preoccupied dealing with the walrus attack.

If there is any confusion between the dates 29 and 30 July in the two sources (Phipps's journal and his 1774 publication), this is accounted for by the fact that the ship's journal is officially recorded in 'sea time', with the days starting and ending at noon, whereas the book is more likely given in land time, with the days starting and ending at midnight.

Racehorse's log next records: 'at 5 AM try'd the Current by the Diver & found it set EbN 2 ᶠᵐˢ in 30 Seconds: The Boat Returned.' This appears to imply that the boat was being used for the trial of the 'diver' – a new device being trialled at this period that, when immersed under water, measured the current in knots. That the ships were carrying this instrument emphasises the scientific importance of the voyage. The log concludes: 'at 8 Nᵒ,(1)Bore SWbS Nᵒ,(2)SSW & Nᵒ (3) NEe ¾N- Sounded 14 ᶠᵐ· Stones & Shells, at ¼ past 8 Tack'd. The *Carcass* in Company.'[36]

The *Carcass*, meanwhile, was standing to the north-east amid the drift ice, her log noting: 'Snow Hill on the NEˢᵗ land E½S abᵗ 5 leaˢ... at 7 off the point of the low flat Island laying off Brandy Bay, sounded 7 fᵐˢ, sail'd thro' stream of drift ice that run of the Main body towards the Island.' The low island referred to is probably Little Table Island. The log records that latitude observed at midnight is given as 80°23′.45N and that: 'Snowhill EbS abᵗ 4 miles Nᵒmost of the Seven Islands' (known today as Sjuøyane). Lutwidge concludes: 'all these 24 Hours very close to the Main body of Ice which we could see join'd the seven Islands, and no appearance of open water between them and the NEˢᵗ land.' The altitude of the sun he records as 8°50′.[37]

By now both commanders would have felt quite optimistic about how far they had progressed northwards. Furthermore, both ships had only once resorted to the use of ice hooks and poles. However, as the journals show, each time they attempted to get north-easterly they found themselves hemmed in between the land and the ice sheet, the Seven Islands effectively wedging in all the ice.

Saturday 31 July
Racehorse's log records: 'D°· Weather, At 2pm tack'd; at 6 & ½ past 7 Tack'd; at 10 Tacked several times close to the main Ice & look'd out for an opening; at 12 Tack'd on finding an opening; Table Island North 2 Miles.' The mean geographical coordinates for Table Island and adjacent Little Table Island are lat 80°48′N, long 20°22′E. Soundings taken between 12.30pm and 1pm reveal a depth about 66 fathoms [396ft/121m], the seabed mud and shells. Then: 'at ½ past 2 made a signal for the Boat; at 4 Table Island NNE 2 or 3 Miles & N° (3) [?] N½E; at 5 being beset by Ice got the Ice Anchors out; at 6 filling Water on the Ice; at 11 a light breeze coming from the Eastward, cast off [from the ice anchors] and endeavoured to bore thro' the Ice; at Noon finding we could not get no farther, got an Ice Anchor out & made fast to the field of Ice. Bearings as before, The *Carcass* to the SE.'[38]

On this last day of July, the *Carcass* was 'turning up to the Eastward between the NEᵗ land and the Islands'. At 10pm, Lutwidge took the ship in among the drift ice close to the main body of pack ice and recorded: 'at 12 Table Island NW½W 2 or 3 miles: there appeared to be no further open water or passage for the Ships, the main body of Ice seeming to be firmly joined from one Island to another: – I went in the Boat for one of these Islands about 5 or 6 miles to the NEᵈ of the Ships, through narrow Channels being obliged to hawl the boat over the Ice in several places.' Here we could again perhaps assume that Nelson took Lutwidge on shore in his four-oared cutter.

Lutwidge continues: 'Here I had an extensive view of the Sea to the Eastward which was entirely frozen over, not like the Ice we had hitherto encountered, but a flat even surface as far as the Eye could reach, which was undoubtedly 10 leagues at least.' This distance is 30 miles (48km). Continuing, he wrote: '[As the weather was] remarkably fine and clear' and the 'Hill [Table Island] was upon 200 Yards [600 feet/182m] above the surface of the Sea,– a compact body Ice joined all the Islands and Lands in sight, and no appearance of Water: except the Stream along the NE^t land, the way the Ships came in.'[39]

It appeared they had reached an impasse. As with their time spent at Moffin Island, we are fortunate that Lutwidge provided an effective visual account of Table Island: 'There was a great deal of drift wood upon the Island, some of it thrown up much higher than the high water mark, and some Cask Staves, which had been also thrown up by the Sea – many Deer's bones laying upon the Ground, and the marks of Bears feet everywhere amongst the Snow. This Island is three or four miles long, very hilly, and no appearance of any Verdure, except on some small spots amongst the broken precipices.'

Though not disclosed within the ship's logbooks, but well depicted in the d'Auvergne/Cleverley engravings, it appears that some 12 men resorted to playing leapfrog on the ice, one wearing a red cap. In his account, Midshipman Floyd recorded: 'Taking advantage, of various pools of water on the ice-floes, the ships were completed with water after which the ship's companies amused themselves by playing leapfrog and other games on the ice. The ice-pilots did not share in the general hilarity of the men: indeed they displayed considerable uneasiness at the position of the ships, being at such an advanced season of the year, so much farther than they had ever been before.'[40] The fact that Midshipman d'Auvergne chose to initially capture the usual sangfroid attitude of the sailors despite the gravity of events certainly provides an insight into his unique record of the expedition. The relatively calm situation did not prevail.

While Lutwidge was out of the *Carcass,* the ice conditions had drastically changed and he remarked: 'When I returned onboard at 6 AM found the drift Ice had nearly beset both the Ships, the *Racehorse* was made fast to a large piece of it, at Noon sounded 95 fathoms [570ft/174m] soft ground. Variation by the mean of 3 Azimuths N 18°:6·W.'[41] While Lutwidge was out of the ship the master and watch officer had intuitively taken immediate action against the sudden ice surge. Alarmingly, this ice state could likewise have been fatally precarious for Lutwidge and Nelson in their frail boat.

Men from the expedition playing leapfrog on the thick ice that surrounded the ships. Illustration from Phipp's book, NMRN.

Both ships were now in a very dangerous position and it would take much resolve by the two commanders and the consolidated efforts of both crews, some 170 odd men, to release themselves from their predicament. This could either mean surviving a long dark Arctic winter or, worse still, possible death in the icy polar wastes, a fate suffered by John Franklin's expedition 74 years later.

12

Icebound and abandoning ship

'Fearless he stood, when frozen floods surround,
And the strong ship in crystal chains was bound: –
When hope has dwindled to the smallest speck,
And crowding ice has risen to the deck;
The ship half coffin'd in the biting frost,
And home and country seem for ever lost;
Undaunted Phipps survey'd the frightful scene,
With heart unconquer'd, and his mind serene.'

THE HARP OF ST HILDA. RICHARD WINTER, 1814.

The above poem is by Richard Winter, a native of Whitby who knew well the local whaler men who ventured into the Arctic. It was written in tribute to those men and to Phipps – whose home, Mulgrave House, was near Whitby – and beautifully captures the awful situation in which Phipps and his expedition ships and their crews had become embroiled.

Phipps had sailed the *Racehorse* and *Carcass* NNE to the Seven Islands (Sjuøyane) located above the part of Spitsbergen called the 'Northeastland'. The islands are 553 nautical miles (637 miles/1,024km) south of the North Pole. If the ships could make an average speed of 5 knots (5.75mph/9.25km/h) in seas that were completely free of any ice, together with sound weather conditions and the right winds, Phipps could theoretically reach his destination and fulfil the purpose of the expedition in five or six days. This optimistic estimate is hypothetical; the Arctic was too unpredictable to allow any such projections to be realistic.

The expedition ships had already been caught by ice floes, which now appeared to be closing fast and locking in around the islands to create an unstable and dangerous situation for which neither Phipps nor Lutwidge was prepared. An entry from one ship's journal describes: 'no appearance of open water between them and the N°land.' The only men present who were familiar with the predicament were the two ice pilots chosen to accompany the expedition. As the two ship's journals further reveal, the scenario was about to become far worse.

Sunday 1 August
The position of the *Racehorse* according to Phipps's journal is Black Point S87°W Walden Island N5°E and Table Island N 57°E, 4 miles. Latitude and longitude are omitted, and wind direction is given as east variable. Despite the situation, the comments entered in the log seem mundane: 'Light Airs and clear Weather. At Anchor alongside a piece of Ice and employed filling water on it. The *Carcass* came near to us and made fast to the same field of Ice. Middle and latter parts of this day Calm.'

The brevity of the ship's journals means that they do not clearly describe the true state of the ice, which, under extreme pressure, was now piling high about the two ships. In his book, Phipps later wrote: 'August 1st. The ice pressed in fast; there was not the smallest opening; the two ships were within less than two lengths of each other separated by ice and neither having room to turn. The ice which had been all flat the day before and almost level with the water's edge, was now in many places forced higher than the main yard by the pieces squeezing together.'[1] Using similar wording, Midshipman Floyd recorded: 'Great pressure was also being exerted by the pack, and the ice, which the day before had been flat and level with the water's edge, was, in places, forced higher than the main yard by the pieces squeezing together.'[2] The drawings created by d'Auvergne and enhanced by John Cleverley in Phipps's book completely dismiss the fact that the ice reaching the main yard must have been at least 30ft (9m) high, but this may be explained by the fact that from an artistic position including this feature would have obscured the ship's hulls. In reality, the height of the ice together with the continuous loud reports of it cracking upon itself and against the ship's hulls must have been terrifying.

Lutwidge recorded *Carcass*'s position more precisely as: 'Beset with Ice amongst the 7 Islands Black point (on the Nt^e land) S67°W 3 or 4 lea^gs West Island N57°W. N^o. [North] Table Island N5°W.' The latitude by observation is noted as 80°36′N, whereas longitude is apparently not recorded. Wind direction is given as ENE veering to NE. The journal entry record is 'Light airs and Calm. PM. laying too amongst the drift Ice, and at 4 PM made fast the Ship to it, and filled our Water Cask from a Pool upon the Ice, at 10 PM cast the Ship loose and made fast to the Ice near the *Racehorse*, finding we drifted to the SE ^t from her. – at 11 AM a large white bear coming over the Ice towards the Ships, was shot and brought aboard the *Racehorse* – at Noon the drift Ice round the ships considerably increased, setting in towards the SW^t Shore from the North and East. some open water between the Ships and that Shore, but no passage to the Westward where they came in. PM Variation Pr Azimuth N17° 33′W.'

The statement about shooting the bear is the only occasion when Lutwidge refers to a single bear but whether this is the same polar bear that Nelson is alleged to have fought is uncertain because the incident is not corroborated. Furthermore, the timing, given as 11am, does not correspond to the accepted Nelson story whereby the young midshipman is said to have stolen out of the ship with his colleague Hughes during the small hours of the night. As this large bear was taken aboard the *Racehorse*, it could be the bear from which Phipps recorded measurements. Alternatively, from what Phipps wrote in his published account of the voyage, it is possible that this bear was eaten on board the *Racehorse*: 'the seamen ate of their flesh though [found it] exceedingly coarse.'[3]

Monday 2 August

In the *Racehorse,* the crew were still busy filling water casks. This done, 'At 12 PM lowr'd down the Topsails. AM employed rousing up the Cables to get at some Beer.' This entry shows that with no wind, keeping the topsails hoisted was pointless and the moving of the cables to get to the beer suggests that there were no dedicated cable tiers fitted in the ship; cables in most small ships being coiled directly upon the casks in the hold. That they needed to get at the beer suggests the ready-use stock had been consumed and also that there was an intention to issue more beer for morale reasons; they were certainly not short of water, thanks to Dr Irving's water distillation apparatus.

In the *Carcass* Lutwidge recorded the weather as: 'Fresh Breezes and Calm, latter part Foggy. AT 10 PM the N° Island NNbW½W, both Ships closely beset with the Ice and no possibility of moving them, as the Wind blew directly in from the open water, which was now over 7 or 8 miles to the Westward.' They were slowly drifting eastwards, the moving ice field gripping the ships – a situation that could become increasingly perilous, especially if pressure built up against the ships' hulls.

Tuesday 3 August

According to Phipps, Tuesday started with fresh breezes, becoming 'foggy with drizzling Rain', the thick fog clearing later. After furling all sails, the crew were next 'employed breaking up the Ground Tier'. This relates to moving out the lower level of water casks in the hold. Then, 'At 6 we begun to cut the Ice with our Ice Saws & Axes in order to warp the ship to the westward. At Noon sawing the Ice to make a Dock for the Ship to lay in.' This gives an insight into Phipps's rationale behind the actions already taken: he needed to lighten the ship of all unnecessary deadweight to ease the task of hauling the ship into the temporary 'dry dock'. To enable the moving of the heavy ground tier of water, all casks were started to allow the contents to run into the bilge, the water then being pumped overboard. The term 'starting' the casks relates to smashing in the wooden cask headers with an axe to drain them quickly of their content. If the casks could be turned from lying 'bung up' then the bungs could be pulled to drain water, thereby avoiding breaking the headers. If necessary, the headers could be later replaced by the carpenter or cooper.

The loss of water had already been compensated for when the other barrels were filled with ice, this water probably being kept temporarily out of the ship. The note about getting access to the beer shows its importance for crew morale and the fact that it was carried instead of water. The creation of an 'ice dock' made good sense as the shape it formed reduced the risk of the hull being crushed by ice. Although cutting out the dock was a last resort, Phipps knew that keeping the crew 'gainfully employed' would distract them from the plight they were in. It's unfortunate that Midshipman d'Auvergne did not produce a sketch of the dock being formed; had he done so we would have insight into Phipps's intentions. However, from the *Carcass*'s journal this idea appears to have been abandoned.

Recording events in the *Carcass* that day, Lutwidge stated: 'Beset with Ice between the No[rth] Land and the Seven Islands. Latitude by Obs[n] 80°:34′ N.' Continuing, he wrote: 'at 4 PM furled the sails, AM both Ships companies employed with the Ice Saws and Axes endeavoring to cut a Passage thro' the Ice for the Ships to hawl thro' to the Westward, the *Carcass* made fast to the Stern of the *Racehorse*, the Weather was remarkably warm at Noon the Tar running upon the side, Anchor Stocks &c, where the Sun shone upon them, the water on the opposite side of the Ship where the Ice had been removed, was freezing on the surface' – such was the strange contrast of their environmental predicament. The ships, Lutwidge remarked, were still drifting to eastward with the ice taking them even further from any open water.

Wednesday 4 August
In *Racehorse*, Phipps simply wrote in his journal: 'Light Airs and Clear Weather Employed as before.' More informatively, Lutwidge noted: 'PM the People employed from both ships as in the morning cutting thro' the Ice ahead of the *Racehorse*; found it answered no purpose, as we did not advance above 2 or 3 Ships length thro the Ice the whole day and the Ships still drifting to the Eastward, some of the Ice we cut thro was eight feet thick.' As cutting through 8ft (2.4m) of ice would be exhausting and needed high levels of energy, meals provided were prepared with a very high calorific content by using fats such as suet, and with the issues of butter and cheese being increased.

Thursday 5 August
Amid the pervading fog Phipps needed to get a better idea of their position and wrote in *Racehorse*'s journal: 'PM Sent two Pilots and

two men over the Ice to Island N°3.[4] to look for an opening, at 6 it being inclinable to fog made the Signal for the Pilots to return which they did at 7 o'clock without having seen any opening. At 8 & 9 AM Sounded 27 to 32 f^m. Muddy Ground. At Noon Table Island bore NbW.'

In *Carcass*, Lutwidge routinely recorded the bearings of the surrounding islands and the weather in his journal entry, then wrote: 'at 8 AM sounded 27 fathoms [162ft/49m] oazy [sic] ground, at 9 am saw Table Island thro' the Fog bearing N15°W, the Ships still drifting to the Eastward. AM kill'd three bears upon the Ice from the Ship.' This fact is fully verified by the entry in *Carcass*'s master's log, which states: 'At 11 AM 3 Large Bears, the Dam[e] & 2 Whelps, Do. Shot them all three & skinned them found the large Bear 6 feet 9 Inches from snout to tale [sic].'[5] Whether this occurrence relates to Nelson's encounter with a polar bear is not clear but the timing of 11am doesn't seem to fit.

Friday 6 August

The latter part of Friday was 'Calm & foggy with Rain'. Phipps remarked that they found the ship driving to the westward. His next comment revealed a far more alarming situation: 'At half past 1 the Ice forced the *Carcass* on board us & carried away her Bumkin which obliged us to heave on our Hawsers. At 5 AM the ship drifted to the Eastward.' The bumkin, or boomkin, is a stout spar projecting beyond the ship's head that extended the position from which the fore course tacks were operated. Two were fitted: one larboard, one starboard. Although it is unclear which boomkin was damaged, this did effectively disable the proper operation of the fore course tacks, but taking into account the fact that the ship was not actually under sail at the time, this hardly mattered. It was not beyond the ability of the boatswain to rig the standing part of the tack block to the related side cathead as a temporary arrangement until the carpenter could later effect repairs to the broken boomkin using a spare yard or timber.

Although Lutwidge omits to mention the damaged bumkin, his journal does record that he: 'sent one of the Pilots to the West Island to view the Ice, and see how far distant the open water was from the Ships, at 7 PM observed the Ice open a little, but soon closed again.' He then again recorded the bearings: 'Table Island bore

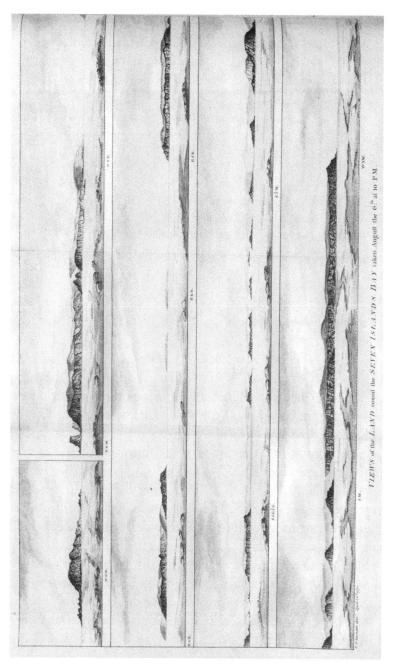

Views of the Seven Islands taken on 6 August 1773. Table Island is shown left in the second view (directed NNW). From Phipp's book, NMRN.

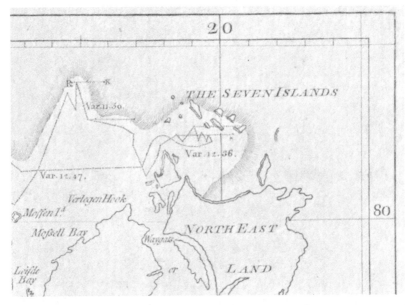

Chart showing the position of the Seven Islands. From Phipp's book, NMRN.

N 26° :00′W, West Island N60°W, Black Point S 88°W, East Island N60°E.' The resultant triangulation of these points provided a reference to compare how much they were drifting easterly. Soundings taken reveal a depth of 25 fathoms [150ft/46m] and Lutwidge closed his log report stating: 'the Ships still drifting with the Ice to the Eastward and a little to the N°ward.'

Even though the direction of drift was somewhat in the direction of their intended destination, being icebound made this both impossible and dangerous; travelling locked in the drifting ice would take months as winter set in.

Despite using ice saws and warping the ships, both vessels were drifting with the ice. Realising the gravity of their situation, Phipps called for Lutwidge to join him aboard the *Racehorse* where they would have discussed contingency plans. Continuously drifting north-easterly towards the Arctic wastes above Russia and Novaya Zemlya, and with the season closing towards winter, whatever decision they jointly concluded must have weighed heavily on both commanders. Faced with no choice, they agreed to abandon the ships and save the men. The fact that the lives of their men were considered to be of greater importance than the expedition objectives says much about the personal qualities of Phipps and Lutwidge.

Although the ships carried bricks, mortar and timber for building shelters, a long winter with insufficient provisions was not ideal. Midshipman Floyd summarised their situation: 'to avoid the melancholy prospect of wintering in such an inclement region Captain Phipps gave orders for immediate service, having previously summoned all officers to his presence and informed them of his probable intention of abandoning both ships.' He added: 'The hopes however, of effecting their release were not abandoned, nor did they intend relinquishing them until all other means of retreat were cut off, but the preparations for equipping the boats we carried out with great alacrity.'[6]

Saturday 7 August

This day saw much activity by everyone involved in both ships. Whether or not Phipps and Lutwidge addressed their ship's companies to explain their proposed course of action is uncertain, but under the circumstances it seems likely that they did so to gain the

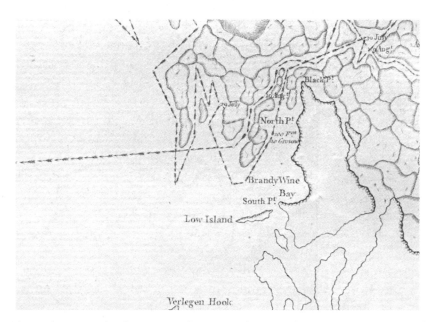

Chart showing the location where *Racehorse* and *Carcass* were trapped in the ice on 30 July and the course taken out reaching Black Point on 10 August. From Phipp's book, NMRN.

trust of the crews. If this were the case then you can picture the scene – upon hearing the shrill boatswain's call piercing the still of the Arctic and the shouts calling 'all hands, all hands', the ship's companies would have mustered on the deck of each ship, clad in an array of winter garments under the sky grey with thick fog. As each commander began addressing his men, perhaps the men's expressions shifted from anxiety and disappointment of failure to hope. Snow and sleet may have begun to fall on the silent standing seamen as the various courses of action were revealed and, once dismissed by their commanders, it's likely that the ships' crews would have promptly set about their business with renewed enthusiasm.

In the *Racehorse* the boatswain, Jonathan Stamford, and his mates would have begun barking various orders to hoist out the boats, as would John Cunningham, boatswain in the *Carcass*. Carpenters would have discussed with their crew what tools, timber and materials were required, while the sailmaker, Tom Spence, would also have gone below to rummage through his stores and gather canvas and twine. Watching over all would be the ship's masters, John Crane in *Racehorse* and James Allen in *Carcass*, the lieutenants busy rallying their men. Somewhere amid this orderly state of urgency, young Nelson would have been busy fulfilling his own tasks preparing the boats.

Racehorse's journal of that day begins: 'The Ship driving with the Ice to the NE, and the ice quite close around us as far as we could see. PM hoisted out our Boats and begun to raise them with light Stantions Tarpaulins and converting our new Canvas into Bread Bags sufficient to contain from 30 to 35 Pounds.' Although hoisting out the boats was a well-rehearsed seamanship evolution, like most naval vessels before c. 1790, the *Racehorse* and *Carcass* did not have davits (fixed cranes) to make this easier.[7] As many of the Greenland whaling ships had been using davits from the early 1600s to enable the speedy launch of their whale-catching boats, it is unfortunate that this feature came so late to men-of-war.[8]

Hoisting out the ship's boats involved using double purchase tackles (one single and one double block) stropped to each of the yard arms of the main and fore course yards, which served as the cranes. From images reproduced by Midshipman d'Auvergne and later enhanced by artist John Cleverley, the boats appear to have been disembarked on the starboard side. In this case the procedure would have been as follows: first the lift tackles of the main and fore course yards were adjusted and secured, ensuring the respective yards were fixed horizontally. Next, the lower block of each yard arm tackle was lowered to deck level; those rigged to larboard (port side) were hooked into eyebolts fitted in the fore or main channel (respective to the yard). Once hauled taut and secured, the related yard was prevented from tilting when coming under load. Next, the lower block of the starboard fore course yard was hooked into the fore-most boat-lifting eyebolt; the starboard main course yard tackle was similarly hooked to the aftermost lifting eyebolt. This all done, tackle rigged to the fore and main mast head burton pendants were hooked into the boat lifting eyebolts – these two tackles provided vertical lift. The boat was then lifted vertically, maintaining a horizontal attitude. Once clear of obstructions the boat was swung out by means of the fore and main course yards, their angles being controlled by the yard braces. Almost simultaneously the yard tackles and vertical lifting tackles were hauled and eased as appropriate as the yards were braced round, swinging out the boat. The yards were then braced square, and with the boat now hanging clear of the ship's side the larboard standing yard tackles were further hauled taut to compensate for the imminent transfer of load. Simultaneously, the yard tackles and vertical lifting tackles were eased, lowering the boat down (usually into the water) but in this case on to the ice, the boat being steadied afore and abaft by the seamen on the ice manhandling the boat's painters (long, loose ropes fixed ahead and astern of the boat). Once steady on the ice, the pairs of yard arm tackles and vertical lifting tackles were unhooked, being hoisted ready for the next boat to be disembarked. Having been lowered over the side, the men on the ice hauled the boat clear of the ship, ready to fulfil its next role.

Understandably, given the involved procedure described above, the introduction of davits into men-of-war proved an invaluable time-saving asset. And because davits gave the ability to launch a boat while the ship was under way, the idea of using boats as a life-saving facility quickly became apparent. It thus became possible to swiftly retrieve men who had fallen accidentally overboard, a change that was fully endorsed within the Royal Navy for morale reasons above all.

Phipps's statement about raising the boats 'with light Stantions' reveals that the carpenter and his crew had constructed a form of

Men on board *Racehorse* getting the ship's boats out on to the ice. Detail from Plate 19.

cradle with sled–like runners to enable the boats to be hauled over the ice with a degree of ease. Logical and practical, Phipps's idea for hauling boats over ice certainly pre-dates similar methods adopted many years later by polar expedition leaders John Franklin in 1847 and Ernest Shackleton in 1916.

While all this was progressing, Phipps wrote: 'At 6 sent a Man with a Lead and Line to the Northward of the ship, as did the *Carcass* to the Eastward; they sounded wherever they could find a crack in the Ice; at half a Mile distance from the Ships, they had from 16 to 14 ^{fms} Rocky Ground. The Ice setting very fast to the NE. AM employed fitting the Boats and making Bread Bags & filling them with Bread, At Noon the Officers & 40 men hauling the Launch over the Ice. Sounded from 14 to 27 ^{fms.}'

On *Carcass*, Lutwidge recorded: 'thick fogs, the Pilot who went to the West Island found the nearest open water was at the West (or Black) point, above 5 leagues distant from the Ships. PM hoisted the Boats out upon the Ice, the People employed in fitting them, making and filling small Bags with Bread, dressing Provisions &c. to carry with the Boats over the Ice; Cap^{tn.} Phipps being resolved to endeavor to save the People, by pushing over to Hackluit's

Men on board *Carcass* bringing boats down on to the ice. Detail from
Plate 19.

headland, and getting on board the Dutch Ships before they left
that part of Spitzbergen.'

Later he noted: 'AM Employed as before, found the Ship still drifting to the Eastward with the body of Ice which enclosed them, one
piece pressing upon another, and rising in heaps all around them,
occasioned, undoubted-ly by the Westerly Winds driving it on to
the Eastward, where it was stop'd by the Islands and the fix'd frozen
Sea behind; at Noon moved the Launches a little to the Westward to
try how they wou'd hawl over the Ice, intending to quit the Ships as
soon as we got them along a few miles towards the open water, unless
the Ice open'd in the mean time, there appeared no probability of
the Ships getting out this Year, as the Season was so far advanced, and
if we attempted wintering, it would be impossible to prevent their
being crushed by the Ice, as they were so great a distance from the
Land, soundings at Noon 14 fathoms [84ft/26m], and the Ships still
drifting (by the Seas) to the Eastward, thick foggy Wea^r.'

Lutwidge's journal account puts their predicament firmly
into perspective: great chunks of the ice continuously piling up
about the ships is quite unimaginable, especially given the inter-
minable cracking and grinding noise that they would generate.

A fiddler sits in the stern sheets playing to keep up the men's spirits as they begin hauling the boats over the ice. Detail from Plate 20.

Cleverley's illustrations worked up from d'Avergne's sketches fail to generate the visual reality of the situation, whereas an unrelated oil painting, *Wreck in the Sea of Ice* painted by the German romantic artist Caspar David Friedrich in 1798 more effectively captures the scenario described by Lutwidge (see Plate 23).

Although John Cleverley captured the entrapped ships and the men hauling the boats on the ice, he fails to account for the fact that rather than wearing the standard sailors' clothing in which they are depicted, the men would have been far more suitably dressed to meet the weather conditions, such as snow and sleet. Also shown is one man in the sternsheets (seats) of a boat playing a fiddle to maintain morale as the men hauled the boats along.

Sunday 8 August
In *Racehorse's* journal Phipps records: 'At 1 PM the People return'd from the Launch. Cut up a Studding Sail to make belts for the Men to drag the Boats over the Ice with.' This suggests that having met some difficulties, another method of hauling was now required. Now furnished with the belts, 'At 3 the Officers and a party of Men went again to haul the Launch along the Ice'. The weight being

hauled must have been considerable; a wooden boat of some 23ft (7m) in length weighed about 2½ tons (5,600lb/2,540kg) even without stocks of provisions.[9]

Conscious of superfluous weight restrictions that had been imposed, Floyd wrote that 'Every man now took care of himself. Each was furnished with a musket and cartouche box and a bag of bread of 30lbs [1.5kg]. Part of the orders from the Commodore [Phipps] were, that no man should carry with him any more clothes than what was on his back, or anything else except his bread and ammunition.' However, Floyd, it appears, himself ignored this directive: 'I therefore went down [below deck] and put on me, two shirts, two waistcoats, two pairs of breeches, four pair of stockings, a large pair of boots, a hat, and stuck a pistol which I had into a canvas belt, which latter at the same time served to keep from falling the few sheets of my journal I had written on the progress of our voyage. The belt was to fasten to the rope to assist dragging a boat.' He then wrote: 'I likewise put in my pocket, a comb, a razor, a pocketbook full of letters, and some pistol shot, also a red woollen cap which I put under my hat, and, thus prepared, I laid myself down about eleven o'clock at night on the deck, and full of thought, fell fast asleep.'[10] That he packed a razor seems odd in the situation but perhaps it was a precious keepsake.

Recording Sunday's events in the *Carcass*'s log, Lutwidge wrote: 'First part light airs and foggy, middle Fresh Breezes and foggy, latter part calm and hazy with fogs, ½ past Noon finding the Ice slack a little the *Racehorse* set her sails endeavouring to press thro' it, the *Carcass* still fast astern of her; at 3 PM the People returned from getting the launches along to the Westward, at 6 both Ships stop'd again by the Ice having got a little way thro' it. At 8 PM hazy saw the Land, Table Island NW¾W, West Island NWbW (Black) Point W¼N, At 4 AM found the Ice press hard upon the Ship, at 11 sent the 2nd and 3rd Lieutenants with 50 men to hawl the Launch over the Ice to the Westward, at Noon found the Ice opening a little, and the Ships moving with it about a mile an Hour to the Westward.' Lutwidge again took bearings of the islands to determine position and distance.

At this point it appears that a fortuitous turn in the weather changed their circumstances; the wind veering round to the NNE suddenly increased in velocity, which had a profound effect upon the ice. Instead of further piling upon itself and entombing the ships, the ice miraculously began to break up. Woken by a great noise, Midshipman Floyd thought everyone had quit the ship and he'd been forgotten. Describing the event, he wrote in his journal: 'I ran up and found everybody hard at work setting the sails, for the wind had shifted in our favour. The fog had cleared up and we perceived by the land that the current had been setting very hard in our favour and it was indeed the greatest work of Providence I had ever seen, to observe how far we had left the rocks, and likewise to see that heavy ocean of ice, of yesterday, everywhere cracking in so short a time. I instantly, as did everybody else, threw off my musket, cartouche box and bread, &c., and lent a willing hand to all that was doing.' As if distracted, he then wrote: 'I cannot help remarking here that the Bruins [bears], whilst we were in our sad condition, came unmolested to our ship, when at another time we should have pursued them with our usual eagerness far surpassing, I am sure, any English fox-hunt.'[11]

Monday 9 August
Racehorse's log for this day records: 'PM hauling the Launch over the Ice. At 3 the Ice opening a little, kept all the Sails set to force the Ship through it; at 7 returned from the Launch to the ship, when we found that she had drove very much to the Westward, and the Ice parting we were employ'd setting the loose pieces from her Bows as the large fields opened.' The fact that they returned to the ship at 7pm implies that the men were given a hearty meal to restore them after their efforts. The journal continues: 'At 9 hoisted in the 6 & 4 Oar'd Boats. At 12 PM [midnight] Fresh Gales with Snow & Sleet. At 1 AM sent a party of Men to bring on board the large Cutter, at 3 hoisted her in. At 4 forcing through the Ice. At 6 the Ice closing upon us we carried out the Ice Hooks & clear'd the Decks [presumably of ice and snow]. At 7 the Ice opened again to the Westward. At 8 cutting the Ice before the Bows and warping as the Ice opened. At 11 the Fog cleared a little when we saw the Launch bearing W½N 1 Mile. At Noon Foggy. Employed forcing the Ship through the Ice as the large fields separated.' Phipps's comments 'we were employ'd setting the loose pieces from her Bows' and 'we carried out the Ice Hooks' show that he was out on the ice leading his men from the front. This leading by example, portrayed in a

painting of Phipps held in the National Portrait Gallery, London[12] (see Plate 12), exemplifies the leadership qualities of this man.

On *Carcass*, Lutwidge reported: 'Light Breezes and foggy. PM forcing the Ships thro' the Ice, at 6 PM the party return'd from the Launches which they had hawled over the Ice 3 or 4 Miles to the Westward, at 8 PM cast loose from the *Racehorse* and set the sails to follow her, at 9 PM sounded 25 fathoms [150ft/46m] and found the Ships drifting with the Ice to the Westward, at 4AM launches ahead thro' the fog bearing WSW, employed in warping thro' the Ice, which was close and heavy, but we found the Ships moving along with it to the Westward.'

Tuesday 10 August

Racehorse's journal records the weather as little wind, foggy with snow and sleet, the men busy warping the ship through the ice. Then 'at 4 the Ice closing, carried out the Hooks & Hawsers to steady the ship'. This suggests that the ship was subjected to some rolling movement, indicating an appreciable flow of water below. Taking advantage of the sudden water current, the log then records that 'At 6 the Ice opening we again warped her through it. At 9 sent an Officer & 25 Men from each ship to bring back the Launches over the Ice to the Ships.' Were they at last free? With 25 men allocated to hauling one boat apiece, each man had a pulling load of approximately 224lb (102kg).

Phipps continues: 'At 3 AM hoisted the Launch up alongside, and the Ice closing again we carried the Hooks out to steady the Ship & furled the Sails.' The hooks he mentions were the ice hooks that they had used previously. Then 'At 7 the Ice opening we loosed the Sails. At 8 saw the Land bearing S10°W. At 8 there being Islands on our Bows, we carried the Hooks out astern to hang the Ship by till they [the ships] separated; at ½ past 9 we got between them & kept the Ship's head in a small opening to the SW.' The action of 'hanging the ship round' by means of an ice anchor is similar to the accepted seamanship manoeuvre known as 'club hauling', which uses the ship's anchor to snag and cause the ship's momentum to swing the ship around faster. In this case, an ice hook rather than an anchor was used – essentially a nautical handbrake turn.

Half an hour later the wind suddenly picked up. Much relieved, Phipps happily wrote: 'At 10 Fresh Gales & hazy, we made all the Sail we could to force her through it, often very hard against the Ice; at 11 we struck an Island of Ice [iceberg] with the Starboard Bow & the lower part of the Best Bower Anchor Stock taking the Ice, broke the Shank of the Anchor close to the Stock, at Noon Fresh Gales and Squally, Running through the Ice, the openings very narrow we very often struck hard against the loose pieces.'

Remarking on this occurrence, Midshipman Floyd noted that 'there was so little room between the two fields of ice between which, as the clearest passage, we must pass, that a large lump of ice caught our anchor on the starboard side, whose circumference was twenty inches of solid iron, and snapped it without stopping the ship in the least'.[13] Writing of the event in his later book, Phipps remarks: 'She struck very hard, and with one stroke broke the shank of our best bower anchor.'[14] Given that the circumference of the wrought-iron anchor was 20in (51cm), the anchor shank being about 6½in (165cm) thick, the forces required to shear wrought iron of this nature would have been considerable – well in excess of 400 Newtons.[15]

The fact that the *Racehorse* continually 'struck hard against the loose pieces' of ice and the velocity of the ship's head slamming into the unforgiving ice would have generated a kinetic force that reverberated through the ship's hull by virtue of her longitudinal keel and keelson. As remarked upon by Midshipman Floyd earlier, these ice collisions jarred the men as they stood, some being unwittingly thrown to the deck. Below decks, the ship's timbers groaned under the sporadic impact; the fact that the ship's bows survived this punishment is testament to the effectiveness of the modifications made by the dockyard shipwright when turning the ship into an icebreaker.

In the *Carcass*, Lutwidge recorded: 'First part calm with light breezes and fogs, middle part light airs with much snow, latter Fresh Breezes and hazey with snow. ½ past Noon saw Table Island bearing N31°E, North Island NNE½E, Black point 55°W; at 9 PM sent 25 men with an Officer to bring the Launch on board, as we found the Ships getting fast to Westward, at 1 AM got the Launch alongside, at Noon the Ice opening very much, and the Ships getting fast along to the Westward.'

With both ships now comparatively free, the crewmen in both ships must have felt elated, especially as they were now relieved from enduring a gruelling and uncertain open boat voyage in icy seas, shrouded in chilling fog, sleet and snow.

Racehorse forcing through the ice on 10 August 1773. From Phipp's book, NMRN.

Wednesday 11 August

Opening his log entry, Phipps wrote: 'Fresh Gales and Squally with Snow. PM Steering through the openings of the Ice. At ½ Past 12 got amongst the loose Ice. At 4 the Westermost of the Seven Islands N41°E 6 Leagues. The Southernmost point of Brandy Bay S31°E 7 Miles. The *Carcass* 3 miles astern.' That they had closed some 25 miles (40km) towards Brandy Bay meant they were making good progress. The log continues: 'At 4 close to the main body of the Ice and a great deal of loose Ice all round us. At ½ past 9 haul'd our wind to make the Ice, At ½ past 11 bore away being near the body of the Ice which bore from N to NW. At 3 AM saw a Ship in the SW Qu^r·

[quarter] At 6 Cloven Cliff S½W 5 or 6 Leagues and Hacluits [sic] head land SWbS.' This sighting was observed 11 hours after being off the 'Westermost of the Seven Islands' and implies that they had covered 120 nautical miles (138 miles/222km), and were making a speed of some 11 knots. Closing his journal entry, Phipps added, 'At Noon haul'd our wind in Shore.' Bringing the ship's helm up, the *Racehorse* hauled a point closer to windward to head landward.

In the *Carcass*'s journal, Lutwidge recorded that they were: 'sailing amongst the loose ice to the Westward, ½ past 1 set Steeringsails, being in open water, ½ past 2 Black point E¾N ab^t [about] 3 lea^s [leagues] at 4 East point of Brandy Bay SE, East side of Wygatt's streights 6°W ab^t 9 lea^s, at 12 saw the Main body of Ice from West to NNW, at 1AM saw a sail in the SW; at 8 AM Westermost land in sight SW 7 or 8 lea^s at 10 abreast of Cloven Cliff bearing ESE 2 or 3 lea^s at 11 down Steering sails, and hoisted in the Launch which had been hung in the Tackles and lashed alongside.' The fact that they had not swayed the launch up and inboard beforehand implies that once the ice was found to be breaking up around the ship they concentrated on setting sails to get the ship moving. Perhaps overlooked when they were getting the ship under sail, leaving the launch lashed alongside under tow had left the boat vulnerable to damage from loose ice. Lutwidge then checked his chronometer, entering into his log: '½ past 4 PM T.K. 2H 49′ 11″ slow'.

Now sailing freely towards the safe haven of Smeerenburg, it must have seemed almost incredible that just a few days ago the ships were still completely beset by ice. Worse still, they had been drifting uncontrollably eastwards into the Arctic wastes of the Barents Sea, the remote archipelago of Franz Joseph Land, the island of Novaya Zemlya and the Kara Sea above and beyond known Russia. Or, they might have attempted the long passage in two open boats with limited provisions and water while endeavouring to keep dry and warm. Whether anyone in England, be it Joseph Banks, Nevil Maskelyne, Nelson's father Edmund or his uncle Maurice Suckling, paused to think about what was happening upon the Royal Navy's first polar expedition we do not know. At a time when any form of news was limited, people simply waited, any doubts and concerns being suppressed until the expected arrival or outcome was well overdue. Aboard the *Racehorse* and the *Carcass* their respective masters and boatswains busily began preparations to anchor. As for young Nelson, the recent experiences and possibility of death must have proved frightening at times for a boy little more than 14½ years of age and, from what we understand, he appears to have disliked the venture. His experience emphasises why it was stipulated that boys were not really wanted on this expedition.

Nelson, walruses, and the incident of the polar bear: myth or reality?

While *Racehorse* and *Carcass* were trapped in the ice, two incidents occurred involving Midshipman Horatio Nelson and some of the region's native animals. In the first encounter, with walruses, it seems that boats from both the *Racehorse* and the *Carcass* were sent off to explore a passage into open water to try to escape their icebound dilemma. Nelson, as coxswain, commanded the cutter from the *Carcass*. In his book, Phipps writes that *Racehorse*'s boat was then used for hunting: 'Having little wind and the weather very clear two of the officers went with a boat in pursuit of some sea-horses [walruses], and afterwards to the low island.'[16]

This hunting expedition soon went wrong, Phipps noting: 'At six in the morning the officers returned; in their way back they fired at, and wounded a seahorse, which dived immediately, and bought up with it a number of others. They all joined in an attack upon the boat, wrested an oar from one of the men, and were with difficulty prevented from staving or oversetting her [the boat]; but a boat from the *Carcass* joining ours they [the walruses] dispersed.'[17] Coming to the rescue in the *Carcass*'s boat was young Nelson. The first Nelson biographer to discuss the incident is Robert Southey, who used Phipps's wording verbatim to describe the incident in his *The Life of Horatio Lord Nelson* (first published in 1813), which indicates that he used Phipps's publication as a source. It is clear that had it not been for Nelson coming to the rescue in the *Carcass*'s boat, this already dangerous situation would perhaps have had far graver consequences; should any man have fallen overboard into the icy waters, he would have died within minutes.

It was this possible outcome that prompted Phipps to record in an appendix to his book the following observation about walruses: 'It is a gregarious animal though not inclined to attack, but dangerous if attacked as the whole herd join forces to revenge any injury received by an individual.'[18]

Of the various Nelson biographers who followed Southey, only Tom Pocock's *Nelson* refers to the walrus incident, this version surmising that the boat in distress was from the *Carcass* and not the *Racehorse* as Phipps declared. With regard to the ship's journals, although reference is made to sending out the boats, there is no mention of the walrus attack and therefore, without formal corroboration, we have to accept that the story only came to light when Phipps published his work in 1774. Nelson himself is not personally mentioned in Phipps's tale, so it appears that Nelson's personal involvement is attributed to Southey's inference that Nelson was in charge of the *Carcass* cutter, which is indeed highly likely.

The story of Nelson's encounter with a second animal, a polar bear, seems to originate from two sources. The first is the famous painting, *Nelson and the Bear*, by the artist Richard Westall, which depicts a young Horatio Nelson standing upon ice floes and attacking a polar bear using the butt of his musket. Born in Norfolk in 1765, Westall was an illustrator of portraits, historical and literary events. Best known for his portrait of Lord Byron, he later became Queen Victoria's drawing master. Besides *Nelson and the Bear*, he also painted four other Nelson-related paintings: *Nelson Boarding a Captured Ship* (20 November 1777), *Nelson Receiving the Surrender of the 'San Nicholas'* (14 February 1797), *Nelson in Conflict with a Spanish Launch* (3 July 1797), and *Nelson Wounded at Tenerife* (24 July 1797).[19] Like *Nelson and the Bear*, these paintings portray Nelson as the ultimate *Boy's Own* hero; few other naval officers received this man–of–action treatment. Westall painted these images of Nelson in action at the behest of John M'Arthur and James Stanier Clarke as illustrative plates for their 1810 biography *The Life of Admiral Lord Nelson, K.B.*

The painting of Nelson and the polar bear, however, is a reconstruction based on conjecture, rather than fact. Nelson had been dead almost a year when Westall first put brush to canvas, so somebody must have told him the story. But who was it? The only person who appears to corroborate the story was the commanding officer of the *Carcass*, Skeffington Lutwidge. This alone gives some credence to the alleged encounter but it also raises the question: did Westall and Lutwidge ever meet? Or did Westall receive the story second-hand? We do not know. Furthermore, how much had Lutwidge embellished his original anecdote or had this been done by others? Nothing directly concerning Nelson's encounter with the bear is recorded in the captain's and master's journals of the *Carcass* although other polar bear sightings are described.

If we ignore Lutwidge and the evidence of the *Racehorse* and *Carcass* journals, our familiarity with the story stems primarily from Nelson biographers, first appearing in Clarke and M'Arthur's *The Life of Horatio Lord Nelson, K.B.* The account given here reads as follows:

'there is an anecdote recollected by Admiral Lutwidge, which marked the filial attention of his gallant coxswain. Among the gentlemen on the quarterdeck of the *Carcass*, who were not rated midshipmen, there was besides young Nelson, a daring shipmate of his to whom he had become attached. One night, during the mid-watch, it was concerted between them that they should steal together from the ship, and endeavour to obtain a bear's skin. The clearness of the nights in those high latitudes rendered the accomplishment of this object extremely difficult: they however seem to have taken advantage of the haze of an approaching fog, and thus escaped unnoticed. Nelson in high spirits led the way over the frightful chasms in the ice armed with a rusty musket. It was not however long before the adventurers were missed by those on board; and as the fog came on very thick, the anxiety of Captain Lutwidge and his officers was very great. Between three and four in the morning the mist somewhat dispersed, and the two hunters were discovered at considerable distance, attacking a large bear. The signal was instantly made for their return; but it was in vain that Nelson's companion urged him to obey it. He was at the time divided by a chasm in the ice from his shaggy antagonist, which probably saved his life; for the musket had flashed in the pan, and their ammunition was expended. *Never mind* exclaimed Horatio *but let me get a blow at this devil with the butt end of my musket and we shall have him.* His companion finding that entreaty was in vain regained the ship. The Captain seeing the young man's danger ordered a gun to be fired "to terrify the enraged animal": This had the desired effect, but Nelson was obliged to return without his bear, somewhat agitated with the apprehension of the consequence of this adventure. Captain Lutwidge, though he could not but admire so daring a disposition, remanded him rather sternly for such rashness, and for conduct so unworthy of the situation he occupied. Being considered by his Captain to have acted in a manner unworthy of his situation, made a deep impression on the high-minded coxswain; who, habitually pouted his lips when agitated, replied, "*Sir I wished to kill the bear that I might carry its skin to my Father*".[20]

Robert Southey's biography cites the above almost verbatim with a few words and the grammar modified for a later audience.[21] Unlike Clarke and M'Arthur, however, Southey does not mention that Nelson's musket was rusty but simply that: 'his musket flashed in the pan' – ie that the weapon misfired. This difference in narrative raises the question: why would Lutwidge suggest that the musket was rusty? Was it an embellishment to expand the story or a ruse to cover something else? The condition of the weapon might raise other questions, let alone how Nelson acquired it and the ammunition so easily from its rightful custodian, the ship's armourer, Josiah Merlein; no armourer worth his salt would allow rusty weaponry. Regarding the misfire, the 'flash in the pan', common with flintlock weapons, it is possible that Nelson may have panicked and either failed to prime the weapon properly or did not fully cock the weapon in the excitement of the moment. Using a musket butt as a club was common practice in battle when such weapons failed to operate or there was insufficient time to reload. In addition, the wooden stock of Nelson's gun might have swollen with damp, rendering the trigger mechanism temporarily useless. Infantry troops engaged on the field at Waterloo suffered this problem after heavy rain before the battle.

Successive Nelson biographers – Carola Oman in *Nelson* (1967), Tom Pocock in *Nelson* (1987) and Christopher Hibbert in *Nelson: A Personal History* (1994) – each repeat the story in a similar fashion, with Clarke and M'Arthur's biography as the sole source of evidence. Oman, however, does also observe that 'In after years Admiral Lutwidge told the bear story with good humour, and Lord Nelson's brother-in-law entered it in a privately printed memoir desired to amuse nieces and nephews of the hero'.[22] Although Oman provides no source for this information, it suggests that Lutwidge was the prime foundation of the story – and the same source used by Clarke and M'Arthur, although the title of their work included the subtitle: *From his Lordship's Manuscripts.*

While we have no date for the polar bear incident, it is most probable that it occurred when the two ships were trapped in the ice and measures were being taken to prepare the boats to get to safety. It is likely that it was this activity that enticed the inquisitive polar bear in the first place – the men on the ice being the bear's next potential meal. Why the incident is omitted from the *Carcass's* journals is obvious: according to the logbook entries, Lutwidge and the ship's master were too preoccupied with preparing and provisioning the boats. The fact that two immature midshipmen foolishly endangered themselves was of little importance to the wider picture the journal was recording. Furthermore, given that all journals would be scrutinised by the Admiralty, should the ships return home safely, any hint of the incident might have raised embarrassing questions about Lutwidge's leadership.

So, since we have no formal evidence to support the legend of Nelson and the polar bear, we can only accept that it did happen on the strength of what Lutwidge later wrote, including his noting of Nelson's excuse that he was trying to obtain a bearskin for his father. While Nelson was appropriately reprimanded by his commander for his foolhardiness, Lutwidge would have taken into account Nelson's quick initiative in saving the boat's crew from the walrus attack. Perhaps most puzzling is why the name of Nelson's fellow miscreant is absent from the story. In all probability, this fellow was 18-year-old Midshipman Robert Hughes, who had befriended Nelson. Five years older than Nelson, his maturity perhaps made Nelson back off from the bear. The other intriguing question is: who came up with the idea of going off hunting bears, Nelson or Hughes? Unless further evidence comes to light, we will simply never know.

13

Respite at Smeerenburg

Having been delayed by their ordeal in the ice, Phipps needed to consolidate his situation and decided that the whaling station of Smeerenburg was the best place in which to resolve matters. By now, both ship's commanders understood that the sea conditions and quantity of ice were far too unfavourable to continue sailing further north. Phipps was also aware that he and the astronomer, Israel Lyons, still needed to gather as much scientific information as possible before sailing home and, with the winter season setting in, time was now against them.

Although Smeerenburg offered a sanctuary in which to over-winter and perhaps build shelters, it was not ideal. For the majority of the winter the site was abandoned by the whaling people and, despite having provisioned for six months, they had concerns that the on-board food stocks were somewhat diminished. They also needed to prepare to overhaul the ships before departing the Arctic regions.

Thursday 12 August
Amid fresh breezes with snow, the two ships slowly made their approach into the safe harbour of Smeerenburg. *Racehorse*'s log recorded: 'At ½ past 1 PM; Came too [sic] with the Best Bower in 13 ᶠᵐ· on the North Bank as did the *Carcass* and veered to ½ a Cable. The outer part of Amsterdam Island N7° 30′ E 3 Miles, and the small Island near Vogle [sic] Sound N49° E distance 6 or 7 Miles.'

Now at anchor, this was an ideal opportunity to rest the men after their earlier ordeal and cover some of the scientific research they were charged with. Phipps wasted no time and 'Sent the Boat with an Officer to look out for a level spot to fix the Astronomical

Instruments'. While the boat steadily pulled away inshore, Phipps ordered his boatswain, Jonathan Stamford, to reinstate his vessel's ground tackle because the shank of *Racehorse*'s bower anchor had been damaged by an iceberg.[1] Stamford gathered his seamen and 'Bent the Best Bower Cable to the Sheet Anchor & shifted [exchanged] it for a Best Bower'. This involved two evolutions: transferring the cable to run out through the starboard hawse hole and then hitching it to the spare sheet anchor ready rigged in its stowage abaft the fore chains.[2]

According to Lutwidge's journal, the *Carcass* anchored in 10 fathoms (60ft/18m) of water but, with a turn of the tide, both ships then needed to moor closer inshore. Phipps records: 'At 7 weighed as did the *Carcass*, at 8 Anchored in Smeeremberg Harbour with the Best Bower, veered to 2/3 Cable & steadied her [the ship] with the Stream Anchor & hawser.' Although the *Carcass* was riding on her best bower, Lutwidge later 'steadied the Ship with the Kedge Anchor to the S°ward'. Laying out the kedge involved using the ship's boats, and Nelson would have been involved. With this done they 'veered to ½ a Cable'. Because the snowy weather was now accompanied by sleet, the anchor party involved found themselves slithering about on the slushy focsle as they went about their business. As for those out in the exposed boats, the driving sleet must have been miserable.

Friday 13 August
Racehorse's log entry notes that the weather comprised 'Fresh Gales with Snow & Sleet'. Phipps then noted that he had: 'PM Sent the Studding Sail Booms with Spars & Sails on Shore to erect a Tent for the Astronomical Instruments. At 6 AM two of the Dutch Ships sailed to the Southward', presumably home for winter with their cargoes of whale oil. Phipps next wrote about the seamen, who were 'Employed in the after hold & getting the Provisions to hand, Sent the Oven on Shore and fixed it for making Bread'. The reasons for doing this are unclear and it raises two questions: first, why could they not use the galley firehearth on board? Second, can it be assumed that the ship was equipped with a portable oven for use on land or should they be stranded?

In the *Carcass*, Lutwidge recorded the ship's position as: 'At Anchor Smeeremberg point NbE½E about ½ a mile, South Gall N 64°W, Cloven Cliff NE½E 9 or 10 miles.' In the remarks column he wrote: 'PM. The People from the *Racehorse* fixing Tents on shore on Smeeremberg point for the Astronomical Instruments &c.'

Meantime, *Carcass*'s seamen, under the supervision of her boatswain, John Cunningham, 'scraped and tarred the Ship's sides'. Lutwidge also records that they saw two of the Dutch whaling ships set sail 'to the Southward thro' Danes Gutt'. Danes Gutt is a south-lying channel dividing Hakluyt's Headland from Danes Island, Danes Island itself lying due north of Magdalena Bay and Magdalena Hook.

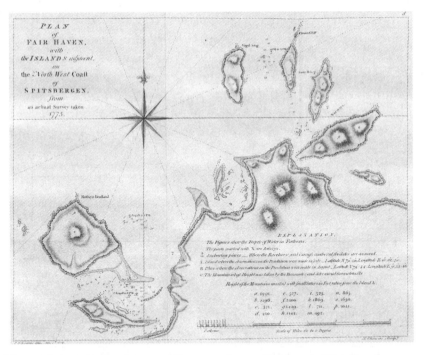

Chart giving the position of Smeerenburg, Hakluyt's Headland and the relative positions of Danes Gutt and Magdalena Bay. From Phipps's book, NMRN.

The Figures show the Depth of Water in Fathoms.

The parts marked with X are icebergs.

[anchor symbol] Anchoring places – Where the Racehorse and Carcass anchored the dates are annexed.

A. Island where the observations on the Pendulum were made in July _ Latitude N79°:50′. Longitude E10°:01′:30″.

B. Place where the observations on the Pendulum were made in August _ Latitude N79°:44′. Longitude E9°:55′:46″.

C. The Mountain whose Height was taken by the Barometer, and determined Geometrically.

Height of the Mountains marked with small letters in Feet, taken from the Island A.

a. 1991	e. 327	i. 325	n. 865
b. 2298	f. 2400	k. 1869	o. 1650
c. 321	g. 1449	l. 711	p. 1041
d. 210	h. 1101	m. 492	

Saturday 14 August

Strong gales, snow and sleet persisted, moderating to clear later. Phipps's log says little: 'At 10 PM veered to a whole Cable. Employed as before Latitude of Smeerenburg point by a reflecting Horizon 78°44′ North.' A reflecting horizon was taken due to visibility problems and required the use of a theodolite, or else a bath of quicksilver (mercury) could be used to create the reflection.

Despite their intentions, neither Phipps nor Israel Lyons could make any real observations until the weather conditions were sufficiently clear. Phipps records that he 'again set up the pendulum but was not so fortunate as before never having been able to get an observation of a revolution of the sun, or any equal altitudes for the time'. They did, however, get an opportunity to determine the refraction at midnight, which 'answered within a few seconds to the calculation in Bradley's table, allowing for the barometer and thermometer'. In sight of Cloven Cliff, Phipps undertook a survey of part of their anchorage of Fairhaven 'to connect it with the plan of the other part'. Meanwhile, Dr Irving trekked up a mountain to measure its height by means of a barometer.[3]

Sunday 15 August
Regardless of the weather, Phipps and Lyons were determined to gather scientific information by undertaking a series of experiments. The 'pendulum' to which Phipps refers was used as part of a geophysical survey to determine two things: the acceleration of gravity at this latitude and any potential time difference.

Possibly assisted by Charles Irving, Lyons and Phipps also set up an instrument known as a dip needle (also called the dip circle or inclinometer), which is used for measuring the inclination, or dip, between the horizon and the earth's magnetic field (dip angle). The apparatus comprises a magnetised iron needle pivoted at the centre of a brass graduated circle, the assembly being mounted so that the needle swings vertically rather than horizontally, as does a compass needle. When the instrument is placed with the plane of the circle

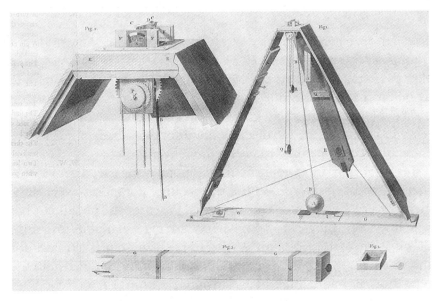

Diagram of the pendulum constructed by George Graham as a means to count individual seconds (it had no minute indicator). See also Chapter 6. From Phipp's book, NMRN.

in the magnetic field vector or meridian of the earth, the needle points in the direction of the earth's magnetic field. When used, the magnetic needle must be accurately balanced so that only magnetic torques are exerted upon it (see Plate 24).

As Lyons and Irving busied themselves with scientific matters, in the *Carcass* the boatswain, John Cunningham, and his men 'stayed the Masts and set up the lower rigging', ready to sail home. Taking observations, Lutwidge recorded: 'Variation by an Azimuth onshore N18°: 30′ W.' The only point recorded by Phipps on Sunday 15 August was 'Latitude of Smeeremberg Point by a reflecting Horizon 79° 44′ North'.

In the *Carcass* that Sunday, her crew 'Blacked the Tops, and Mastheads, and payed the lower masts', the log further stating that Lutwidge 'sent the Longboat to take some bearings and Angles from Hackluit's Island. Alt^{de} L.L. Obs^{d}: 79°:43′N'. This reading matched those calculated by Phipps, who used an alternative observation method. The preservative materials used by *Carcass*'s crew for blacking the mastheads would have been either a mixture of linseed oil or varnish with lamp black (soot), or Stockholm tar thinned with lin(t) seed oil or turpentine. The type used for paying the lower masts was a varnish of rosin or linseed oil.

Phipps used this opportunity to make other observations of the incredible environment in which he and his instruments stood. He noted that some of the most remarkable sights were the large icebergs that filled the valleys between the high mountains, and that where they faced the sea the edge was 'nearly perpendicular with a lively green colour'. What he was describing was what we now call a glacier. A sketch made by Midshipman Philippe d'Auvergne shows that the 'iceberg' was 'about three hundred feet high, with a cascade of water issuing out [of] it'. Further describing the spectacle, Phipps wrote: 'The black mountains, white snow, and beautiful colour of the ice make a very romantick and uncommon picture. Large pieces frequently break off from the icebergs and fall with great noise into the sea: we observed one piece which floated out into the bay, and grounded in twenty-four fathom [144ft/44m]; it was fifty feet [15m] high above the surface of the water, and of the same colour as the Iceberg.'[4]

Monday 16 August
In *Racehorse* the men were 'employed as before', during which time all hands were mustered on deck as Phipps 'Read the Articles of War to The Ship's Company'. As for Lutwidge, he simply recorded: 'Fresh Breezes and hazy, middle part some small rain, Boats employed in watering.'

Tuesday 17 August
Racehorse's journal records: 'PM employed as before. AM the Warrant Officers Airing their Stores and cleaning the Store Rooms out. Loosed Sails to dry', the log entry indicating preparations for sailing. Drying sails involved fully easing off the sheets and partially clewing up the sail and allowing it to hang loosely in its buntlines. In *Carcass's* journal, Lutwidge entered: 'Light Breezes and Cloudy; with Calms. PM sent A Boat round the Ship and to the SW. AM loosed sails to dry, compleated [sic] the watering the Ship, sent a Boat to take some bearings and Angles to the Westward. Ships draught of water {Forward 13^{Ft}: 1". Abaft 12 F^t 7"}.'

Whether or not they completed all the planned scientific experiments is unknown, especially as no record appears to exist about what was intended from the outset. The ship's journals give the impression that due to the enforced delay in the ice, their time for conducting such trials had now become limited. What we do know is that Dr Irving undertook temperature measurements at various depths below sea level, a task for which he created special flasks.

The time available had also become constrained by other factors: winter was setting in, and although the ships carried stores for six months, provisions would be getting short.

Understandably, the ship's logs, being solely for official Admiralty purposes and therefore related to general order', seamanship and navigation, do not account for all the scientific data gathered in the experiments. All information of this nature, jointly gathered by Phipps, Lyons and d'Auvergne, in his capacity as the official expedition recorder, was correlated after the voyage and officially passed to the various scientific bodies including the Royal Society and the community of astronomers working for Nevil Maskelyne at the Royal Observatory in Flamsteed House, Greenwich. Besides

satisfying the academic fraternity, much of this data was also reproduced in tabular form and appendices in Phipps's 1774 account of
the voyage.

If the problems encountered while the ships were trapped in the
ice in the early part of August were not enough to test the endur-
ance of both commanders and their men, the journey home was
equally fraught with difficulties. In his book, Phipps only briefly
gives account of the events that occurred on the return voyage, but
the two ship's logbooks reveal the true gravity of the new situations
they encountered.

Wednesday 18 August

Racehorse's log notes: 'First and middle parts fresh breezes & hazy,
latter fresh Gales & clear. Furl'd Sails', a standard practice undertaken
after drying. Then, 'At 5 the Astronomer went on Shore to take the
Observations for finding the time, the Sun having been hid since
the 15$^{th.}$ The Warrant Officers employed as before, and on taking an
account of their Stores found many articles deficient which were
expended and lost in the Ice.' These apparent losses may not have
been just down to the ice; losses due to neglect were often written
off if suitable circumstances arose.

Thursday 19 August

By now both ships were ready to sail. In his journal Phipps recorded
that they had finished embarking water and that the astronomer,
Lyons, was still 'on shore making Observations for finding the time;
at 8 am Unmoored, and sent the Boat on Shore to bring off the
Instruments with the Tent &c^a. At ½ past 10 weighed and came to
sail as did the *Carcass*. at 11 Calm.'

In the *Carcass*, the men were all on deck at their stations preparing to get the ship under way, one group with the boatswain's
mate, ready manning the capstan, while others with the boatswain
formed the anchor party and heaved out the wooden fish davit to
protrude outboard over the starboard rail while checking its fish
tackle and fish hook were free to run. (A fish davit is a portable
wooden beam employed to hoist and draw up the 'flooks' of the
anchor towards the stern of the ship in order to stow it after it has
been 'catted'.)[5]

Another three men double-checked that the inboard end of the fish davit was well secured in its larboard span shackle, which, bolted to the deck, took the weight of the anchor once 'fished'. Amid this activity, Nelson would have been with his division of seamen, forming part of the after guard, grouped upon the quarterdeck ready to man the ropes and tackles associated with the main and mizzen mast sails.

Lutwidge recorded: 'at 9 AM unmoored as P^r [per] Signal [from Phipps] and hove short, at 10 weighed in company with the *Racehorse*.' With orders given to set her courses and fore-topsail, the *Carcass* slowly began drifting downwind up towards her anchor while the men at the capstan hove in the cable short. Ready at the head of the ship, the focsle party lowered away the cat block and with the shout 'the anchor up and down' (hanging vertical on its cable at the hawse hole), the topsails were fully sheeted home. The resultant momentum caused the ship to jerk the anchor clear of the seabed and the men at the capstan gave a final heave on the cable. Next, one man went over the ship's side and hooked the cat block to the anchor ring, the men manning the cat falls hauling the anchor hard up to the cathead, its shivers squealing as they turned. This done, they next 'fished' the anchor using the fish hook of the fish davit tackle, this being passed around the anchor shank close by the stock. Hauling on the fish tackle falls, the focsle men heaved the anchor up horizontal and 'bowsed' (lashed) it, securing it to the fore channel chains to stow it for sea passage. As the *Carcass* freely got under weigh other sails were set, sheeted home and trimmed by means of their bowlines.

Completing the day's journal entry, Lutwidge next wrote: 'at Noon working out the N°ward.'

Observations recorded in the *Carcass* at midnight that day were: altitude of the sun 2°33´; lat 79°44´N. At 4pm the timekeeper was recorded as 2 hours, 40 minutes and 41 seconds slow. Half an hour later this was 2 hours, 42 minutes and 34 seconds slow; although the timepieces were extremely accurate for this period, their working parts remained subject to temperature and humidity.

Friday 20 August

Due to the unfavourable weather (light airs with rain), Phipps wrote in his log: 'At 2 PM hoisted out a Boat to tow the Ship. At 4 the outer part of Vogle [sic] Sound NEbN and Hacluits head land NWbN 5 Miles. At 12 Hacluits head land SbE 9 Miles. At 4 AM Cloven Cliff SEbE 5 Leagues.'

Saturday 21 August

Although both expedition ships appeared to be making reasonable progress away from Spitsbergen, sea and weather conditions made it hard going. For the first part of the day the ships were sailing under strong gales and squally weather with rain. They were also still encountering drift ice. Phipps wrote: 'Light breezes and cloudy, middle part Strong Gales and Squally.' Although this later turned to light breezes with visibility becoming hazy, his log entry then reads: 'PM Running through a loose stream of Ice. At 3 AM haul'd up WNW the body of the Ice two Cables length from us; At 5 haul'd up again to clear a point of the Ice.' In other words, he luffed the sail, bringing the head of the ship a point or two to weather. He subsequently wrote: 'At 6 bore away to keep along the edge of it.' Finding the need to shorten sail, the log notes: 'At 7 in Top Gal^t. Sails; at 12 in 2^d. Reef Top Gal^t. Sails At 2 AM Tack'd, could not Weather the Ice; at 8 Tack'd & out 2^d. Fore Topsail. At Noon a great swell from the SSW. *Carcass* in Company.'

Meeting similar situations that same day, Lutwidge recorded: 'At 1 PM saw several Fin Fish, at 2 sailed thro' some drift Ice the main body of Ice from SEbE to NEbN, hawl'd to the SW, at 12 in 1st and 2nd reefs.' Like Phipps, Lutwidge had to reef when the wind force turned to gales. His log then states: 'at ½ past 1 AM Tk^d to the Eastward, ½ past 7 Tk^d to the SW, *Racehorse* in Company.' The fin fish to which he refers is probably the cusk or tusk (*Brosme brosme*), a North Atlantic cod-like fish in the ling family Lotidae distinguishable by its long single dorsal fin.

While both ships simultaneously shortened sail by reefing 'at 12', to meet arising wind conditions, the sail configuration was possibly reduced in preparation for tacking to eastward. It was often customary to reduce sail before nightfall to avoid having to shorten sail overnight in darkness should the wind speed unexpectedly increase.

Sunday 22 August

Because the weather had moderated to light winds, visibility deteriorated to fog. Progressing on a course N14°W the ships made little progress, making just 42 miles (78km) that day. Although the ice is recorded as bearing SW to NW some 1½ miles (2.5km) distant, it no longer presented any threat.

Monday 23 August

Although this was the last they saw of any drift ice, general sailing conditions markedly deteriorated as a new weather front came in, Phipps's log recording: 'Fresh Gales and Squally latter part Strong Gales and very thick Weather with Snow.' As visibility worsened the two ships began losing sight of each other, Phipps noting: 'At ½ past 4 PM the *Carcass* fired a Gun which we answered and shortened Sail. At 9 in 2$^{d.}$ Reef Topsails. At 3 AM lost sight of the *Carcass*; made Signals for her; at ¼ past 6 it clearing a little saw the *Carcass* to the NNE 2 or 3 Miles & we shortened Sail. At Noon the *Carcass* in Company.' The *Carcass* was struggling to keep up. Lutwidge's journal records identical weather conditions but adds that they also experienced sleet and 'at 9 PM in 2nd reefs and stood to the SE, *Racehorse* in Company'. Rather oddly, Lutwidge's journal fails to mention firing a gun signal at 4.30pm.

Tuesday 24 August

The wind had considerably eased to light airs and calms, forcing both ships to increase sail. At 9pm the *Racehorse* took out the second reefs of the topsails. At 1am her seamen were again called to go aloft to take 'out all Reefs and set Top Gal^t Sails'. Responding to the increase in sail area, the *Racehorse* began to surge ahead. Similarly acting in response to the change in wind, Lutwidge recorded in his log: 'at 10 PM out 2nd reefs, [and] at 1 AM out 1st reefs, AM bent a new Foresail and the proper Tacks and Sheets. - found by Observation at Noon the ship 13 miles the Southward of her reckoning by the log; corrected by a SSW course, *Racehorse* in Company.'

Observations recorded in *Carcass*'s journal include the altitude of the sun at noon: 24°9´; and the timekeeper at 7.30pm being 2 hours, 29 minutes 35 seconds slow, and one hour later, 2 hours, 39 minutes and 13 seconds slow, the timepiece being affected by barometric pressure change. Lutwidge's log entry raises some interesting points: although the comment referring to bending a 'new Foresail' is itself not unusual, the words appear to imply that they had been using a 'storm foresail' while in the Arctic regions. Setting a shorter storm foresail had the practical advantage of providing greater visibility ahead of the ship in the ice floe conditions. Because this practice was common in whaling ships it can be assumed that the expedition must have been advised to carry this type of sail by whaling people beforehand, or if not by them then certainly by the two ice pilots embarked.[6] The second comment regarding the 'proper Tacks and Sheets' is significant, since it indicates that the associated sheets and tacks of the storm foresail may have been of rope of a lighter and smaller thickness, which, being less prone to build-up of ice derived from sea spray, could be easily shaken to remove ice.

Wednesday 25 August

According to *Racehorse*'s journal, weather conditions changed from calm to 'light breezes with Sleet and Showers of Rain' and then states: 'PM The Ship's head to the Southward and from 9 to 11 D°. from North to West.'

Lutwidge's log entry is more informative: 'P.M. received a Mem° from Capt Phipps (in case of separation) to make the best of my way to the Nore, *Racehorse* in company at Noon.' This directive complied with similar instructions given on the outbound voyage should the ships meet extreme weather. While it appears that the written memorandum was transferred over to the *Carcass,* neither of the ship's journals records boats being lowered to enable this.

Thursday 26 August

Conditions were 'Fresh Gales with rain and thick Wea^r'. Phipps wrote: 'At 6 pm in Top Gal^t Sails; at 7 in 1st & 2nd Reefs of the Topsails, in Spritsail T. S Yard and down Top Gal^t Yards.'[7] The fact that Phipps mentions taking in the spritsail topsail yard confirms that the *Racehorse* was definitely rigged with this sail on her jib boom as opposed to her official spar mast and yard dimension list. Although this feature is omitted in Cleverley's engraving and paintings depicting the earlier events of 7 and 10 August (see pages 201–206 and 209–210), it must have been that d'Auvergne's original sketches erroneously omitted these items. D'Auvergne must have been aboard the *Racehorse* as she and the *Carcass* were 'forcing through the ice' on the 10th, so it follows that the scenes he drew must have been conjectural.

Lutwidge's log entry informs us of 'Fresh Breezes and Cloudy', turning to 'Fresh Gales with Rain and thick Wea^r.' Responding to arising conditions, Lutwidge 'at 7 PM in 2nd reefs and down Topgallan^t yards'. Sending down these yards from all three masts to the deck in each ship was a precautionary measure taken to reduce the top weight and strain on the related topgallant mast rigging, especially as they were expecting the ships to roll heavily in the increasingly turbulent sea state.[8]

Friday 27 August

According to Phipps's log the *Racehorse* was sailing on a course S28°W; her position, lat 72°12′N, long 9°24′W. Her estimated run from Hakluyt's Headland was 151 leagues or 453 nautical miles (521 miles/839km). The journal entry records: 'First part Gales & hazy with Rain, middle moderate & hazy and latter cloudy Weather.' As the wind velocity fell from fresh gales it became very hazy, *Racehorse*'s journal reading: 'at 4 foggy made a [gun] Signal to the *Carcass*, at 7 saw her. At 5 AM Tack'd and out 2nd Reefs of the Topsails. Saw 3 Ships to the Westward. At 10 out 1st Reefs of Main Topsail at Noon found the Ship 11 Miles to the Southward of the Latitude by account.'

The *Carcass* appears to have been sailing under courses and topsails, neither of which were reefed, and the log entry records: 'a great Swell from the SSE, and 5 AM Tk^d to the SE, at 8 saw 3 sail in the SW, standing to the South^{wd} *Racehorse* in company.' The heavy swell made the ships pitch heavily; the lurching decks falling from under their feet would have forced the men to stagger. No doubt safety lines were rigged fore and aft along the upper decks to facilitate movement to and fro with some degree of ease. The three ships seen by both vessels must have been whaling vessels returning home from a season's hunting in the Greenland fishery with their holds filled with a rich harvest of whale oil sealed in barrels. Taking a fix at noon, Lutwidge record the altitude of the sun as L. L. (Lower Limb) 27°14′, relating to the bottom part of the sun's circumference.

Saturday 28 August
Sailing in winds varying from southerly to west by south, the two ships lay on a course S61°W. Lat is logged as 72°9′N, long 10°55′W. Distance run is recorded as 44 miles, giving a speed of just 1.8 nautical miles per hour (2.1mph/3.3km/h). The distance now run from Hakluyt's Headland was estimated as 162 leagues (486 miles or 900km). Progressing steadily in light breezes with fog and rain, Phipps recorded: 'at 3 PM Tacked Ship up Top Gal$^{t.}$ Yards and set the sails.' The *Carcass* in succession 'Tk$^{d.}$ to the Westward'.

Sunday 29 August
The wind still being light, the *Racehorse* 'got the Spritsail Top S$^{l.}$ Yard out'. Phipps appears to have used this square headsail rigged on the jib boom quite frequently as opposed to the square spritsail set on the bowsprit. This suggests that Phipps liked to use the sprit topsail to balance the rig, thus keeping the ship's head on course. The wind effect upon the spritsail topsail relative to the same forces acting upon the fore topsail also helped to drive the ship's head deep to avoid the ship yawing (the side-to-side movement of the bow and stern of the ship, which made steering difficult). When sailing a ship such as *Racehorse,* the upper sails – topsails and topgallants – drive the ship's head down, whereas wind effect upon the courses (the lowermost sails) tends to lift the head upwards. A balance can be met by using different combinations of sails set relative to sea conditions and by steering ability.

Monday 30 August
Racehorse's log records little other than that 'At 3 PM unbent the Mainsail & Fore sail and bent new ones'. As for the *Carcass*, Lutwidge simply notes: 'all these 24 Hours standing to the S$^{o.}$ward. *Racehorse* in Company.' Lutwidge recorded the altitude of the sun as L. L. 28°21′ and his John Arnold's timekeeper at 7am running 2 hours, 32 minutes and 54 seconds slow.

Tuesday 31 August
The weather, it appears, was moderate and cloudy. Phipps wrote in *Racehorse*'s journal: 'At 4 PM shortened Sail for the *Carcass*. At 7 fresh breezes, in Top Gal$^{t.}$ Sails; at 10 brought too [sic] with the

Main Topsail to the Mast to wait for the *Carcass*. At 4 AM Variation by the Sun's Amplitude 19°16′ W.' At noon in the *Carcass* they set the steering sails to attain greater speed. Lutwidge then recorded his observations, that taken by an amplitude being N19°59′W, and that taken by three azimuths being N22°1′W. The altitude of the sun taken at noon is recorded as L. L. 29°32′. At 5am the timekeeper was running 2 hours, 34 minutes and 38 seconds slow, while at 7am it was running 2 hours, 35 minutes and 45 seconds slow.

So far, the homebound voyage from Smeerenburg had been relatively slow and uneventful. The *Carcass* continued to fall behind Phipps's *Racehorse* as she had when sailing out-bound to Spitsbergen in June. For the ship's companies in both vessels this initial southbound journey must have seemed routine and even tedious. Perhaps lulled into a false sense that the voyage would be plain sailing once they made landfall of the Hebrides, they anticipated reaching the Nore in two weeks, but this was not to be. Another weather front, far more violent than the last, was rapidly closing in from the west, the consequences of which would have a marked effect on their progress and the safety of both the ships and men.

14

Division and the storm-tossed voyage home

Part 1: Signs of deteriorating weather

Wednesday 1 September

The first day of September saw *Racehorse* and *Carcass* southward bound, *Racehorse*'s log providing the following details: course S64° W, lat 68°44′N, long 9°3′W. The estimated distance run from Hakluyt's Headland is given as 227 leagues (681 miles/1,095km). From this and figures recorded five days previously, ie 28 August, the ships were averaging a run of 13 leagues (39 miles/63km) per day. This equates to just 0.54 leagues (1.63 miles/2.62km) per hour.

Figures recorded in *Carcass*'s log state the following: course S71°45′W, lat 68°42′N, long 10°8′W. Why these three factors differ from those of *Racehorse* is inexplicable, although Lutwidge does record the distance run as 682 miles (1,098km). In short, the geographical coordinates given in both ship's logs position the vessels west of Norway but still above the Arctic Circle at 66°33′N. *Carcass*'s log notes that experiencing southerly breezes they made sail to the westward and at '½ past 4 AM T^{kd} to the Eastward, saw a sail to the N°ward'.

Thursday 2 September

In *Racehorse* they recorded light airs turning to moderate gales: 'One Sail in the NE Q$^{ur.}$ At Midnight Latitude by the Meridian Altitude of the Moon 68°39′33″N.'

Standing to the NE the *Carcass* set her studding sails, Lutwidge recording the timekeeper running 2 hours, 39 minutes and 1 second slow.

Friday 3 September
At 4pm the *Racehorse* 'shortened Sail for the *Carcass*'. Making sail again 3 hours later and finding the weather turning foggy, *Racehorse* made a 'Signal to the *Carcass* which they answered'. The *Carcass* at 4pm took 'in Steeringsails' and Lutwidge recorded in the log the altitude of the sun at noon and how the timekeeper was running.

Saturday 4 September
Little is recorded in either ship's journals except astronomical observations, Phipps recording: 'At Midnight Latitude by Meridian Altitude of Jupiter 65°27′25″N', while Lutwidge noted the altitude of the sun at noon as L.L. 29°27′, along with chronometer timings. Although progress towards home appeared slow, it was at least steady.

Sunday 5 September
With winds variable between S, SSE and SE, the *Racehorse* was steering S17°W: 'At 3 PM brought to and Sounded 683 ^{fm} [4,100ft/1,255m] soft Ground; At 8 made Sail.' Phipps also notes that he 'Read the Articles of War &$^{ce.}$ to the Ship's Company'. Because it was Sunday, Phipps would also have held divine service as was his duty as captain.

In *Carcass*, Lutwidge estimated that they had run 968 miles (1,558km) and, reiterating Phipps, noted that 'at 3 PM the *Racehorse* sounded and struck Ground about 700 fathoms [4,200ft/1,280m] soft Mud. A.M. a great swell from the SSW.' Other observations were variations by amplitude N20°36′W and by azimuth 20°53′W: the timekeeper at 1.30pm was 2 hours, 39 minutes and 40 seconds slow and at 6.30am 2 hours, 39 minutes and 20 seconds slow.

Monday 6 September
Both ships record seeing 'a sail to the Westward' at about 5pm. An hour later *Carcass*'s log records that they set the steering sails. With the wind velocity increasing this proved risky, so 'at 10 AM carried away a Foretopmast Steeringsail boom'. The 'boom' probably refers to the boom that extended out from the topsail yard. From this the studding sail is suspended by its block and halliard, the tack and sheet of the sail secured to a boom extending from the fore course yard. Such damage to rigging, easily caused by a gust of wind, was not irreparable and could be replaced with a spare or new boom made

by the carpenter. However, sending it aloft again would have proved challenging in heavy seas.

Tuesday 7 September
Racehorse's log records: 'Fresh Gales & and hazy Weather At 4 PM shortened Sail for the *Carcass* At 11 spoke a Dogger[1] from Archangel for Amsterdam. At 5 AM in Top G^{lt} Sails; at 8 set D°.' The fluctuations in wind strength prescribed constant changes of sail.

In *Carcass's* journal, Lutwidge recorded the estimated distance run as 1,190 miles (1,915km), which indicates that the ships were making an average speed of 3 knots. Their geographical position was lat 60°14′N, long 11°44′W. At this point the ship's logs begin to include sightings of other ships as the seaways became busier the further south they sailed. This is particularly evident in *Carcass's* log, which notes: 'at 2 PM saw a sail in the NW, at 10 pass'd Two sail standing to the SW, ½ past 1 AM bore away after the *Racehorse* to the WSW, at 5 AM squally saw four sail to the Southward at 8 two sail in sight to the Westward.' Observations by Lutwidge include the altitude of the sun at noon L. L. 35°29′ and the comment 'By Obs^{n.} of the Sun and Moon dist[ant] 5° 27′15″ E from Greenwich'. Checking his chronometer at 7am, Lutwidge records it as 2 hours, 33 minutes and 59 seconds slow.

Wednesday 8 September
Wednesday's weather was variable and soundings taken by the *Racehorse* at 12.30pm recorded a depth of 56 fathoms (336ft/102m) with fine yellowish coloured sand, and 'At 4 a great swell from the SW. At 4 fired a Shot at a Dutch Fishing Buss[2] to bring her down to us. At 6 AM in 1st Reef Topsails; at 10 in 2^{d} Reefs Fore and Mizzen Topsails.' Replacing sails in such weather was commonplace for the topmen. Although not explained, Phipps had two possible reasons to contact the Dutch fishing buss: to exchange information on weather and sea conditions, or perhaps to purchase fish for the crew.

In *Carcass* they took various soundings, the first, taken at 9.30am, being 50 fathoms (300ft/81m) with fine brown sand, another at 2.30pm the same depth but fine black and white sand. Lutwidge then wrote: 'At 4 PM wore Ship to the SE, the Wind Coming to the Southward With a Great Swell; four Sail in sight. Found the Ship was to the Eastward of her reckoning as by the Longitude made from

Hackluit's headland we should have seen Shetland.' This suggests that Lutwidge had concerns about their whereabouts and probably accounts for Phipps's earlier exchange with the fishing vessel. The next entry notes: 'At 1 AM fresh Breezes with showers of rain, at 5 and unbent the Maintopsail which gave away in the Clew, and bent another, in 1ˢᵗ reefs. At 8 Fresh Gales and Squally.'

Thursday 9 September
The wind according to *Racehorse*'s log was fresh becoming lighter later, committing them to take 'out 2ᵈ·Reefs of Fore & Miz.Topsails', and later tack ship. Although both ships were sailing in company, Lutwidge gives a conflicting report: 'middle Squally with rain, latter part Fresh Gales and Squally, at 8 PM Tᵏᵈ· to the SW. at 2AM a heavy swell from the Southward. ½ past 7 Tkᵈ· to the Sᵒ·ward.'

At this time there was no formal scale for wind speed or type, hence the differing interpretations from the two ships. It would be another 32 years before the naval hydrographer Francis Beaufort introduced the Beaufort scale used today.

Part 2: The storm

The further south they progressed, the worse the weather became. It is unlikely that the crew were given hot food during this time as the short rising-wave motion in these sea areas would have made it hazardous to boil food on the galley firehearth; hard tack and cheese sufficed in such conditions.

Friday 10 September
Racehorse's log records: 'Fresh Gales and Cloudy, middle and latter parts Strong Gales and Squally. At 2 AM close Reeft the Fore Topsail & in 2ᵈ· Reef Main Topsail. Lost sight of the *Carcass*. At 4 took in the Topsails & Reeft the Mainsail; in Spritsail Topsail Yard & down Top Galᵗ· Yards. Shipt a great deal of Water. At 7 set the Reeft Mainsail. At 8 saw the *Carcass* in the NW Qᵘʳ. At Noon under Reeft Mainsail and Foresail.'

Lutwidge made similar notes at the start of the day, 'Fresh Gales and rain', but the weather soon deteriorated to 'Strong gales and Squally winds and great swell from the Westward'. In this swell the *Carcass* laboured, heeling and pitching her bows to plunge through the troughs of sea, her lurching focsle drenched and hazardous.

To ease the ship's situation, it was essential that they quickly shortened sail. Lutwidge wrote: 'at 3 AM close reeft the Topsails and in Fore and Mizentopsails, at 4 in Maintopsail and Struck the Topgallan^t masts, AM secured all the Boats & clear'd the Decks, throwing overboard all the empty Casks and lumber, as the Main Deck was continually full of water.' Sea water cascaded into the living quarters below, saturating all and sundry, the men continuously buffeted and bruised. The log continues: 'scuttled the Launch on the Main Deck and clear'd her ready to throw overboard, if the Gale increased: at Noon the *Racehorse* 5 miles from two leeward bearing SSE.' In scuttling the launch, they stove in her planking with axes to prevent it filling with water and becoming an immovable deadweight they could not heave overboard.

It was during this storm that the two ships parted company. Taking in all three topsails reduced the wind velocity on the upper masts, the effect of which tended to push the vessel beam over; however, at the same time it rapidly reduced the speed of the *Carcass*.

Saturday 11 September

Rachorse's log records: 'Strong Gales and Squally, latter part Fresh Gales and Squally with Rain. PM. Shipt a great deal of Water At 4 it being more moderate set the Fore & Main Topsails close Reeft. At 6 saw a ship to Windward who hoisted English Colours; we answered her by hoisting our Ensign and supposed her to be the *Carcass*. at 8 am set the Miz: Topsail out Reefs & sounded 50 fm. Stones & Sand. At noon close Reeft the Topsails.' Considering the awful conditions encountered it is remarkable that they could still take such accurate soundings.

Carcass's log that day notes: 'First part Strong Gales and Squally with a heavy Sea from the Westward, middle Fresh Gales with Showers of rain, latter squally, at 3 PM set the Main topsail, ½ past more moderate, set Fore and Mizon topsails and bore down to join the *Racehorse* at 5 out reefs [to increase speed] and hoisted the Ensign which she answered.'

On the relative position of the *Racehorse*, Lutwidge wrote: '½ past 7 she bore SEbS 3 or 4 miles, ½ past 8 saw her light bearing SE, sounded 50 fathoms [300ft/91m] fine brown sand: – the Wind shifted from WSW to South, stood to the South West in order to join her supposing her to stand that way as we lost sight of her light when the wind shifted: and 10 PM fired a Gun which was not answered: at Noon close reefed the Topsails.' Observations recorded that day were: altitude of the sun 36°,31´, the timekeeper checked at 7.30am was found to be 2 hours, 53 minutes and 24 seconds slow. The fact that the *Carcass* hoisted her ensign is a reminder that naval ships did not continuously fly ensigns as a matter of course unless necessary. If an ensign were hoisted upside down it would be a signal of distress.

Sunday 12 September

In *Racehorse*, her log records her course as S17°E, long 7°17´W, lat 56°57´N which places her midway between the Orkneys and Stavanger on the Norwegian coasts, the log records the distance run as 459 leagues (1,377 miles/2,550km), the weather as: 'Fresh Gales and hazy, middle and latter parts very Strong Gales and Squally At ½ past 1 PM saw a Ship to the Eastward; took in the Fore & Miz: Topsails and bore down on her.' According to Midshipman Floyd: 'we thought her to be the *Carcass*, with whom we parted company on the night of the storm of the 10th. The men on the yards were pretty confident 'twas her so that in order to join her gain we bore down onto this ship', Floyd adding: 'The sea ran so high and the squall of wind happening when we were abreast of her, that it prevented our sending a boat on board, as we first intended, for we wanted exceedingly to know whereabouts we were.'[3]

As shown in Phipps's journal, it was not the *Carcass* as hoped, but: 'she proved to be a Swedish Ship from Gottenburgh. At 3 wore and made Sail. At 6 spoke Brigg [sic] from Berwick.' Floyd's narrative again gives more detail on the situation: 'She [the Swedish ship] was scarcely out of sight when we spoke a brig from Berwick, but it blew so strong that she could not understand what we asked but guessed we only wanted to know from whence she came which she told us, or else we should not have even known that.'[4] One can envisage the scene between the *Racehorse* and the brig with the rolling sea and wind driving constant spray between them; the two commanders, speaking trumpets in hand; the wind carrying away all words; the wild gesticulations – all to no avail. Phipps's log concludes: 'At 10 Wore and set the Fore Topsail; at 11 took in D°. At ½ past 1AM took in the Main Topsail & haul'd up the Mainsail.'

As Midshipman Floyd recalled, the weather abruptly turned extremely violent: 'there burst upon us like a clap of thunder a most dreadful storm of wind and rain which was so very sudden and unexpected that having not so much the least sign by which we could have foreseen the great violence of it, we had our topsails still out [set] so that we were laid down on our beam ends and the sea made a fair breach over us. We immediately made a seamanlike disposition of our sails, clewing up all of them at once, and bringing-too under a balanced mizzen.'[5]

With the watch officer bellowing 'clew up all courses and topsails' from the quarterdeck, the seamen raced to the bitts, threw ropes off the pinrails and, hauling hand over hand, sweated down the lines, their backs bowing in unison with each pull downwards, drenching seas cascading over them. Using the 'balanced mizzen' allowed them to try to steady the ship's head to windward. With no time to reef the mizzen sail, the after-guard[6] quickly lowered the mizzen gaff and reduced the sail by partially furling it using the brails and resetting the mizzen sheets and tacks accordingly. Irrespective of these actions, Floyd tells us that it took 'the second lieutenant and three men at the helm, which was constantly a lee' to keep the ship's head right.[7]

Although now head to wind, heavy swamping seas enveloped the *Racehorse*, causing all manner of chaos and destruction: 'At 2 shipt several large Seas, one of which stove in the 4 Oar'd Boat and broke the Skid which occasioned her to fall in upon the Deck, it also broke the Launches Gripes[8] and forced her upon the lee Guns &c. filled her full of Water: in going to leeward she [the boat] broke the axletree of the Chain Pump. The Skid which was broke went through the bottom of the 10 Oar'd Cutter. The 6 Oar'd Cutter being stove and the stern lashing giving way, her stern went overboard where she hung by the foremost lashing till the next Sea came & stove her to pieces, we then cut the fore lashing & let the remaining part go overboard. It also wash'd the small Spars, a Studding sail Boom & a Topgal[t] Yard with the sail overboard off the Skids. The Decks being full of Water, bore away Southward and hove all the things which were in the Launch & the remains of the 4 Oar'd Boat overboard. We also stove the Launch and hove her overboard and two of the Guns with their Carriages. The above Seas washed overboard the Harness Casks.'

Within half an hour four boats were disastrously lost. Meanwhile, 'All hands were on deck, whose sole employ then was at the pumps, and holding fast'. Describing the sea that damaged the boats, Floyd writes that it reached 'half way up the topmast head', before falling upon them and that the men clearing the boats were 'working up to their necks in the waste where there was no intermission of shipping water'. He then records that 'the seams in the deck everywhere yawed [opened] so much that it was thought too dangerous to admit us any longer to keep our cannon, two of which were thrown overboard; and as we cut away our spare masts leaving no [now] the deck entirely open, there was no shelter or covering for the men.'

The position of the ship's hull 'frequently lay so long on our side [on their beam ends] that we thought it impossible to recover'. Floyd is referring to the ship's ability to right itself: the science of righting moments working with the ship's natural metacentric height relative to its centre of gravity – an applied science not then fully understood. In conclusion, he wrote: 'the sea, too, was so tremendous a height that when we descended the side of it, it quite too[k] our breath away, and gave us reason to think, when between two of them, that every minute was our last...'[9]

Phipps notes that the strength of the wind was such that 'one of these gales [was], the hardest, I think I ever was in'. Floyd estimated that as a result of the north-westerly gale the ship came within 10 leagues (21.6 miles/40km) of the rugged coast of Norway. The potential danger meant that they set the foresail, 'but judging that this, too would be insufficient, we attempted to set the reefed mainsail, which we had no sooner shown [set] it flew to rags'.[10]

In the *Carcass,* young Nelson would also experience the ravages of the storm and onslaught of the seas, his clothes drenched, while working with others about the heaving decks. In his log, Lutwidge first records that they had run 1,395 miles (2,245km) from Hakluyt's Headland; a difference of just 18 miles (28km) from Phipps's reckoning. Persistently battered by strong gales, with squalls and rain showers, the *Carcass,* like *Racehorse,* desperately needed to shorten sail and at 2pm they took 'in Fore and Mizen Topsails, at 7 set up the lower rigging and wore to the S°ward, at 10 handed the Topsails, ½ past 11 very hard Squalls, the Ship almost water logged from the weight of the water on her Decks, handed the Courses, lowered the lower Yards and brought her too under a balanced Mizen with her head to the SW: at 10 AM something more moderate, reefed the Courses and handed them again and swayed up the lower Yards.' Soundings taken at noon revealed 32 fathoms (192ft/58.5m) fine brown sand, 'and a great swell from the Westward'.

Besides the seamanship skills brought into play by Lutwidge, his master and his boatswain, activity on deck would have been intense regardless of the sea conditions, the gusting wind and the rain. One can imagine how events played out with Lutwidge, the master and his boatswain standing on the heaving deck, their legs braced against the roll of the ship and their clothing damp with spray and salt. Using their shrill 'bosun's calls', the boatswain's mates would have piped down through the hatchways shouting 'all hand, all hands', although most of the men would have been awake anyway.

Taking in the topsails involved letting go the sheets and rapidly hauling in on clewlines and buntlines, drawing the sail close into the yard to prevent the wind 'blowing it out' (tearing the canvas). The topmen, laid out on the yards, would have been handing the reef tackle but because of the urgency of the situation it is doubtful whether the topmen had time to fully furl and stow the sails with their gaskets, although this would have prevented them being blown out. Lowering the course yards was more compli-cated. Besides manning braces to brace in the yards square, the lifts, tye halyards and jeer tackle were manned next and eased, lowering the yard to the deck. At the same time the ratings paid out the sheets as the yard dropped, the seamen hauling on clew-lines and buntlines simultaneously controlling the flapping canvas. A particular point of seamanship revealed in Lutwidge's log is the reefing of the main and fore course sails *before* they 'swayed up the lower yards'. Hoisting up the course yards involved hauling on the halyards (or jeer tackle if rigged). The reasons for reefing the course sails while on deck would, from a safety perspective, have been a practical, seamanlike solution to make a difficult task easier and safer for the men.

Monday 13 September

With the winds easing moderately, Phipps began to get the *Racehorse* in order. Soundings taken at 1pm revealed a depth of 30 fathoms (180ft/55m) with coarse yellowish sand. At 4pm they 'set the reeft Mainsail', the crew clearing the decks. After wearing ship at 4am, the men were 'Employed repairing the Running Rigging which was much damaged and reeved a new Tiller Rope. At 6 set the close reeft Fore & Mizen Topsails; at 7 struck the Topgal^t Masts at 8 set the close reeft Main Topsail.'

The fact that a new tiller rope was reeved through its respective lead blocks indicates that the constant heavy sea motion imposed upon the rudder had been sufficient to snap the rope between helm and tiller. Luckily, the rudder pintles were not dislodged out of their gudgeon braces, which would have led to a far more dangerous problem: complete rudder loss. By good fortune the rudder lock, a wooden chock, integrally wedged into the upper pintles, prevented this from happening.

Alone, the *Carcass* also set more sail to begin making better progress home, all the while looking out for the *Racehorse*: 'at 1 PM set the reefed Courses. at 2 set Main topsail, at 6 set Fore topsail at 8 out 3rd reef Fore topsail and sounded 35 fathoms (210ft/64m) fine brown sand and at 10 and 12 the same soundings at 12 (Midnight) wore to the Westward, at 11 AM fired a Gun to speak with the Dutch ship to the Westward.' Lutwidge was hoping that the Dutch trader had seen the *Racehorse*.

Tuesday 14 September

Tuesday's weather consisted of light to fresh breezes turning to fresh gales and squalls; the *Racehorse* taking in her fore and mizzen topsails and taking 'Soundings at different times from 18 to 40 fm'.

In *Carcass,* they 'spoke a Dutch ship from Archangel bound to Amsterdam sounded 35 fathoms [210ft/64m] fine brown sand, ½ past 3 sent a Boat on board a Prussian Dogger [fishing craft] from Emden', making for the fishing grounds of Dogger Bank.[11] Although the reasons they did this are not entirely clear, it could be that Lutwidge was seeking information about the whereabouts of the *Racehorse*. It can also be assumed that Nelson or Biddle would have been involved with the boat used for this action. The altitude of the sun at noon was recorded as 37°54′.

Now lying to the east of Whitby, the *Carcass* had, according to her log, sailed an estimated distance of 1,505 miles (2,422km) from Hakluyt's Headland. She had approximately 275 miles (443km) to go to reach the Thames estuary. At this point the *Carcass* was still sailing with her topgallant masts struck (lowered), each topgallant mast lashed to its respective topmast, their heels set down upon the lower mast caps. As for *Racehorse*, she was still not in sight.

Wednesday 15 September
Steering S14°E, *Racehorse's* position is recorded as lat 54°33′N, long 8° 59′ W. With running repairs to the rigging complete, they set the fore topsail at 2.30pm, the topmen later going aloft to take out the third reefs of the main topsail. Her fore topsail, as it became apparent once set, must have suffered damage during the storm so they then 'bent a new Fore Topsail'. The procedure for this is identical to that for bending a new foresail described earlier. The wind becoming squally, they close-reefed all topsails and 'at 10 Wore Ship & handed the Fore & Mizen Topsails'; the manoeuvre of wearing ship rather than tacking put less strain on the standing rigging.

Both ships were now unavoidably divided, with the *Carcass* sailing on a course S47°W. Her position was recorded as lat 54°41′N, long 12°46′W, which placed her about 195 nautical miles (225 miles/362km) distant from the *Racehorse*.

Carcass's log recalls: 'First part Fresh Breezes and Cloudy, middle Fresh Gales, latter Strong Gales with some rain, at 3 PM out reefs of the Courses and Topsails, and up Topgall^t masts at 3 AM T^kd to the NW. at 7 in 1st reefs, at 9 close reeft the Top sails at 11 set the Maintopsail, all these 24 Hours upon the Dogger bank and sounding every Hour.'

Although soundings were undertaken as a precautionary measure, the fact that the water depth on the Bank varies between 8 and 19 fathoms (49–118ft/15–36m), meant that its depth was never a grounding threat to Lutwidges's shallow-draughted ship. The real purpose of sounding hourly in this case was to cross-reference their position by comparing the composition of the seabed with other known data.

Thursday 16 September

The weather remained consistently difficult with unexpected squalls necessitating much sail handling. *Racehorse's* log states: 'At 4 PM; Reeft the Mainsail; at 5 set the Fore Topsail & Wore Ship, at 8 set the Miz. Topsail: at 11 handed D°.' When they 'handed D°', they simply let go the mizzen topsail sheets, which allowed them to haul on the clewlines and 'clew the sail' up into the bunt of the yard, the buntlines being simultaneously hauled in order to temporarily shorten sail, to 'hang in its gear'– the entire operation taking far less time than would sending men aloft reefing. The sail could be easily reset by letting go 'bunts and clews' and 'sheeting the sail home' by hauling the sail out on its sheets. According to the log, they later quickly reset the mizzen topsail by this means at 6am.

The log then records: 'At 10 carried away the Parrel of the Main Topsail Yard.' The topsail yard parrel that had given way consisted of a rope and wooden ball 'necklace' arrangement that loosely secured the yard to its respective mast. The parrel rope falls were made fast on deck from where they could be eased or hauled taut to control grip of the parrel upon the mast and hence the yard, this arrangement being applicable to all yards. The material failure of this component was probably due to stresses suffered during the recent heavy storm. Critical to the safe operation of the topsail and its yard, this would have needed immediate remedial attention. Despite the blustering gale and driving rain, a bosun's mate and able rating scaled high aloft with rope to effect repairs – a precarious undertaking as the yard was temporarily loose. Phipps's journal concludes: 'At Noon out 3^d & 2^d Reef T. Sails Sounded at different times from 16 to 25 ^{fm}.'

Meanwhile, in *Carcass*, Lutwidge entered in his journal: 'at 2 PM wore to the SW, set Foretopsail and out 3rd reefs at 7 in 1st and 2nd reefs: At 8 AM several fishing Vessels in sight, at 9 got a pilot from one of them, and wore to the N°ward, at 10 T^{kd} to the SW, sounded every Hour.'

Even though Lutwidge was confident in the navigational skills of his master, James Allen, taking on board a pilot from the fishing vessel who was familiar with the sea area in which they were cruising made good sense. It is not recorded when this 'pilot' was released out from the ship. From this it can be assumed that Lutwidge, having already made up his mind to get inshore of the fishing port of Yarmouth (now Great Yarmouth), also required a competent pilot with local knowledge who could negotiate the four north–south running sand banks of the Scroby Sands lying some 4 miles (13km) off the coast between Caister and the entrance of Yarmouth harbour.

Friday 17 September

Many miles away, the *Racehorse* was still battling through heavy seas, strong gales and squally weather, the ship steering S59°W; her position recorded as lat 53°12′N, long 9°24′W. In his journal, Phipps wrote: 'PM brought too a Swedish Snow from Stockholm for Venice.' We can assume that Phipps was totally unaware of the *Carcass*'s whereabouts and was asking if she had been sighted, then: 'At 2 out Reefs of the Main Topsail; at 7 in 1ˢᵗ & 2ᵈ Reef Topsails; at 9 close Reeft them; At 10 handed the Fore & Miz, Topsails, at 1 AM handed the Main Topsail; at 5 set Dᵒ· – The larboard foremost Main Chain Plate broke, reev'd the laniard in the spare Deadeye and set up the Shroud again.' Chain plates made of flat iron strapping secured the lower rigging shroud deadeyes to the ship's side by a series of preventer bolts, the deadeyes being housed upon the stout horizontal channel boards protruding from the ship's side. The log entry continues: 'At 8 the Wind shifting to the NW Wore Ship set the fore & Miz: Topsails, let 2 Reefs out of the Main & 1 of the Fore Topsails; At 11 out 2ᵈ Reefs.'

Effecting a temporary repair to the damaged shroud chain plate was easy but, unforeseeably they had to 'Put a preventer Gammoning upon the Bowsprit'. They soon faced a far greater problem, since the entire bowsprit was found to be working itself loose as a result of the excessive stresses imposed upon it during the heavy storm conditions. The foremast rigging relied upon the stability of this angled mast, which projected beyond the head of the ship. Normally the bowsprit was held by a gammoning lashing, which comprised a series of thick rope turns passing over the bowsprit and down through the 'knee of the ship's head', the rope turns being 'frapped' (bound) together.

This must have stretched and, as it slackened, the bowsprit would have tended to kick upwards and shudder every time the ship's head pitched into a trough of sea, the constant flexing indirectly affecting the foremast rigging. To alleviate the problem, they needed to rig a 'preventer gammoning' – a temporary lashing arrangement.

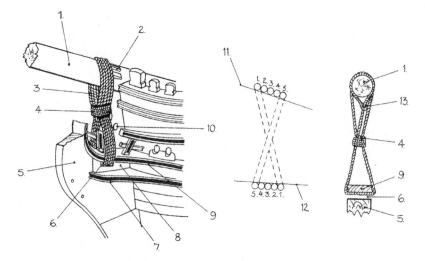

Standard bowsprit gammoning.

Key;

1. Bowsprit
2. Gammoning cleats
3. Gammoning lashing
4. Centre lashing and seizing made from tail of gammoning rope
5. Knee of the ship's head
7. Lower cheek
8. Trailboard
9. Upper cheek and hair bracket
10. Hole for fore stay collar
11. Line of upper surface of bowsprit
12. Line of upper surface of gammoning rope slot in knee of the head
13. Eye spliced into standing end of gammoning rope

Drawing by the author.

Overseen by the boatswain, the task of rigging the turns of rope preventer gammoning in such heavy weather would have been extremely dangerous. With a ship of this size, her bows probably rose so high on the wave crests that the gripe of the stem post was exposed. Those standing on the gratings in the ship's head, passing the new rope over and under the bowsprit would feel the deck drop from under their feet every time the ship lunged into another trough of sea. Anticipating the next lurch, each man became temporarily unbalanced, some even being briefly submerged in the ice-cold sea. As for those laying out on the bowsprit adding

Detail of the men putting on a preventer gammoning as described above. Illustration by Gordon Frickers.

their weight to keep the bowsprit hard down as the preventer turns were rove, they clung precariously astride the gyrating spar as they gazed back inboard, watching the ship's stern far beyond them rise and fall, the thumping sea upon the ship's bow below their dangling feet. With the preventer gammoning finally frapped and hitched and all made safe, the *Racehorse* drove south-west, her larboard anchors awash in the foaming waves. The log recorded: 'Sounded from 14 to 17[fm.]'

At this point the *Carcass* was steering S23°E, her position lat 53°41′N, long 12°54′W. Her bearings and distance at noon are recorded as 'Cromer Lighthouse SWbW four or 5 leagues' (12–15 miles/19–24km). Then a small fishing village, Cromer lies on the north-east coast of Norfolk (East Anglia). The day began with fresh gales and cloudy weather, later turning to strong gales. This changeable weather obliged Lutwidge's master to alter the sail configurations repeatedly to meet the arising circumstances; the crew constantly called on deck to hand wet ropes at the pinrails and topsail bitts. Such frequent activity is clearly evident in Lutwidge's log: 'at 4 PM T[kd] to the NW, at 7 in 3rd reefs, at 8 in Fore and Mizon top^{ls} at 10 in Maintopsail, at ½ past 11 wore to the S°ward. sounding 5 fathoms [30ft/9m], at 4 AM wore to the N°ward, carried away several lanyards of the lower rigging, at 6 set topsails, and out 3rd reefs, at 8 up Topgall^{nt} yards, and out 2nd reefs at 10 made the Land from SWbW to WbS: find the Ship above two degrees to the Eastward of the Reckoning.' The sounding, given as 5 fathoms (30ft/9m), shows they were approaching coastal shoaling water. The lanyards were those rove between the upper and lower shroud deadeyes which, fitted on the channel boards fitted upon the ship's sides, were constantly prone to wetting and damage from heavy seas.

Saturday 18 September

Except for brief notes abut reefing the main and fore topsails, tacking and soundings taken, little is entered in *Racehorses*'s journal and it seems that most of her previous problems had been resolved.

Part 3: Respite for the *Carcass* at Yarmouth Roads

Sailing alone, the *Carcass* slowly closed with the Norfolk coast, the weather clear with fresh breezes. Much relieved after sailing through such horrendous weather, Lutwidge wrote in his log: 'At 10 PM anchored with the Best Bower in 12 fath^s Winterton Ness lights SbW about 4 miles.' (Winterton is about 22 miles/35km from Cromer.) The log then notes: '½ past 4 AM weighed came to sail, At 9 AM anchored in Yarmouth Roads in 7 fathoms [42ft/12.8m].' Once anchored, the bearings taken were: 'Yarmouth Church 15°W. Gullstone Church WSW about 2 Miles.'[12]

Next, Lutwidge wrote: 'At Noon sent away an express to the Admiralty with a journal of the Proceedings of the Voyage.' The 'express' referred to was a hired dispatch rider who, changing horses regularly, travelled at an average speed of 12mph (20kph). Given the distance between Yarmouth and London, Lutwidge's documents should have arrived at Whitehall for Lord Anson's eyes at about 9.30 that evening but, as recorded by the Admiralty secretary, Lutwidge's dispatches and ship's journal were not attended to until the next day. The accompanying letter was recorded and annotated read as follows.[13]

'*Carcass* Yarmouth Roads 18th of September 1773.
[The letter is annotated by the Admiralty Secretary] Rec'd by Express
19th September at ½ pas 1PM.

Sir,

Please to inform my Lord's Commissioners of the Admiralty, that I
anchored in this day with His Majesty's Sloop under my Command,
having been separated by bad weather from the *Racehorse* on the
evening of the 10th instant, in Latitude against this in latitude 57°
38′N, about 20 leagues on the Coast of Norway.

Agreeable to my last Orders from Capt Phipps "in case of separation", I should lose no time in proceeding to the Nore, but the wind
now contrary, I sent this by express, as it is possible from the Weather
we have had, that the *Racehorse* is not yet arrived.

By the enclosed Journal of our Proceedings: their Lordships will
see that Capt Phipps has done everything that was possible (tho'
without Effect) to accomplish a passage Northwards, and that it is
impossible to proceed farther than we did towards the North Pole,
on the West side of Spitsbergen – The Ships repeatedly coasted close
along a firm and solid body of Ice, (extending nearly from East to
West) from the 5th to the 23rd degree of Longitude East of Greenwich:
and from 79° 20′ to 80° 39′ North Latitude, always pushing into the
Ice as far as they cou'd go: where there was any opening... till they
were both enclosed and set fair in it on the 1st August to the Eastward
of Spitsbergen between the North-east Land and the Seven Islands.

I am Sir.
Your most Obedient Humble Servant
Skeff^{tn} Lutwidge'

The letter is signed by the secretary Philip Stephens Esq.

The urgent dispatch of the *Carcass*'s journal to the Admiralty was
a prudent action on Lutwidge's part to inform their Lordships that at
least one ship from the expedition had made it home safely, Lutwidge
assuming that Phipps in the *Racehorse* was either still making her way
to the Nore or, worse, lost at sea. It seems that similar sentiments
concerning the loss of the 'other ship' had occurred in the *Racehorse*,
Midshipman Floyd again bringing this to our attention: 'we took

it for granted that the *Carcass* must have foundered, for we still saw nothing of her, and as she was somewhat deeper than we were, we concluded, from the bad hand that had been made of it, she could not have swam it out.'[14] Floyd's journal ends abruptly at this point, perhaps with intention to conclude later. Although Floyd's comment about the possible foundering of the *Carcass* seems like a reasonable assumption by *Racehorse*'s officers, in fact it was most unlikely because the difference in draught between *Racehorse* and *Carcass* was just 1ft (0.31m), the former being 13ft (0.4m), the latter 12ft (0.37m). Moreover, *Racehorse* was the heavier ship.

Sunday 19 September
Still out at sea, the *Racehorse* was contending with squally weather and rain, her crew unremittingly called aloft due to the fluctuating wind conditions. Phipps's journal entries record: 'At 8 PM close Reeft and handed the Fore & Miz: Topsails; close reeft the Main Topsail & clued up the Mainsail.' Clewing up this sail provided greater visibility for the quartermasters manning the helm on the quarterdeck. The log then notes that they were sailing: 'Under the close reeft Main Topsail and Foresail 'till the Squall blew over, then made Sail. At 12 Wore Ship; at 4 AM set the Fore & Miz: Topsails, at 6 out 3$^{d.}$ reef Fore & 2$^{d.}$ of Main Topsails. At ½ past 9 Tack'd and out reefs. Sounded from 14 to 17$^{fm.}$.' The continuous sail handling on all three masts must have been exhausting for the topmen; their one consolation was that with all topgallant masts struck there were at least no topgallant sails to contend with. What is noticeable about the ship's journals is the fact that neither of them mention setting lower and topmast staysails. Triangular in shape and set fore and aft on the stays between masts, their use in keeping the ship steady would have certainly proved invaluable under their circumstances or when hove to.

Taking advantage of Sunday's weather, which was recorded as fresh breezes and fair, that afternoon *Carcass*'s men began to 'set up a standing rigging fore and aft'. This, consisting of the forestays supporting each respective lower, top and topgallant mast, had been much stressed during the bad weather of the previous weeks. Tightening up the stays involved heaving up on the lanyards that ran between the hearts turned into the lower end of each stay and its respective collar. While the crew were doing this they 'veered

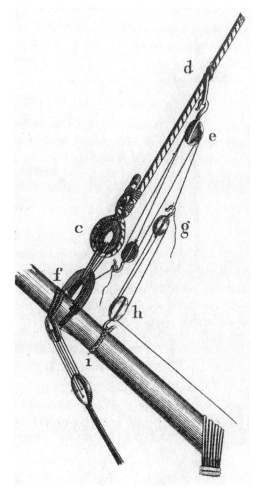

c. Wooden heart turned into lower
   end of fore stay
d. Selvagee
e. Double block of luff tackle hooked
   to selvagee
f. Standing heart lashed to bowsprit
g. Single block of second luff tackle
h. Double block of second luff tackle
i. Rope strop securing lower double
   block to bowsprit

Method for tightening the upfore lower mast stay upon the bowsprit.
From Darcy Lever.

to ½ a Cable' and 'aired the spare sails', which, brought up out
of the ship's sail rooms, were opened out to dry, as they would
have been wetted by the ingress of sea water during the stormy
weather.

Monday 20 September
At sea, the *Racehorse* continued to encounter gales and squalls, her
crew reefing and handing her topsails as before. Further rigging

damage occurred: 'At 11 the Strap [strop] of larboard Main Topsail Sheet Block broke; fixed a new one.' When this block failed the lower outer corner of the topsail would have flapped uncontrollably until the topsail sheet could be got under control. This was done by hauling upon both the sails' clewlines and making good the repair when the clew of the sail was snug up into the bunt of its respective yard. When they 'fixed a new one', a 15in (38cm) shoulder block had to be manhandled along the main yard and stropped to its respective yard arm – an easy task in harbour but not on a pitching ship in a squall.

In the *Carcass*, little happened except that they 'moored a Cable each way SSW and NNE'. Setting out two anchors provided greater security against the strong tidal flow.

Tuesday 21 September
Sailing on a course S24°W, the position of the *Racehorse* was lat 52°17′N, long 9°18′W; the bearing and distance at noon recorded as 'Catwick EbS 55 miles', putting the ship WbN of what Phipps has either misspelled (or phonetically spelled), the Dutch west coast fishing village of Katwijk. This location indicates that the storm force winds encountered had driven the *Racehorse* much further to the east in the North Sea than Phipps had hoped when trying to make landfall on England's East Anglian coast. Second, Phipps's easterly position close to Holland explains why the *Carcass* and *Racehorse* had completely failed to reunite. The chart showing their voyage home, reproduced in Phipps's book of 1774, makes good sense. It seems that Phipps was accidentally driven east, but did he deliberately make for the Dutch coast for safety? An alternative theory is that he drove easterly to attain sufficient sea room to bear down against prevailing winds and make landfall on the Suffolk coast of England, a distance of about 130 nautical miles (150 miles/241.5km).

As for the day's events, weather conditions appear to have moderated to fresh gales and cloudy, Phipps's log recording: 'At ½ past 2AM saw the Land bearing from SbE to EbS off shore 4 Leagues Stood on Shore by our Lead into 7^{fm} Water Catwick Church SE½S 3 or 4 Miles. At 6 AM out 2^d. Reef Topsails' as they prudently closed toward the unfamiliar shoreline.

Meanwhile, lying in Yarmouth Roads Lutwidge recorded 'Fresh Gales and Cloudy middle Squally'. Realising that a new weather front was imminent, after conferring with his master Lutwidge made preparations to meet this sudden change: 'At 4 PM struck the Topgall^t masts and got them down AM cleared the Hawse sent the Long boat for water.' This would have been another opportunity where Nelson, as coxswain, would run the boat to the watering point ashore. It is probable that this would have been to the hand pump located at nearby Gullstone (Gorleston).

Wednesday 22 September
Sailing off the Dutch coast under topmasts, only the apparently moderate weather conditions encouraged Phipps to reinstate the ship's full rig: 'At 3 PM up Top Gal^t Masts got the Top Gal^t Yards, across & set the Top Gal^t Sails; At 6 set Stud^g Sails.'

1	Mast head eye formed in end of stay
2	Serving of the eye
3	Parcelling
4	Mouse made up of spun yarn
5	Eye set up at extreme end of stay
6	Seizing and canvas cap
7–9	Seizing
10	Worming of the stay
11	Upper heart, set up in stay
12	Lanyard
13	Eye seizing
14	Eye seized in end of collar
15	Lower heart set up in collar
16–17	Seizing
18	Seizing and canvas cap
19	Collar
20	Serving of the collar

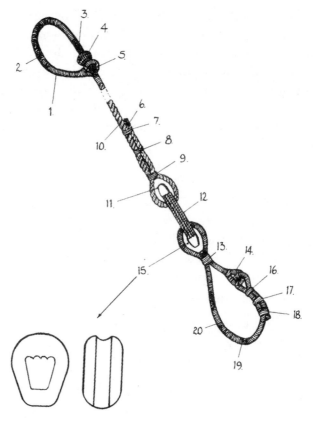

Detail of main stay and heart.

Raising the topgallant masts was relatively easy. This involved hauling down on the top tackle rove through a shiver (sheave) integrally
fitted vertically into the heel of the mast. This then ran through
blocks stropped either side at the topmast cap, the falls running
down to the bitts on deck, the topgallant mast shrouds and forestays
reconfiguring to their taut state once the mast was fully hoisted
and the locking fid driven through the heel. Five hours later the
light winds turned to hard squally gales, compelling Phipps to take
down the studding sails and later shorten sail: 'At 1 AM close Reeft
the Fore & Miz: Topsails and handed [furled] them.' They further
reduced sail: 'At 2 close reefed the Main Topsail and down Top Gal^t:
Yards: At ½ past 5 hauled up the Mains^le & Wore Ship. Saw the Land
NWbN to NNW.'

The log entry for the *Carcass* reads: 'For the most part Strong Gales and Squally, sometimes rain, PM the Longboat returned with water, at 10 struck Yards and Topmasts.' Although not in use, the masts and yards were reduced on this occasion to alleviate the stresses imposed upon the rigging stays and shrouds by the current weather conditions. The striking of masts and yards could generally be completed by professional seamen in half an hour.

Thursday 23 September
As the *Racehorse* progressed slowly southwards, her course S50°E, Phipps was totally unaware of the whereabouts of the *Carcass*. He was also oblivious to the fact that Lutwidge's dispatch about the expeditionary voyage had already been delivered to the Admiralty and read by Anson and other senior admirals. Realising from Lutwidge's report that Phipps was unaccountably still at sea and divided from the *Carcass* must have raised both professional and personal concerns at the Admiralty.

Friday 24 September
The *Racehorse* was still off Holland with her log recording: 'Moderate and cloudy latter part fresh Gales with Rain. At ½ past 1 PM out all Reefs saw the Land bearing from SEbS to SbE distance 6 Miles. At ½ past 3 Tack'd, in 2^d & 3^d Reefs of Main Topsail. At 4 Schorven S½E 3 or 4 Leagues.' Phipps's entry relating to 'Schorven' is somewhat mystifying as there is no place listed on the east coast of England of similar spelling. Taking account of the chart of their homebound voyage in Phipps's book, it is likely that the journal is referring to the Dutch fishing port of Scheveningen, Phipps's spelling being either phonetic or his understanding of the pronunciation. Scheveningen also makes good sense as the earlier log entry 'Caterwick', relating to Katwijk, lies just north of Scheveningen. The identification of these two places shows how far east the *Racehorse* had been driven.

Phipp's journal continues: 'At 8 saw the Land from the WbN to NW. At 9 Tack'd, Orfordness Lighthouse WSW 4 leagues. At 11 out 3^d & 2^d Reefs of the Fore & Miz: Topsails. Tack'd occasionally.' At this time, Orfordness (Orford Ness) lighthouse was simply a pair of wooden leading lights built in 1637. The sight of land must have been a source of elation for Phipps and the men of *Racehorse's* crew considering what they had endured on their passage home: damage to rigging, the incident of the bowsprit and the loss of the boats. If they had reflected on their experience when beset in the ice in the early days of August, any prospect of getting home must have seemed unbelievable.

With the weather moderating to 'Fresh Gales and Cloudy', Lutwidge prepared to get to sea to complete his journey towards the Thames estuary: 'at 6 PM got up the Topmasts and Yards and set up the Topmasts rigging, at 7 AM got up Topgall^t masts, unmoored, at 9 weighed, working along the Coast of England to the SW, at 10 got up the Topgall^t yards.' From a modern perspective, manually raising six individual masts and six yards in just four hours is a considerable feat. The one factor that may have made their job easier was that the mast and spars of the *Carcass* were relatively light in comparison to those of other contemporary men-of-war.

Saturday 25 September
Enduring less irksome weather, *Racehorse* made her approach towards the Suffolk coastline, the log stating: 'Employed turning to Windward. At 4 Orford Church NNE the Lighthouse NEbE off Shore ½ Mile. At 6 anchored with the Best Bower in 7^{fm} & veered to a whole Cable. Balsey Cliff WbS 5 or 6 Miles & Ouzly [sic] Church NWbW 4 miles. At 7 AM up Top Gl^t Masts & got Top Gl^t Yards a cross. At 9 set up the rigging fore & aft.' The place Phipps refers to as 'Balsey' is today called Bawdsey and that given as 'Ouzly' is in fact Hollesley.

Part 4: The reunion and home

Sunday 26 September
Racehorse's position at noon is recorded as: 'At Single Anchor under the West Rocks.'[15] At the start of the day Phipps's journal states: 'PM Weighed came to Sail, out Reefs & set Top Gal^t Sails. At 7 came to with the Best Bower in 6½ ^{fm} Water. At 7 AM join'd Company and Anchored here His Majesty's Sloop the *Carcass*.'

The reunification of the two ships must have been a boost in morale for both Phipps and Lutwidge. As well as the stress on men and ships, both commanders had been anxious that their sister ship had been lost in heavy seas. Both ships could now weigh anchor and proceeded south together.

The *Carcass*'s log records: 'At Single Anchor. Languard [Landguard] Fort NNW. Harwich Church NW. Buoy of the Gunfleet WSW.' This puts Lutwidge off the joint estuary of the River Orwell and River Stour.[16]

Monday 27 September

At 2pm the *Racehorse* weighed and came to sail with the *Carcass*, 'the weather; Moderate and cloudy, middle part variable with Rain, the latter fresh breezes and cloudy.' The log entry records: 'Employed turning to windward [south-westerly], the wind being SWbS veering to WSW. At ½ past 8 Anchored with the Best Bower in 8 ^{fm} & veered to a whole Cable.' Weighing again at 6am they began 'turning up the Swin' (a well-used navigable channel sometimes called the King's Channel) and 'At ½ past 10 Anchored in Shoe hole with the best Bower & veered to 2/3 of a Cable.' This refers to the anchorage ground of 3½ fathoms (6ft/1.8m) officially named as 'Horse Shoe Hole' in the Thames estuary, midway between Maplin Sands to the north and Reculver Towers on the Kent coast to the south. *Racehorse*'s position at noon is recorded as: 'Shoe Beacon NWbN Half A Mile', the *Carcass* lying at single anchor a mile off the Whitaker Beacon.

Tuesday 28 September

Waiting to catch the right tide flow, *Racehorse*'s log notes: 'At 5 PM Employed turning to Windward; at 9 Anchored with the best Bower in 7 ^{fm} Water. The Nore light W ¼ S3 Miles. Weighing again at 6am the ship progressed turning to windward and At 11 Bore away. At Noon the Sheerness Garrison SWb½S, 4 or 5 Miles.' The *Carcass*, which was also anchored at the Nore, also weighed, got up her fore-topsail and proceeded to Deptford.

That the two ships appear to be consistently anchoring and weighing is down to three factors: 1 the wind direction was often not suitable: according to the log books it was generally SSW to WSW; 2 changes in the tide relative to the opposing wind direction; 3 anchoring overnight was a precautionary measure taken because the approaches into the Thames estuary were busy with many heavily laden craft bound for London.

Wednesday 29 September
Phipps recorded the weather as 'Moderate breezes and clear'. He then wrote:'At 1 pm anchored with the best Bower in Sea Reaching in 9 ^{fm}. The Nore Light SE. Sheerness Garrison SSW ½ W. At 6 fired a Gun & made the Signal for a Boat.' The *Racehorse* and *Carcass* then parted company, with Phipps recording:'At 6 am Weighed and came to Sail. Standing up the River. Fired two Guns as a Signal for our Boat.'

That same day Lutwidge entered in *Carcass*'s journal: 'at 3 pm fired a Gun as a Signal for the Boat, ½ past 5 weighed working up to Galleons [Reach], at 8 got abreast of Leigh roads, at 11 past Gravesend, came on board 5 Customs and Excise Officers, at 1 AM Anchored in Longreach, Purfleet N½W about 2 miles, at 7 weighed: at ½ past 10 Anchored in Galleons in 3 fathoms [18ft/5.5m], at Noon came alongside a Hoy for the Gunner's Stores.'

Wednesday 29 September was Midshipman Horatio Nelson's 15th birthday. How he celebrated, if indeed he did, is uncertain as he left no record. And with all that was going on in the *Carcass* as she tried to make her way up to Galleons Reach, her midshipmen would have been too preoccupied to take part in such celebrations.

Thursday 30 September
In light breezes the *Racehorse* made her way up the Thames, Phipps writing:'Employed in turning up the River At 2 PM Anchored with the Best Bower in Galleons reach in 5 ^{fm} & veered to a whole cable.' After enduring the Arctic pack ice and ravages of the wind and sea, the *Racehorse* was at last home and safe from further assault, or so it seemed. Phipps concluded Thursday's log entry: 'On the turn of the Tide an East Indiamen run foul of us and carried away our Jibb Boom & Spritsail Yard.'

15

Paying off the ships

A Navy Board Warrant sent to Deptford and dated 22 September 1773 stated simply: 'The *Racehorse* and *Carcass* Sloops to be laid up.'[1]

Once the Warrant was received, the process of decommissioning both ships and discharging their crews and stores began. It is probable that all supernumeraries immediately left the ship at the earliest opportunity, the astronomer, Israel Lyons, eager to report back to the Royal Observatory Greenwich, being one. Others would have included Dr Charles Irving and his African assistant, Olaudah Equiano,[2] who lodged in Irving's home in Pall Mall. As for the four hired Greenland pilots, they would on receipt of pay owed return to their profession within the whaling fleet.

With the expedition complete, both ships had to be taken out of service. This involved various processes before they could be formally decommissioned and paid off. Although both terms virtually mean the same thing, the former relates to the relinquishment of command and dispersal of the commissioned naval officers, while the latter applies to giving final payment and release of the ship's company. Prior to this, much work had to be undertaken before the ships were laid up 'in ordinary' (reserve) or passed into the hands of the appointed naval dockyard. The most urgent task always related to the ship's armament with its associated hazards.

Racehorse pays off at Deptford

Thursday 30 September

Phipps's log entry reads: 'Came alongside a Hoy to take the Guns and Gunner's Stores in.' All ordnance-related work was overseen by the ship's gunner, John Fenton, working with a gang of men and Board of Ordnance overseers sent from Woolwich Arsenal. To this end Phipps 'Steady'd the ship with the Kedge Anchor', the action of which counteracted any movement created when hoisting the heavy guns off their carriages and over into the hoy. Prior to disembarkation, all gun tackles and breeching ropes had already been removed. Next, each gun barrel was released from its carriage by knocking out the retaining cotter pins and flipping over the hinged cap-squares that clamped the gun's trunnions. All necessary paperwork was completed, including making account of the guns that had been thrown overboard during the storm.

Once all guns had been 'swayed' out of the ship, the carriages were hoisted out into the hoy. While this was progressing, preparations for taking out all the gunpowder were put in train, with the hoy of the *Racehorse* hoisting a plain red danger flag indicating that explosives were being transported. This was necessary not only for naval requirements, but also because the Thames at this point was full of mercantile traffic going upriver to the docks at Wapping and beyond or down to the sea. Under normal circumstances, powder would have been conveyed into a separate powder hoy but as the *Racehorse* was carrying little powder this was probably unnecessary. Along with full powder barrels, spent powder casks that had been 'knocked down' were also disembarked. The staves, together with their headers and hoops, were bundled and tagged as individual units. Spent casks were equally dangerous as they carried residual volatile powder. It was imperative that all magazines were completely free of powder and made-up cartridges. The next thing disembarked was the solid iron round shot, along with all musket shot. Finally, all other stores and equipment rammers, wadhooks, sponges and all other gunnery paraphernalia were taken out of the ship into the hoy, all this work being undertaken by groups of the ship's company. This completed, Phipps wrote, 'at 10 AM Weighed and came to sail'. The *Racehorse* moved to an alternative mooring.

Friday 1 October
'At 2 PM came on board the Ordinary Men and assisted in securing the Ship alongside the Terror Bomb.' Once this was done, *Racehorse's* ship's company were 'Employed unbending the Sails & unrigging the Ship'. The next day at 2pm the *Racehorse* was 'transported alongside the Vestal'. The task of unrigging continued, the majority involving secondary running rigging associated with the sails. At this time, the primary running rigging relative to the masts and yards remained in place as it was needed for the removal of such items.

Those referred to as the 'ordinary men' were generally naval ratings who were either unattached to any specific commissioned vessel, unfit for active sea service, or naval pensioners. In short, this was an organised team of professionally able men who provided manpower supporting ships and their crews where directed by an officer of the Ordinary. The Ordinary itself was a department of the Navy Board appointed to cover routine expenses related to the maintenance of ships and dockyards. Naval ships laid up or undergoing repair and maintenance were said to be laid up in 'ordinary'. As for the ratings involved, such work provided a supplementary income to a pension, the system itself providing 'jobs for the boys'. The log mentions two other vessels: the *Terror* and the *Vestal*. The former, a Basilisk class bomb vessel launched in 1740, was quite similar to Lutwidge's *Carcass*; the other was a 32-gun fifth-rate frigate launched in 1757, which, though just 16 years old, would be broken up in 1775.

Sunday 3 October (week of)
The men were 'employed as before and sending the Officers Stores on Shore'. Monday's work was similar, by which time all the topgallant and topsail yards had been sent down. Following this, all topgallant masts and topmasts were lowered, unshipped and removed into the dockyard for overhaul. All associated standing and running rigging, including blocks and deadeyes, would have been inspected and 'laid apart' for later reuse in the ship after anything defective had been replaced or condemned – that not condemned being recycled. Concerning the matter of returning the ship's boats, most had been lost.

By Tuesday, most of this was complete and the men had started 'getting the Sea Stores ready to be Surveyed', the survey jointly undertaken by the *Racehorse*'s purser and Woolwich dockyard representatives. With the surveys completed by Wednesday, the men were next 'Employed getting the Sea Stores on Shore and clearing the after Hold'. Thursday was spent 'sending the Cables and Provisions on Shore', while on Friday, 8 October all were busy 'unrigging the Main Mast and sending the Rigging and Main Yard on Shore'. Rather oddly, no mention is made of the fore and mizzen masts.

Saturday 9 October
Phipps simply records: 'Employed returning Stores and cleaning the ship.' Next day: 'The Warrant Officers and People employed as before. AM Wash'd the Ship. Received some Fresh Beef.' On the Monday, they began 'returning the Boatswain's Stores … Spirits and Wines' being returned the following day.

Wednesday 13 October
Phipps's last log entry notes: 'Fresh Gales and Squally with Rain. PM employed sweeping and cleaning the Ship. The Master Attendant came on board and visited the Officer's Store Rooms &c. AM the Ship was Paid off', the log concluding with Phipp's signature.

Racehorse's ship's company were paid and dispersed, some returning home to families, others seeking another position in a Royal Naval ship or employment within a vessel operating in the mercantile fleet, the East India Company being one relatively lucrative choice. Within three years, those still serving in the Royal Navy would find themselves deployed aboard the more standard men-of-war, frigates and line-of-battle ships, operating on the North American station at war against the rebel Americans.

Carcass pays off at Deptford

Thursday 30 September
Lutwidge wrote: 'D° Wea^r P.M. got out of the Guns and Gunner' Stores … these obviously being sent into a Hoy at 9 weighed and came to sail.' The *Carcass*, like the *Racehorse*, was not without misfortune: 'at 10 got foul of a large Transport and carried away

the larboard Mizen shrouds and part of the Channel.' That both ships suffered collisions highlights what may have been a common occurrence in the crowded confines of the River Thames at this time. Continuing his record, Lutwidge wrote: 'at 1 AM anchored at Deptford and warp'd alongside the Sheer Hulk, at 6 unbent the sails began to unrig, at Noon stripp'd the Topmasts and got them down.' The reference 'warp'd' relates to pulling (warping) the ship along by her cable, which, made fast to a fixed point, is hauled in by means of the capstan. The 'Sheer Hulk' mentioned is a vessel (usually redundant for sea service) rigged with tall sheer legs (two heavy poles rigged with large blocks and tackle) used for lifting out masts.

Friday 1 October
The log recorded: 'D° Wea^r. Employed returning the Sails, Yards &c. A.M. unrigging the Ship, getting out the Provisions and empty Casks.'

Saturday 2 October
Carcass's log noted: 'First part Fresh Breezes in Cloudy, middle and latter light breezes and fair, employed returning stores, hawled the launch up, got out the Cables and Anchors.' The log entry next day reads: 'Light Breezes and fair, PM got the Cables ashore.'

Monday 4 October
'Fresh Breezes, sometimes rain, A.M. starting the water and getting out the Casks, got out the Booms.' 'Starting the water' involves taking out the bungs, which allows the barrels to empty into the bilge, the discarded water then being pumped overboard using the ship's bilge pump.

Tuesday 5 October (week of)
The log continues: 'D° Wea^r. Employed returning the Booms and Anchors, returned the spare Sails and rigging.' Next day, the 'First part light Breezes and fair, PM transported to the side of the Hulk, AM returning Boatswain's and Carpenter's Stores.' Thursday's log entry simply reads: 'Fresh Breezes with rain employed as before.' Work undertaken on Friday and Saturday generally comprised 'returning

stores'. The log entry for Sunday 10 October records: 'Ditt° Wea^r P.M. returned the Spirits, Wine and some empty Casks.'

Monday 11 October
The weather was squally with rain easing to fresh breezes and fair later, the log entry reading: 'A.M. unrigged the Main Yard and stripp'd the Mainmast, employed returning the rigging and other Stores.' Tuesday and Wednesday were spent returning stores and cleaning the ship.

Thursday 14 October
Lutwidge's last entry in the *Carcass*'s log simply reads: 'Moderate and fair, PM employed cleaning the ship A.M. she was paid off.' Lutwidge concluded the journal with his signature.

Carcass's ship's company, like that of the *Racehorse*, would be dispersed either home or to other ships, naval service or mercantile, their careers governed by the vagaries of fortune and politics. Both Phipps and Lutwidge presented themselves at the Admiralty to give account to Lord Anson and his Board, as well as to the Royal Society. For their endeavours and leadership Commander Phipps and Commander Lutwidge were both promoted to full captain. For a brief while both men enjoyed a degree of celebrity before resuming active duty in command of other ships. Phipps presented a silver pocket watch to each of his *Racehorse* officers and midshipmen as a token of gratitude for their loyal support throughout their most strange voyage.

Despite all they had contributed towards exploration, the dark clouds of war against the American colonists were looming in the futures of both the men and the ships of the polar expedition. Not only would this transatlantic Civil War affect the fates of the individual men from both ships, but it would also determine the fate of the *Racehorse* and *Carcass* as fighting ships of war.

HM Ships Racehorse and Carcass
following the 1773 voyage

HM ship Racehorse

Returning into Deptford on 29 September 1773, *Racehorse* was moored alongside the wall and paid off, and received a 'small fitting', costs being £4 12s 0d for her hull, masts and yards, and £149 7s 3d for rigging and stores: a total of £153 19s 3d.[1]

During the 15-month period that *Racehorse* was laid up, the ensuing political unrest between Britain and her American colonists worsened; war, it appeared, was inevitable. When the Royal Navy began to mobilise, the *Racehorse* was not exempt, and in January 1775 the ship was recommissioned under the command of James Orrok. She was reconverted into a bomb vessel at a cost of £2,679 1s 3d and, more befitting to her new role, renamed by Admiralty Order HMS *Thunder* on 24 October 1775.[2]

On the same date, the 63-year old Orrok was superseded by Commander James Reid. Although Orrok was perfectly capable of dealing with *Racehorse*'s refit, he was now considered too old to hold such an active post. Reid was younger, an experienced bomb vessel commander who had previously held command of Lutwidge's ship *Carcass* before her Arctic reconversion.

The American War of Independence

Commander Reid soon received orders to join Commodore Sir Peter Parker's squadron being deployed to serve in North America.

Parker hoisted his broad pennant in the 50-gun fourth-rate *Bristol*[3] and assembled his ships off Cork, where a large force of troops under Lord Cornwallis were embarked. Nelson later served in *Bristol* as 3rd Lieutenant in 1778.

Parker sailed at the end of January 1776 and once the newly named *Thunder* was out of the dockyard, Reid sailed to join Parker on 23 February. Parker's main objective was to support a combined operations attack upon the American rebels at Charlestown, South Carolina. The *Thunder* arrived with Parker's squadron and transports off Cape Fear, North Carolina, in May. Parker's first role was to transport 2,500 troops under the command of General Clinton and land them on Long Island, Charleston. The aim of these troops was to wade across the channel between Long Island and Sullivan's Island and assault the fort. Supported by the Navy, Parker's second role was to carry out a naval bombardment to breach the defences, an objective well suited to the bomb vessel *Thunder* with its 13in and 10in explosive shells. After landing the troops, Parker's squadron sailed south, arriving off Charleston in early June. His squadron now comprised the following ships.[4]

Parker's squadron at the attack on Fort Sullivan (Moultrie) 28 June 1776[5]

Name	Guns	Rate	Commander
Bristol	50	4th	John Morris
Experiment	50	4th	Alexander Scott
Actæon	28	5th	Christopher Atkins
Active	28	5th	William Williams
Solebay	28	5th	Thomas Symonds
Syren	28	5th	Christopher Furneaux
Sphinx	20	6th	Anthony Hunt
Thunder	8	Bomb	James Reid
Friendship	22	6th	?

The American rebels, led by patriot Colonel William Moultrie, had taken up defence inside a wooden palisade fort located at the southern end of Sullivan's Island on the north side of Charlestown harbour. Named Fort Sullivan at the time, it was later renamed Fort Moultrie. Moultrie's defenders, comprising the 2nd South Carolina Regiment and a company of the 4th South Carolina Artillery, numbered 435 men. The intention of the attack was to bombard the garrison into submission while General Clinton's British troops attempted an assault from landward. The attack commenced on Friday 28 June, the ships weighing anchor at 10.30am.

By 11.15am, Parker had disposed his ships with the *Bristol, Experiment* and *Active* anchored in line ahead to the eastward 400 yards (366m) off shore to open a direct fire upon the fort. At the same time the frigates *Actæon, Sphinx* and *Syren* passed by the fort, stationing themselves westward to protect the major ships from fire ships. The *Thunder,* protected by the *Friendship,* anchored south-east ahead and outside the other ships at a range of about 1½ miles (2.4km) from the east bastion and commenced firing her shells into the fort, their high trajectory meeting their mark.

Despite Parker's able planning, the assault began to falter. First, the shallow depth of water prevented the ships getting in close; second, and unexpectedly, the fort's soft palmetto log walls actually absorbed the British shot like a sponge, nullifying the anticipated effect of splinter injuries on the garrison lying within, who were able to maintain a vigorous return of fire. Moreover, the springs[6] holding the *Bristol* in position were shot through when the ship swung round with the tide, exposing her vulnerable stern to the continuous barrage of gunfire from the fort. Unable to manoeuvre out of the line of fire, the *Bristol* suffered considerable casualties as the shot smashed in through her stern, passing longitudinally through the gun decks. The quarterdeck was so devastatingly raked that those manning it sustained high casualties, Captain John Morris being instantly killed. Only Parker remained standing, though his breeches had been blown off, leaving his backside exposed, and he was stuck by splinters, which slightly wounded his knee and thigh.

The entire situation was exacerbated when despite the best efforts of the *Thunder* lobbing her bombs into the fort, her explosive shells appeared totally ineffective. Reporting on this later, Moultrie said that although 'most of them fell within the fort we had a morass in the middle which swallowed them instantly and those that fell in the sand were immediately buried'.[7]

Believing that range required compensating, the *Thunder*'s artil-lerymen increased the firing charges, the amplified recoil effect of which led to her mortars breaking out of their mounts; with her mortar beds cracked, the *Thunder* had to discontinue firing. Parker's attack was further thwarted when the *Actæon, Sphinx* and *Syren* each ran aground upon unmarked sandbars; the *Actæon* and *Sphinx* collided and became entangled in the process, the *Sphinx* completely losing her bowsprit. Unable to add their weight of gunfire against the fort, Colonel Moultrie's position was soon alleviated, Moultrie later reporting: 'Had these three ships effected their purpose, they would have enfiladed us in such a manner, as to have driven us from our guns.'[8]

Although the *Sphinx* and *Syren* were successfully refloated, the *Actæon* remained hard aground. By evening, Parker was compelled to withdraw. Bearing the brunt of the American fire, the *Bristol* suffered considerably, with 40 killed and 71 wounded. Her main and mizzen mast rigging was shot through by chain shot, the main mast severely wounded with nine shot.[9] Marginally less damaged, the *Experiment* still sustained 29 killed and 56 wounded, while the frigates *Active* and *Solebay* each suffered 15 killed.[10] As for the *Actæon* now hard aground, she was abandoned and although set on fire she was boarded by patriots who looted the ship's stores and fired her guns upon the British ships, the rebels quitting the wreck before fires reached her magazines and the ship blew up.[11]

Commenting on the American defence, one British observer remarked: 'their fire was surprisingly well served' and it was 'slow, but decisive indeed; they were very cool and took care not to fire except their guns were exceedingly well directed'.[12] American casualties amounted to just 12 killed and 25 wounded.[13] The rebel victory at Sullivan's Island galvanised the patriots' drive for independence; the Declaration of Independence itself was signed at Philadelphia just six days later, on Thursday 4 July 1776.[14]

After this action, command of the *Thunder* was taken over by Commander Anthony James Pye Molloy, the ship remaining deployed off the north-eastern American seaboard. In April 1778, James Gambier took over command of the *Thunder*, by which date France was now actively supporting the American cause, a French Royal Naval fleet under Admiral Jean Baptiste Charles Henri Hector d'Estaing being now close at hand. Operating off Sandy Hook on 4 August 1778, the *Thunder* unfortunately fell in with the French 74-gun ships *Hector* and *Vaillant* from d'Estaing's squadron. After a brief exchange of fire *'pour l'honneur de pavillon'* ('for the honour of the flag'), the *Thunder* was overwhelmingly outgunned and, losing her masts, was captured and later burned. Gambier and two surviving crew were later released.[15]

HM Ship *Carcass*

Following the polar expedition, the *Carcass* came to 'At single anchor in Gallions' [Reach] Wednesday 29 September 1773.' Next day the ship was 'Lash'd Long Side the Sheerhulk at Deptford.' Soon afterwards the crews were dispersed and on 14 October both the *Carcass* and *Racehorse* were paid off'.

With war against Britain's rebel American colonists imminent, the *Carcass* was recommissioned under Commander James Reid on 21 January 1775. Taken into dock at Deptford ten days later, the *Carcass* was refitted for her impending service abroad. Fully completed at a cost of £345 17s 7d for her hull mast and yards, and £657 6s 4d for rigging and stores, the ship left the dockyard on 28 March.[16] During the second week of April the *Carcass* made her way down the Thames to the Nore and anchored EbN off Sheerness Light and SW 1½ miles (2.4km) off Sheerness Garrison. At noon on 10 April, the *Carcass* weighed and sailed for the North Foreland, where she was deployed to escort an outward-bound convoy of merchantmen and in company with her previous companion HM Sloop *Racehorse* made sail for Senegal on the West African coast. The ten-week voyage on escort duties was quite uneventful and the *Carcass* returned to Spithead on Wednesday 19 August and proceeded up Channel to the Downs, finally anchoring at the Nore on 31 August.

Two days later, the *Carcass* was 'moored alongside a hulk at Sheerness' disembarking her guns and stores. The ship then moved upriver, arriving at Woolwich on 5 September. David Ogilvie, who had served as master in the *Carcass* since 21 January 1775, made his last log entry on 13 September 1775: 'Sent the Marines on Shore to March to Chatham Head Qtrs the Commissioner came down &

paid the Ship off.'[17] Next day, the ship was immediately docked and refitted at a cost of £2,613 18s 4d.[18]

On 21 November, the *Carcass* was recommissioned as a sloop under the command of Robert Dring, the ship being relaunched the following day. Dring remained in command until he was superseded on 2 February 1777, during which time the *Carcass* appears to have been deployed in home waters escorting convoys and undertaking policing duties, stopping and searching vessels as necessary.

On 3 February 1777 command passed to John Howarth. One month later, the *Carcass* went into dock at Portsmouth for minor repairs and to have her sheathing removed, the overall expenses amounting to £853 0s 5d. Sailing on 29 March, *Carcass* resumed her previous duties.[19]

In 1778 we find the *Carcass* deployed in the West Indies. Her master's log records that she arrived at Gross Islet Bay, St Lucia, on Friday 13 February and had to land 18 sick men next day. On Tuesday 17 February, the log states that *Carcass* spoke with the 24-gun *Seahorse* and learned that a French fleet had been seen off Grenada. Signals were immediately made to Admiral Byron and his squadron, the *Carcass* in company, was sent 'in pursuit of French fleet. Ad^m made signal for the Ships to Engage as they came up in succession. Ad^m Barrington and the headmost ships began to engage the Enemy, we begun to engage soon after They bore away Ad^m made sign^l to pursue them and begun the Engagement again.'[20]

A running engagement between the fleets continued into the next day with the *Carcass*'s log recording: 'Left off firing being at two greater distance Ad^m made sign^l for the fleet to gather, Saw the lights of the French fleet bearing away at SBN. Had our sails and Rigging very much Damaged and 8 men Killed and 14 wounded.'[21]

By the Sunday, the *Carcass* had been at sea for a considerable period so the commander 'Put the ship's company to 2/3 Allowance of Beef & Pork'. Although damaged, the *Carcass* sailed into Basse Terre Roads, St Kitts on 27 February to make good her rigging and restock provisions. By 6 March she was back at sea in company with the ships *Maidstone* (28 guns) *Deale Castle* (20 guns) and *Sphinx* (20 guns), at which time it was understood that the French fleet lying off the island of Nevis numbered '7 ships of the line 7 frigates and 3 sloops'.

After this, the *Carcass* resumed more normal duties operating between the British West Indian possessions and Bermuda, with Howarth succeeded in command by Edward Edwards on 22 April. Disease in ships serving on the West Indies station was quite common and the ship's log records many instances where prevention was undertaken, such as 'washed between decks with Vinegar and Soap', and 'Smoak'd Ship between decks'. Back in harbour for the first part of June 1778, the crew were engaged in refitting the ship, during which process the main mast was removed temporarily. On Saturday 20 June the *Carcass*'s log records: 'arrived HM ships *Proserpine*, Commodore Hotham and the *Albermarle*.'[22] The *Albemarle*, a sixth-rate frigate of 28 guns, would come under the command of Captain Horatio Nelson in 1782.

Three days later *Carcass* was ready to go to sea: 'Came on B^d a pilot and took charge of the Ship, Hauled [in] the Boats and made sail.' By 25 June the ship lay 'off Martenico' and on Friday 3 July, while cruising at sea, she 'spoke with Boreas'.[23] The *Boreas*, another 28-gun sixth-rate frigate, would also later be commanded by Captain Horatio Nelson in 1783.

The *Carcass* remained on the West Indies station for a few years. During this period command passed to John Young on 9 December 1780; Edward Herbert on 12 June 1781; and John Young again from 30 July 1781 until the ship was recalled back to England. Arriving at Woolwich on 16 November 1781, the *Carcass* was paid off on 4 December the same year. In February 1782 the *Carcass* was 'Surveyed afloat at Woolwich', and was found 'in want of a Middling Repair'. The cost of refitting a somewhat obsolete vessel seemed prohibitive and the work was deferred. Finally, on 5 August 1784, the *Carcass* was sold for £320.[24]

17

The officers and men after the voyage

With the polar expedition concluded, the men of the ships were dispersed into the fleet once their ships had been paid off. Some would enjoy an active role within the Royal Navy, others made their mark elsewhere in society. As for the common seamen, who tend to simply disappear from history, through archival research, for example in ship's muster books, it may be possible to identify them in other Royal Naval ships. For those who entered the mercantile fleet, traceability would prove more difficult. Others, influenced by their Arctic experience, perhaps sought employment in the whaling ships where pay could be better. Whoever they were, officers or seamen, their experiences on the expedition must have had a profound effect on their general outlook.

The men from the *Racehorse*

Constantine Phipps
On his return from the voyage, Constantine Phipps was immediately promoted to full captain. A couple of years later, following the death of his father on 13 September 1775, Phipps succeeded as 2nd Baron Mulgrave (Ireland). In December 1777, Phipps was elected into Parliament as MP for Huntingdon. That same year Lord Sandwich appointed Phipps as one of the Lords of the Admiralty Board, a position he held until April 1782. During his time on the Board, Phipps became the Admiralty's principal speaker in the House of Commons. He also became one of Sandwich's closest colleagues – a relationship made clear in Sandwich's letter to Phipps of January 1779:

'How much I long for your return to town and how lamely business goes on in your absence; when anything in which this office is concerned comes to be agitated in Parliament, I really know not what we shall do without your assistance.'[1] Phipps was apparently not the most brilliant of parliamentary speakers but being a master of his subject it seems he rarely failed to convince even a hostile house.

Just a couple of years after the polar expedition ended, Britain was embroiled with the American War of Independence (1775–83). Phipps soon found himself back on active sea service and in 1776 he was placed in command of the 64-gun ship *Ardent*. In the spring of 1778 he took command of the 74-gun *Courageux* as part of Admiral Augustus Keppel's Channel Fleet, Keppel flying his flag in the 100-gun *Victory*. On 27 July that same year the *Courageux* undertook a leading role in the indecisive First Battle of Ushant against a French fleet commanded by the comte d'Orvillier. During this engagement, Phipps led the attack upon the French 90-gun *Ville de Paris*, although the French ship escaped due to confusion between Keppel's two divisions, Admiral Sir Hugh Palliser's rear division failing to closely engage at the crucial point of battle. When the fleet returned, Phipps was called to Whitehall to give evidence at the court martial investigating Keppel's failure to capture or destroy d'Orvillier's fleet and Phipps came to the defence of Palliser.[2] For the *Victory* (later Nelson's flagship at Trafalgar in 1805), this was the ship's first major naval engagement.

When Admiral Sir Hugh Palliser was forced to resign in April 1779, Phipps became a leading member of the Admiralty Board and Sandwich's principal adviser in all professional matters, although he remained at sea. He stayed remarkably well informed by maintaining a continuous correspondence with Sandwich. As early as December 1777 Phipps became one of the principal architects of a plan to abandon the American War of Independence as a sideshow, with a view to making a concentrated strike in the West Indies before the French could fully intervene. This strategy could have changed the course of the war, perhaps bringing it more swiftly to a conclusion. However, government indecision prevailed, the French Navy was able to mobilise fully and the war carried on for a further six years when Spain and Holland interceded in alliance with France in 1778.

When a combined Franco-Spanish fleet entered the Channel in June 1781, Phipps had been directed to command a significant raid upon Flushing. This, however, had to be cancelled at the last minute. Phipps then submitted a plan to consolidate a large naval force in the Caribbean, which, if adopted by the ministry, could have left the Channel and North Sea with minimal defensive forces. Fortunately, when the North administration fell in 1782, the proposal was abandoned, saving both Sandwich and Phipps potential embarrassment. Phipps remained in command of the *Courageux* until 1781, serving under Admirals Charles Hardy, Francis Geary, George Darby and Richard Howe, all flying their flags in the 100-gun *Victory*. On 4 January 1781 Phipps captured the 32-gun French frigate *La Minerve* in heavy weather off Brest.[3]

On 3 September 1783, the Treaty of Versailles recognised the autonomy of the American colonies, ending the American War of Independence. The *Courageux* was paid off and once back on shore Phipps never went to sea again. He remained as MP for Huntingdon until 1784, when he next became MP for Newark. In April that year, Phipps took on the position as Paymaster of the Forces and on 18 May 1784 he was appointed commissioner for the affairs of India, the administrative role of the Lords of 'Trade and Plantations'. Now aged 43, Phipps finally married on 20 June 1787, his 18-year-old bride being Anne Elizabeth Cholmley (1769–88). The marriage was tragically short, as Anne died in childbirth the following year, leaving Phipps a daughter as the only Mulgrave heir. Despite this misfortune, Phipps continued actively working in his various posts until ill health forced him to resign in 1791. On retirement, he was created Baron Mulgrave in the peerage of Great Britain. For his services, Phipps was also made a Fellow of the Royal Society and the Society of Antiquaries.

Aged just 48, Phipps died at Liège on 10 October 1792 and was buried on 29 October at Lythe, Yorkshire. Summarising Phipps's character, NAM Rodger remarked: 'Mulgrave was not an original thinker; his conventional attitude to the rewards of office and influence caused the reforming Sandwich some embarrassment, and he vainly opposed the introduction of carronades, a new type of gun which played a significant part in the Navy's recovery from the worst days of the American war. In his virtues, however, he was typical of Sandwich's naval followers; he was not showy or well known, but a thorough seaman with a deep knowledge of the Navy, who built up the finest naval library in England and founded his political position on his professional mastery.'

The officers

Henry Harvey

Following the Arctic voyage, *Racehorse's* first lieutenant, Henry Harvey, was immediately promoted to commander and had an active career spanning the course of three different wars. With the onset of the American War of Independence he was promoted commander going into the 14-gun sloop *Martin* on the North American station. He was involved with the siege of Quebec on 6 May 1776, afterwards joining Vice Admiral John Montagu's squadron off Newfoundland protecting convoys against rebel colonists as they sailed from the St Lawrence River. On 9 May 1777 Montagu posted Harvey into the 24-gun frigate *Squirrel,* deployed out of St John's in February 1778 on escort convoys to Africa. That November, Harvey was appointed to his former commanding officer's commission in the new 32-gun frigate *Convert* escorting convoys in the Irish Sea and off Scotland, during which time he briefly took command of Phipps's 74-gun *Courageux* while it was fitting out.

Back in the *Convert,* Harvey was briefly involved with the relief of Jersey when the French attempted to capture the Channel Islands in May 1779. He next found himself involved in search of the American Continental Naval commander John Paul Jones off Ireland, whose success against British shipping earned him the title 'Father of the American Navy'. In December 1779, Harvey joined Admiral Sir George Rodney's fleet in the Leeward Islands of the West Indies, much of the time shadowing the now ever-present French warships. When naval command in the West Indies was temporarily held by Admiral Sir Samuel Hood, Harvey fought with Hood at the Battle of St Kitts (Battle of Frigate Bay) on 25 and 26 January 1782 between the British fleet under Rear-Admiral Sir Samuel Hood and a larger French fleet under Admiral François-Joseph Paul, Marquis de Grasse Tilly, Comte de Grasse. With Rodney he again saw action against de Grasse at the Battle of the Saintes on 12 April 1782. That December he was appointed to the 32-gun *Cleopatra*, in which he returned home to England and paid off the ship in April 1783.

Briefly unemployed until 1786, Harvey took command of the 28-gun frigate *Pegasus* for service on the North American station. This proved difficult as his first lieutenant was Prince William Henry, who expected to hold command once at sea.[4] However, Harvey handled the situation with 'such discretion as secured to him the lasting friendship of His Royal Highness'.[5]

Within weeks Harvey transferred into the 28-gun *Rose*, jointly operating with the *Pegasus* in peacetime manoeuvres off North America. Serving with him as a midshipman in the *Rose* was his eldest son, Henry, who unfortunately drowned in a shipboard accident. When the *Rose* paid off in 1789 Harvey went 'on the beach' on half pay. Following the Spanish armament during the Nootka Crisis of 1790, Harvey, like many officers, was recalled into service and given consecutive command of the 74-gun ships *Alfred* and *Colossus*.

Following the outbreak of the French Revolutionary War Harvey took command of 74-gun *Ramillies*, in which he was present with Admiral Lord Howe's fleet at the battle of the Glorious First of June in 1794. During this action Harvey distinguished himself by rescuing his brother John's ship *Brunswick*, which had become entangled with the French 74-gun *Vengeur du Peuple*. Although saved, John Harvey died of wounds received in this action.[6]

Promoted to rear admiral, Harvey hoisted his flag in the 98-gun *Prince of Wales* commanding the North Sea squadron and in June 1795 participated at the Battle of Groix, after which he supported Sir John Borlase Warren's invasion at Quiberon Bay. In April 1796, Harvey was made commander-in-chief of the Leeward Islands Station where in 1797 he supported the landing of Lieutenant General Sir Ralph Abercrombie's army to capture Trinidad from the Spanish.[7]

Coming up to 57 years of age, Harvey was looking to retire. Returning to England, he raised his flag in the 100-gun *Royal Sovereign* as second-in-command of the Channel Fleet until the Peace of Amiens in 1801 when he formally retired from the Navy as vice admiral. Promoted to full admiral in 1804, Harvey settled with his wife, Elizabeth, in Walmer, Kent. Here he died peacefully in 1810, survived by his wife and three of his five children. His son Thomas later became an admiral in his own right.[8]

Cuthbert Adamson

Racehorse's second lieutenant, Cuthbert Adamson, was not promoted beyond lieutenant after the voyage. Perhaps his Arctic experience and naval life in general disillusioned him as he subsequently retired on half pay and died in November 1804. Adamson married twice, his second wife, Mary Huthwaite, bearing him a son named John (born 3 September 1787), who went on to become a scholar of Portuguese and under-sheriff of Newcastle, in which role he passed the Municipal Corporation Act in 1835.[9]

Thomas Graves

After Lieutenant Thomas Graves was paid off from the *Racehorse* he sailed to North America in 1774 with his uncle Vice Admiral Samuel Graves in the 50-gun *Preston*, the Admiral assuming command of the North American station that July. In 1775 Thomas Graves was appointed command of the six-gun armed schooner *Diana* deployed in the prevention of smuggling, which was becoming more problematic as colonial insurrection increased. When Graves took the *Diana* from Boston into the Charles River on 27 May 1775 he was attacked by an insurgent force of 2,000 men. The ship ran aground and was set on fire and in the affray Graves was severely burned.[10]

Graves then commanded other tenders between Boston and Rhode Island until he was recalled to rejoin his uncle in the *Preston* and returned to England. Soon he was back on the North American station in the same ship, this time under Commodore William Hotham. On his promotion in 1779 he took command of HM Sloop *Savage*, operating on the West Indies and North American stations, and advanced to post rank in May 1778. In the absence of Commodore Edmund Affleck, he commanded the 74-gun *Bedford* in the Battle of the Chesapeake on 5 September. Remaining in the *Bedford* as Affleck's flag captain, Graves was involved in two significant naval actions. The first was the Battle of St Kitts (Battle of Frigate Bay). Fighting with distinction, the *Bedford* suffered just two killed and 15 wounded. The second engagement was the Battle of the Saintes (Battle of Dominica) on 9 and 12 April 1782 under the same British and French commanders. In this instance the *Bedford* suffered just 17 wounded and the British victory prevented the French and Spanish from invading Jamaica. That autumn Graves assumed command of the former French 36-gun frigate *Magicienne*. In this command Graves fought a very severe action with the French *Sybille* on 2 January 1783. Both vessels were wrecked before parting without conclusion: the dismasted *Magicienne* took two weeks to get into Jamaica; the *Sybille* was captured that February by HM Ship *Hussar*.[11]

After the ending of the American War of Independence, Graves spent time in France until the start of the French Revolutionary War in 1793. Despite the need to man the fleet with experienced men, it was not until October 1800 that Graves, now aged 53, was appointed command of the 74-gun *Cumberland* attached to Lord St Vincent's Channel Fleet. However, having been promoted to Rear Admiral of the White on 1 January 1801, that March Graves hoisted his flag in the 64-gun *Polyphemus* with Sir Hyde Parker's fleet proceeding to the Baltic to challenge the Danes. Shifting his flag into the 74-gun *Defiance*, Graves fought as second-in-command under Rear Admiral Horatio Nelson at the Battle of Copenhagen on 2 April 1801. For his services, Graves received the thanks of Parliament and appointment as Knight Commander of the Bath. In poor health, Graves retired from active service although his flag remained flying in the 98-gun *Foudroyant* stationed in the Bay of Biscay from 1804 to 1805. Promoted to vice admiral on 9 November 1805 and admiral on 2 August 1812, Thomas Graves died at Woodbine Hill, near Honiton, on 29 March 1814.[12]

Thomas Floyd
The career of Midshipman Thomas Floyd after his polar experience was sadly short. What we do know is that after the voyage Floyd spent some three-and-a-half years serving in the Mediterranean with little prospect of promotion and became so disillusioned that he was ready to quit the service. Encouraged by his peers to persevere, he served as a lieutenant in the 74-gun *Conqueror*, commanded by Captain Thomas Graves (formerly of the *Racehorse*) in May 1777, sailing to reinforce Howe and Byron's squadron on the North American station. In a letter dated June 1778 he states that the entire crew of the *Conqueror* were suffering the effects of scurvy and that only ten men were fit enough to stand on deck. Probably affected by scurvy himself, Floyd died in October 1778 aged just 29, while the *Conqueror* was stationed off Sandy Hook.

Philippe d'Auvergne

After the Arctic voyage, Philippe d'Auvergne entered into the 64-gun *Asia*, which in 1775 was stationed in Boston Harbor supporting the British forces fighting against the American militia. During this time, he was given charge of the *Asia* boats carrying soldiers to attack the town of Lexington and continued this role at Boston and at Bunker Hill and was also on board one of the ships that bombarded nearby Falmouth, setting fire to the town. Promoted to acting lieutenant, d'Auvergne served in the 50-gun *Chatham,* commanding the flat-bottomed boats with hinged gateways[13] landing troops on Long Island, during which he came under considerable fire when crossing to Manhattan Island.[14]

D'Auvergne was then assigned into the 50-gun *Preston*, flying the flag of Admiral Shuldham commanding the fleet in Boston. Shuldham, impressed with d'Auvergne's abilities, commissioned him lieutenant on 2 June 1777, giving him command of the eight-gun galley *Alarm*, in which he captured the 24-gun continental naval ship *Delaware* on 25 October 1777 and on 27 May 1778 landed marines at Fogland Ferry, successfully destroying the guardhouse.[15] When French frigates arrived at Rhode Island in late July 1778, d'Auvergne was ordered to scuttle the *Alarm* to avoid capture. Finding himself on shore, d'Auvergne was appointed the rank of major commanding the naval brigade.[16]

Returning to England, Auvergne was appointed first lieutenant in the 32-gun *Arethusa*, which on 18 March 1779 fought the French *L'Aigrette* off Ushant. Making her escape, the *Arethusa* struck a rock off the coast of Molène and although 13 escaped the remaining 187 crew, including d'Auvergne, were taken prisoner by the French and interned in Carhaix, Brittany.[17] Exchanged with French prisoners of war and returned to England in 1780, he was given command of the 26-gun sloop *Lark*, which in 1781 sailed as part of Commodore George Johnston's invasion fleet to the Cape of Good Hope to punish the Dutch for their alliance with the French.

At Porto Praya, Johnston's ships were attacked by a French squadron sent to help the Dutch and the *Lark* and other ships were damaged. Despite failing to land at the Cape, Johnston's squadron did capture a number of Dutch vessels. This success was mainly due to the intelligence report d'Auvergne submitted to Commodore Johnston, the details of which were based on information gathered from the *Active* after the capture of the Dutch East Indiaman *Heldwoltenlade* on 1 July. Not surprisingly, Johnston described d'Auvergne as a 'very promising young officer'.[18]

Promoted on to master and commander on 21 August 1781, d'Auvergne took command of the ten-gun cutter *Rattlesnake*, which with the 50-gun *Jupiter* was deployed to survey the remote volcanic islands of Trinidade and Martin Vaz north-east of Brazil to establish if they were suitable as a base for outward-bound Indiamen. Caught in a storm during the evening of 21 October, the *Rattlesnake* lost her anchor cable and ran on shore. Wishing to claim the islands for Britain, Commodore Johnston agreed to d'Auvergne and some of his crew staying on the tiny island, temporarily. However, it was not until 27 December 1782 when the 50-gun HMS *Bristol,* escorting an East Indiaman, passed by and saw the distress signals that all were rescued and taken to Madras.[19]

As with his previous loss of the *Alarm*, d'Auvergne would eventually face a court martial for the loss of the *Rattlesnake*, although he was acquitted. While in India, d'Auvergne met Muhammed Ali Khan Wallajah, the Nawab of Arcot. The Nawab asked d'Auvergne to make a petition to the king to reclaim his state, which he had been forced to surrender to the East India Company. On his return to Britain in 1783, d'Auvergne successfully raised the Nawab's petition, winning back his state. Soon after he was promoted to post captain, but 'on the beach' due to the peace with France, d'Auvergne spent three years travelling the Grand Tour, during which he spent a winter with Godefroy de La Tour Auvergne, the 6th Duke of Bouillon, in Normandy. As the duke's only heir was a disabled son and d'Auvergne had a bloodline connection with the family that had been previously proven, he readily adopted Philippe as the rightful heir with the title Prince of Bouillon. Bestowed upon him in 1786, this was formalised as 7th Duke of Bouillon in 1791 on the death of the duke's unfortunate son.

On 11 June 1786, d'Auvergne was elected a Fellow of the Royal Society and in 1787 he published his research work, *An Account of the New Improved Sea-compasses*. That same year the Admiralty appointed him as revenue officer for Jersey, giving him the 20-gun sixth-rate ship HMS *Narcissus* for this duty, but he resigned in 1789 due to ill health.[20]

In 1793, the island of Jersey found itself on the front line with revolutionary France, and its governor, Alexander Lindsay, tried to open communications between England and the French Royalists. However, before he could complete the task, he was posted to Jamaica. In 1794, the Admiralty posted d'Auvergne as a temporary replacement as commander of the floating batteries and gunboats defending Jersey from the Jacobins. In the September, d'Auvergne was officially appointed to the role with the title of *Administrateur des Secours Accordes aux Emigrés* (Administrator of Relief Grants to Émigrés). His duties were to: command a division of armed vessels to cover the Islands; open communications with the continent, to obtain information on hostile enemy movements; maintain communications with the insurgents in Western Provinces and to distribute assistance to the lay French emigrants in the Islands.[21]

D'Auvergne was provided with £30,000 a month by the British government's secret service, to which he reported directly, becoming effectively a spymaster. He also caused unrest in France and set up communications with the French Royalists through a network of spies and insurgents while smuggling arms, ammunition and supplies to them across the 14-mile (22.5km) stretch of water to the French mainland.[22]

When peace was declared with Republican France through the Treaty of Amiens on 25 March 1802, d'Auvergne lost the command of Jersey and had to retire on a captain's half pay. The Jersey émigrés he had supported were granted an amnesty by Bonaparte to return home. Moreover, although d'Auvergne's spy ring had diminished either through capture or had signed Bonaparte's declaration, he continued to collect intelligence from France, particularly about the large force Bonaparte was amassing at Brest.

When hostilities resumed in 1803, d'Auvergne was given the 44-gun frigate *Severn* to reinforce Jersey's defences, although the ship was unfortunately wrecked the following year. Promoted to rear admiral in 1808, d'Auvergne assumed command of naval ships in the Channel Islands. When Bonaparte confirmed an order to confiscate all assets of d'Auvergne's Bouillon family in 1809, he granted d'Auvergne's Château de Navarre to his divorced wife, Josephine. In time, the loss of d'Auvergne's estates left him with considerable financial difficulties. Suffering with ill health, d'Auvergne was forced to stand down from his role in 1812, after which he returned to London. He was also bankrupt, owing £12,000 in Jersey alone, and sadly committed suicide at Holmes' Hotel, London on 18 September 1816, aged 61. He was buried in St Margaret's Church, Westminster. Despite his desperate situation at his death, he still held the grand title of Monsignor His Serene Highness Philippe Duc de Bouillon d'Auvergne, of Jersey by the Grace of God and the will of his people.[23]

Able Seaman Gustav Weston (Olaudah Equiano)
In 1775, Equiano's supportive colleague, Dr Irving, embarked on a new project cultivating a sugar plantation on Jamaica and the Mosquito Coast in Central America. Trusting Equiano in preference to anyone else, he recruited him on the grounds of his African background and Igbo language to help select slaves and manage them as labourers on the plantations. Equiano initially declined on the grounds of his deep-rooted abhorrence of slavery, but having been given advice from friends and a certificate justifying his character, he eventually consented to the venture.[24] The certificate contained the following recommendation on his character:

'The bearer, Gustavus Vassa, has served me several years with strict honesty, sobriety, and fidelity. I can, therefore, with justice recommend him for these qualifications; and indeed, in every respect I consider him as an excellent servant. I do hereby certify that he always behaved well, and that he is perfectly trust-worthy Signed Charles Irving.'

Understandably, Irving had to provide Equiano with this certificate in order to satisfy the authorities in both Jamaica and the Mosquito Coast that Equiano was a bona fide 'free man', not to be mistaken for any black slave still living and working in these places.

The project having failed, Equiano returned to London and worked as a hairdresser and, expanding his activities, also learned to play the French horn and joined various debating societies. Further travels took him to Philadelphia in 1785 and New York in 1786, after which he settled in London. The experience of his travels led to his involvement with an abolitionist movement supported by the Quakers, which sought to end the slave trade. The kindness and freedom that Equiano had earlier received from Quaker Robert King (see p. 125) clearly influenced his mindset, along with the espousal of freedom and self-determination by the rebel American colonists. In 1786, Equiano became a member of the 'Sons of Africa', a group of 12 black men from London who were campaigning for the abolition of the slave trade. The following year the Society for Effecting the Abolition of the Slave Trade was founded by a denominational group of Anglicans who could directly influence Parliament. As Quakers could not become MPs, Equiano decided to become a Methodist to allow him to fully participate in the debate. Many friends and religious benefactors encouraged Equiano to write and publish his life story and, financially supported by philanthropic abolitionists, his autobiography *The Interesting Narrative of the Life of Olaudah Equiano or Gustavus Vassa, The African* was published in 1789. The book included such stirring paragraphs as the following impassioned argument against slavery: 'O, ye nominal Christians might not an African ask you – Learned you this from your God who says unto you, Do unto all men as you would men should do unto you? Is it not enough that we are torn from our country and friends to toil for your luxury and lust of gain? Why are parents to lose their children, brothers their sisters, or husbands and wives? Surely, this is a new refinement in cruelty, which, while it has no advantage to atone for it, thus aggravates distress, and adds fresh horrors even to the wretchedness of slavery.'[25]

The book soon became immensely popular with abolitionists and, travelling widely, including to Scotland, to promote his work, Equiano became a moderately wealthy man. It is one of the earliest books published by a black African writer and undoubtedly had an impact on abolitionists such as Granville Sharp and William Wilberforce, whose efforts led to the Act of Abolition being passed by both Houses of Parliament and given Royal Assent on 25 March 1807. In years to come, Equiano's work would influence other human and civil rights activists, including Martin Luther King.

Now aged 47, Equiano was living in Cambridgeshire and married a local Englishwoman, Susanna Cullen, at St Andrew's Church, Soham on 7 April 1792, the bride taking the surname of Vassa. The couple had two daughters: Anna Maria (1793–97) and Joanna (1795–57). Susanna died in February 1796 aged 34. Heartbroken, Equiano died barely a year later, on 31 March 1797. Soon after his death their elder daughter died aged just four. The younger child, Joanna Vassa, inherited Equiano's considerable estate of £950 (more than £80,000 today). Always positive in his outlook, Equiano's approach to life is summed up in this reflective paragraph: 'I believe there are few events in my life which have not happened to many: it is true the incidents of it are numerous, and did I consider myself a European, I might say my sufferings were great; but when I compare my lot with that of most of my country men, I regard myself as a particular favourite of Heaven, and acknowledge the mercies of Providence in every occurrence of my life.'[26]

The men from the *Carcass*

Skeffington Lutwidge

Like Phipps, Lutwidge was immediately promoted to captain in recognition of his able command on the Arctic voyage. In August 1775, Lutwidge was appointed to command the 28-gun sixth-rate HMS *Triton* and sailed to North America in March the following year. During the American War of Independence Lutwidge was continually in active service, at first deployed in the St Lawrence River between 1777 and 1778. On 10 April 1777, he was promoted commodore and commander-in-chief of the British naval forces based at St John's on Lake Champlain, jointly working with General Guy Carleton. Lutwidge's command included gunboats prefabricated in both England and Quebec. Once assembled and manned by Royal Naval personnel, these were deployed to combat the American vessels busy patrolling the lake. The gunboats were also used to escort and protect the British army units preparing to invade the colonies.[27]

On 2 July 1777, General John Burgoyne lay siege to Fort Ticondero. When it fell four days later, Lutwidge led the naval forces pursuing the American rebel forces retreating in boats across Lake Champlain.[28]

Superseded as commander by Captain Samuel Graves on 4 October 1777, Lutwidge resumed duties commanding the *Triton*, in which he captured the American privateer *Pompey* on 13 June 1778. In early 1779, the *Triton* sailed for Britain to be refitted and recoppered, after which Lutwidge returned his ship to the North American station, capturing the American privateer *Gates* on 29 September 1779. Next attached to Admiral George Rodney's fleet, Lutwidge was involved in the capture of a Spanish convoy on 8 January 1780 and during the night of 16 and 17 January took part in the action against the Spanish squadron under Don Juan de Lángara off Portugal. Generally named as the First Battle of Cape St Vincent, it is also known as Rodney's 'moonlight battle' as it took place at night. It was also the first major British naval victory over their European enemies during the American War of Independence and proved the value of copper-sheathing the hulls of warships.[29]

Lutwidge's final duty in the *Triton* during the American war was to escort a convoy to Minorca and then to the Leeward Islands, after which he briefly took command of the 74-gun third-rate ship *Yarmouth*, sailing her back to Britain with American prisoners of war and paying her off on arrival in March 1780. The *Yarmouth* had previously fought with the American Congress frigate *Randolph* commanded by Nicholas Biddle, who served under Lutwidge in the *Carcass* as an able seaman.

Almost immediately Lutwidge was posted to the new 36-gun fifth rate HMS *Perseverance*, and by September found himself deployed once more to the North American station. While on passage across the Atlantic, Lutwidge recaptured the 20-gun sixth-rate *Lively* on 29 July, which had been taken by the French more than two years earlier on 10 July 1778.

Lutwidge spent two further years on the North American station, during which time he captured many American privateers: the *General Green* on 30 August 1781; the *Raven* on 1 April 1782; and the *Diana* on 29 August 1782. At the conclusion of the American war in 1783, the *Perseverance* was recalled and paid off.[30]

Although Britain was once more at peace, Lutwidge remained actively employed and was given command of the 64-gun third-rate HMS *Scipio* in November 1786, the *Scipio* then serving as guard ship on the River Medway.[31] Three years later, the French Revolution took place and in December 1792 Lutwidge put into commission the new 74-gun third-rate HMS *Terrible*. On the outbreak of the French Revolutionary War, in April 1793 he sailed in the *Terrible* to join the Mediterranean fleet commanded by Admiral Samuel Hood. Promoted to Rear Admiral of the Blue on 12 April 1794, Lutwidge was further promoted to Rear Admiral of the White on 4 July that same year. Promoted once more, Lutwidge became Vice Admiral of the Blue on 1 June 1795.[32] Posted as Commander-in-Chief, The Nore, in 1797 Lutwidge hoisted his vice admiral's flag aboard the 90-gun second rate HMS *Sandwich*. When the *Sandwich* was paid off that September, Lutwidge shifted his flag into the newly appointed guard ship, the former Dutch 64-gun warship renamed HMS *Zealand*, that October. On 14 February 1799, Lutwidge was elevated to Vice Admiral of the Red, hoisting his flag in the 64-gun *Overyssel*, which had been captured from the Dutch on 22 October 1795.[33]

The year 1800 saw Lutwidge posted as commander-in-chief in the Downs and promoted Admiral of the Blue on 1 January 1801. It was in this year that his former midshipman in the *Carcass*, Horatio Nelson (now ranked Vice Admiral), was deployed under Lutwidge's overall command operating in the 38-gun fifth-rate frigate *Medusa* off the French coast, harassing the French invasion flotillas near Boulogne and Calais.[34]

Lutwidge received further promotions throughout the Napoleonic war: Admiral of the White on 9 November 1805 and Admiral of the Red on 31 July 1810. Sadly, this year saw the death of his wife, Catherine. Retired from his long active Royal Navy career, Lutwidge died at his estate of Holmrook on 16 August 1814, aged 78, with no children to succeed him. A distant relation was his great-nephew Charles Lutwidge Dodgson, better known as Lewis Carroll.[35] (Skeffington Lutwidge's nephew, Major Charles Lutwidge, who sold the Holmrook estate to him, was the father of Carroll's mother, Fanny.) A monument to Lutwidge's memory was raised in the parish church in Irton, Cumbria, in the form of a stained-glass window.[36]

Horatio Nelson

Fifteen-year-old Midshipman Nelson moved out of the *Carcass* with a gross wage of £8 12s 6d, the net sum amounting to £8 2s

2d after deductions of 10s 4d, and returned into the *Triumph* a far more confident young man, having taken great strides in 'lessons of seamanship, resourcefulness and resolution'.[37]

In Nelson's absence in the Arctic, his uncle Maurice Suckling had arranged for him to join the 24-gun sixth-rate frigate *Seahorse*, commanded by Captain George Farmer, which was part of a squadron assembling at Spithead for deployment in the East Indies under Commodore Sir Edward Hughes; the *Seahorse* sailed in company on 19 November 1773.[38]

On 19 February 1775, Nelson experienced his first taste of battle when the *Seahorse* was attacked by boats belonging to a hostile Indian prince, Hyder Ali. Having contracted malaria, Nelson was transferred into the 24-gun *Dolphin* on 14 March 1776 at Bombay and sent home to England. The *Dolphin*, which had earlier circumnavigated the world under John Byron, was now under the command of Captain James Pigott, and had been recalled for overdue disposal.[39] Of the attentive care he received on the homebound voyage, Nelson later said that Pigott's 'kindness at the time saved my life'.[40]

Once home, Nelson went to Bath to recuperate from his tropical illness but he would suffer from recurring fevers throughout his life. On 1 October 1776, Nelson entered as an acting fourth lieutenant into the 64-gun *Worcester* on convoy duty in the Channel and on 9 April 1777 he passed his lieutenant's exam in London, giving him a Master of Arts degree. Previously given the King's Commission as lieutenant, he now joined the 32-gun *Lowestoffe* as second lieutenant. The ship, commanded by Captain William Locker, sailed for deployment in the West Indies to uphold the Navigation Acts by blockading American vessels. While in this ship, Nelson captured his first prize, the American brig *Resolution*, as the only officer willing to get into the sea boat and board the vessel in the heavy sea conditions. Impressed by Nelson's zeal, Locker gave him temporary command of the small schooner *Little Lucy* in November 1777, in which, between January and April 1778, Nelson independently captured his first prize ships. On 5 September 1778, Nelson was appointed first lieutenant in Commodore Sir Peter Parker's 50-gun flagship *Bristol*. Later promoted to commander, Nelson was appointed into the 12-gun brig *Badger* on 8 December that year, the vessel being deployed off Jamaica against American privateers.

Promoted to post captain, Nelson was given command of the 28-gun *Hinchingbroke* on 1 September 1779 at Port Royal to cruise off the Mosquito coast of South America between Cartagena, and in January 1780 received orders to undertake an expedition against the Spanish forts on the San Juan River, Nicaragua. He accompanied 'one Ship 2 Briggs 3 Sloops and the Royal George tender' carrying some 200 troops. The expedition proved extremely difficult, with men suffering from yellow jack and malaria, and Nelson himself plagued with fevers and dysentery; the entire force had to retire. While Collingwood took command of the *Hinchingbroke*, Nelson was appointed commander of the 44-gun *Janus* but was too ill to actually take command.[41]

Returning home to Bath to convalesce, Nelson was next given command of the 28-gun *Albemarle* at Woolwich where, on 23 August 1781, he 'hoisted my Pendant'[42] and spent the next two years escorting convoys to the St Lawrence River, New York and the Baltic. He was also present at the failed attempt to capture Turk's Island in the West Indies in March 1783. On 3 September that year, the Treaty of Versailles ended the American War. Although at peace, Royal Naval duties continued and Nelson was given command of the 28-gun nine-pounder frigate *Boreas*. Assuming command on 24 March 1784, he sailed from St Helen's Roads off Portsmouth on 19 May for Barbados.

In the West Indies, he would meet new challenges, responsibilities and marriage to Frances Nisbet. With the American war concluding, Nelson, like many, returned to England and found himself unemployed 'on the beach' on half pay, residing with his wife at his father's home in Norfolk and living the life of a country gentleman. This interlude was short-lived.

Bankrupt France collapsed into turmoil with the Revolution and ensuing war. When King Louis XVI was guillotined in 21 January 1793, Britain's Royal Navy, anticipating war, was fully mobilised. As part of this process, the 64-gun ship HMS *Agamemnon* was recommissioned under Nelson's command. After provisioning, Nelson sailed the *Agamemnon* to join the fleet lying at the Nore and then sailed to join the Mediterranean fleet under Vice Admiral, the Viscount Samuel Hood.[43]

From this point on, Nelson would rise in rank and reputation to prove a formidably tenacious adversary to the French. The man who at 14 years old had once walked the decks of the *Carcass* amid the threat of Arctic ice would die in battle off Cape Trafalgar in October 1805 while walking the quarterdeck of his 100-gun flagship *Victory*, winning the hearts and minds of the British nation.[44]

Nicholas Biddle

Also nurtured out of the *Carcass*, the fledgling American Navy would also have its hero: Able Seaman Nicholas Biddle. Serving honourably under Lutwidge's command as coxswain, once paid off from the *Carcass* Biddle returned home to Philadelphia, probably serving his passage in one of the many westward-bound merchantmen. Following the outbreak of the American War of Independence, the Pennsylvania Committee of Safety sought capable seamen, and especially those with Royal Navy experience; professionally, Biddle was an ideal candidate. On 1 August 1775, the committee placed Biddle in command of the armed galley *Franklin*, which was put into service under the control of Continental Congress together with some 13 row galleys. Built at Philadelphia at a cost of £550 and all being fitted with a single gun mounted in the bow, these gunboats were all deployed on the Delaware River under the overall command of Thomas Read, the first naval officer to attain the rank of commodore in command of the Continental Naval fleet. The vessels were to be used to oppose hostile incursions made by the British Navy upholding the imposed Trade and Navigation acts on colonial merchant shipping and smugglers alike.[45]

In December 1775, Biddle was commissioned into the Continental Navy as one of the first five captains of what would become the United States Navy and given command of the 14-gun brig *Andrew Doria*, in which Biddle fought in the Continental Navy's action against the 20-gun sixth-rate HMS *Glasgow* on 6 April 1776.[46]

When the *Andrew Doria* sailed with the American Commodore Esek Hopkins to New Providence, Biddle proved a successful commander, capturing numerous armed merchantmen, including two armed transports carrying 400 reinforcements for the British Army in North America. However, the raid on New Providence by the fledgling American Navy was not without problems as many of the colonial seamen were stuck down with smallpox, though Biddle's ship *Andrew Doria* was not affected. Biddle's earlier Royal Naval training had stood him in good stead for, besides keeping a clean ship to combat potential disease, he had wisely had all his crew inoculated against smallpox beforehand.[47] As Biddle's ship was disease-free, Hopkins transferred his sick into the *Andrew Doria* for passage home and hospitalisation.[48]

Biddle's success continued, so much so that after capturing many ships when cruising off the Newfoundland Banks, when the *Andrew Doria* returned into port only five seamen remained on board, the rest out crewing the prizes.[49]

On 6 June 1776, the Continental Congress appointed Biddle to command of the USS *Randolph*, a 32-gun frigate built recently in Philadelphia. Although violent storms dismasted his ship off the Delaware Capes, Biddle's superb seamanship brought *Randolph* into Charleston for repairs. Sailing again for the West Indies on 4 September 1777, Biddle captured the 20-gun sixth-rate *True Briton* and her three-ship convoy. Biddle's luck, however, was to change dramatically: operating off Barbados, the *Randolph* engaged the British 64-gun ship of the line HMS *Yarmouth* on 7 March 1778. Instead of attempting to flee from his more heavily armed adversary, Biddle boldly decided to engage. One eyewitness reported that the frigate held her own during the 20-minute engagement, appearing 'to fire four or five broadsides to the Yarmouth's one'. Gallantly though Biddle defended the *Randolph*, the powerful guns of the *Yarmouth's* broadsides soon took effect. Just after Biddle was severely wounded, shot penetrated the *Randolph's* powder magazines. Almost immediately the ship exploded, killing all but four of the 305 on board, Biddle included. The loss of *Randolph* was a serious blow to the fledgling Continental Navy.[50]

18

Later Arctic expeditions

The Treaty of Paris, signed on 10 February 1763, concluded the Seven Years' War (the French and Indian War – the first ever war fought on a world scale). Prussia and Austria, which had been fully involved in the struggle on the European front, signed a separate agreement – the Treaty of Hubertsburg – on 15 February 1763. Both treaties marked the beginning of British supremacy outside Europe, with Great Britain agreeing to uphold the protection of Roman Catholicism in the New World. Besides Britain gaining predominance over much of France's possessions in North America, the window of peace created by the Treaty enabled Britain to resume uninterrupted trading with the West Indies. Moreover, through the increasingly powerful support of the Honorable East India Company (HEIC), she was free to expand her commercial ties with the lucrative markets of India. Added to these mercantile assets, Britain could now use her Royal Navy in the pursuit of exploration, itself becoming a parallel arm to the ensuing 'age of enlightenment'.[1] The Admiralty, backed by the Royal Society, had already seen the navigator Captain James Cook undertaking extensive exploration into the Pacific and South Seas between 1768 and 1771, and Cook would continue to explore new seas and lands until his death in 1779.

Despite increasing momentum in the field of exploration, Phipps's 1773 polar expedition was the last serious attempt by the Royal Navy to seek a northerly trading passage to the East for 72 years. The delay was not because Phipps's expedition had to some degree failed, nor was it a matter of financial resources; Cook sailed on his third voyage in 1776. The main factor was global politics. Despite the many advantages created by the hard-earned peace enabled through treaties of Paris and Hubertsburg in 1763, the recent conflict had left smouldering dissatisfaction in England's American colonies. Within three years of young Nelson's and Biddle's return from the Arctic, instability and political disenfranchisement led to the Declaration of American Independence by the colonists in Philadelphia on 4 July 1776 and soon developed into what was effectively a transatlantic civil war. Soon the Royal Navy was back on a war footing and any British voyages of exploration were abandoned until after the end of the American War of Independence (1775–83).

Even then, the only exploratory voyage undertaken by Britain after 1783 was the ill-fated expedition of Lieutenant William Bligh. Given command of HM armed transport *Bounty*, Bligh's objective was to collect breadfruit plants from Otaheite (now Tahiti) in the Society Islands and transport them to Jamaica in the Caribbean to be replanted as a staple diet source for the slave population. This enterprise, supported by the Royal Navy, had Royal Society involvement in the form of botanist David Nelson and his assistant William Brown from Kew. The Board of Longitude also provided Bligh with Kendall's chronometer K2, which had previously been used by Phipps. Bligh departed from Portsmouth on 23 December 1787 sailing for Cape Horn but was unable to make passage this way against adverse winds and treacherous seas. He was forced to go eastwards via the Cape of Good Hope and the *Bounty* finally anchored in Matavai Bay in Otaheite on Sunday 26 October 1788 after travelling some 27,086 nautical miles (31,170 miles/50,163km). After successfully gathering 1,000 plants, Bligh sailed in early April 1789 for the Caribbean. On Tuesday 28 April 1789, Bligh was faced with a notorious mutiny.[2]

While the year 1789 was calamitous for Britain, it was much more so for France. The American War of Independence had left France extremely vulnerable; she was virtually bankrupt from supporting the American rebellion against Britain and successive poor harvests had generated further discontent against the aristocracy. The result was revolution within six years of the end of the American war, ignited when a mob in Paris, urged on by shouts of *liberté, equalité* and *fraternité*, stormed the Bastille on 14 July

1789. This event sparked off a revolution of unprecedented scale. Complete turmoil ensued under the self-imposed Jacobin rule of the National Convention with its bloody reign of terror led by Maximilien Robespiere's Committee of Public Safety. When the French King Louis XVI was beheaded on 21 January 1793, Britain declared war on France on 1 February 1793, while her ally Austria turned against the French revolutionary government that April. The ensuing French Revolutionary War enveloped all of Europe and involved some 16 countries, until a brief peace was agreed in 1801. This, however, turned out to be a mere intermission as war started up again in 1803 in what became known as the Napoleonic Wars against the rule of the French general Napoleon Bonaparte, who had been crowned Emperor of France in 1802.

This new conflict continued until Bonaparte's formidable army was finally defeated by Britain and her five allied forces under Field Marshall Wellington at the Battle of Waterloo on 18 July 1815. As a result of these conflicts, for 22 years – from 1793 to 1815 – Britain's Royal Navy fought constantly on a global scale, leaving no room for exploration in any form.

When the Second Treaty of Paris was signed on 20 November 1815, finally ending the long period of war against France, Britain entered a period known as *Pax Britannia*. Following Nelson's complete annihilation of the operational capabilities of the French and Spanish navies at the Battle of Trafalgar of 21 October 1805, Britain's Royal Navy gained the freedom to re-establish its peace-time roles. This included policing the seas against piracy, upholding the Navigation Acts and supporting, where necessary, the general abolition of the slave trade.

At the same time the Royal Navy could start to think about exploration again, including seeking the fabled north-west passage. Although the desire to find a shorter trading route to the East was still an objective, the emphasis now lay with the navigation and charting of unknown seas and territory. It had been more than 40 years since Phipps, Lutwidge and the young Nelson had returned to England after their voyage in 1773 and all three were now dead, the former two by natural causes, Nelson dying at the Battle of Cape Trafalgar on 21 October 1805.

The expeditions of 1818

From 1804, Sir John Barrow held the post of Second Secretary to the Admiralty under the First Lord of the Admiralty Lord Melville. When Melville received a request from Joseph Banks at the Royal Society to make another attempt to seek the north-west passage, Barrow had two ships prepared: the *Dorothea* and the *Trent*. Overall command of the expedition was appointed to Captain David Buchan in the *Dorothea*. Commanding the *Trent* was Lieutenant John Franklin. Franklin, who had earlier served at Trafalgar as a signal midshipman in the 74-gun ship *Bellerophon*, had recently undertaken exploration work in the Arctic regions of Canada. The first lieutenant in the *Trent* was Frederick William Beechey – the son of the celebrated portrait artist William Beechey by his second marriage.[3] Like Phipps's 1773 expedition, both ships carried whaler men as ice pilots, one 'ice master' being the experienced Whitby whaling captain, William Scoresby.[4]

Buchan was instructed first to proceed to the Bering Strait and, if possible, to aim for the North Pole. Should he not succeed he was to 'endeavour to pass between Greenland and the east coast of America into the sea call[ed] Baffin Bay, for the northern limits of which as it appears in the charts there is little or no authority, and thence by Davis' Strait to England'.[5]

On reaching Spitsbergen, the ships became icebound. After being trapped for three weeks, the ships were freed when northerly winds helped to break up the ice. While attempting to proceed through a narrow channel in the pack ice they resorted, as had Phipps earlier, to using ice anchors to drag the ships and eventually reached a northern latitude 80°34′N. Turning westward, they proceeded towards Greenland where they encountered bad weather and were driven towards the pack ice. Measures were taken to protect the ships' hulls, the *Trent* rigging fenders made of cables, walrus hides and square iron plates, but all was in vain: 'all parts appear to be equally predictable at present one unbroken line of furious breakers in which events pieces arise with the evening subsiding the waves crashing together carrying such a noise that it was the greatest difficulty we could make our orders heard by the crew.'[6]

Approaching the edge of the ice, Lieutenant Beechey recorded the moment of impact: 'each person instinctively secured his own hold and with his eyes fixed upon the mast, waited in breathless anxiety the moment of concussion. It soon arrived – the brig cutting her way through the light ice, came in violent contact with the main body. In an instant we all lost our footing the masts bent with the impetus, and the cracking timbers from below bespoke a pressure which was calculated to awaken our serious apprehensions. The vessel staggered under the shock, and for the moment seemed to recoil; but the next wave, curling up under the counter, drove her about her own length within the margin of ice.'[7]

Stranded and buffeted between the ice floes, the *Trent* rolled profusely, her crew unable to stand against the violent movement. Beechey records: 'The motion indeed was so great the ship's bell, which in the heaviest gale of wind never struck itself, now tolled so continually that it was ordered to be muffled.'[8]

Fortunately, after setting more sail, the motive forces enabled the *Trent* to split ice floes 14ft (14.25m) thick, allowing her to escape from danger. With the *Dorothea* much battered by the ice, Buchan prudently decided to sail home, with Franklin reluctantly following in the *Trent*. Having reached just 80°34′N, they had achieved little more than Phipps.[9]

Totally obsessed with polar exploration, John Barrow published his scholarly book on the subject in 1818 under the title: *A Chronological History of Voyages into The Arctic Regions*. Typical of publications at that time, it had an extensive subtitle given as: *Undertaken chiefly for the Purpose of Discovering a North East and North West passage between the Atlantic and the Pacific from the earliest period of Scandinavian navigation to the departures of the Recent Expedition under the orders of Captains Ross and Buchan.*

The first publication of its kind, this work stands alone: pages 303 to 311 are devoted to Phipps's 1773 voyage while pages 364 to 379 cover the 1818 expedition of Buchan and Franklin. Modern research from primary source documents have brought new light to details disclosed in Barrow's book.[10]

Influenced by the earlier theories of Daines Barrington, Barrow firmly believed in the existence of a polar current that flowed between the Bering Strait and the Davis Strait. Using proof based upon drifting harpooned whales, Barrow submitted a proposal regarding the need to correct the 'defective geography of the Western Arctic' and ascertain the 'existence of a Northwest passage from the Atlantic to the Pacific'.[11]

Fully aware that the Russians were also seeking a route across the polar regions, Barrow believed that it was of national importance that the British, having actively sought this route on and off since the 16th century, should be the first to succeed. Realising what the Royal Navy could offer in furthering exploration, Barrow arranged a second voyage under the command of Captain John Ross in the *Isabella,* accompanied by the *Alexander* commanded by Lieutenant William Edward Parry. The expedition sailed on 18 April 1818 and met Captain Buchan's expeditionary ships at Lerwick on their return home from Spitsbergen and Greenland. Despite their best efforts, however, Ross and Parry achieved very little apart from making corrections to the charts of Baffin's Island and the surrounding seas and forging good relationships with the native Inuits of Greenland and Baffin's Island.

A third expedition was arranged in 1819, this time under the command of Parry in the *Hecla* bomb vessel, accompanied by the former gun brig *Griper,* commanded by Lieutenant Matthew Liddon. Passing up through Lancaster Sound they steered westwards along what is now called the Parry Channel, reaching longitude 110°W that September and the outermost of the Canadian Arctic islands, which they named Melville Island after the first Lord of the Admiralty. With provisions for two years' travel, Parry records that they had: 'a large supply of fresh meats and soups, preserved in tin cases by Messrs Donkin and Gamble, of Burkitt's be its essence of malt and hops and of the essence of Spruce, was also put on board, besides a number of other extra stores adapted to cold climates and a long voyage. The anti-scorbutic consisted of lemon juice (which forms a part of the daily rations on board His Majesty's Ships), vinegar, sauerkraut, pickles and herbs and the whole of the provisions which were the very best quality stowed in tight casks to preserve them from moisture or other injury. As a matter of experiment, a small quantity of vinegar in a high concentrated state, recommended and prepared by Dr Bollman, was also put on board, and was found of essential service, the greater part of the common kind being destroyed by the severity of the frost. In order to save storage only a small proportion of biscuit was received; flour which had been previously kiln dried with great care being substituted in its place.'[12]

Before wintering on Melville Island, they had to move the ships into the chosen harbour before ice set in fully. Of this Parry wrote: 'it was necessary to cut a channel of more than two miles in length, through which the ships were drawn to their winter quarters. For three days both ship's companies were employed in this arduous task, in which officers and men shared alike.' The text continues: 'Up to their knees in water with the thermometer at zero not a complaint was heard, and when the ships at length, at 3 PM. on the 26th September reached their station in Winter Harbour, the event was hailed with three as hearty cheers as ever burst from the lips of British seamen.'[13]

Parry and his men were the first ever naval expedition to over-winter, setting a precedent that all further expeditions would follow. The ships were roofed over with padded cloth for insulation, and throughout the winter they undertook scientific observations including ones relating to meteorology and magnetism. The health of the two crews remained generally good as, besides the foodstuffs described above, the men lived on game such as caribou and musk oxen, the quantity of which amounted to 3,766lb (1,700kg) during the 12 months that they lived on Melville.

As required, they modified their clothing with hides and other animal materials to combat frostbite. Boredom was relieved by schooling, amateur dramatics and musical entertainment. In June 1820, they undertook a journey overland using handcarts carry-ing tents, preserved meat and other necessities. That August they departed Melville Island to attempt to sail further westward for the Bering Strait. However, they were soon prevented by dense pack ice some 40–50ft (12–15m) thick; the furthest point they made was Cape Dundas (113°46′W). Finding no passage to the south, Parry decided to return to England via the Davis Strait, naming various headlands, coasts, capes and islands on his way and reaching home in 1820. Despite failing to traverse westward to the Bering Strait, Parry's expedition was a success; not only was it of huge geograph-ical importance but they had gained invaluable knowledge about surviving in the Arctic regions.

The Franklin expedition

In May 1819, John Franklin, now holding the rank of captain and with the recommendation of John Barrow, embarked on an expedition backed by the Hudson Bay Company and with the support of Sir Alexander Mackenzie of the North-West Company; Mackenzie himself having reached the coast of the polar sea on 14 July 1789. Sailing from Gravesend in the *Prince of Wales*, this was the first of Franklin's successful overland expeditions involving the use of boats to navigate the various Canadian rivers, the Copper River and the Mackenzie River to reach Prince Rupert's Land. Franklin returned in 1822 and took a second journey into the polar sea between 1825 and 1827. Sadly, Franklin was not to be so fortunate when he sailed on his fourth expedition to seek the north-west passage in HM ships *Erebus and Terror* 18 years later.

Sailing from Greenhithe on the Thames in east London on 19 May 1845, Franklin's crew consisted of 24 officers and 110 men. Although technology for steam-powered ships was still relatively new, both the *Erebus* and *Terror* were powered by reciprocating steam engines that drove a single screw at a speed of 4 knots (4.6mph/7.4km/h). These vessels were the first steam ships with a screw propeller to be employed for polar exploration, the propeller being retracted up into the hull to protect it from damage.[14]

Like the *Racehorse* and the *Carcass* of 1773, the *Erebus* and *Terror* were purposely modified to suit their task, with bows reinforced with heavy beams and plates of iron. Besides the hull being sheathed with additional layers of planking, their holds were also subdivided into watertight compartments. For buoyancy and stability, the spaces between the compartments and hull were filled with coal and compacted coal dust. Both ships were also fitted with an internal steam heating system for the comfort of the crew.[15] Once prepared, the ships were stocked with three years' provisions that consisted of conventionally preserved foodstuffs together with some 8,000 tinned items supplied through provisioner Stephen Goldner. Both vessels had previously seen service in the Antarctic with James Clark Ross between 1841and 1844.[16]

Despite their thorough preparations, Franklin's two vessels became icebound in the Victoria Strait near King William Island around latitude 68°N in the Canadian Arctic. While this predicament paralleled that of his predecessor Phipps, the two situations were completely different. Phipps got free within ten days, primarily because the weather conditions changed and the ice broke up, while the temperatures off Spitsbergen were not as severe. Franklin experienced temperatures far lower because of the extensive land mass nearby. The entire expedition, with 129 men, including Franklin, was lost.[17]

Hearing no news from Franklin after two years, public concern grew about the fate of the expedition. Lady Franklin, members of Parliament and British newspapers all urged the Admiralty to send out a search party. In response, the Admiralty set up a three-part search plan beginning in 1848. This consisted of an overland rescue party, led by Sir John Richardson and John Rae down the MacKenzie River and two seaborne searches made by HM ships *Enterprise* and *Investigator* – the former under overall command of Captain Ross, who had previously sailed to the Arctic with William Parry in 1818. The sea search concept was for one ship to enter the Canadian Arctic archipelago through Lancaster Sound, and the other to approach from the Pacific side, but their endeavours proved fruitless. Worse still, the *Investigator*[18] became beset in ice at Banks Island and was finally abandoned in June 1853.[19] Much prompted by Lady Franklin, further searches were made from 1850 onwards, none of which revealed the whereabouts of Franklin, his ships or men. Although it was accepted that the expedition had been lost without trace, searches continued involving British and American vessels, some of which visited the coast of Beechey Island. Here they found some expeditionary relics and the graves of three crewmen. While surveying the coast south-east of King William Island in 1854, the explorer John Rae was able to acquire some relics and stories about the Franklin party from local Inuit people. This, and the graves previously found, gave rise to much speculation about the tragic circumstances surrounding Franklin's expedition.

At the behest of Lady Franklin, another search was made by Captain Francis Leopold McClintock, who took command of a small schooner-rigged steam yacht named the *Fox* that had been privately purchased in Aberdeen for this task by Lady Franklin. Once fitted out for Arctic conditions, McClintock sailed from Aberdeen in

1857 with a crew of 25 to begin his search from Repulse Bay. Francis was no stranger to the Arctic, having sailed with Ross in 1848–1849, and was highly experienced at travelling with man-hauled sledges, covering 1,320 miles (2,124km) in 105 days. Faced with a hard-freezing winter, McClintock and his crew were forced to overwinter from September to April 1858 and did not reach Beechey Island until August. Meeting another extreme winter with the seaways of Peel Sound blocked by ice, they spent another winter on shore. In February the following year, McClintock met some Inuit who told him that a ship had been crushed by ice off King William Island, but while the crew had landed safely it seemed that some white people had starved to death on an island.

In April 1859, McClintock and his second-in-command Lieutenant Hobson set out on sledges towards the east coast of King William Island where they split to circumnavigate the island in opposite directions. McClintock met other Inuit who sold him items from Franklin's expedition, and he was also told that many of the people from the ship had died as they walked to the 'great river'. McClintock and his team then went south where they found a partially exposed skeleton. In early May, when both sled teams reunited on the western side of King William Island, Hobson's party found a 28ft (8.5m) boat equipped with sled runners for hauling over ice. The boat was loaded with clothing, equipment, two loaded shotguns and various provisions including 45lb (20kg) of chocolate. The boat also contained two headless skeletons, which appeared to have been eaten by wolves. Noting that the boat was not facing towards their intended destination, the Great Fish River, Hobson deduced that they had decided to turn back to the ships. His party then pressed onwards to Cape Felix and on 5 May found the only surviving documents from the expedition: two single messages left by Franklin's officers, Captain Crozier of the *Terror* and Commander Fitzjames of the *Erebus*. Each was found inside piled stone cairns; one to the north, the other south.[20]

The first note read as follows:

'28th May 1847, HM Ships *Erebus* and *Terror* Wintered in the Ice in Lat. 70° 05′ N. Long. 98° 23′ W. Having wintered in 1846–7 at Beechey Island in Lat. 74° 43′ 28″N. Long. 91° 39′15″W after having ascended Wellington Channel to Lat 77° and returned by the west side of Cornwallis Island. Sir John Franklin commanding the Expedition. All well.' An added footnote with signatures records: 'Party consisting of 2 officers and 8 men left the Ships on Monday 24 May 1847. G.M. Gore Lieut.

Chas. F. Des Voeux Mate.'

The second message, dated 1848, was written in the margins of the same sheet of paper and forebodingly reported:

'HM Ships *Erebus* and *Terror* were deserted 22 April, 5 leagues NNW of this [hav]ing been beset since 12th Septr. 1846. The officers and Crews consisting of 105 souls, under the command of Capt. F.R.M. Crozier landed here Lat. 69° 37' 42" N. Long. 98° 41'. Sir John Franklin died on 11 June 1847 and the total deaths in the Expedition has been to date 9 officers and 15 men.

James Fitzjames Captain of *Erebus*

FRM Crozier Captain and Senior Officer'

The added note reads: 'And start tomorrow 26th for Backs Fish River.'[21]

It seems that Crozier and his 105 survivors were attempting to haul the boats towards the Back's Fish River to get to the nearest Hudson's Bay Company outpost. Already undernourished and inadequately clothed, and some beset with tuberculosis and scurvy, the crews were very vulnerable to the freezing climate. McClintock and Hobson also found that some of the bones had knife marks on them, suggesting that Franklin's starving men had turned to cannibalism in their attempts to survive.

McClintock returned to England in September 1859 bringing the news of Franklin's lost expedition. He was knighted while the *Fox*'s officers and men shared a £5,000 parliamentary reward. Despite their efforts, they had failed to find any trace of Franklin's two ships, *Erebus* and *Terror*.

In 1992, an archaeological examination of the site on King William Island where McClintock had discovered the bones provided further details of what had happened to Franklin's men. Forensic scientist Anne Keenleyside revealed that the bodies contained elevated levels of lead, and her examinations also found many cut marks 'consistent with de-fleshing'. In 2015, a study in the *Journal of Osteoarchaeology* also noted that: '35 bones had signs of breakage and "pot polishing", which occurs when the ends of bones heated in boiling water rub against the cooking pot they are placed in', which 'typically occurs in the end stage of cannibalism'.

The elevated levels of lead found in the bodies suggests that the men were suffering from lead poisoning from the lead solder used to seal the tinned food products, a fault caused by hasty manufacturing processes. An alternative theory is that the lead poisoning was caused by the ship's water system components.

Recent events add new dimensions to the Franklin Arctic story. According to Inuit folklore, HM ships *Erebus* and *Terror* hold historic and cultural significance, local legend suggesting that at least one of the ships was seen north-west of the Adelaide Peninsula prior to its sinking. The Inuit also speak about their attempts to salvage all manner of items from the ships before they sank.

Understanding that Inuit oral history held the key to unlocking the mystery surrounding Franklin's ships, Parks Canada set up the Victoria Strait Expedition in 2008 to seek out Franklin's two ships. Led by nautical archaeologist Ryan Harris and Marc-André Bernier, the expedition worked closely with the Inuit to conduct research and plan the search. Deploying the icebreaker CCGS (Canadian Coast Guard Ship) *Sir Wilfrid Laurier* off the coast of Nunavut in the quest, the cost of the six-week search was CDN$75,000. Also involved in the search were the Canadian Hydrographic Service (CHS), who contributed high-resolution photography, high-definition video and multi-beam sonar equipment to scan measurements upon the Arctic ocean bed. The combined technological effort together with the 19th-century Inuit oral testimony gathered by McClintock's expedition proved so successful that they did indeed find Franklin's lost ships *Erebus* in 2014 and *Terror* in 2016. Perhaps overlooked is the fact that on 25 July 2010 Parks Canada had also successfully found the wreck of HM ship *Investigator*, which had been lost during Ross's expedition to find Franklin in 1848.[22]

First discovered, on 2 September 2014, was Franklin's own ship HMS *Erebus,* the wreck of which was lying beneath the ice in about 11 fathoms (66ft/20m) of water. Its position was south of King William Island off Victoria Strait and near the eastern stretches of the Queen Maud Gulf off Ugjulik on the western coast of the Adelaide Peninsula. Formal identification of the vessel was made by comparing the shape of the ship against the original ship plans held in the National Maritime Museum at Greenwich, London. The key element in identifying the wreck was one of the ship's iron boat davits. The *Erebus* had been preserved in very good condition. Although dismasted, the preservation of the hull fabric was due to the freezing temperature of the water and the absence of bacteria and other organisms that normally invade and consume wooden ships. Before the wreck could be accessed, a hole had to be bored down through ice 6ft 8in (2m) thick, through which archaeological divers made 14 dives to explore and confirm the wreck's identity. Later dives uncovered a host of relics, including the ship's bell. It is hoped that journals or diaries may be also recovered, the content of which may reveal other secrets surrounding the disappearance of Franklin's 1845 voyage.

Almost to the day, two years later, on 3 September 2016, a Parks Canada marine archaeological team aboard the *Martin Bergmann* found the *Terror*. An Inuk crew member, Sammy Kogvik, had suggested a diversion in course to Terror Bay in King William Island, off Nunavut, where he and a friend had seen what looked like a mast rising out of the sea ice on a fishing trip. The wreck was discovered lying at a depth of 13 fathoms (78.7ft/24m) in the middle of the uncharted bay 60 miles (96km) south of where it was believed to have been crushed in the ice. The ship's wreck was well preserved with her three masts broken off but standing, her hatches closed and her provisions intact.[23, 24]

Adrian Schimnowski, the expedition leader of the research ship, remarked that the vessel found was 'a perfect time capsule', noting that 'it was located right where an Inuit hunter said it would be'. Canadian Rear Admiral John Newton remarked that both vessels were found 'just 31 miles apart from each other'. Considering the circumstances in which Franklin had found himself, this proximity is hardly surprising.

Speaking further about the day they discovered the *Terror*, Schimnowski noted that 'the *Terror* seemed to be listing at about 45 degrees to starboard on the seabed'. But on the third dive with a remotely operated vehicle, 'we noticed the wreck is sitting level on the seabed floor not at a list – which means the boat sank gently to the bottom'. Lying some 13 fathoms (80ft/24m) down, 'the wreck is in perfect condition, with metal sheeting that reinforced the hull against sea ice clearly visible amid swaying kelp. A long, heavy rope line running through a hole in the ship's deck suggests an anchor line may have been deployed before the *Terror* went down.'

The wreck reveals her 20ft (6.1m) long bowsprit still extends straight out from the bow. The wreck is in such good condition that the glass panes of three of her four stern cabin windows – where her commander, Captain Francis Crozier, slept and worked – remain intact. The wreck also reveals that the vessel had been well prepared for winter before she sank. A ROV (Remotely Operated Vehicle) sent in to capture images of the wreck entered the mess hall, went into a few cabins and found the food storage room with plates and one can on the shelves, as well as two wine bottles, tables, empty shelving and a desk with open drawers.[25] A crucial detail in the identification of the ship was a wide exhaust pipe rising above the upper deck, which is in the precise location where a smokestack rose from the locomotive engine that was installed in the belly of the *Terror* to power the ship's propeller.

While it appears that both the *Erebus* and *Terror* initially became ice-bound together at the same longitude and latitude before being abandoned, there are still a number of questions about why the two became separated. Although Crozier's note states that both ships were deserted on 22 April 1848, what we don't know is whether Crozier had previously moved all men into the *Terror* to consolidate resources after the death of Franklin and the 24 other men recorded on 11 June 1847. If this was the case, was Crozier still acting under Franklin's orders to attempt to complete the north-west passage on Franklin's behalf in the *Terror* with all current survivors once the ship eventually became ice-free? Alternatively, after three years away and some loss of life it is very probable that Crozier had firmly decided to sail for home with the survivors once the *Terror* was free. This was not to be: Crozier abandoned the *Terror* and took to the frozen land with the remaining crew who, compelled to resort to cannibalism to survive, all perished miserably.

As to finding the *Erebus* and *Terror* lying segregated quite some distance apart, in time the hull of one or both became crushed and as ice eventually melted, one vessel completely foundered; alternatively, the other vessel may have simply drifted within its ice cocoon.

The difficulties of operating sail-powered vessels within the ice-bound high latitudes made it almost impossible for Phipps to reach his prime objective: the North Pole. Even with the advent of mechanical steam power, Franklin's *Erebus and Terror* expedition, undertaken 70 years later, still proved navigationally problematic. It was not until 204 years after Phipps's intrepid voyage that a surface vessel was able to reach the 'top of the world'. This was achieved by the Russian-built nuclear-powered icebreaker *Artika* commanded by Captain Yury Kuchiev, which reached the North Pole at 9:40 Moscow time on 17 August 1977 when undertaking what was considered a 'scientific-practical experimental voyage'. With a displacement of some 23,000 tonnes, the *Artika* could break through ice 5 metres thick; an advantage well beyond the imagination of commanders Phipps and Lutwidge.

19

Conclusions

When British naval commanders Constantine Phipps and Skeffington Lutwidge sailed from the Nore in June 1773, they were going to an environment as unknown to them as the moon was to the astronauts of the 1960s. Although expeditions of discovery were still being undertaken in the Pacific by explorers such as Captain James Cook, Admiral Louis-Antoine de Bougainville and others, few ventured into the icy wastes of the Arctic seas surrounding what is today Svalbard. The only sailors then willing to risk these lonely, hazardous waters were the 'Greenland men', whalers who pursued their financially rewarding business, regardless of the dangers. From leaving the Nore and returning to anchor in Galleon's Reach, the voyage spanned just three-and-a-half months, a relatively brief period compared to Anson's circumnavigation between 1740 and 1744 and the later exploration voyages of Byron, Bougainville and Cook. However, besides its hostile environment, this alien untouched world was almost bereft of fellow humans. Phipps, his men and ships were totally isolated from assistance – or the possibility of calling for it – should they have met trouble. The character and skill of the commanders and their crews and the robustness of the ships would prove crucial in the survival of the expedition and what they were able to achieve.

The commanders and their leadership

Both Phipps and Lutwidge were notable for their ship-handling capabilities in the most extreme sea conditions and their management of their ship's companies under difficult and unexpected circumstances. As Vice-Admiral Cuthbert Collingwood noted some 30 years after Phipps's voyage: 'Nothing is achieved without good order and discipline.' Discipline, not to be confused with punishment, went hand in hand with leadership while the awareness of responsible leadership demonstrated by both commanders proved the key to the success of this voyage. They had no issues with insubordination or failure to respond to orders throughout the entire voyage, demonstrating that leadership is about achieving 'a cheerful and willing obedience' with one's peers or subordinates. Professional seamen were used to obeying orders regardless of the circumstances facing them, whether they be the 'dangers of the sea', the force of the gale or 'the violence of the enemy',[1] or on this specific voyage, the menace of the ice. It was the combination of discipline and leadership that proved so effective when it was decided to abandon the *Racehorse* and *Carcass* and haul the boats to open sea. Each man in the ship's companies knew this decision could have had fatal consequences but both commanders understood that their seamen would rise to the challenge set before them.

The value placed on each individual member of the ship's companies for the tasks they undertook in the most unusual of surroundings should not be underestimated, Midshipman Nelson included. Few, if any, of the officers and able-bodied seamen had ever sailed in such seas or endured the extreme cold in which they were working. During this voyage, Nelson would encounter examples of strong leadership that would carry him through his career, while Nicholas Biddle, his Philadelphian fellow coxswain in the *Carcass,* would take this same authority into the fledgling United States Navy.

Discipline seems to have been maintained effectively throughout the six-month period that the *Racehorse* and *Carcass* were under commission for the expedition. Just one man of the 172 borne in the two ships was punished and this was for theft in the *Carcass* when outbound at Whitby on Tuesday 15 June: 'Punished Richard Dingle for Theft by running the Gauntlet.'[2] Rather oddly, this event is not recorded in the standard captain's and master's journals but appears to have come from an alternative *Carcass* journal.[3] Dingle, aged 25, was serving in the ship as carpenter's crew. As a felony, theft was deemed to be particularly antisocial as it affected all men, officers and seamen alike. Therefore, rather than receiving a formal flogging the offender was punished by 'running the gauntlet', which meant that the beating was meted out by the whole ship's company as the miscreant passed between the assembled lines of men. Lutwidge used this single opportunity to firmly establish his own and the king's authority, demonstrating also that he fully supported his ship's company on matters of justice. The subtle message given out by the way he dealt with the punishment helped to establish the bond he would need when calling the men to put themselves out far beyond their designated duties. Lutwidge's actions also reciprocated the sentiments of Phipps, their overall commander.[4]

Acclaim must also be given to the four Greenland pilots borne within the ships. Though referred to little in the ship's journals, these experienced men were ever-present, providing professional advice to the ship's commanders, masters and boatswains alike. This was especially important when trying to con the ships through the ice or laying out ice anchors. Although a short reference is made to 'sending' them 'on board the *Racehorse*' to meet and discuss the situation, less obvious in the records is the frequency with which their advice would have been called upon on a watch-by-watch basis with regard to relatively minor dangers or problems as they occurred.

The crew lists show men of varying ages, nationality and ethnic backgrounds and despite these differences there seems to have been no prejudice in any form within the ship's companies. Not only did each man apparently work happily with his shipmate, but there was also no division in pay according to ethnicity: Equiano received the appropriate wage for his rating of able seaman, as did the Madagascan seamen. When the *Racehorse* paid off, Equiano, like others in the ship's company, received a watch from Phipps. This gesture, showing appreciation for a 'job well done', highlights Phipps's qualities as a commander and his personal character.

With the exception of the ice pilots, who had sailed the Arctic on many previous occasions, the entire adventure must have influenced all those who sailed. Given the many trials they endured, the lieutenants and midshipmen would have each discovered much about their inner strengths and failings, factors that very much influenced their careers. Some became noteworthy leaders attaining flag rank, others did not. With regard to the warrant officers, of whom we know little, it seems likely that the experience fortified their professional capabilities; the same could be said for most of the ratings, although Able Seaman Biddle would soon assume command of his own armed vessel opposing the British Royal Navy a few years later.

Not including the commissioned and professional warrant officers, the ship's muster books clearly show that most of the men volunteered to enter into the ships for the duration of the voyage, in the same way that merchant seamen 'signed on' in mercantile vessels in the 20th century. Although the ship's journals note that the Admiralty sanctioned an impressment 'rendezvous' to be set up in London, the men entering from this source were not the forcibly 'pressed men' that we often associate with the Georgian Navy; the heavy-handed and indiscriminate practice of impressment generally only occurred during times of war. As professional seamen with an expectation of a degree of hardship, most would have been grateful simply to have escaped from possible death in the icy wastes and may have thought no more of it except to recall their story to family and others.

For one man, his experience trapped in the ice was life-changing. When Olaudah Equiano initially signed on into the ship he had expectations of fame and adventure, but facing imminent death in the Arctic, he came to doubt the reasoning behind the voyage. Reflecting on this in his book, he wrote: 'that our Creator never intended we should find an ocean passage to the North Pole ... I had had fears of death hourly upon me, and shuddered at the thoughts of meeting the grim king of terrors in the natural state I then was in, and was exceedingly doubtful of a happy eternity if I should die in it.' He now 'began to seriously reflect on the dangers I had escaped, particularly those of my last voyage'. Salvation, he hoped, was earned, not given, deserved, not granted. He had committed, according to the Church of England, the sin of self-sufficiency by assuming that reliance on his 'own strength' alone would bring him spiritual comfort: 'I rejoiced greatly; and heartily thanked the Lord for delivering me to London, where I was determined to work out my own salvation...'[5]

Apart from Phipps and Equiano, the only other person who has left us any idea of his personal experience of the voyage is Midshipman Thomas Floyd, whose unofficial journal notes were compiled and published by his family in 1879, more than a century after the voyage. Floyd's account gives an intriguing insight into the more mundane workings in the ship, including some below decks 'grumbling' from the seamen – observations rarely recorded in the 18th century. Although midshipmen were encouraged to keep a journal, Nelson does not appear to have left any written record. Perhaps he did but it was lost or because he was personally unhappy about the voyage, it was later discarded; if he had done, it would have provided an incredible insight into the general story.

The ships

When converted to withstand the rigours of sailing in Arctic conditions and crushing from ice, the robustly built *Racehorse* and *Carcass* were at the forefront of 18th-century technology. Although both ships did suffer considerably on the voyage home it was probably no more so than any other vessel would have done under the circumstances. Despite the ice and heavy seas their hulls survived intact, maintaining an objective of warship design: to remain a 'fighting floating gun platform'.[6]

The impact on the vessels of driving into the ice was substantial, causing, as both Phipps and Floyd described, men to be 'flung to the deck' as kinetic forces reverberated throughout the hulls. This was not just a single shock but an unremitting series of impacts far greater in force than that sustained when riding into heavy seas, where the force from buffeting water is easily dispersed. That these ships withstood the strain imposed by the unrelenting ice says much about the work of the dockyard shipwrights and those involved in redesigning the ships to sail in the Arctic. After the voyage both vessels were 'taken in hand' by dockyard shipwrights, surveyed and refitted. There are no records of what the surveys revealed about damage sustained from the ice, but it is probable that the leading edge of each vessel's stem post and 'knee of the head' would have been superficially damaged by constant impact, as would the foremost hull planking. Whether any impact damage was transferred to the keel and keelson, or the additional strength members added to the ship beforehand, we do not know. Even in modern steel-built ships, chunks of floating ice create a scouring effect along the length of a ship's hull. The same abrasive forces would doubtless have impacted the surfaces of the external planking of the *Racehorse* and *Carcass*, especially on the strakes of timber and wales running longitudinally close to the waterline.

The ships' rudders were particularly vulnerable, and careful measures had to be taken to ensure that they were not damaged. The ship's journals note that the rudder ropes that transmitted movement between the ship's wheel (helm) via the tiller to the rudder stock were occasionally replaced due to wear by constant movement. Given the number of helm changes required when manoeuvring the ships through the ice, the need for frequent tiller rope replacement is quite understandable. And given how well the ships maintained their hull integrity and performance under adverse conditions, it is ironic that the ship's journals reveal that both *Racehorse* and *Carcass* unfortunately suffered superficial impact damage from other shipping passing down the Thames while lying at anchor in the safety of Galleon's Reach at the end of the voyage.

The rig of the ships

Providing the motive power to drive the ships, the masts, yards, sails and associated rigging sustained some damage but this was common in all 18th-century sailing vessels, especially when such equipment was made of natural materials – wood, hemp and flax – all of which were constantly under a wide range of stresses imposed by weather conditions and the motion of the ship. As items failed, running repairs were undertaken daily by the boatswain and sailmaker, who held coils of varying sizes of hempen cordage, pulley blocks, canvas and twine in their stores. Except for the stormy conditions met on the return voyage, there seem to have been no real failings caused by the icy conditions at Spitsbergen. The ship's journals give many references to 'setting up the rigging' – an action that demanded periodical tightening up of the standing (supporting) rigging, which inevitably stretched under continuous stress-loading conditions. This should not be viewed as component failure but as standard maintenance and good ship's husbandry. That the ships did not lose spars and masts during the strong gales and stormy weather met on the return voyage is undoubtedly due to this careful maintenance, along with good seamanship.

Seamanship

'Good seamanship' encompasses not only navigation, steering, knotting and splicing ropes, reeving tackles and setting sails, but also the ability to foresee potential problems arising from the sea, wind and weather conditions before the situation becomes unmanageable and potentially leads to the loss of ship and life. A key aspect of seamanship is the implementation of preventative measures; according to the ship's logs, both captains sent down topgallant and topsail yards and likewise struck topgallant and topmasts on many occasions as a matter of safety to avoid damage or loss. Such actions also reduced the stresses imposed on the standing rigging when the ship was riding and rolling in heavy seas. The set of the sails could also have an adverse effect on the safety of the ship. Both ship's logs record the setting or taking in of sails as well as reefing or taking out reefs, both of which were a response to varying or unexpected wind conditions and strength, and are a good demonstration of the adage: 'A good master knows how much sail to set, but the better master knows when to take sail in.' Unless one has worked aloft in a square-rigged ship, it is impossible to imagine the difficulty of manhandling the ropework and sails when working the rig in such freezing conditions. Despite the problems met in the ice or in the midst of a storm, at no time did the commanders or ship's masters put the ships and men in jeopardy, demonstrating both the exemplary practical seamanship and professionalism of the Georgian Navy.

Ground tackle

The ship's anchors and their associated cables suffered no material failure except when the *Racehorse* fractured the shank of her best bower anchor in collision with a small iceberg. As Midshipman Floyd recalls in his journal, the anchor shank was 20in (51cm) in circumference and 6.0375in (15.34cm) thick. Given that the anchor was made of tough wrought iron, the strength of ice cannot be underestimated. Modern tests have proved that old ice is so strongly formed that when made into a bullet it can be cleanly fired through steel plate.

The ship's boats

On no occasion did the materials of these key items of ship's equipment fail, nor were they at any time misused by their coxswains,
Biddle and Nelson. They proved sound even when towed across
rugged stretches of the ice when the men were making a bid to
open water, although some were irreparably damaged or wrecked
during the stormy weather on the return voyage home. However,
given the extreme seas this was not unexpected.

The ships' sailing abilities

The two ship's logbooks reveal a marked difference between the
Racehorse and the *Carcass*. Phipps's journal carries many references
relating to *Racehorse* reducing sail or even heaving-to to allow the
Carcass to catch up with the *Racehorse*. Lutwidge's journal also
records many occasions when they had to set steering (studding)
sails to make more speed to keep up with the *Racehorse*. Although
both ships were similarly rigged as sloops, the difference in sailing
capability relates to the form of their hulls. While both had been
modified with strengthening timbers for the ice conditions, their
original construction was different: the *Racehorse* being French-
built as a privateer, the *Carcass* built as a robust British bomb vessel.
French ships were designed with finer lines below the waterline at
the point of entry through the water at the stem and at the buttocks
running towards to the stern, giving a far speedier ship that suited
French strategy. As a result, the *Racehorse* was initially of far lighter
construction in terms of timber scantlings (measurements) in order
to give her greater speed.[7] The journals clearly delineate the comparative damage sustained by the two ships during the stormy weather
on their return voyage: the *Racehorse* is recorded as suffering considerable injury to her hull, which fits with the fact that lighter French
vessels were less able to sustain sea-keeping on blockade duty than
were British warships.

The *Racehorse* and the *Carcass* found themselves at the forefront of
sailing technology in Arctic conditions and were effectively Britain's
first icebreakers. When embarking on the voyage, Phipps, Lutwidge,

Nelson and the other officers and men could not have envisaged that what they were attempting would become a relatively routine procedure in the years to come.

Navigation

It is clear from the two ship's journals that, in terms of navigation, the voyage was a complete success. Many astronomical fixes were taken to find positions of longitude and latitude with which, using the two different chronometers borne in the ships, they could determine the comparative accuracy of the chronological tables they carried. By accurately fixing the positions of longitude and latitude they could correct pre-existing charts and create new ones. Many other astronomical observations were also made and much of the recorded data was brought home for analysis by the astronomers at the Royal Observatory at Greenwich and the Board of Longitude. At this period, gaining mastery of navigation and astronomy was important in maintaining Britain's primacy at sea when compared to other world powers, especially France.

The ship's journals

Excluding the period when the *Racehorse* and *Carcass* became separated during the terrible storm on the homeward voyage, both journals generally run parallel to each other. However, although Phipps and Lutwidge shared common objectives in accordance with the instructions in the Admiralty orders, there is a marked difference in their form, which reflects the diverse characters of the two men. Of the two, Phipps's journal is far more concise, straightforward and no-nonsense and, although he occasionally records some points relating to damage, such as 'the larboard foremost Main Chain Plate broke, reeved a lanyard in the spare deadeye and set up the shroud again', he then simply wrote: 'Put Preventer Gammoning upon the Bowsprit' as a matter of fact and reported little else. When recording that they changed the mainsail, Phipps omits to tell us that, as Midshipman Floyd noted, the sail had 'blown to rags'. In general, Phipps's log entries remain impartial and keep to the facts, mainly because he was all too aware that his journals, as with those of any other sea officer, would be heavily scrutinised by the Admiralty on their return.

Lutwidge, on the other hand, is more observant and inclined to record specific details, so from his journals we get a far greater picture of Spitsbergen and its geographical features. He appears the more benign commander, with an empathetic and more jovial personality – qualities that would have won him the affection of his men. Although seven years older than his expedition leader and perhaps less educationally advantaged, Lutwidge appears to have relished the opportunity to make the most of the scientific and other observational opportunities that the expedition offered.

Scientific discovery and other observations

Published in 1774, Phipps's record of the voyage in the form of his book was a British response to the publication in France of Bougainville's account of his expedition. Not only does Phipps's book give a descriptive account of the voyage and its progress, but he also ensured that it contained significant information about the fauna and flora of the islands, in written form or as sketches and drawings. The work also contains a host of appendices related to data collected from the various observations, including gravitational surveys by pendulum and temperature observations of the sea at predetermined depths. It would be the first of many academic publications and pamphlets covering British voyages of exploration – another indication of the expedition's success. Phipps's journal can be considered of significant importance, perhaps equivalent to Captain Cook's writings on his first voyage.

Record keeping

Though this is not clear from the *Racehorse*'s journal, the person charged with collating and recording details of astronomical and scientific observations was Midshipman Philippe d'Auvergne. As potential King's Officers, all midshipmen were encouraged to sketch for a variety of reasons. They recorded harbours, anchorages and the lie of the land together with enemy fortifications, and such records were maintained as part of the Admiralty's espionage strategy.[8] Encouraged by Phipps, d'Auvergne maintained a journal for this purpose in which he also used his artistic skills, sketching a wide variety of the geographical features and spectacles of the Arctic. He also recorded the local flora and fauna; his excellent drawings stand testament to his extraordinary abilities. While carrying out his many duties, d'Auvergne was also involved with the officers and men exchanging visits or undertaking experiments.

So invaluable were his illustrations that Phipps had many of the on-site sketches engraved by the artist John Cleverley the Younger and used them in his book. Most notable are the view of Hakluyt's Headland to Cloven Cliff on 4 July, the glacier at Magdalena and those relating to *Racehorse* and *Carcass* being beset in the ice; the last two being worked up into paintings by Cleverley. Unfortunately, it is unlikely that d'Auvergne's account and sketches still exist in their original form. And while Phipps and others saw d'Auvergne as an important contributor to the voyage, Horatio Nelson did not. Apparently, the serious attitude d'Auvergne applied to his scientific obligations caused irritation on Nelson's part. Given his age, this unreasonable behaviour suggests a degree of jealousy or even narcissism. D'Auvergne, it appears, suffered with Nelson's pointed antagonism throughout his service career.

Cartography, depth soundings and sea currents

Phipps and Lutwidge jointly undertook a considerable amount of cartography of what was then a somewhat obscure group of islands beyond the North Cape and Greenland that had only been formally mapped as recently as 1758. The journals show both men consistently taking bearings at specific points on the various islands of the northern part of the Svalbard archipelago. The logbooks show that great attention was given to taking soundings, the depths of which were carefully marked on the charts they possessed or amended accordingly. This can be seen in the marked-up charts printed in Phipps's 1774 book.[9]

Not only did these regularly recorded soundings show the sea depth in fathoms (1 fathom being 6ft/1.82m), but they also provided information about the geological composition of the seabed: whether it was rocky, shingle, sandy, or mud ooze, the sampling substance of which attached itself to the sticky tallow inserted into the base of the sounding lead.[10] Painstaking as it seems to do this, this data was essential in identifying whether the seabed was suitable for safe anchoring. This information also gave the ship's commanders the ability to determine their position by cross-referencing the data with previously recorded figures.

They also measured the speed and direction of sea currents. Not only was this important for chart work, but it was also necessary to test the new scientific apparatus being carried for this purpose. It is possible that the device to which Phipps refers in his journal as a 'diver' was similar to the one described by Mr Henry de Saumarez as being 'For measuring the Way of the Ship at Sea', in *Philosophical Transactions* No.391 dated November 1725. Other data recorded was the influence of gravity in high latitudes, the experimental pendulum apparatus carried being used to discover such information.

Pendulum and water experiments

The pendulum experiments that Israel Lyons and Phipps performed provided much data about gravity, velocity and the accurate recording of time. The recordings were passed to the academics of the Royal Society for evaluation and were later published as an appendix in Phipps's 1774 record of the voyage. Dr Irving also carried out many experiments related to water, most of which were associated with water density and temperature at predetermined depths. This was achieved by an improvised system using bottles devised by himself and Phipps. This data was apparently compared with similar experiments carried out by Irving at the Nore to determine a working datum prior to sailing. Air temperatures were also recorded in light and shade.

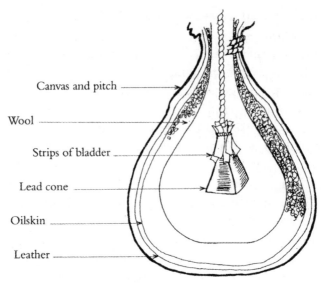

Canvas and pitch

Wool

Strips of bladder

Lead cone

Oilskin

Leather

Dr Irving's water flask experiment.

Chronometers

Two chronometers were carried: that manufactured by Larcum Kendal (K2) in the *Racehorse*, the other made by John Arnold, in the *Carcass*. Both were trialled in accordance with strict written instructions provided for their operation.[11] From the journals it appears that Lutwidge paid greater attention to recording the accuracy of Arnold's timepiece compared to the notes recorded about K2 in the *Racehorse*'s journal. This was probably because Israel Lyons, as the Astronomer Royal, would have been keeping his own official records on the accuracy of chronometer K2. All the data recorded from the timekeepers was collated by Israel Lyons, the details of which, together with the various astronomical observations made, were recorded in Phipps's book in a series of tables titled *Observations for finding Longitude by the Time-keepers*. These calculations appear to have been undertaken every two days.[12]

Astronomical observations

The ship's journals record numerous notes about the sighting of celestial bodies, primarily the sun, the moon and planet Jupiter. Lyons measured the altitude of these with brass sextants of Hadley's patent, made by Dolland, of 18in (45.7cm) radius, and 'Captain Phipps with a smaller of four inches radius made by Ramsden'.[13] While observations of the sun at noon were routine, the observations of the moon were, along with the chronometer readings and their calculated offset relationship relative to the fixed time at Greenwich Meridian, used to determine longitude. From this data, Lyons prepared a series of tables entitled *Observations for finding Longitude by the Moon* for the Royal Observatory. These are also reproduced in Phipps's book. As for the joint relationship between observations of the moon with Jupiter, these were similarly collated by Lyons and published in Phipps's book.[14]

Observations about the ice

Some of the most important data that came out of the expedition was the wealth of information about icebergs, ice floes, drift ice and glaciers. As the logbooks show, Phipps and Lutwidge made a deliberate effort to describe the various types of ice conditions and the hazards they encountered. This proved invaluable to future explorers preparing for similar expeditions into the Arctic and, later, Antarctica. Perhaps their most terrifying experience was when compacted drift ice closed in on the ships, forcing up great chunks of ice about them. These towered to a height level with the main yard, some 50ft (15.24m) above the main deck. The ship's journals use the word 'iceberg' for what we would call a glacier – a logical term as they appeared like an 'ice mountain' – whereas what we would today call an iceberg, the journals refer to as an 'ice island', which, as they appeared semi-floating on the sea, again seems sensible. For some reason, neither of the journals mention the need to remove ice from the ships' decks, which implies that this task had become utterly routine and regularly carried out by the watch on deck.

Notes on the animals encountered in the Arctic

Although Phipps was the first European to collate any data about polar bears, his notes were rather rudimentary, simply recording the size and weight of the particular animal with a few observations. Although the two ship's journals have various entries abut wildlife – be it bears, walruses or reindeer – most of these relate to the animals being shot as sport; the indiscriminate hunting and killing of rare animals with no consideration for the ramifications was typical at the time. As Midshipman Floyd remarked, it was all undertaken 'like an English fox-hunt'. In his book, Phipps records that the reindeer and polar bear were killed and eaten, as was the Arctic fox – his comment on the latter being: 'We ate the flesh of one and found it good meat.'[15]

Of the polar bear, he notes that: 'This animal is much larger than the black bear' and notes its dimensions in detail (see page 154–56).[16]

Commenting on the whale being sought after by the 'Greenland men', Phipps simply notes: 'We saw few of them during our stay.'[17]

The appendices in Phipps's book also cover birds, fish, crustaceans and worms. It appears that crabs were indirectly collected when trawling, which indicates that both ships had trawl nets to catch fish to supplement their diet. This was not uncommon; various naval ship journals of the period verify the presence of such nets, the 32-gun frigate *Lowestoffe* in which Nelson later served being one example.[18]

One of the crab types found by Phipps was *Cancer boreas,* later described by Arctic explorer William Scoresby: 'This singular species was first discovered and figured by Captain Phipps. was found in the stomach of a seal.'[19] The fact that the crab was found inside a seal, as was the crab *Cancer ampulla,* suggests that Phipps was carrying out dissections during the voyage.[20] It seems that dissections and other scientific investigations were deliberately omitted from the *Racehorse*'s journal, as the details were of no formal interest to the Admiralty. In his later two-volume work on the Arctic regions, Scoresby also noted that he had found *Cancer ampulla* inside a shark. Another crab species attributed to Phipps was *Cancer pulex*: 'taken out by Captain Phipps in a trawl net near the coast of Spitzbergen.'[21] Scoresby also noted *Ascidia galatinosa* and *Ascidia rustica*: 'Taken by Captain Phipps in a trawl net on the North side of Spitzbergen.'[22] It appears that the worm species *Sipunculus lendix,* 'adhering, by its snout to the inside of the intestines of an Eider Duck', was brought back to England where, at Phipps's request, it was dissected and analysed by the

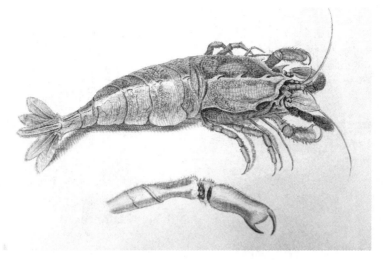

Illustration of *Cancer nugax* from Phipps's book, NMRN.

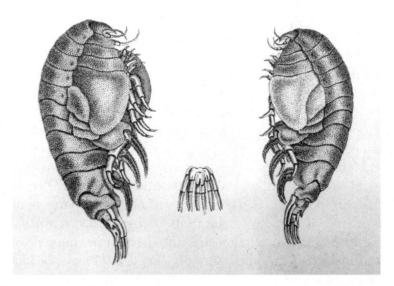

Illustration of *Cancer ampulla* from Phipps's book, NMRN.

eminent surgeon and member of the Royal Society, John Hunter.[23] According to Phipps, Hunter 'informed me that he had seen the same species of animal adhering to the intestines of whales'.[24] It is likely that the illustration of this species reproduced in Phipps's book was initially drawn by Hunter.

Illustration of *Buccinum carinatum* from Phipps's book, NMRN.

Arctic flora

Unlike many other explorers, Phipps and Lutwidge did not bring back a wide variety of unusual plants such as those obtained by Bougainville during his circumnavigation or collected by Joseph Banks during James Cook's first expedition. While the expedition did make some contribution to botany it was not of great significance, and, as Phipps stated in his book, his involvement with other pressing duties 'rendered it impossible for me to make many observations on its natural productions'.[25] What's more, although he did provide brief descriptions of flora and wildlife, he was not a naturalist in the true sense and it is possible that this part of the book required assistance from others more familiar with the subject, whether they were present on the voyage or not. If any examples were collected, it is likely that none survived the effects of the stormy weather they encountered on the way home.

Success or failure?

Phipps's 1773 expedition did not achieve its main objective of reaching the North Pole. Their orders were to proceed 'to the Northward

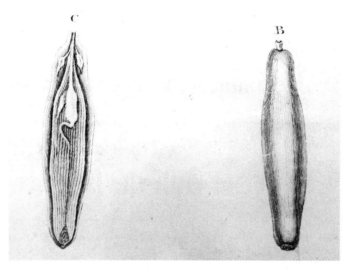

Illustration of *Sipunculas lendix* from Phipps's book, NMRN.

Illustration of *Synoicum turgens* from Phipps's book, NMRN.

and passing between Spitzbergen and Greenland proceed up to the North pole or as far towards it as you shall be able.'[26] Unfortunately, with the ice floes becoming so densely packed, the ships could not make passage much beyond Nordaustandet (Northeastland) at lat 80°0′.0N long 18°38′.0E, nor progress any further to the north-east as they had hoped. The expedition's furthest point north was lat 80°48´.N, long 4°43´.E on 27 July.[27] The lateness of the season meant that attempting a north-east passage was out of the question.

However, the voyage did achieve a number of its aims: numerous scientific experiments were carried out and new technology such as the chronometer proven; new maps were made and old ones corrected; and much data was collected about the local environment, its flora and fauna. No men were lost and the ships' modifications proved remarkably robust under the conditions. The commanders' instincts not to abandon the ships when they became trapped in the ice proved to be sound.

The story of Phipps's (and Nelson's) Arctic voyage concludes at the end of September 1773 with Nelson transferring into the 24-gun frigate *Seahorse*. All the other men were also dispersed, most into anonymity while others made their own historical contributions in Georgian society. It is now some 245 years since Phipps and Lutwidge sailed from the Nore in *Racehorse* and *Carcass* on the first Royal Naval adventure into the Arctic. In their wake followed many others from various nations: naturalists, scientists, geologists and a number of prospective miners. Today, the Arctic encourages new forms of exploration: small well-equipped cruise ships convey a reserved number of travellers into this isolated region. Meanwhile, climate change and melting ice pose a huge environmental threat to the land where Nelson allegedly encountered a polar bear.

Perhaps the ultimate question remains: what would have been the effect on history had Phipps and his crew, and in particular the young Nelson, suffered a similar fate to Franklin and died in the icy wastes? History is governed by accidental or unintentional events, the repercussions of which generate the fortune or tragedy of man. While Westall's painting *Nelson and the Polar Bear* depicts legendary heroism on a national scale, Phipps, Lutwidge and some 172 men in two rather stubby little ships remain the principal heroes of this extraordinary story of polar exploration.

Peter Goodwin
Khenu-Ankh-Ka, Southsea, May 2018

Appendix 1: Extract from progress book (refit history) of HMS Racehorse and Thunder (Source: TNA.ADM. 180/3 (entry [folio] 623))

At what Port	Arrived	Docked or Grounded	When Sheathed	When Graved	When Launched	Sailed	Nature of Repair	Charge of Hull, Masts & Yards £. s. d	Rigging & Stores £. s. d.	Total £. s. d	Observations
Deptford	20 July 1757	-	-	-	-	16 Aug 1757	Ditto	485.8.9	1786 3 9	2211 8 6	Admty Ordr 11 April 1758. To fit her as a Fire ship
Sheerness	30 Dec 1757	13 Jan 1758	-	Tarred Jan 1758	14 Jan 1758	23 Jan 1758	Refitted	162 5 3	203 15 10	448 1.1.	Admty Ordr 5th Sepr 1758 to fit her for a Bomb to Carry two Mortars [1 of 13 inch., 1 of 10 inch. [see Note 1]
Sheerness:											Surveyd afloat 7 Oct 1763. [see Note 2]
Deptford	26 Mar 1773	27 Mar 1773	Doubled April 1773	Graved April 1773	22 April 1773	21 May 1773	Fitted	1503 18 5	1387 3 3	2891 1 6	Fitted for a voyage towards the North Pole

Notes:

1. Guns listed as 8 in number 6 Pounders, 12 Swivels and 70 Men. The ship then went into Chatham.
2. Found to be in good Condition but that she will require docking before she proceeds to Sea for which she may be fitted in 16 days Estd for the Hull £120 (*Not reported to the Admiralty*)
3. Author's note: On 24 October 1775 *Racehorse* was renamed *Thunder* by Admiralty Order and consequently refitted for this purpose. Unfortunately, the progress book covering this vessel does not appear to have been continued within the primary source document.

Appendix 2: Extract from progress book (refit history) of HMS Carcass (Source: TNA. ADM. 180/3)

At what Port	Arrived	Docked or Grounded	When Sheathed	When Graved	When Launched	Sailed	Nature of Repair	Charge of Hull, Masts & Yards £. s. d	Rigging & Stores £. s. d.	Total £. s. d	Observations
Rotherhithe	Began	28 Sep 1758		Jan 1759	27 Jan 1759	Built		3,759. 11. 6		3,757. 1. 6	
Ditto	4 June 1761	4 June 1761		June 1761	5 June 1761	5 June 1761	Ditto as a Sloop	275. 4. 10	1,071. 2. 1	1,346. 7. 9	Admty Ord.r 25 May 1761 to Refit her as a Bomb
Ditto	12 Nov 1761	14 Nov 1761		Nov 1761	16 Nov 1761	7 Dec 1761	Ref as a Sloop				Survey'd Afloat 24th Feb.y 1763 & found to want Sm.ll Rep.r
Ditto	2 Feb 1762	23 Feb 1762		Feb 1762	24 Feb 1762	11 Mar 1762	Refitted as a Bomb	138. 11. 7	588. 8. 6	727. 10. 1	Est.d for Her Hull &c £419 and 6 Weeks; Not reported to Admty.
Sheerness	25 Mar 1773	27 Mar 1773	Sh'd Apr 73	Apr 1773	17 Apr 1773		Fitted				Fitted for a voyage towards the North Pole, May 1773
Ditto	19 Apr 1773	19 Apr 1773			22 Apr 1773	30 Apr 1773	Refitt'd	1,193. 15. 5	1,701. 13. 3	2,895. 8. 8	[Ditto]
Woolwich	16 Nov 1781										Surv'd Afloat at Woolwich Feb 1782 & found to want Middlg Repair

Author's note: HMS *Carcass* was sold on 5 August 1784 for £320

Appendix 3: *Quality of Sailing Report for HMS* Racehorse

The OBSERVATIONS of the Quality of His Majesty's Ship *Racehorse*
(Source: PRO. Adm. 95/30/45)

		Ft.	Ins.	
Her best Sailing Draft of Water when Victualled and Stored for Channel Service	{ Afore	13	2 }	or as much lighter (at the same Difference) as she is able to bear Sail
being given this 14th Day of Oct.r 1773	{ Abaft	13	6 }	

Her Lowest Gundeck Port will be above the surface of the Water............................Not recorded.

	In a Topgallant Gale..................	*goes Six knots*
	In a Topsail Gale......................	*Six [knots]*
Query the 1st........	How she Steers, and how she Wears and Stays	*Steers very well, wears quick and stays well unless in a Head Sea*
	Under her... {Reeft Topsails...................	*Four and a Half [knots]*
	Courses......................	*Never tried.*

And Query, Whether she will Stay under her Courses....................... *Never tried.*

2nd. In each Circumstance above mentioned (in Sailing with Other Ships) in what Proportion she gathers to Windward, and in what proportion she forereaches, and in general her Proportions in leeway.. *Generally falls to leeward and a Stern making one Point more leeway than any other Ship & in general one point and a half and two points.*

3rd. How she proves in Sailing thro' all the variations of the Wind from its being two feet abaft the Beam, to its Veering forward upon the Bowline in every Strength of Gale, especially if a stiff Gale and a Head sea, and how many Knots she runs in each Circumstance and how she carries her Helm.. *In a stiff gale two Points, abaft the beam 9 ½ and 10 knots, before the Beam 8 and upon a bowline 6 ½ & 7 [knots] She in general carries a weather helm.*

4th. The most knots she runs before the Wind; and how she Rolls in a trough of Sea........ *Eight knots and rolls greatly.*
5th. How she behaves in Lying Too, or a Try, under a Mainsail also under a Mizon balanc'd... *Never tried.]*

6th. What a Roader she is, and how she Careens....................................... *She being very stiff she is a very good roader*

7th. If upon Trial the best sailing Draft of water given as above should not prove to be so what
is her best sailing Draft of Water................................... {Afore { Abaft

	Ft.	Ins
	14	0
	13	6

8th. What is her best Draft of water when victualled for six Months, and Stored for { Afore
Foreign Service.................................... { Abaft

9th. What height is her lowest Gundeck-Port above the Surface of the Water...... { Afore
{ Midships
{ Abaft

10th. Trim of the Ship...

Note: Unfortunately no sailing report exists relating to *Racehorse* as fitted as an expeditionary sloop consequently the above relates to her common role as a bomb vessel where under the name *Racehorse* or later as *Thunder*.

Ft.   Ins.
14   0
13   6   *best draught of water for sailing*
No response answer is written

Her best trim by the head Note put the most part of her iron ballast betwixt the bomb bed beans makes her roll easy and much less.
By the Head 5 or 6 Inches; and the masts upright

James Orrock

Appendix 4: Quality of Sailing Report HMS Carcass

The OBSERVATIONS of the Quality of His Majesty's Ship *Carcass*
(Source: PRO. Adm. 95/30/45)

	Ft.	Ins.	
Her best Sailing Draft of Water when Victualled and Stored for Channel Service { Afore	12	8 }	or as much lighter (at the same Difference) as she is able to bear Sail
being given this *14th* Day of Oct *1773* { Abaft	12	2 }	

Her Lowest Gundeck Port will be above the surface of the Water................ 4   8

In a Topgallant Gale........................ goes Five or Six knots

In a Topsail Gale........................ goes about Six knots

Query the 1st...... How she Steers, and how she Wears and Stays .... Steers very well, wears quick and stays well unless in a Head Sea

Under her... {Reeft Topsails........................ Six goes about three knots or more, pitches much in a head Sea

{Courses........................ goes about three knots, pitches heavy, otherwise behaves well.

never had occasion to try her, but think she will

2nd. In each Circumstance above mentioned (in Sailing with Other Ships) in what Proportion she   Carries sail long, and is weatherly but does not forereach
gathers to Windward, and in what proportion she forereaches, and in general her Proportions in
leeway.......................

3rd. How she proves in Sailing thro' all the variations of the Wind from its being two feet abaft the   Pitches very heavy when close hauled, goes very easy with the Wind on the Beam; and
Beam, to its Veering forward upon the Bowline in every Strength of Gale, especially if a stiff Gale   Ships a good deal of Water, sometimes in the Waste, carries her helm in general rather
and a Head sea, and how many Knots she runs in each Circumstance and how she carries her   Weatherly.
Helm........................

4th. The most knots she runs before the Wind; and how she Rolls in a trough of Sea........   goes Ten knots, rolls very deep, but Easy

5th. How she behaves in Lying Too, or a Try, under a Mainsail also under a Mizon balanc'd...   Lays too very well, but takes in Water in the Waste when she Falls Off

6th. What a Roader she is, and how she Careens........................   Rides well, but pitches much in a Head swell

329

7th. If upon Trial the best sailing Draft of water given as above should not prove to be so { Afore { Abaft .... —

Ft.   Ins.
As above

8th. What is her best Draft of water when victualled for six Months, and Stored for { Afore { Abaft ....

Ft.   Ins.
13   3
12   9

9th. What height is her lowest Gundeck-Port above the Surface of the Water...... { Afore { Midships { Abaft

Ft.   Ins.
About 4 feet

10th. Trim of the Ship...........................

By the Head 5 or 6 Inches; and the masts upright

Lutwidge Cap.ᵗ

Appendix 5: *Notes about commanding officers of HMS* Racehorse *and as renamed* Thunder

Captain James Gambier, who took command of *Thunder* in April 1778, was captured by the French on 14 August 1778. Later released as an exchanged POW, he rose to flag rank fighting in the *Defence* at the battle of the Glorious First of June 1794, Basque Roads 1799, and the bombardment of Copenhagen on 2 September 1807. Appointed Admiral of the Fleet 22 July 1830, he died 19 April 1833.

(Sources: TNA. ADM 346/20/21; 346/23/2)

Appendix 6: Notes about commanding officers of HMS Carcass

Captain Edward Edwards, who took command of the *Carcass* in later years, also commanded the frigate *Pandora* seeking out the mutineers from the *Bounty*. With Edwards on this voyage was former *Bounty* crew member Midshipman Peter Haywood. On the return voyage from Pitcairn Island, the *Pandora* foundered on the Great Barrier Reef on 29 August 1791 and four of the ten mutineers were captured and 31 of *Pandora*'s crew died when the ship was destroyed. Edwards and the other survivors – 89 men and 10 prisoners – were forced to make an arduous open boat voyage to Timor and then onwards to Batavia (Jakarta). This was the second time in two years that Haywood found himself in an open boat making for the safety of the Dutch East Indies.

(Source: Hough, Richard, *Captain Bligh and Mr Christian: The Men and the Mutiny*, Hutchinson, 1972, passim)

Appendix 7: Ship's Muster Book HMS Racehorse 23 April–28 June 1773
(Source: TNA. ADM. 36/490)

Statement given at head of page reads:

'*Race Horses* [sic] Complement 90 Men. Began Wages the 16th, and Extra Petty Warrant Victualling at Deptford the 19th of April 1773. Ended Extra Petty Warrant the 11th of May following and began Sea Victualing the next day.'

'MUSTER–TABLE of his Majesty's Ship *Race Horse* between the 19th April and the 30 June 1773'

Author's note: Column 9, 'Further notes from muster', has been added to the original muster book columns by the author to include additional notes – i.e. whether the man was promoted or reclassified etc, as well as where they were discharged or deserted (run).

SB No.	Date Entered	Whence & whether Prest or not	Place & Country where Born	Age	Surname	First Name	Rank Title or Rate	Further notes from muster	D, DD, or R	Time of Discharge
1	11 April	Pr Comn 16 April	–	–	Phipps	Constantine	Captain			
		Pr Comn 16 April	–		Harvey	Henry	1st Lieutenant			

Notes: SB No. = Ship's Book Number, **D** = Discharged, **DD** = Discharged dead, **R** = Run [Deserted]

(Continued)

Appendix 7: (Continued)

SB No.	Date Entered	Whence & whether Prest or not	Place & Country where Born	Age	Surname	First Name	Rank Title or Rate	Further notes from muster	D, DD, or R	Time of Discharge
		Pr Comn 16 April	–	–	Graves	Thomas	3rd Lieutenant			
	19 April				Stamford	Jonathan	Boatswain			
5					Oyne	John	Gunner	Discharged to Bonetta	D	10 May
					Williams	Jonathan	Carpenter 2nd	Exchanged to Vestal	D	20 May
					Galbraith	Daniel	Cook	Superannuated	D	5 May
		Deptford	Edinburgh	26	Thane	Samuel	Able Seaman	4 June – Master's Mate		
			Jersey	21	D'Auvergne	Philip	Able Seaman	4 June – Midshipman		
10			Kirkaldie Scotland	28	Miller	David	Able Seaman	4 June – Master's Mate		
			Shrewsbury, Shropshire	21	Floyd	Thomas	Able Seaman	4 June – Midshipman		
			Upsal [Uppsala] Sweden	30	Walden	Frederick	Able Seaman	4 June – Midshipman		
			Limerick, Ireland	24	Scott	George	Able Seaman	4 June – Midshipman		

No.	Date	Age	Surname	Forename	Origin	Rating	Remarks		
		29	Jones	Thomas	Drogherday, Scotland	Able Seaman	4 June – Quartermaster		
15		30	Pendry	Alexander	Topsham, Devon	Able Seaman	To Nore	D	30 May
17		30	Johnson	Thomas	London	Able Seaman	4 June – Captain's Clerk		
18	19 April Deptford	22	Bates	Josiah	Newark, Notts.	Able Seaman			
		23	Hamilton	William	Leith, Scotland	Able Seaman			
20		28	McCarty	Charles	Dublin	Able Seaman			
		21	Owen	Thomas	Deptford	Able Seaman	4 June – Carpenter's Crew		
		33	Vian Parnell	William	Plymouth, Devon	Able Seaman	4 June– Bosun's Mate		
		37	Roberts	William	Hemsworth	Able Seaman	At Deptford	R	7 May
25		33	Guy	William	London	Able Seaman	At Deptford	R	7 May
		40	Larkin	William	Chatham	Able Seaman	At Deptford	R	7 May
		25	Robertson	Jonathan	Whitehaven, Cumberland	Able Seaman	At Deptford	R	7 May
		20	Scorpen	Charles	Naples, Italy	Able Seaman		D	
			Widows Man	(1)		Able Seaman	Admiralty Order to enter none sent effective May 1		
30		–	Widows Man	(2)		Able Seaman	Ditto		
	20 April Pr Warrant 20 April		Crane	John		Master			

335

(*Continued*)

Appendix 7: (Continued)

SB No.	Date Entered	Whence & whether Prest or not	Place & Country where Born	Age	Surname	First Name	Rank Title or Rate	Further notes from muster	D, DD, or R	Time of Discharge
			Pool [sic], Dorset	35	Shepherd	Robert	Able Seaman	4 June – Quarter Gunner		
			North Shields	22	Stone	Thomas	Able Seaman			
34			Saltash, Devon	29	Hoblin	Thomas	Able Seaman	4 June – Quarter Gunner		
35	20 April	Pr Warrant 20 April	–	–	Strong	John	Purser			
		Deptford	Gosport	22	Sproul	Andrew	Able Seaman	At Whitby	R	11 June
			Bath	34	Wyett	Jonathan	Able Seaman	4 June – Boatswain's Mate		
			Titchfield, Hampshire	29	Freewater	Daniel	Able Seaman			
			Titchfield, Hampshire	25	Freewater	Jonathan	Able Seaman			
40			Madagascar	30	Syfax	John	Able Seaman			
			Berwick	30	Blackadder	Josiah	Able Seaman	At Deptford	R	26 June
			Brampton (sic) Kent	24	Stubbs	William	Able Seaman	At Deptford	R	9 May
			Leghorn, Italy	28	Joseph	John	Able Seaman			
			Newcastle	21	Cowens	Thomas	Able Seaman	At Deptford	R	May
			Waterford	31	Haley	John	Able Seaman	At Deptford	R	7 May

No.	Date	Entered	Birthplace	Age	Surname	Forename	Rating	Note		Date
45			Killeton, Cornwall	29	Arthur	Charles	Able Seaman			
			Chelsea	23	Cooper	George	Able Seaman			
			Kinsale, Ireland	24	Flynn	David	Able Seaman	At Deptford	**R**	7 May
			Fareham, Hants		Gold	John	Able Seaman	4 June – rated but illegible		
50	23 April		London	24	Guire	Charles	Able Seaman	At Deptford	**R**	7 May
51			Berwick	21	Leach	Alexander	Able Seaman	4 June – Carpenter's Mate		
	23 April	Deptford	Southampton	23	Sidney	William	Able Seaman			
			London	21	White	John	Able Seaman	At Whitby	**R**	11 June
			Lambeth, Surry [sic]	31	Dalton	William	Able Seaman	At Deptford	**R**	4 May
55			Falkland, Fifeshire	23	Blake	Alexander	Able Seaman	4 June – Purser's Steward		
	24 April		Egham, Surry [sic]	31	Plym	Richard	Able Seaman	4 June – Gunners Mate		
	26 April		Saffron Walden, Essex		Lucas	Charles	Able Seaman	4 June – Midshipman		
		Pr Comn 16 April	Plymouth	23	Moses	Peter	Able Seaman		**D**	4 May
					Adamson	Cuthbert	2nd Lieutenant			
60	26 April	Deptford	Guernsey	37	Collis	William	Able Seaman		**D**	26 May
			Dublin	34	Fling	John	Able Seaman			
			Aberdeen	23	Smith	James	Able Seaman			
			Belfast, Ireland	21	Trimble	Jonathan	Able Seaman			

(Continued)

Appendix 7: (Continued)

SB No.	Date Entered	Whence & whether Prest or not	Place & Country where Born	Age	Surname	First Name	Rank Title or Rate	Further notes from muster	D, DD, or R	Time of Discharge
65			Philadelphia	22	O'Carny	James	Able Seaman			
	28 April		Bristol	33	Robinson	Richard	Able Seaman	At Sheerness	D	9 June
			Wakefield, Yorkshire	25	Baker	Josiah	Able Seaman			
			London	31	Carpenter	George	Able Seaman			
	29 April		Stockholm	40	Roos	Peter	Able Seaman			
	29 April	Deptford	Stockholm	29	Sodestrom	John	Able Seaman			
70			Stockholm	30	Hagg	Nelis	Able Seaman			
			Gottenburgh [sic]	22	Lindgreen	Jonathan	Able Seaman			
			Gottenburgh [sic]	24	Dalton	Jonas	Able Seaman	At Deptford	R	9 May
			Calmas, Sweden	26	Lundguist	Hans	Able Seaman	At Deptford	R	1 ?
	26 April	Pʳ Warrant 26 April			Irving	Charles	Surgeon			
75	29 April	Pʳ Warrant 24 April	From HMS *Egmont*		Mair	Alexander	Surgeons Mate			
	30 April	Deptford	London	34	Spry	John	Able Seaman	At Deptford	R	7 May
	1 May		London	30	Easterman	Jonathan	Able Seaman	At Deptford	R	12 May
	3 May		Gottenburgh [sic]	22	Malm	Alexander	Able Seaman			
			Dalkeith, Scotland	27	Finley	William	Able Seaman	To 4 June – Carpenter's crew?		
80			Pisquata	26	Shepherd	John	Able Seaman			
			Boston, New England	23	Haines	Alexander	Able Seaman			

Notes 1. Pisquata. This probably relates to the Pisquata River in New Hampshire rather than a town 3. Those from Gothenburg may have joined as a group from another ship.

338

No.	Date	Entered	Born	Age	Surname	Forename	Rating	Disposal		
	5 May		Sweden	22	Hans	Philemon	Able Seaman	At Deptford	R	9 May
			Sweden	22	Anderson	Peter	Able Seaman			
			Keldon [sic] Essex		Richmond	Jonathan	Able Seaman			
85	8 May	Deptford	Lisbon	37	Olivia	Anthony	Able Seaman	At Deptford	R	3 May
			London	28	Jackson	Samuel	Able Seaman	At Deptford	R	9 May
	10 May		Gottenburgh	30	Christian	Swin	Able Seaman			
	11 May		Limerick, Ireland	24	Higgins	Samuel	Able Seaman			
			Kilmarden, Ireland	22	Jackson	George	Able Seaman	At Deptford	R	4 May
			Waterford, Ireland	22	Bacchus	Peter	Able Seaman			
90			Sothwark [sic]		Wise	Richard	Able Seaman	4 June – Carpenter's Crew		
	Pr Warrant 10 May				Fenton	John	Gunner			
	14 May		Leith	21	McIntire	Jonathan	Able Seaman			
			Nº. [North] Shields	24	Ditchburn	Barthlomew	Able Seaman	4 June – Quartermaster		
			Nekin, Suff[olk]	21	Ellsden	Benjamin	Able Seaman			
			Virginia	44	Roberts	Mark	Able Seaman			
5			Kinsale, Ireland	43	Brian	Edward	Able Seaman		D	9 May
			Berkstead? Sussex	36	Clifton	Jonathan	Able Seaman	4 June – Sailmaker's Crew		

Notes 1. Keldon = Kelvedon. 2. Nekin in Suffolk cannot be identified. 3. Berkstead, Sussex is probably Buxted, near Uckfield.

(Continued)

Appendix 7: (Continued)

SB No.	Date Entered	Whence & whether Prest or not	Place & Country where Born	Age	Surname	First Name	Rank Title or Rate	Further notes from muster	D, DD, or R	Time of Discharge
			Droitwich, Worcester[shire]	22	Bostock	Josiah	Able Seaman			
100			Amsterdam	26	Valentine	Joshua	Able Seaman			
			Stockholm	20	Marbeck	Lawrence	Able Seaman			
102	6 May	*Barfleur*	Bushfort [sic], Antrim	25	Dunken	Roberts	Masters Mate			
	17 May		Derry, Ireland	27	Lowall	David	Able Seaman	4 June – [ship's] Corporal		
			Exeter	20	Godfrey	Johnathan	Able Seaman			
105			S° [South] Carolina	28	Weston	Gustav	Able Seaman	Galleons Reach	R	26 May
			London	29	Stubbins	Edward	Able Seaman			
			Philadelphia	24	McCaul	William	Able Seaman			
			Dagnam [sic] Essex	25	Parin	Henry	Able Seaman	4 June – Quartermaster's Mate		
			St Andrews, Fife	30	Moor	Jonathon	Able Seaman			
110	28 April	Pr Warrant 11 May	Ladykirk, Berwick		Sharpe	Alexander	Able Seaman	11 May – Cook		
	21 May	Pr Warrant 21 May			West	Josiah	Carpenter	[Replaced previous]		

Notes: 1. Bushfort = Bushforde Antrim. **2.** No. 105 Gustav Weston is in fact Olaudah Equiano. **3.** Dagnam = Dagenham.

340

	27 May	27 May	Cork	25	Simmons	William	Able Seaman
		Pr Warrant 24 May	Limehouse	22	Spence	Thomas	Sailmaker
		Pr Warrant 25 May			Wellsted	Richard	Armourer
115		Sheerness	Portsmouth	21	Sandall	Osmand	Able Seaman
			Deptford	23	Kingsley	John	Able Seaman — To 4 June – Carpenter's Mate
					York	Richard	Able Seaman
	31 May				Hill	William	Able Seaman
119	1 June	1 June			Ribley	Matthew	Able Seaman
	1 June	(Sheerness)			Treeble	John	Able Seaman
					Turnbelle	Fursley	Able Seaman
	12 June	12 June (Whitby)			Lore	John	Able Seaman

Notes:

1. The last entry, John Lore, replaced the man who 'Run' at Whitby.
2. The document is jointly signed by the captain, master, purser and boatswain.
3. After these signatures an additional note is entered which reads:
   'Supernumerary Borne for victuals only 1 May 73–26 May Woolwich. – Israel Lyons.' [This relates to the appointed Astronomer Royal].
   The document is again signed by the three named signatures stated above.
4. An additional page is added to the above muster list, which is titled: 'A List of Men Run from His Majesty's Ship Racehorse; The Honorable Const. J. Phipps Commander between the 19th April & 30th June 1773.' The list comprises 17 men, dates Run and where.

341

Appendix 8: *Ship's Muster Book HM Ship Carcass 23 April–28 June 1773*
(Source: TNA.ADM. 36/567)

Statement given at head of page reads:

'Carcass Complement 90 men to the 1st of June 1773 then 80 men Pr. Admiralty Order. Began Wages the 16th, and Extra Petty Warrant Victualling the 21st of April 1773. Ended Extra Petty Warrant Victualling the 19th May 1773.'

'MUSTER–TABLE' of his Majesty's Ship Carcass between the 19th April and the 30 June 1773'

Author's note: Column 9, 'Further notes from muster', has been added to the original muster book columns by the author to include additional notes – i.e. whether the man was promoted or reclassified etc, as well as where they were discharged or deserted (run).

SB No.	Date Entered	Whence & whether Prest or not	Place & Country where Born	Age	Surname	First Name	Rank Title or Rate	Further notes from muster	D, DD or R	Time of Discharge
1	21 April	Pr Commn 16 April	-	-	Wykham	George	3rd Lieutenant			
-					-	-	Widows Man (1)			
					-	-	Widows Man (2)			
	21 April	Sheerness Ordin'ry	-	-	Cunningham	John	Boatswain			

Notes: SB No. = Ship's Book Number, **D** = Discharged, **DD** = Discharged dead, **R** = Run [Deserted]

1. Penton = Paignton **2.** Yeoman of the Powder Room no longer needed once gunpowder stowed.

No.	Date	Entered	Birthplace	Age	Surname	First name	Rating	Note	D	Date
	–			–	Ramsey	John	Gunner			
	–			–	Purcell	Abraham	Carpenter			
5	–			–	Yarworth	Thomas	Cook		D	12 May
	22 April	Sheerness Ordy	Penton* [sic] Devon	32	Searle	Richard	Able Seaman	1 May – Master's Mate		
			Dartford Kent	36	Western	Richard	Able Seaman	1 May – Midshipman		
					Dean	Charles	Able Seaman	1 May – Midshipman		
	–		London	20	Creswell	John	Able Seaman			
10	–		Limerick Ireland	34	Farrell	Patrick	Able Seaman	To 1 May – Yeoman of the Powder Room	D	1 May Pr Order
	23 April		Bristol	41	Hancock	Samuel	Able Seaman		D	27 May Pr Order
	–		Fifeshire North Britain	29	Finley	Thomas	Able Seaman	1 May – Ship's Corporal		
	–		Isle of Man	21	Quaile	Peter	Able Seaman			
	25 April		Bexley Kent	32	Fowler	Henry	Able Seaman			
15	27 April	Pr Warrant 20 April		–	Wallis	William	Surgeon			
	16 April	Pr Commn 16 April		–	Baird	John	1st Lieutenant			
17	22 April	London Ord.	Galloway North. Britain	23	Hasty	John	Able Seaman		D	28 May Pr Order.

(Continued)

Notes: 1. North Britain relates to Scotland.

Appendix 8: (Continued)

SB No.	Date Entered	Whence & whether Prest or not	Place & Country where Born	Age	Surname	First Name	Rank Title or Rate	Further notes from muster	D, DD or R	Time of Discharge
18	19 April	Pʳ Warrant 20 April	–	–	Parry	John	Purser			
	30 April	Sheerness Ordy	Paisland? Suffolk	22	Vollge	Lazarus	Able Seaman			
20	–	Pʳ Warrant 20 April	–	–	Allen	James	Master			
	–	Chatham Volunteer	Chatham	35	Scott	John	Able Seaman			
	22 April	Whitehaven Volr	Wicklow Ireland	35	Shelton	Mathias	Able Seaman			
	30 April	Pʳ Warrant 20 April		–	Wallace	Thomas	Surgeon's Mate			
	23 April	London Redezvous	Lincoln	25	White	John	Able Seaman			
	29 April		–	–	Holland	Edward	Able Seaman		D	23 May Pʳ Order
			Cork Ireland	26	Haley	David	Ordinary Seaman		D	27 May Pʳ Ord
	5 May	Sheerness Ordy	–	–	Jones	Thomas	Able Seaman		D	28 May Pʳ Ord
	23 April	London Redezvous	Dublin	34	Smith	Thomas	Able Seaman			
			Scarborough	36	Green	John	Able Seaman			
30	1 May			28	Cook	William	Able Seaman			
	4 May		Denmark	23	Thompson	Lutway	Ordinary Seaman		D	28 May Pʳ Ord
	2 May		Hull, Yorkshire	40	Sampson	Charles	Able Seaman			

Notes: 1. Paisland could be Pakefield Suffolk near Lowestoffe [Lowestoft]. **2.** David Haley was discharged because as an ordinary seaman he was considered 'inexperienced' for this voyage. **3.** Lutway Thompson was discharged for the same reason.

344

Date		Place	Age	Surname	Forename	Rank	Remarks		Date
3 May		Bristol	42	Lane	William	Able Seaman	8 May – Quartermaster's Mate		
4 May		Tottenham Middlesex	29	Petty	James	Able Seaman			
–	Pr Commn 16 April	–	–	Lutwidge	Skeffington	Commander			
1 May		Petworth Sussex	36	Mitchener	Thomas	Able Seaman	Unfit to proceed the voyage	D	11 June
–		Russia	28	Beaver	John	Able Seaman			
22 April		London	24	Rushworth	Edward	Able Seaman	8 May – Midshipman		
7 May	Sheerness	Burnham Norfolk	16	Nelson	Horatio	Midshipman			
9 May	Sheerness Ordy	Isle of Wight	23	Cass	James	Able Seaman			
–		Isle of Wight	20	White	Edward	Able Seaman			
	London Rendezvous	London	21	Butler	Richard	Able Seaman		D	27 May Pr Ord
4 May		London	39	Brown	William	Able Seaman		D	28 May Pr Ord
8 May		Bristol	30	Nelson	Peter	Able Seaman		R	28 May Ditto
7 May		Harwich Essex	21	Flowers	John	Able Seaman		D	28 May Ditto

Notes: 1. There were two people with the surname Nelson in the ship.

(Continued)

345

Appendix 8: (Continued)

SB No.	Date Entered	Whence & whether Prest or not	Place & Country where Born	Age	Surname	First Name	Rank Title or Rate	Further notes from muster	D, DD or R	Time of Discharge
	3 May		Bamf [sic] North Britain	22	Wright	James	Able Seaman		D	27 May Pr Ord
	-		Dumfries North Britain	22	Onion	William	Able Seaman			
	7 May		London	25	Foyle	James	Able Seaman		R	14 May Pr Ord
	5 May	From Resolution	Edinburgh	20	Smith	James	Able Seaman			
	4 May		Philadelphia	25	Biddle	Nicholas	Able Seaman	11 May – Coxswain		
	2 May		Madagascar	23	Brown	Joseph	Able Seaman			
	10 May	From Resolution	Liverpool	35	Lawrence	Thomas	Able Seaman	11 May – Boatswain's Mate		
	30 April		London	29	Hall	William	Able Seaman	11 May – Carpenter's Crew		
	4 May		Stonehold Glouc'shire	32	Jackson	William	Able Seaman		D	27 May Pr Ord
	6 May		Clovelly Devon	34	Rose	John	Able Seaman		D	27 May Pr Ord
	10 May	Sheerness	Deptford Kent	23	Arman	Samuel	Able Seaman		R	28 May Ditto

	Date	Source	Place	Age	Surname	First name	Rating	Note		
	4 May	London Redezvous	Kildare Ireland	27	Doyle	James	Able Seaman		D	27 May Pr Ord
	–		London	23	Willis	John	Ordinary Seaman			
60	9 May		New York	37	Green	John	Able Seaman			
	10 May		Cork, Ireland	24	Malone	John	Able Seaman			
			Lowestoffe Suffolk	23	Manning	James	Able Seaman			
69	16 April	Pr Comn 16 April		–	Pennington	Josiah	2nd Lieutenant			
70	13 May	Pr Warrant 11 May		–	McLean	Alexander	Cook			
	6 May	From *Resolution*	London	28	Bernam	Edward	Able Seaman	3 June – Sailmaker's Crew		
	–		Wivelscombe Somerset	26	Marsh	William	Ordinary Seaman		D	27 May Pr Ord
	23 April		Dublin	32	English	Thomas	Able Seaman		D	27 May Pr Ord
	2 May		London	40	Shaw	Robert	Able Seaman		D	27 May Pr Ord
5	29 April		Edinburgh	41	Frazer	James	Able Seaman		D	27 May Pr Ord
	4 May		Bridgenorth Shropshire	48	Worthy	Josiah	Able Seaman		D	27 May Pr Ord
	27 April		Worcester	21	Goodman	John	Able Seaman		D	27 May Pr Ord
	29 May		Lancaster	37	Young	John	Able Seaman			

Notes: 1. Lowestoffe = Lowestoft. **2.** Wivelscombe relates to Wiveliscombe.

(*Continued*)

SB No.	Date Entered	Whence & whether Prest or not	Place & Country where Born	Age	Surname	First Name	Rank Title or Rate	Further notes from muster	D, DD or R	Time of Discharge
	30 May			37	Grant	James	Able Seaman		D	27 May Pr Order.
	27 May		London	33	Solias	Peter	Able Seaman		D	Ditto
	28 May		Newport Pembrokeshhire	27	Davis	Daniel	Able Seaman		D	Ditto
	1 May		Manchester	23	Taylor	James	Able Seaman		D	27 May Pr Ord
			Kinsale Ireland	25	Collins	Jeremiah	Able Seaman			
			Dublin		Mc Lane	John	Able Seaman		D	27 May Pr Ord
85			Liverpool		Holly	Robert	Able Seaman			28 May Pr Ord
86	2 May	15 May *Resolution*	Wrexham Denbighshire	33	Price	James	Able Seaman		D	28 May Pr Ord
	5 May		Cork Ireland	26	Cantillon	James	Able Seaman			
	2 May		Forfar North Britain	19	Edwards	Thomas	Able Seaman		D	27 May Pr Ord
	–		Waterford Ireland	22	Shirley	Edward	Able Seaman		D	27 May Pr Ord

No	Date	Source	Place	Age	Surname	Forename	Rank	Promotion	Discharge
90	27 April		Whitney Oxfordshire	20	Pritchard	John	Able Seaman		
	-		Québec	20	Wicker	John	Able Seaman		D 22 May
	-		St. John's Norfolk	23	Colt	James	Able Seaman	15 May – Qtr Gunner	
	21 May	Sheerness	Yarmouth [Norfolk]	25	Cropley	William	Gunners Mate		
	28 May	Supy[?] list	Bristol	21	Willis	Francis	Able Seaman		
	6 May		Canterbury	20	Steele	Edward	Able Seaman		
	5 May		London	20	Gray	James	Able Seaman		
	22 April		Greenwich	20	Stuteville	Charles	Able Seaman		
	30 April		Ripley, Surrey	33	Knight	Aaron	Able Seaman	29 May – Boatswains Mate	
100	16 May		St Peter's Kent	23	Carrrell	James	Able Seaman		
			Rossheen ? North Britain	33	Monro	John	Able Seaman		
	12 May		Dublin	35	Bradley	Josiah	Quarter Master		
	6 May		London	25	Toms	John	Able Seaman	29 May – Midshipman	
103	22 April	Supy[?]. List	Dublin	25	Mulock	Joshua	Able Seaman	29 May – Master's Mate	

Notes: 1. Rosheen (in Scotland) cannot be identified.

(Continued)

349

Appendix 8: (Continued)

SB No.	Date Entered	Whence & whether Prest or not	Place & Country where Born	Age	Surname	First Name	Rank Title or Rate	Further notes from muster	D, DD or R	Time of Discharge
	30 April		Southampton	29	Williams	John	Able Seaman			
5	5 May		Edinburgh	29	Paterson	William	Able Seaman			
	17 May		London	32	Bond	John	Able Seaman			
	16 May		Glasgow	28	Stephen^son	John	Able Seaman			
	22 April		Plymouth	27	Burges	James Gee	Able Seaman	29 May – Master's Mate	D	23 May Pr Ord
	5 May		London	18	Praper	Richard	Ordinary Seaman	29 May – Able Seaman	D	27 May Pr Ord
110	17 May	Pr Warant 14 May	London	22	Merlien	Josiah	Armourer			
			Chatham	30	Cockerell	John	Carpenter's Mate	Carpenter		
	22 May		Barking, Essex	40	Smith	William	Carpenter's Mate			
			London	35	Bread	John	Sailmaker's Crew			
114			London	17	Robinson	James	Clerk			

Notes: The list is signed by the captain and purser.

350

Appendix 9: Place names of the Spitsbergen archipelago and their modern Norwegian Svalbard equivalents

Amsterdam Island	Amsterdamøya
Dane's Gat	Danskegattet
Deadman's Island	Lihholmen
Cloven Cliff	Klovningen
Fair Haven	Fair Haven
Hakluyt's Headland	Hakluythovden
Hinlopen Straits	Hinlopenstretet
Low Island	Lägøya
Magdalena Hook	Magdalenehuken
Marble Island	Skrifter or Svalbard og Ishavet
Moffen Island	Moffen
North East Land	Nordaustlandet
Outer Norway	Ytre Norskøya
Phipps Island	Phippsøya
Prince Charles Island	Prins Karls Forland
Seven Islands	Sjuøyane
Smeerenberg	Smeerenburg
Vogel Sang	Fuglesangen
Walden's Island	Waldenøya

(**Source:** Savours, Ann, "'A very interesting point in geography'": The 1773 Phipps Expedition towards the North Pole', *Arctic Institute of North America Vol 37, No 4*, December 1984, pp402–425)

Note: As shown at least two of those names resulting from the 1773 expedition survive today. *Walden Island* is named after midshipman John Walden who, along with two pilots, landed on the westernmost island of the archipelago on 5 August 1773. Other islands named after expedition members are Phippsøva and Nelsønova or Siuøvane. Cummingøva is named after watchmaker, Alexander Cummings, who made the pendulum used by Phipps's expedition.

Appendix 10: The warrant officers and petty officers of HMS Racehorse and Carcass

Warrant Officers

	Racehorse	Carcass
Title	Name	Name
Master	John Crane	James Allen
Boatswain	John Stanford	John Cunningham
Carpenter	Josiah West	Abraham Purcell
Gunner	John Fenton	John Ramsey
Purser	John Strong	John Parry
Surgeon	Charles Irving	William Wallis
Surgeon's mate	Alexander Mair	Thomas Wallace
Armourer	Richard Wellsted	Josiah Merlien
Cook	Alexander Shaw	Alexander MacLane
Sailmaker	Thomas Spence	
TOTAL	10	9

Notes: **NA**= not appointed.

Petty Officers

	Racehorse	Carcass
Title	Name	Name
Boatswain's mate	Jonathan Wyatt	Aaron Knight
Gunner's mate	Richard Plym	William Cropley
Carpenter's mate	Alexander Leach	John Cockerell
Carpenter's mate	John Kinsley	NA
Master's mate	Dunkern Roberts	Joshua Mulock
Master's mate	Samuel Thane	Richard Searle
Master's mate		James Gee Burgess
Quartermaster	Thomas Jones	NA
Quartermaster	Bartholomew Ditchburn	John Thompson
Quartermaster's mate	Henry Perin	William Lane
Quartermaster's mate	Samuel Thane	NA
Ship's corporal	?	Thomas Finley
Quarter gunner		James Colt
TOTAL	10	10

Notes: **NA**= not appointed.

Appendix 11: Complement of the rank and ratings borne in HM ships Racehorse and Carcass when they sailed

(Source: Compiled from both ship's muster books, this list includes those re-rated or reappointed. This excludes the supernumeraries and those formally discharged or run.)

Rank, Title or Rating	Racehorse	Carcass	Rank, Title or Rating	Racehorse	Carcass
Commander	I	I	Boatswain's mates	I	2
Lieutenants	3	3	Gunner's mates	I	I
Master	I	I	Quarter gunner	2	I
Boatswain	I	I	Yeoman of the powder room	NA	I
Gunner	I	I	Armourer	I	I
Carpenter	I	I	Carpenter's mates	2	I
Purser	I	I	Carpenter's crew	3	2
Cook	I	I	Sailmaker	I	NA
Surgeon	I	I	Sailmaker's crew	I	2
Surgeon's mate	I	I	Ship's corporal	I	I
Midshipmen	5	6	Purser's [ship's] steward	I	NA
Master's mates	2	3	Ice pilots	2	2
Captain's clerk	I	I	Coxswain	NA	I
Quartermaster	I	I	Able seamen (of unspecified role)	30	41
Quarter master's mates	I	I	Supernumeraries	I	I
Sub Totals	**22**	**24**		**47**	**57**

Note: NA = Not Appointed

Total *Racehorse* **69** *Carcass* **81**

Appendix 12: Ship's company's national identity of HM ships Racehorse and Carcass.

Racehorse

Of the 120 men who initially entered into on *Racehorse*'s ship's books, 62 per cent (72) appear to be of English origin. Of this figure, 12 were from the greater London area. The remaining 38 per cent comprised the following mixed nationalities:

Colonists	British Isles			Foreign					
American	Channel Islanders	Irish	Scots	Italian	Dutch	Madagascan	Portuguese	Swedish	Total
6	2	12	9	2	1	1	1	12	46

Carcass

Of the 112 men who initially signed on *Carcass*'s ship's books, 71 per cent (79) appear to be of English origin. Of this figure, 17 were from the greater London area. Including Midshipman Horatio Nelson (ship's book number 39) there were three people from Norfolk; the remaining 29 per cent comprised the following mixed nationalities:

Colonists	British Isles				Foreign				
American	Canadian	Irish	Manxman	Scots	Welsh	Danish	Madagascan	Russian	Total
2	1	12	1	10	2	1	1	1	32

Appendix 13: Specifications for a 6-pounder carriage gun

Like all Royal Navy vessels, both *Racehorse* and *Carcass* were armed for defensive needs. As the ship's journals show, the guns were consistently used for signalling communication between each ship, especially within the dense foggy situations encountered. The size of naval 6 pounder guns issued from the Board of Ordinance were supplied in just two cuts (types): long or short. Long–cut guns of this calibre were 8ft (2.44m) long, the shorter cut, 6ft (1.83m) in length. Because there is no evidence about which size was carried, for practical reasons it is assumed that both vessels were armed with the short type, the specifications of which are as follows.

Item	Misc.	Measurement.	Total	Metric
Length of piece (barrel) (see Note 1)	–	6ft	–	1.83m
Calibre	19.6	–	–	–
Bore diameter [A]	–	3.69in	–	93.74mm
Windage [A–D] (see Note 2)	–	0.2in	–	5.08mm
Diameter of trunnions	–	3.69in	–	93.74mm
Weight of piece (gun barrel) [B]	–	16 cwt 2 quarters 0lb	1,848lb	838.24kg
Weight of carriage [C]	–	3 cwt 1 quarter 6lb	370lb	167.83kg
Total weight of gun [B+ C]	–	19 cwt 3 quarters 6lb	2,218lb	1,006.7kg
Shot weight [D]	–	6lb	–	2.72kg
Shot diameter	–	3.49in	–	88.65mm
Proportional weight of shot to gun	286.2	–	–	–
Weight standard of gunpowder charge	–	2lb	–	0.92kg

Maximum range (at 6 degrees' elevation)	–	1,500–1,610 yards	0.8–0.91 miles	1.37–1.47km
Point blank range (no elevation)	–	320 yards	0.2 miles	0.29km
Number of gun's crew (see Notes 3 & 4)	–	4	–	–

Notes:

1. Length is taken from muzzle to the breech, ie does not include cascabel for recoil rope.
2. Windage is the clearance measurement difference between shot diameter and bore diameter: about 1/10in (2.54mm).
3. This figure relates to operating the gun using round shot in action.
4. The fact that guns were being used for signalling by blank firing with such a reduced powder charge meant that one man could easily operate them safely as there would be no recoil under these circumstances.
5. Because the larger-cut long 6 pounders were 2ft (61cm) longer, their related weight dimensions are 20 per cent greater. As for their other specifications, these remain as given above.
6. Signalling charge would have been no greater than ½–1lb (226.8–454g).

Appendix 14: *Miscellaneous Admiralty and Navy Board letter book instructions related to preparing HM ships* Racehorse *and* Carcass *in 1773*

(Source: TNA. ADM. 95/94, p395)

Deptford 16 Febr^y: *Racehorse to be fitted for a voyage to the North Pole.*
Sheerness 16 Febr^y: *Carcass D°.*
Deptford 24 March: *Racehorse Sloop to be supplied with Ice Saws.*
Sheerness 24 March: *Carcass Sloop to be supplied with Ice Saws.*
Deptford 29 March: *Ice hatchets to be provided and sent to Sheerness for the Carcass Sloop.*
Sheerness 29 March: *Do received Sheerness*
Sheerness 27 March: *Carcass*
Deptford 4 March: *Racehorse to be dismantled as far as may be necessary.*
[Note: This relates to taking down the bomb beds and shell rooms].
Sheerness 26 March: *Carcass Sloop to be refitted in Preference to other Works.*
Sheerness 3 April: *Carcass Sloop to employ Men such extra on her as day light will permit.*
Sheerness 5 April: *To Proceed in fitting according to former orders.*
Deptford 9 April: *To take out her bomb beds & make other alterations.*
[Note: This relates to *Racehorse*].
Deptford 12 April: *Racehorse to build three Cabins in her.*
Sheerness 13 April: *Captain Lutwidge late of the Carcass Sloop having requested she as soon to be recommission'd, that the undermentioned boats may be provided as they are the most suitable for the intended voyage Vizt:*

The Sloops proper Long boat, One Launch of 26 feet One six oar'd Cutter One four oar'd Gig (of large dimensions).
Also that a Bulkhead may be fitted for the Afterpart of the Fore Castle in the same manner as the present Bulkhead of the Quarter Deck. These are to direct & require You to fit a Bulkhead to the Afterpart of the forecastle as

desired, and to supply the Sloop with the proper L^{ong} boat, and a Cutter of 25 feet, which we have in Store, unappropriated. The Launch and Gig we have contracted for here and Ordered to be sent to Sheerness for &c. HW JW JB GN

Deptford 14 April: To make gratings over the tiller as proposed. [Note: This relates to *Racehorse*].
Sheerness 19 April: *Pursuant an Order from fron the R^t. Hon ble The Lords Commissioners of the Admt^y of the 16th Inst: These are to direct & require you to cause His Maj st^y' Sloop Carcass Sloop at your Port, to be fitted out for a Voyage towards the North Pole & Stored in all respects proper for said voyage. And the Clerk of the Cheque is to enter Ninety Men as her compe^{nt} [complement] according to the scheme on the other side [of the paper] hereof &c. GW, CM (N?).*

1 *Commander.*
3 *Lieutenants.*
1 *Master.*
1 *Boatswain.*
1 *Gunner.*
1 *Carpenter.*
1 *Purser.*
1 *Surgeon.*
1 *Cook.*
3 *Master's Mates.*
6 *Midshipmen.*
1 *Captain's Clerk.*
2 *Quarter Masters.*
1 *Quarter Master's Mate.*
2 *Boatswain's Mates.*
1 *Coxswain.*
1 *Master Sailmaker.*
1 *Sailmaker's Crew.*
1 *Steward.*
1 *Corporal*
90 *Able Seamen*

Deptford 19 April: An identical letter is addressed to the *Racehorse*.
Deptford 20 April: *Racehorse Sloop to make the alterations proposed. The*

Master Shipwright & his Assistant having acquainted the distance of the Forecastle of the Racehorse Sloop from the Crosspiece of the topsail Sheets [bitts] *to where the Booms are for the Boats to lay on insofar that there're is no Lodgement than a foot at each end which by working the Ship, they may come down & be of bad consequence and propose to lengthen the Forecastle Two beams further aft and to have a Cabbin at the afterpart each side by which means there will be no room to Stow several seamen under the afterpart and to have a Bulk^{hd} at the after part of the same: These are to direct & require you to cause the same to be done accordingly for R^c. HP JW EM GM [?M]*

Sheerness 21 April: *These are to direct & require you to supply the Racehorse Sloop with a Green Kersey cloth and you are to supply her with Taylors Blocks and the Tacks & Sheets to be of small sizes as Captain Phipps shall desire.*

Sheerness 21 April: *Carcass to have a berth put up for the Pilots.*

Deptford 30 April: *Racehorse to be fitted with ports or half ports.*

Deptford 5 May: *Carcass Sloop with several stores.*

Deptford and Sheerness 7 May: *Racehorse (& Carcass) to be supplied to be provided with several particulars.*

Deptford 22 September: *Racehorse & Carcass Sloops to be laid up.*

List of primary sources

The National Archives, Kew, London

TNA ADM 2 98	Admiralty Orders & Warrants
TNA ADM 36 7490	Ship's Muster Book HMS *Racehorse*
TNA ADM 36 7567	Ship's Muster Book HMS *Carcass*
TNA ADM 51 757	Commander's Journal HMS *Racehorse*
TNA ADM 51 381	Commander's journal HMS *Racehorse*
TNA ADM 51 167/ Part 3	Commander's Journal HMS *Carcass*
TNA ADM 52 157	Master's Journal HMS *Racehorse*
TNA ADM 52	Master's Journal HMS *Racehorse*
TNA ADM 55	Master's Journal HMS *Carcass*
TNA ADM 95 94	Navy Board & Admiralty: Office of Comptroller of Navy: Reports, Estimates, Orders & Papers relating to ship building & repairs
TNA ADM 95	Quality of Sailing Report HMS *Racehorse*
TNA ADM 95 30/45.	Quality of Sailing Report HMS *Carcass*
TNA ADM 106	Navy Board Instructions to Master Shipwright Sheerness Dockyard 1773
TNA ADM 180 3 (623)	Ship Progress Book HMS *Racehorse* and HMS *Thunder*
TNA ADM 180	Ship Progress Book HMS *Carcass*

The National Maritime Museum Greenwich, London

NMM ZAZ 6566 J2200	HMS *Racehorse*: Inboard profile decks 1758 (Fireship).
NMM ZAZ 6567 J2199	HMS *Racehorse*: Profile & upper deck 1758
NMM ZAZ 6568 J2198	HMS *Racehorse*: Section at bomb bed 1758 (Bomb).
NMM ZAZ 6569 J2197	HMS *Racehorse*: Lines & profile 1773 (Arctic).
NMM ZAZ 6570 J2193	HMS *Racehorse*: Platforms 1773 (Arctic).
NMM ZAZ 6571 J2194	HMS *Racehorse*: Upper deck 1773 (Arctic).
NMM ZAZ 6572 J 2195	HMS *Racehorse*: Quarter deck & Forecastle (Arctic)
NMM ZAZ 6573 J2196	HMS *Racehorse*: Quarterdeck 1773 (Arctic)
NMM ZAZ 5629 J1446	HMS *Carcass*: Profile, decks & sections 1758
NMM ZAZ 6563 J8000	HMS *Carcass*: Inboard Profile & sections with details 1773 (Arctic).
NMM ZAZ 6564 J7999	HMS *Carcass*: Decks as a Sloop
NMM ZAZ 6565 J7998	HMS *Carcass*: Decks 1768 as sloop with modifications

The National Royal Navy Museum Portsmouth

RNM 1996/67/2 *A Voyage towards the North Pole at His Majesty's Command 1773*. Constantine Phipps (original copy).

Admiralty Library: Royal Naval Historical Branch

Correspondence D/NHB/22/1 March 2005. BR (Admiralty Book of Reference BR 1333. Naval Distilling Plant Theory and Operation (1945).

Other sources

Mulgrave Castle MSS

Glossary

A

Aback A sail is aback when sheeted to windward.

Abaft Towards the stern of ship.

Abeam At right angle to a ship's fore and aft centreline. Any object which lies outside a vessel at right angles to ship.

Aboard On board or in a ship.

About A ship is said to go about when turning from one tack to another

Aloft Up above; up the mast or in rigging.

Ahull Lying too without any sail set in a gale.

Astern Beyond the ship's stern

Athwart Across the ship. Opposite to fore and aft

A-try Lying under a trysail in a gale.

Aweather Towards the windward, or weather side.

B

Back To sheet the clew a sail to windward. The wind is said to back when it changes direction.

Back stay Supporting standing rigging preventing mast bending forward.

Beam Breadth of a vessel. Transverse timber supporting a deck.

Beam-ends A vessel is said to be on her beam ends when so excessively heeled that her masts are horizontal.

Bear away To put the helm up to windward to turn the ship further away from the wind.

Bearing The direction of an object expressed in degrees or a compass pint from a ship's fore and aft line from the direction of the bow, stern, or beam. If at 45 degrees off the stern can be expressed as a quarter.

Beat To tack or make progress to windward taking by a zig zag course, the wind first on one side then on the other.

Becalmed A ship is said to be becalmed when there is no wind sail hanging lifeless providing no motive power.

Belay Make fast a rope to a pin cleat or other object.

Bend To fasten a rope to another or to and object or a sail to its spar (opposite: unbend).

Berth Sleeping place in the ship. Place for a ship in a dock or alongside a jetty.

Bight Bend or loop in rope.

Bobstay Standing rigging securing the bowsprit down to the head of the ship.

Board To make a, board is setting off on a tack.

Bowse Down (or in) a rope. To haul taut a rope.

Broach Action of the ship to slew round against the position of the helm in a heavy sea so that wind is brought abeam.

Bulkhead Partition within the ship.

Bulwark Side of a ship's hull or safety rail running along upper decks.

Bitts Located on deck at the base of a mast these comprise two vertical timbers with a crosspiece fitted with belaying pins (see *Belay*) and pulley sheaves for topsail sheets.

Boomkin (or *Bumkin*) Angled projecting spar beyond bowsprit to secure foresail sheet blocks.

Bunt Middle lower part of a square sail.

Buntlines Ropes to hoist bunt of sail.

C

Cable Heavy rope attached to the anchor made to a length of 120 fathoms (219.5m). Made by laying up three complete ropes with a left-handed twist. Measured by circumference, in *Racehorse* these were 15 inches (380mm) and *Carcass* 12.5 inches (317mm), i.e. ½ inch for every foot of ship's breadth. If anchoring in greater depth a second cable was bent to the other.

Carry away To break loose.

Cast away To turn a ship's head on to chosen tack when getting under way from anchor.

Centre of effort Combined point of sail area plan upon which wind forces act.

Centre of gravity Combined point of ship's weight and buoyancy (see *Metacentric height*).

Chains (and *Chain plate*) Fixture at ship's side to which mast shrouds are secured either in the form of iron strap or longitudinal broad plank housing the deadeyes.

Claw off To beat away from the shoreline.

Cleat Fitting for temporary securing a rope

Clew Lower outer corner of a sail to which a clewline is rigged

Clewline Rope(s) used to hoist the clew of sail up into its yard.

Close hauled A vessel is said to be close hauled when sailing just off the wind (6 points) her sails being trimmed to attain best advantage. Synonymous with *sailing on a bowline, sailing taut* or *on a wind*.

Compass point Division on a compass card; a thirty second part of a circle i.e. 11 ¼°.

D

Dead reckoning An account of a ship's position at sea with regard to course made good and distance run in knots.

F

Fall Hauling point of a rope.

Fall off A ship is said to fall off when tending to bear off the wind.

Fore stay Supporting standing rope preventing the mast bending backward and forward.

Fox Short length of rope.

G

Gudgeon Metal eye fitted on after face of a stern post in which the rudder pintle (pin) sits.

H

Hang-off To hold.

Heel to List or roll over.

Helm Tiller or wheel to steer a vessel.

Head sail Triangular sail (jib) rigged to the bowsprit or jibboom.

Halyard (halliard) Rope with tackle used for hoisting yards, staysails or head sails.

Heave-to Trim sails in order to bring the ship to a standstill. A ship so stopped is said to be hove-too. The alternative is to 'come to'.

Hounds Position on lower mast to which standing rigging (shrouds and stays) are attached.

I

In One is said to be in a ship not on a ship. e.g. He served in HMS *Racehorse*.

In irons A vessel is said to be in irons when unable to bring the ship's head through the wind when attempting to turn onto another tack.

K

Kedge Small anchor used for steadying the ship of for hauling vessel off when she has run aground.

Kevel Finger and thumb type cleat for securing running rigging.

Knee Stout timber bracket with two arms locating deck beams to ship's side. Hanging knee in vertical plane; lodging knee in horizontal plane.

Knot Measure of speed at sea: 1 nautical mile (6,080 feet/1.852 km) per hour.

L

Larboard The left-hand side of a vessel when looking forward towards the ship's bow. (Today more commonly termed port side).

Latitude Geographical position north or south of the earth's equator expressed in degrees, [°], minutes ['] and seconds ["] of the arc with the suffix N or S.

Lee Opposite side to which the wind is blowing (alternative expression is leeward).

Lee helm A ship is said to carry a lee helm when it has a tendency to turn her bow away from the wind thus helm must be kept to leeward.

Leeway The amount of sideways movement a ship makes through the water.

Lie-to To cause a ship to keep her head steady in a gale by means of staysails in order to prevent heavy seas tumbling into her (Lying-to).

Longitude Positional distance east or west of the Greenwich meridian [0°] expressed in degrees minutes and seconds with the suffix E or W. Of, expressed in degrees and minutes.

Loose ice A number of pieces of ice near each other but through which a ship can move.

Luff Fore edge of a fore and aft sail or weather side leach (edge) of a square sail. To luff is to bring the ship's head up to windward.

M

Metacentric height (gm) This is the measurement of the initial static stability of a floating body calculated as the vertical distance above or below the ship's centre of gravity (CG). The greater the metacentric height above CG the better the stability righting moment acting against overturning.

Miss stays A vessel is said to miss stays when it fails to come about and falls back onto her previous tack (see *In irons*)

N

Nautical mile Based on the circumference of the earth, it is equal to one minute of latitude. i.e. (6,080 feet/1.852m).

O

Offing Position at a distance from shoreline.

Off and on When a ship beating to windward approaches a shore on one tack and recedes from it on another, i.e. standing off and on.

Overhaul To gain a position ahead of an accompanying vessel by setting more sail.

P

Painter Rope attached to a boat's bow.

Parrel Wood and rope neckless fitting to keep the center of a yard or the jaws of a gaff boom close in to the mast.

Pay off When a ship head falls off to leeward, she said to pay off.

Pintle Pin-like fitting on rudder that engages with a gudgeon to form a hinge about which the rudder rotates.

Port The left-hand side of a vessel when looking forward towards the ship's bow. (originally called larboard after earlier term laden board – loading side.

Q

Quarter Direction 45° off the bow or stern.

R

Run To sail before the wind.

Running rigging All that associated with the operational movement and control of yards and sails.

S

Sails

Square sails associated with the *Racehorse* and *Carcass* are:

Fore mast Lower (or course), topsail, topgallant sail and topmast and topgallant studding sails.

Main mast As per foremast.

Mizzen mast Topsail and topgallant sail only.

Bowsprit Spritsail and outer spritsail.

Fore and aft sails associated with the *Racehorse* and *Carcass* are:

Fore mast Fore staysail, topmast staysail and jib.

Main mast Main stay sail, middle staysail and topmast staysail.

Mizzen mast Mizzen sail (set on a gaff and boom, mizzen staysail and topmast staysail.

Seizing Rope used to bind two ropes together.

Set The direction in which a vessel is moved by a current or tidal stream.

Set to Hoist or make sail.

Shake out To let out a reef in a sail.

Sheets Ropes used to control the clew of a square sail and after clew of a staysail.

Shrouds Standing rigging providing transverse support to masts and bowsprit, their lower ends secured to the chain plates (or channels) by means of deadeyes.

Shiver (sheaver) Wooden pulley wheel set in a bock or fixed component.

Starboard The right-hand side of a vessel when looking forward towards the ship's bow.

Stays Supporting standing rigging preventing mast bending backward

Sternsheets Aftermost part of open boat.

Stiff A vessel is said to be stiff when carrying enough sail without heeling too much.

Swell Long easy waves with crests that do not brake.

T

Tack (noun) 1. Ropes used to control and haul forward the clew of a lower square sail. 2. Rope used to haul out the clew of a studding sail (stunsail) to the end of its boom. 3. Rope used to control the fore clew of a staysail.

Tack (verb) To go about and change course when sailing sail close hauled against the wind in a zig zag manner by alternating from larboard to starboard (opposite to wearing). Also, a point of sailing close to wind as the vessel will go with advantage.

Tackle Purchase formed by the connection of a rope fall with two or more blocks.

Tiller Wooden steering shaft slotted into rudder head.

Tye Halyard associated with hoisting yards.

U

Under way Vessel is said to be under way when not anchored.

Up and down An anchor cable is said to be up and down when it has been hauled in until it is vertical.

Up helm The act of putting the helm to windward in order to bear away.

W

Weatherly Term given to a ship capable of sailing close to the wind.

Weigh Act of hoisting up anchor to get under way.

Wear The act the turning a vessel about onto another tack by passing the stern through the wind. Wearing is the opposite manoeuvre to tacking.

Y

Yaw A vessel is said to yaw when not holding a steady course but swings side to side.

Adapted from the *Sailor's Word Book of 1867* by Admiral W.H. Smyth and *Falconer's New Universal Dictionary of Marine 1815*.

Endnotes

CHAPTER I INTRODUCTION

1 Journal of Captain Skeffington Lutwidge, commanding HM Sloop *Carcass* TNA. ADM. 51/167 Part 3.

2 Jones, Evan T and Condon, Margaret M, *Cabot and Bristol's Age of Discovery: The Bristol Discovery Voyages 1480–1508*, University of Bristol, November 2016, passim.

CHAPTER 2 THE EARLY ARCTIC EXPLORERS

1 Francesco, Guidi-Bruscoli, 'John Cabot and his Italian Financiers', *Historical Research*, 2012.

2 Weare, GE, *Cabot's Discovery of North America,* London, 1897, p116.

3 Smugglers' City maritime history course, Department of History, University of Bristol. See also Williamson, James A, *The Cabot Voyages and Bristol Discovery Under Henry VII*, Cambridge University Press, 1962, pp212–214.

4 Fabyan, R, *The Great Chronicle of London*, London, 1533.

5 Jones, Evan T and Condon, Margaret M, *Cabot and Bristol's Age of Discovery: The Bristol Discovery Voyages 1480–1508*, University of Bristol, November 2016. See also Hakluyt, R, *The Principal Navigations, Voyages, Traffiques & Discoveries of the English Nation*, Hakluyt Society Vol. 5, London, 1885–1890, pp84–91.

6 Op cit Jones and Condon.

7 McDermott, J, *Martin Frobisher: Elizabethan Privateer,* Yale University, 2001, p123.

8 McGhee, R, *The Arctic Voyages of Martin Frobisher: An Elizabethan Adventure,* Canadian Museum of Civilisation, 2001, Washington University Press, Seattle, 2001, p38.

9 Op cit McGhee, R, p41.

10 Op cit McDermott, J, p127.

11 Op cit McGhee, R, p43.

12 Op cit McGhee, R, p47.

13 Op cit McGhee, R, pp28–47.

14 Op cit Hakluyt, R, pp137–138.

15 Op cit McGhee, passim.

16 The Navy Royale, which had become very much formalised into an integrated unit under the Tudor dynasty, became the Parlimentarian Navy under Cromwell after the overthrow of the monarchy in 1649. The title Royal Navy, as we know it today, became officially recognised with the restoration of monarchy under Charles II in 1660.

17 Op cit Hakluyt, R, 282–283.

18 Op cit Hakluyt, R, p282.

19 Op cit Hakluyt, R, p292.

20 Op cit Hakluyt, R, pp292–303.

21 Op cit Hakluyt, R, pp309–316.

22 de Veer, Gerrit, *The Three Voyages of William Barents to the Arctic Regions (1594, 1595 & 1596)*, Hakluyt Society, London, 1927, passim.

23 Op cit de Veer, passim.

24 Op cit de Veer, passim.

25 Bear Island became the subject matter of the eponymous novel by Alistair MacLean, which was made into a film in 1979.

26 Op cit de Veer, Gerrit, passim.

27 Ibid.

28 Ibid.

29 Andrist, R, *Heroes of Polar Exploration*, London, 1963, pp29–30. See also op cit de Veer, Gerrit, passim.

30 Op cit de Veer, Gerrit, passim.

31 Markham, Clements, *The Voyages of William Baffin, 1612–1622*, Hakluyt Society, London, 1881, p21.

32 Ibid, passim.

33 Ibid.

34 Villiers, A, *Monsoon Seas: The Story of the Indian Ocean*, McGaw-Hill Book Company, 1952, passim.

35 Butts, Edward, *Henry Hudson: New World Voyage*, Toronto, 2009, pp12–14. See also Conway, WM, *No Man's Land*, Cambridge, 1906, passim.

36 Founded by Royal Charter on 1 December 1600, The Honourable East India Company (HEIC), often abbreviated (EIC), was also colloquially named the John Company.

37 Op cit Butts, E, pp12–14.

38 Formerly known as the Vereenigde Oost Indicshe, abbreviated (VOR), this was the equivilent of the British East India Company.

39 Savours, Ann, *The Search for the North West Passage,* Chatham Publishing, 1999, pp24–25. See also Hearne, Samuel, *A Journey from Prince of Wales's Fort in Hudson's Bay to the Northern Ocean, in the Years 1769, 1770, 1771, and 1772,* London, 1795.

40 Gerrit de Veer's works, later translated by William Philip and edited by Charles T Beke, were published by the Hakluyt Society in 1853 under the title *A True Description of Three Voyages by the North-east towards Cathay and China: Undertaken by the Dutch in the Years 1594, 1595 and 1596.* In 1927 the Hakluyt Society republished a revised work under the title *The Three Voyages of William Barents to the Arctic Regions: 1594, 1595 & 1596.*

CHAPTER 3 CIRCUMNAVIGATION, LONGITUDE
AND THE ROYAL SOCIETY MISSION FOR EXPLORATION

1 Goodwin, P, *The Influence of Industrial Technology and Material Procurement on the Design Construction and Development of HMS Victory and 18th Century Naval Warships,* Master of Philosophy dissertation, Institute of Maritime Studies, University of St Andrews (1998), pp44–58.

2 A contemporary model of the *Dolphin* is retained within the collections of the National Maritime Museum, Greenwich, London.

3 For reasons unknown, Carteret's account of his voyage in the *Swallow* was not wholly accepted by the Admiralty, so he wrote his own version, which was published posthumously by the Hakluyt Society in 1965.

4 Rigby, N and van der Merwe, P, *Captain Cook in the Pacific,* National Maritime Museum, 2002, p24.

5 *Secret Instructions to Lieutenant Cook 30 July 1768,* National Library of Australia, 2005.

6 Op cit Rigby, N, and van der Merwe, P, p24.

7 *London Gazetteer,* 18 August 1768.

8 Villiers, A, *Captain Cook, The Seaman's Seaman,* Penguin, 1969, passim; and Beaglehole, JC (Ed), *The Journals of Captain James Cook on his Voyages of Discovery: Volume IV The Life of Captain James Cook,* Hakluyt Society, 1974, passim.

9 Royal Society Council Minutes, 1769–1782, Vol. 6:158.

10 Savours, Ann, '"A very interesting point in geography": The 1773 Phipps Expedition towards the North Pole', *Arctic Institute of North America Vol 37, No 4,* December 1984, pp402–428.

11 Phipps, C, *A Voyage Towards the North Pole: Undertaken by His Majesty's Command, 1773*, London, 1774, pl0.

12 Op cit Savours, A, pp402–428.

13 Experiments measuring gravity by means of a pendulum were to be undertaken as a potential alternative means of determining longitude based on theories proposed by Isaac Newton.

14 Sobel, D, *Longitude: The True Story of a Lone Genius Who Solved the Greatest Scientific Problem of His Time*, Walker & Company, 1996, p12.

15 Op cit Sobel, D, p53.

16 Op cit Sobel, D, passim.

17 Op cit Sobel, D, pp74–79.

18 Gould, T, *The Marine Chronometer: Its History and Development*, London, 1923, passim.

CHAPTER 4 THE SERVICE HISTORY OF HM SHIPS *RACEHORSE* AND *CARCASS* PRIOR TO 1773

All journal quotes related to HMS *Racehorse* are sourced from TNA ADM. 180; 180/3; 52/994; 51/882/7; 346/23/3.
All journal quotes related to HMS *Carcass* are from TNA. ADM. 52/552.

1 Goodwin, P, *The Bomb Vessel Granado 1742*, Conway Maritime Press, 1989, p7.

2 Op cit TNA. ADM. 180/3.

3 Op cit TNA. ADM. 180.

4 Ibid.

5 Ibid.

6 Op cit Goodwin, P, passim. See also Ware, C, *The Bomb Vessel: Shore Bombardment Ships of the Age of Sail*, Conway Maritime Press, 1994, p42.

7 Op cit TNA. ADM. 180/3.

8 Clowes, WL, *The Royal Navy: A History from Earliest Times to 1900,* vol. 3. 1715–1793, London, 1906, p206.

9 Reid, S, *Quebec 1759: The Battle That Won Canada*, Osprey Publishing, 2003, p25.

10 Op cit Clowes, WL, pp 207–208.

11 'Flatboats' were flat-bottomed troop-landing craft that were able to carry some 30 men. Built in semi-kit form, they had been carried over in the holds of the troop transports, probably stacked inside each other minus their thwarts (seats). Quickly assembled on deck with their thwarts rigidly bracing the hull, the flatboats were simply lowered into the water ready for troops to embark.

12 Op cit TNA. ADM. 52/994.

13 Ibid.

14 Anderson, F, *Crucible of War: The Seven Years' War, and the Fate of Empire in British North America, 1754–1766*, Faber & Faber, 2000, p345.

15 Op cit TNA. ADM. 52/994. See also TNA. ADM. 51/882/7.

16 Eccles, WJ, *The Canadian Frontier, 1534–1760,* Holt, Rinehart and Winston of Canda Ltd, 1969, p180.

17 Op cit Reid, S, p44.

18 Because the master's journal of the *Racehorse* is poorly written, the various transcribed extracts have been corrected where necessary to maintain sense.

19 Op cit TNA. ADM. 52/994.

20 Originally owned by a farmer named Abraham Martin.

21 Op cit TNA. ADM. 52/994.

22 Ibid.

23 Lloyd, C, *The Capture of Quebec,* The Macmillan Company, 1959, passim.

24 Op cit TNA. ADM. 52/994.

25 Op cit ADM. 51/882/7. See also Goodwin, P, *Nelson's Ships: A History of the Vessels In Which He Served 1771–1805,* Conway Maritime Press, 2002, pp41–42.

26 Op cit TNA. ADM. 52/994.

27 Ibid.

28 Op cit TNA. ADM. 180/3.

29 Ibid.

30 Ibid.

31 Goodwin, P, *The Influence of Industrial Technology and Material Procurement on the Design, Construction and Development of H.M.S. Victory,* D.Phil. Dissertation, Scottish Institute of Maritime Studies, University of St Andrews, 1998.

32 The first trial using copper sheathing was adopted for the 32-gun frigate *Alarm* in 1761. Following the relative success of this experiment, the 24-gun fifth-rate *Dolphin* was similarly sheathed for Byron's circumnavigational voyage (1764–66) and Wallis's global voyage (see chapter 2). Despite having been fully proven on two long voyages, the practice of copper sheathing would not be formally introduced until c. 1780, due to its prohibitive production cost. However, in the years preceding this date the copper industry, formerly confined to Wales and Cornwall, became consolidated and expanded upon by the industrialist entrepreneur Thomas Williams, the 'Copper King'. Besides vastly improving smelting techniques and production resources, Williams provided

copper bolts and sheathing plates at rates more acceptable to the needs of the Admiralty and the purse of its Navy Board. Furthermore, despite its deterrent properties against worm, marine crustaceans and weed, copper proved far lighter in weight than wooden sheathing boards. These advantages created speedier ships. As an added benefit, ships only needed to be recoppered every four to six years, as opposed to sheathing board, which had to be replaced biannually. Coppering also eliminated docking every six to eight months for graving, ships simply being carreened for breaming – a simpler alternative for removing marine growth without the need for a dock, which was often unavailable. Regardless of the above, the *Racehorse* did not survive long enough to acquire the benefits of copper sheathing introduced c. 1780.

References: Goodwin, P, *The Construction and Fitting of the Sailing Man-of-War 1650–1850*, Conway Maritime Press, 1987, pp226–227; Lavery, B, *The Arming and Fitting of English Ships of War 1600–1815*, Conway Maritime Press, 1987, pp56–65;

Op cit Goodwin, P, *The Influence of Industrial Technology...*, passim; Rowland, J, *Copper Mountain,* Anglesey Antiquarian Society, 1981, pp22–37; Harris, JR, *Copper King*, Liverpool, 1964, pp47–49; and Harris, J, *Industrial Espionage and Technology Transfer: Britain and France in the Eighteenth Century,* Aldershot, 1998, passim.

33 Op cit TNA. ADM. 180/3.
34 Op cit TNA. ADM. 346/23/3.
35 Op cit TNA. ADM. 180/3.
36 Op cit Ware, C, p42.
37 Op cit TNA. ADM. 180/3
38 Op cit Ware, C, p42; see also Lyon, D, *The Sailing Navy List*, NMM, 1992, p99.
39 Op cit Goodwin, p33.
40 Op cit TNA. ADM. 180/3.
41 McLynn, F, *1759: The Year Britain Became Master of the World,* Grove Press, 2011, pp236–241.
42 Op cit McLynn, F, pp236–241.
43 Op cit Clowes, WL, p196. See also op cit Mclynn, F, pp236–241 and Corbett, JS, *England in the Seven Years' War Vol 2 1759–1763*, 2nd edition, London, 1992, pp23–25.
44 Op cit TNA. ADM. 180/3
45 Op cit TNA. ADM. 52/552.
46 Op cit Goodwin, P, *The Influence of Industrial Technology...*, passim.
47 Op cit TNA. ADM. 52/552.
48 Ibid.

49 Op cit TNA. ADM. 180/3.
50 Ibid.
51 Ibid.

CHAPTER 5 COMMISSIONING AND FITTING OUT THE SHIPS

Note:
All journal quotes related to HMS *Racehorse* are sourced from TNA ADM. 180/3; 95/94; 51/757; 51/157; 52/57.
All journal quotes related to HMS *Carcass* are from TNA. ADM. 51/167/3.

1 TNA. ADM. 95/94.
2 Ibid.
3 Ibid.
4 Ibid.
5 Ibid.
6 Floyd, T, *A Midshipman's Narrative of [Capt. C. J. Phipps's] Polar Voyage – 1773*, London, 1879, pp87–88.
7 TNA. ADM. 51/157 and op cit TNA. ADM. 180/3.
8 Op cit TNA. ADM. 95/94.
9 Op cit Floyd, T, p87 Floyd. T. *A Midshipman's Narrative of [Capt. C. J. Phipps's] Polar Voyage – 1773*. London 1879. pp.87–89. See also Ware, C, *The Bomb Vessel: Shore Bombardment Ships of the Age of Sail*, Conway Maritime Press, 1994, pp96–97.
   With respect to the construction and modifications undertaken in *Racehorse*, the following extant ship draughts held in the National Maritime Museum collections have been consulted:
   HMS *Racehorse* 1757: Vizt.
   1 ZAZ 6573 (J2196). Quarterdeck 1773 (Arctic Voyage)
   2 ZAZ 6572 (J2195). Quarterdeck & forecastle 1773 (Arctic Voyage)
   3 ZAZ 6571 (J2194). Upper deck 1773 (Arctic Voyage)
   4 ZAZ 6569 (J2197). Lines & Profile 1773 (Arctic Voyage)
   5 ZAZ 6570 (J2193). Platforms 1773 (Arctic Voyage)
   6 ZAZ 6566 (J2200). Inboard profile, Decks 1758 (Fireship)
   7 ZAZ 6566 (J2700). Quarterdeck & forecastle 1758 (Fireship)
   8 ZAZ 6567 (J2199). Profile & Upper Deck (Bomb).
   9 ZAZ 6568 (J2198). Section at Bomb bed (Bomb).

10 National Maritime Museum Drawing Nos. 4415, 4416 and 6456, Box 66. See also Ware, C, *The Bomb Vessel: Shore Bombardment Ships of the Age of Sail*, Conway Maritime Press, 1994, pp96–97.

11 Goodwin, P, *The Influence of Industrial Technology and Material Procurement on the Design, Construction and Development of H.M.S. Victory,* M. Phil. Dissertation, Scottish Institute of Maritime Studies, University of St Andrews, 1998.

12 Op cit Goodwin, P, *The Influence of Industrial...* px71–76. See also Goodwin, P, *The Construction and Fitting of the Sailing Man-of-War 1650–1850,* Conway Maritime Press, 1987, pp95–98; and Lavery, B, *Ship of the Line Volume 1,* London, 1983, pp140–151 and *Volume 2,* London, 1984, pp41–45.

13 Op cit Floyd, T, pp87–88.

14 Op cit TNA. ADM. 51/157.

15 Goodwin, P, *The Haynes Owners' Workshop Manual: HMS Victory 1765-1812: An Insight into Owning, Operating and Maintaining the Royal Navy's Oldest and Most Famous Warship,* Haynes Publishing, 2012, pp40–41.

16 Op cit TNA. ADM. 51/157.

17 Shingle ballast comprised pebbles of no greater than 1½–2in (3.8–5cm) in size. This served two functions: 1, to form a bed on which to set down the ground tier of water casks to prevent them moving when the ship rolls; 2, to act as compensating ballast that could be shifted in baskets to alter the trim of the ship as provisions, water, stores, shot and powder were consumed.

18 Op cit TNA. ADM. 51/157.

19 Gilbert, KR, *The Portsmouth Block-making Machinery,* HMSO for the Science Museum, 1965, passim. See also Coad, J *The Portsmouth Block Mills,* English Heritage, 2005; passim and Coad, J, *Naval Architecture of the Royal Navy,* Over Wallop, 1989, p78; and McDougal, P, *Royal Dockyards,* London, 1982, pp132–134.

20 The revolutionary mass-production machinery referred to was the brainchild of émigré French engineer Marc Brunel who had the machines manufactured by prominent London engineer Henry Maudslay. Brunel's mass-production ingenuity concept was later adopted by car manufacturer Henry Ford.

21 Op cit TNA. ADM. 95/94 and TNA. ADM. 51/157.

22 Op cit TNA. ADM. 95/94.

23 Op cit TNA. ADM. 51/157

24 Ibid.

25 Goodwin, P, 'The Application and Scheme of Paintworks in British Men-of-War in the late Eighteenth and early Nineteenth Centuries', *Mariner's Mirror,* Vol. 99:3, August 2013, pp275–286.

26 Op cit TNA. ADM. 51/157.

27   Small lengths of twisted rope made for use as seizings.

28   Op cit TNA. ADM. 51/157.

29   Ibid.

30   Ibid.

31   Op cit TNA. ADM. 95/94.

32   Ibid.

33   Op cit TNA. ADM. 51/157.

34   Ibid.

35   Sandwich was visiting in his official capacity as First Lord of the Admiralty primarily because he fully endorsed the forthcoming expedition. The French dignitary was the Comte de Guines, Adrien-Louis de Bonnières, who had been appointed ambassador to the English Court at St James by the French Queen Marie-Antoinette in 1768.

36   Op cit TNA. ADM. 51/157.

37   Ibid.

38   The Nore relates to a sandbank at the mouth of the Thames Estuary defining where the River Thames meets the North Sea and is the closest anchorage to Sheerness Dockyard.

39   Op cit TNA. ADM. 51/157.

40   The term 'People' was commonly used in 18th-century ship's journals when referring to the ship's crew or ship's company. Moreover, the term was extensively quoted in society in reference to the collective or general public, hence its significant use within the American Declaration of Independence, in which the word 'People' is used on ten occasions.

41   Op cit TNA. ADM. 51/157.

42   Ibid

43   Ibid.

44   TNA. ADM. 95/94.

45   Op cit TNA. ADM. 51/167/3.

46   Op cit TNA. ADM. 51/167/3 and op cit TNA. ADM. 95/94.

47   Op cit TNA. ADM. 95/94.

48   Ibid.

49   Op cit TNA. ADM. 51/167/3 and op cit TNA. ADM. 95/94.

50   Ibid.

51
   • Wales are the strakes of heavy planking that run longitudinally just above the waterline, binding the ship timbers (frames) at the ship's greatest breadth. In addition, their inherent strength counteracts the flexing effects of hogging and sagging on the ship's hull

when it is riding in a trough of sea or balanced between two wave crests. 'Doubling' (sometimes referred to as 'furring') with 2½in (63.5mm) oak planking also added strength, with the extra skin of 2in (50.8mm) planking placed upon the hull planking.

- Riders are internal frames of considerable scantling that provide greater hull strength in the transverse plane.
- Breast hooks are large curved timbers wrought in the horizontal plane across the inboard faces of the timbers forming the ship's bow in the lower part of the hull of the ship; the hawse pieces thereby providing greater strength to the ship's bow structure. These are usually duplicated with similarly formed timbers at each deck level called deck hooks.
- Sleepers are large baulks of fashioned timber fitted longitudinally across the floors of the ship within the lower regions of the bow and stern that serve a similar function to the riders. All riders and breast and deck hooks, the sleepers included, were fastened with substantial iron bolts driven from within.

52 Op cit TNA. ADM. 51/167/3.
53 TNA. ADM. 95/94.
54 Op cit TNA. ADM. 51/167/3.
55 Ibid.
56 Lever, D, *The Young Sea Officer's Sheet Anchor: Or a Key to the Leading of Rigging and to Practical Seamanship*, London, 1819, passim.
57 HM ships named *Resolution* jointly serving in the Royal Navy were: 1, the 74-gun third-rate ship *Resolution* that was launched at Deptford in 1770 and which remained in service until broken up in 1813; 2, Cook's *Resolution* – formerly the North Sea collier *Marquis of Granby*, launched at Whitby in 1770 and purchased into the Royal Navy in 1771 at a cost of £4,151 (the equivalent to £490,777 today). Operating as a transport, she was captured by the French on 9 June 1782; 3, the armed cutter HMS *Resolution* purchased in 1779, which foundered in the North Sea in 1797.
58 Op cit TNA. ADM. 51/167/3. With respect to the construction and modifications undertaken in *Carcass*, the following extant ship draughts held in the National Maritime Museum collections have been consulted:

HMS *Carcass* 1759: Vizt.
1 ZAZ 6564. (J7999). Decks 1773 as Sloop 1773.
2 ZAZ 6565. (J7998). Decks 1768 as Sloop with mods etc.

3   ZAZ 5629. (J1446). Profiles decks & sections 1758.

4   ZAZ 6563. (J8000). Inboard profile & section with details 1773 (Arctic voyage).

59   Harland, J, *Seamanship in the Age of Sail,* Bloomsbury Publishing, 1984, passim.

60   Op cit TNA. ADM. 51/167/3.

61   Ibid.

62   Ibid.

63   Op cit Harland, J. p96 and p103. See also op cit Lever, D, passim; and Hutchison, W, *A Treatise on Practical Seamanship,* London, 1777, passim.

64   Op cit TNA. ADM. 51/167/3.

65   Ibid.

CHAPTER 6 EQUIPPING THE SHIPS FOR THE ARCTIC VOYAGE

Note:

All journal quotes related to HMS *Racehorse* are sourced from TNA. ADM. 51/167; 95/94; 55/157.

1   Op cit TNA. ADM. 95/94.

2   Op cit TNA. ADM. 51/167.

3   Reid, S, *The Flintlock Musket: Brown Bess and Charleville, 1750–1865,* Bloomsbury, 2016, p15

5   Op cit TNA. ADM. 51/167.

4   Op cit Reid, S, passim.

6   Op cit TNA. ADM. 51/167.

7   Op cit TNA. ADM. 95/94.

8   Ibid.

9   Ibid.

10   Ibid.

11   Ibid.

12   Dunn, R, *The Telescope: A Short History,* Bloomsbury, 2011, passim.

13   Cummings also invented the 'S' bend applied to toilet discharge pipework.

14   The same design is discussed and illustrated in *The Philosophical Transactions of the Royal Society,* v. 62 (1772), pp476–480.

15   Burney, W, *Falconer's Universal Dictionary of the Marine,* London, 1815, p123.

16   Op cit TNA. ADM. 95/94.

17   de Pagés, *Travels Around the World in the Years 1767, 1768, 1769, 1770& 1771,* London 1772, p246.

18 Floyd, T, *A Midshipman's Narrative of [Capt. C.J. Phipps's] Polar Voyage 1773*, London, 1879, p96.

19 Ballantyne, RM, *Fast in the Ice. Adventures in the Polar Regions*, London, 1863.

20 This information was jointly provided by Olaf Janzen and John Harland.

21 Op cit TNA. ADM. 55/157.

22 Op cit TNA. ADM. 95/94.

23 Oxford Dictionary, online.

24 Op cit TNA. ADM. 55/157.

25 Op cit Floyd, T, p99.

26 Op cit TNA. ADM. 95/94.

27 Ibid.

CHAPTER 7 PROVISIONING, SUPPLIES AND SHIP'S FACILITIES
FOR AN ARCTIC VOYAGE

Note:

All journal quotes related to HMS *Racehorse* are sourced from TNA ADM. 51/167; 55/157.

1 What is referred to as 'bread' was actually biscuit made from flour, water, and sometimes salt. In their manufacture, these were baked twice to make them impervious to damp, hence the colloquial name 'hardtack'. They were generally kept in bags and it was essential they was kept completely dry, as damp could give rise to weevil infestation; weevil larvae were often present in flour. Various extant ship's log books include statements that refer to 'the people picking the bread', a reference to crew members sorting and removing deteriorating bread to avoid further contamination.

2 Op cit TNA. ADM. 51/167.

3 Op cit TNA. ADM. 2/98 p300. Note: *Racehorse* and *Carcass*.

4 Op cit TNA. ADM. 51/157.

5 Op cit TNA. ADM. 51/167/3.

6 Op cit TNA. ADM. 95/94.

7 Pepsyian MSS. Adm letters X, 44 Magdalene College, Cambridge. Also cited in Goodwin, P, *The Construction and Fitting of the Sailing Man-of-War 1650–1850*, Conway Maritime Press, 1987, p163. See also Naval Distilling plants BR, Admiralty Library, Naval Historical Branch, Portsmouth.

8 *Carcass* as fitted and platform plans 1173. NMM. 4421A Box 66. *Racehorse* lines profile 1773 NMM. 6456 Box 66.

9 'Fearnought' is a rough, heavy, undyed woollen cloth.

Note:

All journal quotes related to HMS *Racehorse* are sourced from TNA. ADM. 36/7490; /L/E/17A.

All journal quotes related to HMS *Carcass* are sourced from TNA. ADM. 51/381; 51/167; 36/567.

1 In hindsight, if Lieutenant Bligh had been provided with marines aboard the ill-fated *Bounty* the mutiny he faced in April 1789 may not have occurred.

2 Clowes, WL, *The Royal Navy: A History from Earliest Times to 1900,* vol. 3. 1715–1793, London, 1906, pp242–244.

3 Op cit Clowes, WL, pp247–249.

4 Stephen, L, 'Phipps, Constantine John', *Dictionary of National Biography,* 1896, p231.

5 The *Boreas* was later commanded by Nelson on the West Indies station, where it upheld the Navigation Acts being enforced against American traders.

6 Laughton, JK, *Dictionary of National Biography 1885–1900 Vol. 22,* passim.

7 Ibid, passim.

8 Both the *Modeste* and *Centaur* were former French warships that had been captured by Admiral Edward Boscawen's squadron at the Battle of Lagos in 1759. Op cit Clowes, WL, p212.

9 Acholona, Catherine, 'The Igbo Roots of Olaudah Equiano', *Research in African Literatures Vol. 21, No. 2, Dictatorship and Oppression,* Indiana University Press, 1990, pp124–128.

10 Olaudah, Equiano, *The Interesting Narrative of the Life of Olaudah Equiano, Or Gustavus Vassa, The African,* London, 1789, *passim.*

11 Ibid.

12 Ibid.

13 Ibid.

14 Ibid.

15 Op cit TNA. ADM. 326/7490.

16 Floyd, T, *A Midshipman's Narrative of [Capt. C. J. Phipps's] Polar Voyage – 1773,* London, 1879, p73.

17 Op cit NMM. ADM. /L/E/17A.

18 Op cit TNA. ADM. 51/381.

19 Op cit TNA. ADM. 51/167.

20 MOD Admiralty Library correspondence: D/NHB/22/1: March 2005.

21 Sugden, J, *Nelson: A Dream of Glory*, London, 2004, p80.

22 Op cit TNA. ADM. 36/567.

23 Ibid.

24 Ibid.

25 Pocock, T, *Horatio Nelson*, London, 1987, pp10–11.

26 Op cit Pocock, T, p13.

27 William Biddle (1630–1712) and Sarah Kempe (1634–1709) acquired extensive rights to more than 43,000 acres (170km²) of lands in Quaker West Jersey and first settled at Burlington. Successive generations – William Biddle (1698–1756) and John Biddle (1698–1756) – later moved to the expanding city of Philadelphia.

28 Op cit TNA. ADM. 36/567.

29 Op cit TNA. ADM. 51/167.

30 Op cit TNA. ADM. 36/567.

CHAPTER 9 THE VOYAGE NORTH AND THE SPITSBERGEN ARCHIPELAGO

Note:

All journal quotes related to HMS *Racehorse* are sourced from TNA. ADM. 51/757:

All journal quotes related to HMS *Carcass* are from TNA. ADM. 51/167 PART 3.

1 Worsley, D, *The evolution of an Arctic Archipelago: The Geological History of Svalbard*, Den Norske Stats Oljeselskap AS, 1986, passim.

2 Arlov, Thor, *A Short History of Svalbard*, The Norwegian Polar Institute, Oslo, 1994, passim.

3 Op cit Arlov, pp42–44.

4 Floyd, T, *A Midshipman's Narrative of [Capt. C.J. Phipps's] Polar Voyage 1773*, London, 1879, pp106–107.

5 An extant sketch of Blacktail Beacon dated 1831 clarifies its existence.

6 'Brought to' means stopping the ship making progress by 'heaving to', which is achieved by backing the sails on one mast. This causes the wind effect of one sail to counteract the effect on the other.

7 Hollesley Bay lies just north of the estuary of Rivers Stour and Orwell.

8 Dimlington in the East Riding of Yorkshire lies on the promontory north of the River Humber and is today the site of Easington Gas Terminal for North Sea gas.

9   Op cit TNA. ADM. 36/567.

10 A dead light is a cover for one of the stern cabin windows (lights).

11 1 league = 3 miles or about 5km.

12 Op cit Floyd, T, p110.

13 To 'ware', ie 'wearing ship', is a manoeuvre used when sailing down-
    wind and involves the ship being 'put about' (turned) with the wind
    across the stern, whereby the wind direction is transferred from one
    side of the vessel to the other. The alternative manoeuvre used when
    sailing head to wind is to tack, which is to suddenly turn the ship's
    head through the wind whereby the sails are taken back, causing the
    ship to fall off the wind on to the other tack (direction). Tacking is
    only fully successful if the ship is 'making good way' (momentum)
    through the water. If the vessel makes insufficient way and/or the sails
    don't catch the wind to bear the ship off on to the opposite tack, the
    vessel could fall off on to her previous tack and, temporarily stopped
    in the water, she is said to have missed stays, ie not bringing the wind
    on either side.

14 The above log entry clarifies various points:
    (i) Young Nelson, as coxswain, would have been involved in convey-
         ing the Carcass's lieutenant over to the Racehorse in the cutter.
    (ii) Jan Mayen is a volcanic island in the Arctic Ocean covered
         with glaciers located at 70°59′N 8°32′W (approximately 370
         miles/600km north of Shetland).
    (iii) Cherry Island is today known as either Bear Island or Bjørnøya and
         lies 146 miles (235km) due south of Svalbard in the Barents Sea.

15 The snow referred to by Phipps and Lutwidge is a square-rigged
    vessel with two masts fitted with a trysail mast stepped immediately
    abaft the main mast, rigged with a loose-footed gaff sail.

16 Car. II St.9. 1661. See also Rodger, NAM, Articles of War: The Statutes
    which Governed our Fighting Navies 1661, 1749 and 1866, Kenneth Mason,
    1982, passim; and Goodwin, P, HMS Victory Pocket Manual 1805: Admiral
    Nelson's Flagship at Trafalgar, Conway, 2015, pp55–56.

17 In navigation, an azimuth is the direction of a chosen celestial object
    from the observer, expressed as the angular distance from the north
    or south point of the horizon to the point at which a vertical circle
    passing through the object intersects the horizon.

18 Taking account of recent global warming, according to Ketil Isaksen
    of the Norwegian Meteorological Institute the normal yearly average
    temperature in Svalbard (Spitsbergen) today is -6.7°C (20°F).

19 Hisdal, V, *Svalbard: Nature and History*, Norwegian Polar Institute, Oslo, 1998, pxx.
20 Op cit TNA. ADM. 51/757.
21 Phipps, C, *A Voyage Towards the North Pole: Undertaken by His Majesty's Command, 1773*, London, 1774, p70.
22 Op cit Phipps, C, p183.

CHAPTER 10 PROBING NORTH AMID THE ICE FLOES TO VOGEL SANG

Note:

All journal quotes related to HMS *Racehorse* are sourced from TNA. ADM. 51/757.

All journal quotes related to HMS *Racehorse* are sourced from TNA. ADM. 51/167 Part 3.

1   Op cit TNA. ADM. 51/157.
2   Op cit TNA. ADM. 51/167 Part 3.
3   Op cit TNA. ADM. 51/157.
4   Op cit TNA. ADM. 51/167 Part 3.
5   Op cit TNA. ADM. 51/157.
6   Op cit TNA. ADM. 51/167 Part 3.
7   Op cit TNA. ADM. 51/157.
8   Op cit TNA. ADM. 51/167 Part 3.
9   Op cit TNA. ADM. 51/157.
10 Regarding this sailing evolution, preferred practice in the Royal Navy was to heave to by means of backing the main topsail against the mast rather than using the fore topsail. Harland, J, *Seamanship in the Age of Sail*, Bloomsbury, 2015, p228.
11 Op cit TNA. ADM. 51/167 Part 3.
12 Ibid.
13 Ibid.
14 Op cit TNA. ADM. 51/157.
15 Op cit TNA. ADM. 51/167 Part 3.
16 Floyd, T, *A Midshipman's Narrative of [Capt. C. J. Phipps's] Polar Voyage – 1773*, London, 1879, pp138–139.
17 Op cit TNA. ADM. 51/157.
18 Ibid.
19 Ibid.
20 Op cit TNA. ADM. 51/167 Part 3.
21 Op cit Floyd, T, p141.
22 Op cit TNA. ADM. 51/157.

23   Farrow, Courtney, *The History of Hull's Whaling Industry*, 2017, passim. See also Credland, AG, *The Hull Whaling Trade: An Arctic Enterprise*, Hutton Press Ltd, 1995, passim.
24   Op cit TNA. ADM. 51/157.
25   Op cit Floyd, T, pp142–143.
26   Op cit Floyd, T, p143.
27   Phipps, C, *A Voyage Towards the North Pole: Undertaken by His Majesty's Command, 1773*, London, 1774, p42.
28   Op cit TNA. ADM. 51/157.
29   Op cit Floyd, T, p144.
30   Op cit TNA. ADM. 51/167 Part 3.
31   Op cit TNA. ADM. 51/157.
32   Op cit TNA. ADM. 51/167 Part 3.
33   Op cit Floyd, T, p145.
34   Op cit TNA. ADM. 51/157.
35   Op cit TNA. ADM. 51/167 Part 3.
36   Op cit TNA. ADM. 51/157.
37   Op cit TNA. ADM. 51/167 Part 3.
38   Op cit TNA. ADM. 51/57.
39   Op cit Floyd, T, p147.
40   Op cit TNA. ADM. 51/167 Part 3.
41   Op cit Floyd, T, p147.

CHAPTER II PROBING NORTH-EASTERLY AMID DRIFT ICE TO THE SEVEN ISLANDS

Note:
All journal quotes related to HMS *Racehorse* are sourced from TNA. ADM. 51/757; 36/7490.
All journal quotes related to HMS *Racehorse* are sourced from TNA. ADM. 51/167 Part 3.

 1   Phipps, C, *A Voyage Towards the North Pole: Undertaken by His Majesty's Command, 1773*, London, 1774, p41.
 2   Op cit TNA. ADM. 51/157.
 3   Ibid.
 4   TNA. ADM. 51/167 Part 3.
 5   Lifting the anchor to see if it is clear does appear a rather odd evolution from a seamanship perspective.
 6   Op cit TNA. ADM. 51/167 Part 3.
 7   Lever, D, *The Young Sea Officer's Sheet Anchor: Or a Key to the Leading of Rigging and to Practical Seamanship*, London, 1819, p24.

8   TNA. ADM. 51/167 Part 3.
9   TNA. ADM. 51/157.
10 TNA. ADM. 51/167 Part 3.
11 TNA. ADM. 51/157
12 TNA. ADM. 51/167 Part 3.
13 TNA. ADM. 51/157.
14 TNA. ADM. 51/167 Part 3.
15 TNA. ADM. 51/157.
16 TNA. ADM. 51/167 Part 3.
17 TNA. ADM. 51/157.
18 TNA. ADM. 51/167 Part 3.
19 TNA. ADM. 51/157.
20 TNA. ADM. 51/167 Part 3.
21 Op cit Phipps, C, pp51–52.
22 TNA. ADM. 51/157.
23 TNA. ADM. 51/167 Part 3.
24 TNA. ADM. 51/157.
25 TNA. ADM. 51/167 Part 3.
26 TNA. ADM. 51/157.
27 TNA. ADM. 36/7490.
28 TNA. ADM. 51/167 Part 3.
29 TNA. ADM. 51/157.
30 TNA. ADM. 51/167 Part 3.
31 Ibid.
32 TNA. ADM. 51/157.
33 Op cit Phipps, C, pp 57–58.
34 TNA ADM. 51/167. Part 3.
35 TNA. ADM. 51/157.
36 Ibid.
37 TNA. ADM. 51/167 Part 3.
38 TNA. ADM. 51/157.
39 TNA. ADM. 51/167 Part 3.
40 Floyd, T, *A Midshipman's Narrative of [Capt. C. J. Phipps's] Polar Voyage – 1773*, London, 1879.
41 TNA. ADM. 51/167 Part 3.

CHAPTER 12 ICEBOUND AND ABANDONING SHIP

Note:
All journal quotes related to HMS *Racehorse* are sourced from TNA. ADM.
51/757.

All journal quotes related to HMS *Carcass* are sourced from TNA. ADM. 52/1639 Part 7; 51/167 Part 3; 55/12.

1 Phipps, C, *A Voyage Towards the North Pole: Undertaken by His Majesty's Command, 1773*, London, 1774, p61.
2 Floyd, T, *A Midshipman's Narrative of [Capt. C. J. Phipps's] Polar Voyage – 1773*, London, 1879, pp187–188.
3 Op cit Phipps, C, p183.
4 With the exception of Table Island, Little Table Island and Walden Island, the smaller of the seven islands were not formally named but instead numbered in the ship's journals. One of these, today named Rossøya, lies at lat 80°49´.44N, which is still some 569 nautical miles (655 miles/1,054km) from the North Pole.
5 Op cit TNA. ADM. 52/1639 Part 7.
6 Op cit Floyd, T, pp191–192.
7 Goodwin, P, *The Construction and Fitting of the Sailing Man-of-War 1650–1850*, Conway Maritime Press, 1987, pp213–214.
8 Harland, J, *Seamanship in the Age of Sail,* Bloomsbury Publishing, 1984, pp284–285.
9 Belts of similar nature were later used by Captain John Falcon Scott and his team to haul their sledges to the South Pole in 1912.
10 Op cit Floyd, T, pp199–200.
11 Op cit Floyd, T, pp200–201.
12 Portrait of Constantine Phipps by an unknown artist: NPG. This depicts Phipps using a half pike as a supportive staff in his right hand while gesticulating direction with his hat in his left hand. Behind him, amid the blur of snow and sleet, the men are hauling the boats.
13 Op cit Floyd, T, pp202–203.
14 Op cit Phipps, C, p68.
15 Given that we do not know the mass of the iceberg or speed of the ship (m/s) but only know the mass of the iron, the forces imposed cannot be calculated.
16 Op cit Phipps, C, p57.
17 Op cit Phipps, C, p58.
18 Op cit Phipps, C, p184.
19 Most Nelson biographies include at least two of these Westall images.
20 Clarke, J and M'Arthur, J, *The Life of Horatio Lord Nelson, K.B.*, abridged version, London, 1810, pp7–9.
21 Southey, R, *The Life of Horatio Lord Nelson*, London, 1906, pp7–8.
22 Oman, C, *Nelson*, Sphere, 1967, p16.

CHAPTER 13 RESPITE AT SMEEREMBURG

Note:

All journal quotes related to HMS *Racehorse* are sourced from TNA. ADM. 51/757.

All journal quotes related to HMS *Carcass* are sourced from TNA. ADM. 51/167 Part 3; 55/12.

1 Most ships carried four main anchors: the best bower (heaviest, hung to starboard); the second bower (of slightly lesser weight, hung to larboard); and two sheet anchors, which, marginally lighter, were carried as spares, one each side. In addition, they carried a stream and a kedge anchor.

2 The best bower is always hung to starboard when sailing in the northern hemisphere, this position being relative to prevailing winds.

3 Phipps, C, *A Voyage Towards the North Pole: Undertaken by His Majesty's Command, 1773*, London, 1774, pp69–70

4 Op cit Phipps, C, p70.

5 Burney, W, *Falconer's Universal Dictionary of the Marine*, London, 1815, p152.

6 The prominent Whitby whaler man William Scoresby would later develop a system comprising a spar rigged to the bunt (foot) of the foresail that could be easily raised by ropes to aid visibility.

7 Op cit TNA. ADM. 51/157.

8 Op cit TNA. ADM. 51/167/Part 3.

CHAPTER 14 DIVISION AND THE STORM–TOSSED VOYAGE HOME

Note:

All journal quotes related to HMS *Racehorse* are sourced from TNA. ADM. 51/757.

All journal quotes related to HMS *Carcass* are sourced from TNA. ADM. 51/167 Part 3; 55/12.

1 The 'Dogger' with which Phipps hoped to exchange information was a specific type of vessel commonly operating in the North Sea fishing for cod. Two-masted, they were rigged with a gaff main sail and lateen mizzen.

2 The 'Fishing Buss' was a herring buss – a round-bilged vessel with a round bow and stern about 65ft (20m) long with a broad deck giving space to process the catch on board. Rigged with two or three masts,

the mainmast and foremast (if present) could be lowered during fishing, leaving only the mizzen mast upright. It was square rigged on the main mast, with a gaff rigg on the mizzen, and had a long bowsprit with jib boom with three headsails. The main course and topsail could be reefed.

3 Floyd, T, *A Midshipman's Narrative of [Capt. C.J. Phipps's] Polar Voyage 1773*, London, 1879, p223.

4 Ibid.

5 Op cit Floyd, T, p224.

6 The after guard were the division of seaman dedicated to operating the sails and rigging of the mizzen mast.

7 Op cit Floyd, T, p225.

8 1. The gripes relate to the special shaped timber chocks fitted upon the skid beams crossing the deck. 2. The harness casks relate to the lidded tubs used for steeping the salted meat in fresh water prior to cooking.

9 Op cit Floyd, T, p225–227.

10 Op cit Floyd, T, p227.

11 Dogger Bank is a large sandbank in a shallow area of the North Sea about 20 leagues (62 miles/100km) off the east coast of England, which proved a productive fishing ground for cod. The name comes from the Dutch fishing boats called 'doggers', which were gaff-rigged on the main mast, and carried a lugsail on the mizzen, with two jibs on a long bowsprit. Generally short and broad-beamed, these small boats were ideal for trawling or line fishing.

12 1. Yarmouth is now called Great Yarmouth, differentiating it from Yarmouth on the Isle of Wight. 2. Gullstone is now Gorleston, which lies on the south bank of the River Yare at Great Yarmouth.

13 Op cit TNA. ADM.55/12.

14 Op cit Floyd, T, p228.

15 These rocks are the Red Crag cliffs just north of the port of Felixstowe on the north side of the River Orwell.

16 1. Landguard Fort is located on the peninsular south of the town of Felixstowe and was the site of the last opposed seaborne invasion of England by the Dutch in 1667 and the first land battle of the Royal Marines. Initially built in the early 18th century, today the fort is an English Heritage site. 2. The peninsula formed in the joint estuary of the Rivers Orwell and Stour was once the site of the Royal Navy boys' training establishment HMS *Ganges* (at which the author and his elder brother Derek entered the Royal Navy as Junior Mechanical Engineers, the former in 1966, the latter in 1963).

CHAPTER 15 PAYING OFF THE SHIPS

Note:

All journal quotes related to HMS *Racehorse* are sourced from TNA. ADM. 51/757.

All journal quotes related to HMS *Carcass* are sourced from TNA. ADM. 51/167 Part 3.

1 TNA. ADM. ADM 95/94
2 Equiano, O. *The Interesting Narrative of the Life of Olaudah Equiano Or Gustavus Vassa, The African.* London, 1789.

CHAPTER 16 HISTORY OF HM SHIPS *RACEHORSE* AND *CARCASS* FOLLOWING THE 1773 VOYAGE

Note:

All journal quotes related to HMS *Racehorse* are sourced from TNA. ADM. 57/757.

All journal quotes related to HMS *Carcass* are sourced from TNA. ADM. 51/167 part 3; 52/1639; 52/1640.

1 Op cit TNA. ADM. 180/3.
2 Ibid.
3 Horatio Nelson would later serve in the *Bristol* as third lieutenant, rising to be the ship's first lieutenant when the ship was stationed in the Caribbean. See also Goodwin, P, *Nelson's Ships: Nelson's Ships: A History of the Vessels In Which He Served 1771–1805,* Conway Maritime Press, 2002, chapter 7.
4 Clowes, WL, *The Royal Navy: A History from Earliest Times to 1900,* vol. 3. 1715–1793, London, 1906, pp372 –379.
5 Ibid.
6 Springs in this case are mooring ropes attached to the anchor cable used to hold or pivot a ship in a fixed position when anchored to prevent the ship swinging on her anchor as tide changes; position is maintained by hauling or easing these ropes as required.
7 Op cit Clowes, WL, p374.
8 Wilson, DK, *The Southern Strategy: Britain's Conquest of South Carolina and Georgia, 1775–1780,* Columbia, SC: University of South Carolina Press, 2005, p49.
9 Op cit Goodwin, P, *Nelson's Ships,* pp66–68.

10 Morrill, D, *Southern Campaigns of the American Revolution,* Nautical and Aviation Pub Co of Amer, 1993, p25.

11 Op cit Wilson, DK, p52.

12 Ward, C, *The War of the Revolution,* Macmillan, 1952, pp674–678.

13 Russell, DL, *Victory on Sullivan's Island: the British Cape Fear& Charles Town Expedition of 1776,* Haverford, Pennsylvania, 2000, p220.

14 Op cit Morrill, D, p25.

15 The *Racehorse* (*Thunder*) discussed above is not to be confused with that bearing the same name given to the mercantile vessel *Hercules* purchased by the Royal Navy at Jamaica in 1776. This particular *Racehorse* was captured by the Continental Navy brig *Andrew Doria* on 24 December 1776, and had previously been commanded by the American Nicholas Biddle. Coincidentally, Biddle had served in the *Carcass* on the 1773 polar expedition.

16 Op cit TNA. ADM. 180.

17 Op cit TNA. ADM. 52/1639 and TNA. ADM. 180.

18 Op cit TNA. ADM. 180.

19 Ibid.

20 Op cit TNA. ADM. 52/1640.

21 Ibid.

22 Ibid.

23 Op cit Goodwin, P, Chapters 11 and 12.

24 Op cit TNA. ADM. 180.

CHAPTER 17 THE OFFICERS AND MEN AFTER THE VOYAGE

1 Mulgrave Castle MSS.

2 Clowes, WL, *The Royal Navy: A History from Earliest Times to 1900,* vol. 3. 1715–1793, London, 1906, pp413–419.

3 Goodwin, P, *Nelson's Ships: A History of the Vessels In Which He Served 1771–1805,* Conway Maritime Press, 2002, pp141–151

4 Prince William, later King William IV, had on more than one occasion not proved a good sea officer.

5 Laughton, JK, 'Harvey, Sir Henry', *Dictionary of National Biography 1885–1900 Vol. 22.*

6 Op cit Clowes, WL, pp226–236.

7 Op cit Laughton, JK, 'Harvey, Sir Henry'.

8 Ibid.

9 Teeder, HR, 'Adamson, John (1787–1855)', *Dictionary of National Biography*, London: Smith, Elder & Co, 1885–1900.

10 Laughton, JK, *'Graves, Thomas (1747–1814)'*, *Dictionary of National Biography*, London: Smith, Elder & Co, *1890*.

11 Gardner, R, *The Navies of the American Revolution 1775-1783*, Naval Inst Pr, 1996, p159.

12 Op cit Laughton, JK, 'Graves, Thomas'.

13 These boats 'fitted with gates' are effectively the forerunners of the landing craft used during World War II for the invasion of Normandy in June 1944. Whether d'Auvergne influenced the design of those used at Manhattan Island is conjectural.

14 Op cit Gardner, R, pp24–27.

15 TNA. Colonial Office Correspondence, CO 5/96. Considering his intellect, it is highly probable.

16 Ashelford, J, *In the English Service: The Life of Philippe D'Auvergne*, Jersey Heritage Trust, 2008.

17 Op cit Clowes, WL, pp24–25.

18 TNA. CO. 5/96.

19 Nelson had served in the *Bristol* as third lieutenant in 1778.

20 Op cit Ashelford, J, passim.

21 Ibid.

22 Ibid.

23 Ibid.

24 Equiano, O, *The Interesting Narrative of the Life of Olaudah Equiano Or Gustavus Vassa, The African*. London, 1789, passim.

25 Ibid.

26 Ibid.

27 Op cit Clowes, WL, pp358–369.

28 Mahan, T, *The Major Operations of the Navies in the War of American Independence*, Sampson Low, Marston & Co, 1913, pp47–48.

29 Syrett, D, *The Rodney Papers: Selections From the Correspondence of Admiral Lord Rodney*, NRS. Vol 2 Ashgate Publishing, 2007, pp309–311. See also op cit Gardner, R, pp27–29.

30 Winfield, R, *British Warships in the Age of Sail 1793–1817: Design, Construction, Careers and Fates*, Seaforth Publishing, 2008, p208.

31 Ibid.

32 MOD Admiralty Library Correspondence D/NHB/22/1: March 2005

33 Lyon, D, *The Sailing Navy List*, NMM, 1992, p239.

34 Op cit Goodwin, P, *Nelson's Ships*, pp222–229.

35 Clark, A, Lewis Carroll: A Biography, Littlehampton Book Services Ltd, 1979, p11.

36 Welsh, F, *The Companion Guide to the Lake District*, Companion Guides, 2000, p287.

37 Sugden, J, *Nelson: A Dream of Glory*, Henry Holt & Co, 2002, p80.

38 Op cit Goodwin, P, *Nelson's Ships*, pp39–50.

39 Colledge, JJ, *Ships of the Royal Navy: An Historical Index, Vol 1*, Newton Abbot, 1969, p167.

40 Op cit Sugden, J, p103. See also TNA.ADM. 36/7583, *Dolphin* muster book; and ADM. 33/6325 *Dolphin* pay book.

41 Op cit Goodwin, P, *Nelson's Ships*, pp83–84.

42 TNA.ADM. ND 51 24/3.

43 Op cit Goodwin, P, *Nelson's Ships*, p27. See also Pocock, T, *Horatio Nelson*, London, 1987, p28.

44 Goodwin, P, *Ships of Trafalgar: the British, French and Spanish Fleets, October 1805*, Naval Institute Press, 2005, pp28–29. See also op cit Goodwin, P, *Nelson's Ships*, p259; and Goodwin, P, *HMS Victory Pocket Manual 1805: Admiral Nelson's Flagship at Trafalgar*, Conway, 2015, pp115–141.

45 Paullin, Charles Oscar, *The Navy of the American Revolution: its administration, its policy and its achievements*, Cleveland USA, 1906, p374.

46 Coincidently, when Nelson commanded HM Brig *Badger* in 1778 he witnessed the destruction of the *Glasgow* when it accidentally caught fire when anchored in Montego Bay, Jamaica. Disregarding the imminent danger from the stricken ship's magazines, which could blow up at any time, Nelson and his crew rescued the Glasgow's crew. (Oman, C, *Nelson*, Sphere, 1967, p27. See also op cit Pocock, T, p28.)

47 Although smallpox inoculation is credited to Edward Jenner, who officially proved its success in 1796, the practice had been adopted far earlier in Africa, India and the Ottoman Empire. While travelling in the latter region in 1717, Lady Mary Wortley Montagu witnessed a peasant woman performing inoculations. On returning to Britain, she had her children inoculated during an outbreak in 1721. When Boston, Massachusetts, was struck by smallpox that same year, leading churchman Cotton Mather saw one of his enslaved African workers perform inoculation and zealously promoted the practice, which reached Biddle's home town of Philadelphia in due course.

48 Miller, Nathan, *Sea of Glory: A Naval History of the American Revolution*, Naval Institute Press, Annapolis, 1974, pp110–112.

49 Clark, William Bell, *Captain Dauntless: The Story of Nicholas Biddle*, Louisiana University Press, Baton Rouge, 1949, passim. See also

McGrath, Tim (August 2015). *I Fear Nothing*, Naval History (United States Naval Institute), 2015, p2.

50 Allen, Dardner W, *A Naval History of the American Revolution, Volume 1,* Houghton Mifflin Company, 1913, pp296–298. See also op cit Clark, William Bell, passim.

CHAPTER 18 LATER ARCTIC EXPEDITIONS

1   The East India Company was often colloquially named John Company.

2   Hough, Richard, *Captain Bligh and Mr Christian: The Men and the Mutiny,* Hutchinson, 1972, passim. See also Alexander, C, *The Bounty,* Harper Collins, 2003.

3   William Beechey painted the well-known full-length portrait of Nelson now displayed in St Andrew's Hall, Norwich.

4   Coleman, EC, *The Royal Navy in Polar Exploration: From Frobisher to Ross,* Stroud 2006, p153.

5   Beechey, FW, *A Voyage of Discovery Towards the North Pole,* London, 1843, p10. Quoted from Savours, Ann, *The Search for the North West Passage,* Chatham Publishing, 1999, p43.

6   Op cit Beechey, FW, p10.

7   Op cit Beechey, FW, p43.

8   Parry, the Rev Edward MA, *Memoirs of Rear Admiral Sir W Edward Parry Kt,* London, 1872, p60.

9   Op cit Savours, A, p43.

10 Barrow, J, *A Chronological History of Voyages into The Arctic Region,* London, 1818, passim.

11 Ibid.

12 Op cit Savours, A, p57.

13 Op cit Parry, the Rev Edward MA, p100.

14 A similar mechanical system used for raising a propeller can be seen on the 1860 warship HMS *Warrior* preserved in the Historic Dockyard, Portsmouth.

15 Hutchison, G, *Sir John Franklin's* Erebus and Terror *Expedition: Lost and found,* NMM, 2017, p42.

16 Op cit Savours, A, p180.

17 Neatby, Leslie H & Mercer, Keith, 'Sir John Franklin', The Canadian Encyclopedia, Historica Canada, retrieved 18 September 2015.

18 Op cit Savours, A, pp188–189.

19 The sunken wreck of this *Investigator* was discovered lying in Mercy Bay at the northern tip of Aulavik National Park by Parks Canada archaeologists in 2010.

20 Op cit Hutchison, G, pp126–133.
21 Lambert, A, *The Gates of Hell: Sir John Franklin's Tragic Quest for the North West Passage*, Yale University, 2009, pp276–281.
22 Op cit Hutchison, G, p1152.
23 The *Guardian*, 12 September 2016.
24 The *Martin Bergmann* is operated by the Arctic Research Foundation, which is backed by Waterloo-area entrepreneurs Tim MacDonald and Jim Balsillie.
25 The *Guardian*, 12 September 2016.

CHAPTER 19 CONCLUSIONS

Note:

All journal quotes related to HMS *Racehorse* are sourced from TNA. ADM. 51/544; 2/98; 51/157.

All journal quotes related to HMS *Carcass* are sourced from TNA. ADM. 51/167 Part 3; 55/12.

1 The Royal Naval Prayer.
2 Vincent, E, *Nelson: Love and Fame*, London, 2003, p21.
3 TNA. ADM. 51/167 PART 3 and 55/12.
4 Although this event is referenced in *Nelson: Love and Fame,* the source is not identified.
5 Equiano, O, *The Interesting Narrative of the Life of Olaudah Equiano Or Gustavus Vassa, The African.* London, 1789, p161.
6 Goodwin, P, *The Influence of Industrial Technology and Material Procurement on the Design, Construction and Development of H.M.S. Victory*, M. Phil. Dissertation, Scottish Institute of Maritime Studies, University of St Andrews, 1998.
7 It was this French practice of lighter construction that often proved detrimental to their ability to withstand the effects of British gunfire in battle, hence French ships more readily sustained far greater casualties.
8 The best example in this type of intelligence recording is the sketch made of the fortified tower at Mortella Point, Corsica, which was unsuccessfully attacked in February 1794 by the British warships *Fortitude* (74 guns) and *Juno* (32 guns). The resultant drawings provided the blueprint for all the defensive 'martello' towers built around the southern coast of England.
9 Phipps, C, *A Voyage Towards the North Pole: Undertaken by His Majesty's Command, 1773*, London, 1774, *passim.*

10 Sounding leads, about 18in (47.7cm) long, with an integral eye to attach the line, were made with a concave hollow 1–1½in (25.4–38.1mm) deep in its base. Filled with sticky tallow, this picked up seabed contents including sand and shells.

11 Op cit TNA. ADM. 2/98 pages 301–302.

12 Op cit Phipps, C, pp222–250.

13 Op cit Phipps, C, p222.

14 Op cit Phipps, C, pp251–253.

15 Op cit Phipps, C, p186.

16 Op cit Phipps, C, pp184–86.

17 Op cit Phipps, C, p186.

18 TNA. ADM. 51/544. See also Goodwin, P, *Nelson's Ships: A History of the Vessels In Which He Served 1771–1802*, Conway Maritime Press, 2002, p56.

19 Scoresby, W, *An Account of the Artic Regions: with a history and description of the Northern Whale-Fishery,* Edinburgh, 1820, p542.

20 Ibid.

21 Ibid.

22 Op cit Scoresby, W, p543. See also Phipps, C, p194.

23 John Hunter (1728–1793) of the Royal College of Surgeons undertook the dissection, preservation, collection and displaying of dissected body parts – 'anatomical preparations' – in London during the second half of the 18th century.

24 Op cit Phipps, C, p194.

25 Op cit Phipps, C, p183.

26 TNA. ADM. 2/98 pp302–304.

27 TNA. ADM. 51/157.

Bibliography

Acholona, Catherine, 'The Igbo Roots of Olaudah Equiano', *Research in African Literatures Vol. 21, No. 2, Dictatorship and Oppression*, Indiana University Press, 1990.

Alexander, C, *The Bounty*, Harper Collins, 2003.

Allen, Dardner W, *A Naval History of the American Revolution, Volume 1*, Houghton Mifflin Company, 1913.

Anderson, F, *Crucible of War: The Seven Years' War, and the Fate of Empire in British North America, 1754–1766*, Faber & Faber, 2000.

Andrist, R, *Heroes of Polar Exploration*, London, 1963

Arlov, Thor, *A Short History of Svalbard*, The Norwegian Polar Institute, Oslo, 1994.

Ashelford, J, *In the English Service: The Life of Philippe D'Auvergne*, Jersey Heritage Trust, 2008.

Ballantyne, RM, *Fast in the Ice: Adventures in the Polar Regions*, London, 1863.

Barrow, J, *A Chronological History of Voyages into The Arctic Region*, London, 1818.

Beaglehole, JC (Ed), *The Journals of Captain James Cook on his Voyages of Discovery: Volume IV The Life of Captain James Cook*, Hakluyt Society, 1974

Beattie, O and Geiger, J, *Frozen in Time: The Fate of the Franklin Expedition*, London, 1987.

Beechey, FW, *A Voyage of Discovery Towards the North Pole*, London, 1843.

Burney, W, *Falconer's Universal Dictionary of the Marine*, London, 1815.

Butts, Edward, *Henry Hudson: New World Voyage*, Toronto, 2009.

Clark, A, *Lewis Carroll: A Biography*, Littlehampton Book Services Ltd, 1979.

Clark, William Bell, *Captain Dauntless: The Story of Nicholas Biddle*, Louisiana University Press, Baton Rouge, 1949.

Clarke, J and M'Arthur, J, *The Life of Horatio Lord Nelson, K.B.*, abridged version, London, 1810.

Clowes, WL, *The Royal Navy: A History from Earliest Times to 1900,* vol. 3. 1715–1793, London, 1906.

Coad, J, *Naval Architecture of the Royal Navy*, Over Wallop, 1989.

Coad, J, *The Portsmouth Block Mills*, English Heritage, 2005.

Coleman, EC, *The Royal Navy in Polar Exploration: From Frobisher to Ross*, Stroud, 2006.

Colledge, JJ, *Ships of the Royal Navy: An Historical Index, Vol 1*, Newton Abbot, 1969.

Collins, R, *The Basques*, Blackwell, 1990.

Conefrey, A, and Jordan, T, *Icemen: A History of the Arctic and its Explorers,* Boxtree, 1992.

Conway, WM, *No Man's Land*, Cambridge, 1906.

Conway, WM, *The History of Svalbard from its Discovery in 1596 to the beginning of the Scientific Exploration of the Coast*, Cambridge 1906.

Corbett, JS, *England in the Seven Years' War Vol 2 1759–1763*, 2nd edition, London, 1992

Credland, AG, *The Hull Whaling Trade: An Arctic Enterprise*, Hutton Press Ltd, 1995.

de Veer, Gerrit, *The Three Voyages of William Barents to the Arctic Regions (1594, 1595 & 1596),* Hakluyt Society, London, 1927.

Dunn, R, *The Telescope: A Short History*, Bloomsbury, 2011.

Eccles, WJ, *The Canadian Frontier, 1534–1760,* Holt, Rinehart and Winston of Canda Ltd, 1969.

Equiano, O, *The Interesting Narrative of the Life of Olaudah Equiano Or Gustavus Vassa, The African*, London, 1789.

Fabyan, R, *The Great Chronicle of London*, London, 1533.

Farrow, Courtney, *The History of Hull's Whaling Industry*, 2017.

Fleming, F, *Barrows Boys*, London, 1998.

Floyd, T, *A Midshipman's Narrative of [Capt. C. J. Phipp's] Polar Voyage – 1773*, London, 1879.

Francesco, Guidi-Bruscoli, 'John Cabot and his Italian Financiers', Historical Research, 2012.

Franklin, J, *Journey to the Polar Sea, in the Year 1819-20-21-22*, London, 2000.

Gardner, R, *The Navies of the American Revolution 1775-1783*, Naval Inst Pr, 1996.

Geiger, J, and Mitchell, A, *John Franklin's Lost Ship: The Historical Discovery of HMS Erebus,* Harper Collins, 2015.

Gilbert, KR, *The Portsmouth Block-making Machinery*, HMSO for the Science Museum, 1965.

Goodwin, P, *HMS Victory Pocket Manual 1805: Admiral Nelson's Flagship at Trafalgar*, Conway *Maritime Press*, 2015.

Goodwin, P, *Nelson's Ships: A History of the Vessels In Which He Served 1771–1805, Conway Maritime Press, 2002.*

Goodwin, P, *Ships of Trafalgar: the British, French and Spanish Fleets, October 1805*, Naval Institute Press, 2005.

Goodwin, P, 'The Application and Scheme of Paintworks in British Men-of-War in the late Eighteenth and early Nineteenth Centuries', *Mariner's Mirror*, Vol. 99:3, August 2013.

Goodwin, P, *The Bomb Vessel Grenado 1742,* Conway Maritime Press, 1989.

Goodwin, P, *The Construction and Fitting of the Sailing Man-of-War 1650–1850*, Conway Maritime Press, 1987.

Goodwin, P, *The Haynes Owners' Workshop Manual: HMS Victory 1765-1812: An Insight into Owning, Operating and Maintaining the Royal Navy's Oldest and Most Famous Warship*, Haynes Publishing, 2012.

Goodwin, P, *The Influence of Industrial Technology and Material Procurement on the Design, Construction and Development of H.M.S. Victory*, M. Phil. Dissertation, Scottish Institute of Maritime Studies, University of St Andrews, 1998.

Gould, T, *The Marine Chronometer: Its History and Development*, London, 1923.

Goodwin, P, *The Ships of Trafalgar: The British French and Spanish Fleets October 1805*, Naval Institute Press, 2005.

Hakluyt, R, *The Principal Navigations, Voyages, Traffiques & Discoveries of the English Nation*, Hakluyt Society Vol. 5, London, 1885–1890.

Harland, J, *Seamanship in the Age of Sail,* Bloomsbury Publishing, 1984.

Harris, J, *Industrial Espionage and Technology Transfer: Britain and France in the Eighteenth Century*, Aldershot, 1998.

Harris, JR, *Copper King*, Liverpool, 1964.

Hearne, Samuel, *A Journey from Prince of Wales's Fort in Hudson's Bay to the Northern Ocean, in the Years 1769, 1770, 1771, and 1772*, London, 1795.

Hisdal, V, *Svalbard: Nature and History*, Norwegian Polar Institute, Oslo, 1998.

Hough, Richard, *Captain Bligh and Mr Christian: The Men and the Mutiny,* Hutchinson, 1972.

Hutchison, G, *Sir John Franklin's Erebus and Terror Expedition: Lost and found*, NMM, 2017.

Hutchison, W, *A Treatise on Practical Seamanship*, London, 1777.

Jones, van T and Condon, Margaret M, 'Cabot and Bristol's Age of Discovery: *The Bristol Discovery Voyages 1480–150. 8*', University of Bristol, November 2016.

Lambert, A, *The Gates of Hell: Sir John Franklin's Tragic Quest for the North West Passage*, Yale University, 2009.

Laughton, JK, *Dictionary of National Biography 1885–1900 Vol. 22*.

Lavery, B, *Ship of the Line Volume 1*, London, 1983, and *Volume 2*, London, 1984.

Lavery, B, *The Arming and Fitting of English Ships of War 1600–1815*, Conway Maritime Press, 1987.

Lloyd, C, *The Capture of Quebec*, The Macmillan Company, 1959.

Lever, D, *The Young Sea Officer's Sheet Anchor: Or a Key to the Leading of Rigging and to Practical Seamanship*, London, 1819.

London Gazetteer, 18 August 1768.

Lyon, D, *The Sailing Navy List*, NMM, 1992.

Mahan, T, *The Major Operations of the Navies in the War of American Independence*, Sampson Low, Marston & Co, 1913. Markham, Clements, *The Voyages of William Baffin, 1612–1622*, Hakluyt Society, London, 1881.

May, WE, *The Boats of Men of War*, Caxton Editions, 1999.

McDermott, J, *Martin Frobisher: Elizabethan Privateer*, Yale University, 2001.

McDougal, P, *Royal Dockyards*, David & Charles, 1982. McGhee, R, *The Arctic Voyages of Martin Frobisher: An Elizabethan Adventure,* Canadian Museum of Civilisation, 2001, Washington University Press, Seattle, 2001.

McGrath, Tim (August 2015). 'I Fear Nothing', Naval History (United States Naval Institute), 2015.

McLynn, F, *1759: The Year Britain Became Master of the World,* Grove Press, 2011.

Miller, Nathan, *Sea of Glory: A Naval History of the American Revolution*, Naval Institute Press, Annapolis, 1974.

Morrill, D, Southern Campaigns of the American Revolution, Nautical and Aviation Pub Co of Amer, 1993.

Oman, C, *Nelson*, Sphere, 1967.

Pagés, Monsieur de, *Travels around the World in the Years, 1767, 1768, 1769, 1770, 1771,* Paris, 1792.

Parry, the Rev Edward MA, *Memoirs of Rear Admiral Sir W Edward Parry Kt*, London, 1872.

Paullin, Charles Oscar, *The Navy of the American Revolution: its administration, its policy and its achievements*, Cleveland USA, 1906.

Phipps, C, *A Voyage Towards the North Pole: Undertaken by His Majesty's Command, 1773*, London, 1774.

Pocock, T, *Horatio Nelson*, London, 1987.

Reid, S, *Quebec 1759: The Battle That Won Canada*, Osprey Publishing, 2003.

Reid, S, *The Flintlock Musket: Brown Bess and Charleville, 1750–1865*, Bloomsbury, 2016.

Rigby, N and van der Merwe, P, Captain Cook in the Pacific, National Maritime Museum, 2002.

Rodger, NAM, *Articles of War: The Statutes which Governed our Fighting Navies 1661, 1749 and 1866*, Kenneth Mason, 1982.

Rowland, J, *Copper Mountain*, Anglesey Antiquarian Society, 1981 *Russell, DL, Victory on Sullivan's Island: the British Cape Fear& Charles Town Expedition of 1776, Haverford, 2000.*

Russell, DL, Victory on Sullivan's Island: the British Cape Fear& Charles Town Expedition of 1776, Infinity Publishing, 2000.

Savours, Ann, '"A very interesting point in geography": The 1773 Phipps Expedition towards the North Pole', *Arctic Institute of North America Vol 37, No 4*, December 1984.

Savours, Ann, *The Search for the North West Passage,* Chatham Publishing, 1999.

Scoresby, W, *An Account of the Artic Regions: with a history and description of the Northern Whale-Fishery,* Edinburgh, 1820.

Smyth, Admiral WH, *The Sailor's Wordbook*, London 1867.

Sobel, D, *Longitude: The True Story of a Lone Genius Who Solved the Greatest Scientific Problem of His Time*, Walker & Company, 1996.

Southey, R, *The Life of Horatio Lord Nelson*, London, 1906.

Stephen, L, *Dictionary of National Biography*, 1896.

Sugden, J, *Nelson: A Dream of Glory*, Henry Holt & Co, 2002.

Syrett, D, *The Rodney Papers: Selections From the Correspondence of Admiral Lord Rodney*, NRS. Vol Ashgate Publishing, 2007.

Teeder, HR, 'Adamson, John (1787–1855)', *Dictionary of National Biography*, London: Smith, Elder & Co, 1885–1900.

Villiers, A, *Captain Cook, The Seaman's Seaman*, Penguin, 1969.

Villiers, A, *Monsoon Seas: The Story of the Indian Ocean*, McGaw-Hill Book Company, 1952.

Vincent, E, *Nelson: Love and Fame*, London, 2003.

Ware, C, *The Bomb Vessel: Shore Bombardment Ships of the Age of Sail*, Conway Maritime Press, 1994.

Ward, C, *The War of the Revolution*, Macmillan, 1952.

Weare, GE, *Cabot's Discovery of North America,* London, 1897.

Welsh, F, *The Companion Guide to the Lake District,* Companion Guides, 2000.

Williamson, James A, *The Cabot Voyages and Bristol Discovery Under Henry VII,* Cambridge University Press, 1962.

Wilson, DK, *The Southern Strategy: Britain's Conquest of South Carolina and Georgia, 1775–1780, Columbia, SC: University of South Carolina Press, 2005.*

Winfield, R, *British Warships in the Age of Sail 1793–1817: Design, Construction, Careers and Fates,* Seaforth Publishing, 2008.

Worsley, D, *The evolution of an Arctic Archipelago: The Geological History of Svalbard,* Den Norske Stats Oljeselskap AS, 1986.

Acknowledgements

Foremost I thank Vice-Admiral Sir Alan Massey KCB CBE former Second Sea Lord, and my primary line manager during my former role as Keeper and Curator of his flagship HMS *Victory,* for kindly contributing the foreword to this book.

I also thank the following people for their invaluable contributions and assistance: friend and colleague Master Mariner Lieutenant Commander Frank Scott, RN (Retired) for his innumerable contributions regarding navigation and seamanship relative to square rigged sailing ships needed to clarify details; Andrew Choong and Jeremy Michell, Ship Plans and Photographs Department of the National Maritime Museum Greenwich, London for supplying much needed draughts and information about HM Ships *Racehorse* and *Carcass* employed for the exploratory voyage. Also, at the National Maritime Museum, Emma Beech, Emma Lefley and Scarlet Faro, for supplying illustrative material. Heather Johnson, Archive Collections Curator, National Museum of the Royal Navy, Portsmouth, for access and illustrations from Constantine Phipps's original 1774 record of the voyage and Jenny Wraight, Head Librarian Naval Historical Branch Admiralty Library, HM Naval Base Portsmouth.

My thanks are also due to Susan Lumas, Naval Dockyards Society and former Archivist at the National Archives Kew for her advice regarding the search for documents. Also, the staff of the National Archive Kew, London, the Rijksmuseum Amsterdam, Tate Britain, the Royal Collections, and the United Kingdom Hydrographic Office, Taunton. I also thank Doctor Ann Shirley (formerly of the Scott Polar Research Institute Cambridge, for her advisory contribution.

I particularly thank my friend and colleague the marine artist Gordon Frickers for generously creating his incredible painting *HM Sloop Racehorse North Sea Storm Arctic Expedition 1773* capturing her precarious situation on Friday 17 September, and sincerely thank him for our many historical research discussions undertaken to produce this accurate work.

Most of all I graciously thank my wife Katy: Registrar Portsmouth City Museums and Archives Service. Katy proved an invaluable professional assistant when searching and transcribing innumerable documents from the National Archives. Added to this I inevitably thank her for her treasured support and patience throughout the exacting process of compiling this book.

Peter Goodwin. *Khenu Ankh Ka,* Southsea, 10 May 2018.

Index

INDEX